FREE BUSINESS STUFF From the INTERNET

Vince Emery

CORIOLIS GROUP BOOKS

Publisher	Keith Weiskamp
Editor	Denise Constantine and Maggy Miskell
Proofreader	Kathy Dermer
Interior Design	Rob Mauhar
Cover Design	Bradley O. Grannis
Layout Production	Rob Mauhar

The Coriolis Group, Inc.
7339 E. Acoma Drive, Suite 7
Scottsdale, AZ 85260
Phone: (602) 483-0192
Fax: (602) 483-0193
Web address: http://www.coriolis.com

ISBN 1-883577-82-9 : $19.99

Printed in the United States of America

10 9 8 7 6 5 4 3 2 1

Dedication

Though we are not related, we share the name "Vincent." Besides that name, we received other qualities in common as gifts from our parents. Our fathers, both self-made businessmen, passed along their entrepreneurial spirits. Our mothers, both working women, taught us the importance of taking pride in a job and the satisfaction of reaching our goals.

This book is our gift to them.

Contents

Tools for Internet-Based Businesses 91

Entrepreneurs, Startups, and Home Businesses   133

For Retailers   215

Accounting and Finance   231

Tax Reduction 275

More Profitable Investing 289

Doing Business Internationally   319

Business Law, Trademarks, Copyrights, and Patents   351

Resources to Help You Buy Better Stuff Cheaper   373

Logistics and Transportation   389

Manufacturing   405

A Free Lunch for Economists   421

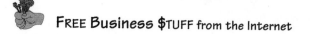

For Businesswomen   447

Five Star Sites   463

Index   467

FREE $TUFF

You see, Mr. Gittes, most people never have to face the fact that, at the right time and place, they're capable of—anything!

Noah Cross (John Huston)
Chinatown

Head Start

In a hurry to make money from the Internet? Even better, are you tight with a buck and in a hurry to make money from the Internet?

Yes? Then this is the book for you.

What you get here are hundreds of Internet resources, each one selected strictly for its power to help your bottom line and for its price tag of zero. That's zilchola. *Free.*

Software, books, newsletters, databases, spreadsheets, job sources, magazines, advice from experts, and what have you: We cherry-picked the best Internet stuff available that passed our Scrooge McDuck test. All resources included in this book are available free and can *fatten your wallet*—by increasing your sales, by saving your time, or by saving your money.

To find these winners, we slogged through hundreds of hours of useless crud. (Don't worry, we wore rubber gloves.) Next, we examined the winners as closely as a customs inspector.

Then we clearly explained them (or tried to) in easy-to-understand business language. You don't have to scratch your head over technobabble. (Though you may scratch your head while puzzling out our jokes. We figure a light style makes this book fun to use, and easier to apply. No law says business has to be boring, right?) When a resource has both good and bad points, we point out what's worthwhile and what wastes time. This means we often give you time-saving details that other books skip. Sidebar panels and illustrations provide examples of resources in action.

Pat and I hope all our digging and description saves you weeks of research time. (Besides, this book's bright green cover makes it faster to find on your cluttered desk.)

How to Put This Book to Work

One Hollywood critic summed up the phone book as, "Great characters, but not much of a plot."

Change "characters" to "stuff" and you can say the same thing about *FREE Business $TUFF From the Internet*. This book is not tightly-plotted like *Gone with the Wind* or even *I Love Lucy*. You don't need to read this book in front-to-back

order. In fact, we encourage you to skip around and read the parts that most interest you. We hope you find this book to be like a box of Crackerjacks: You can dip in anyplace and start snacking, but once you do it's hard to stop—and you'll find lots of ways to receive free prizes.

Start by browsing the table of contents, find something that looks rewarding, and jump in. For instance, if advertising makes your heart beat faster, read the chapter on *Marketing, Advertising, and Publicity*. If you are keen on manufacturing, read the *Manufacturing* chapter.

Two chapters in this book will profit *everyone*. (This means you.) One is this chapter, which gives you background plus some extremely handy tips.

The other chapter you must read is Chapter 2, *How to Find Business Stuff on the Internet*. There is a whole world of great business stuff, but we couldn't cram it all into one book. Chapter 2 is your key to finding all the great resources that we didn't have the space to give you. If you have *ever* been frustrated by trying to find stuff on the Net, read Chapter 2. (Us? Frustrated by the Net? Naaah! Well, maybe a bit. But only when the computer's turned on.) Because Chapter 2 is more valuable than almost any other Net book you own, we added gray thumb tabs on the outside edges of the pages to make it more accessible.

The Stars That Guide Us

As you peruse our compendium of free business stuff, you'll think you're seeing stars. Don't worry, the only kind of stars you'll see are printed ones. You'll see a rating of up to ☆☆☆☆☆ stars to the right of each business resource's name.

The more stars you see, the bigger the payoff. If you read our descriptions and two or more resources seem equal, the stars will save you time by helping you decide which resource will be more valuable to you. For instance, which of the dozens of accounting resources in this book do you want to visit first?

(If you want a quick look at just the very, very best stuff, turn to our appendix of five star resources, the ones we rated highest in the whole book.)

Stars indicate *usefulness for business* and no other factor—not cute graphics, not ease of use, and not clever writing. We care only what makes your cash register ring. Here is what the different ratings mean:

☆☆☆☆☆	Highest rating. Rarely given. Extremely valuable for most businesses.
☆☆☆☆	A superior resource. One of the best of its kind. Very useful for many businesses.
☆☆☆	Recommended. Either *somewhat* useful for *many* businesses, or *very* useful for *some* businesses (or by people in certain positions).
☆☆	Useful only for a small number of specialized businesses.

You won't find any one-star resources listed. Why waste your time? We threw out thousands of losers that didn't cut the mustard. For example, both the Advertising Hall of Fame and the Accounting Hall of Fame have Internet sites. While interesting, neither site gives you a profitable return on the time you invest to visit them. This book gives you only winners that deliver the goods. Winners with more stars deliver more value.

At least, your latently talented authors think they deliver more. Our evaluations reflect our own points of view. When you use one of our multi-starred resources, you may find that it meets your needs differently than we expected. Sometimes that will happen because everything on the Net changes so often and we might not have accurately anticipated your needs. We joke about this elsewhere in the book, but *if you think one of our ratings was way off, send us email and let us know*. You'll find our email addresses at the end of this chapter. Our ratings may not be as accurate as gospel truth, but the stars should give you a workable guide to what's good, what's better, and what's best.

"The stars above us govern our conditions," said William Shakespeare in *King Lear*. You'd almost think he was talking about this book.

What Are Those Little Flags For?

The Internet is worldwide. The last time we looked, full Internet access was available in 90 countries (plus the continent of Antarctica), and 168 countries could exchange email across the Net.

This gives you tremendous opportunities if you want to invest in or trade with businesses in other countries. With that in mind, we've included dozens of resources dealing with business in several countries. We haven't limited you to U.S.A. stuff only.

To help you find stuff more quickly for the countries where you do biz, if a resource is useful mostly to businesses in only one country, we added that country's flag to it. For example, the newsgroup **can.taxes** discusses Canadian taxes. We put a Canadian flag to the right of its name. The Maple Leaf flag indicates that this resource will be most useful for Canadian businesspeople, and for people in other countries who do business in Canada or invest in Canadian businesses.

If a resource in this book doesn't have a flag, it will be useful for businesses worldwide, or at least for businesses in several countries. So when you read this book, look for the flagless resources as well as those with your country's flag.

Please note that just because a resource comes from a particular country does not mean that it will necessarily get that country's flag. Many Canadian and British resources, for example, are useful for businesspeople in any country.

Also, note that there are many more flagless country-specific resources and sub-resources. This next section tells you how to find those.

Where to Find the Most Stuff Fastest

Okay, you've read the chapter on the subject that thrills you the most. You love the free stuff you've found. Do you want to find even more on your topic? The answer is a big fat "YES!" And here's how to find it.

First, let's set the stage. We had a perpetual puzzle writing this book: When a resource is useful for more than one area of business, where do we put it? For instance, the online version of the print periodical *JOE* (Job Opportunities for Economists), qualifies as a resource for economists, as a resource for job hunters, and as an electronic publication. Our solution was to stick *JOE* in the chapter *A Free Lunch for Economists* and to put references to it under several different headings (**economic resources**, **job opportunities**, *JOE*, and **newsletters**) in the index of this book.

Some people love indexes and use 'em a lot. Whether that's you or not, the index of this book is by far the fastest way to find many of the tucked away goodies. This index is not an afterthought. It was written while we wrote the book.

Some things you can find in the index:

- **Sub-resources**—Many of the hundreds of resources that received full-length reviews have sub-resources. You won't find these sub-resources in the table of contents, but you will find hundreds of them in the index.

- **Unreviewed resources**—Many business resources link to or are affiliated with full-blown resources that we mention but didn't review for a variety of reasons. Some were too new. Many are so specialized that we figured few of our readers would need them, even though they are excellent resources for a very small quantity of businesses. Again, these are not in the table of contents, but you'll find them in the index.

- **Job opportunities**—Descriptions of job openings in the book are listed under the heading **job opportunities**.

- **National resources**—As we mentioned above, a resource with a flag will be most useful for companies in that country and by companies doing business with that country. But many countries offer resources useful for businesses in several countries. Rather than give them 27 flags apiece, we list them in the index under the appropriate countries. For examples, look under **Canadian resources**, **British resources**, or **French-language resources**. When a resource is multinational overall and contains sub-resources for a specific country, you'll find those country-specific sub-resources under that country's heading.

- **Publications**—We mention more than 100 online publications in this book. Our quandary over categorizing them: How do we determine what is a magazine, what is a newsletter, what is a newspaper, and what is a journal? These classifications are highly subjective. Our solution was to give you all books or book-like online publications under the index heading **books** and all periodicals under the heading **newsletters**. We know that's simplistic, but it's also the most useful way for you to find online pubs.

- **Internet-based business stuff**—This book provides you business resources available over the Internet, but our chapter *Tools for Internet-Based Businesses* gives you resources aimed at companies who use the Net as their main business channel. Businesses that use the Internet for their bread and butter, so to speak. Look in the index under the word **Internet** first, but you can find additional resources for Internet-based businesses under the index heading **Internet and business**.

- **Stuff for software companies**—Several excellent resources on the Net help the people who run software companies, including marketing, R&D, distri-

bution, and legal resources. We listed these under the heading **software** in the index. This heading also contains all references to software programming and to software programs themselves. Information specific to either Windows or Mac software is listed under **Windows** or **Macintosh resources**.

So even if you don't normally use indexes, it might be profitable for you to spend a few minutes browsing through this one. It's by far your quickest way to find a lot of the good free stuff in this book.

How Our Resource Descriptions Work

Each description of a resource starts with its name and its rating of stars. Then our review follows, which tells you what to expect from that resource, who it's for (when that isn't obvious), and what its advantages and disadvantages might be.

After the main text of each review, you'll see a line that says, "**How.**" "**How**" tells you what Internet tool you need to reach a certain resource: Email, Gopher, FTP, the World Wide Web, newsgroups, or (very rarely) Telnet. Most businesspeople use email and the Web. Fortunately, you can reach almost all Internet resources with your Web browser. Once you know how to browse the Web, you can use the same techniques to reach Gopher, newsgroup, FTP, and Telnet resources from the same browser you already use.

After "**How,**" the next line says "**Where.**" This tells you the Internet address for this resource. Sound simple? It is. But some people get confused by Internet addresses, so here's a quick explanation.

There are a number of different "types" of resources on the Internet, each one uses a different set of communications *protocols* for getting online. Some Internet sites are Gopher servers and others are FTP servers. Other sites use Telnet, and still others require a World Wide Web browser.

When you use a Web browser, you name the type of resource you're accessing by entering its protocol followed by its Internet address. This long, hieroglyphic-like statement, which you'll see a lot of in this book, is called a *Uniform Resource Locator* (or *URL* for short).

In this book, we assume you are using a Web browser, so you can reach any Internet location by typing its protocol followed by its address. For Web sites, the protocol is *HyperText Transfer Protocol*, which is *HTTP* for short. So a typical Web site address might look like this:

http://login.eunet.no/~presno/bok/i.html

(We warned you it would look like hieroglyphics.) Most (but not all) Web browsers assume that any address you type is a Web site unless you indicate otherwise. This is a great feature, because you don't have to type in the **http://** part of the address above. Instead, just enter:

login.eunet.no/~presno/bok/i.html

Many Web addresses begin with **www.**, making them easy to identify as a Web site. In this book, when a Web address starts with **www.** the **http://** is omitted, because it's obvious that **www.anywhere.com** is a World Wide Web site. Also, with most browsers (including any version of Netscape from 1.0 forward), the **http://** is not needed. In other words, Netscape automatically assumes that any address you type in is a Web site. If Netscape can't find an address as a Web site, it will check to see if it is a Gopher or FTP address. So consider this to be a shortcut: Omit **http://** whenever you type in a Web address. It's just not needed.

For other types of Internet resources, you will need the full URL. Don't panic; that's the way they are listed. An Internet address beginning with **gopher://** is a Gopher site. One that begins with **ftp://** is an FTP site. (Predictable, huh?) One that starts with **news:** (no slashes!) is a newsgroup. Just type the full URL into your Web browser and it will take you that site.

On most Web browsers, if you try entering an FTP address or a Gopher address into your Web browser and it doesn't work, you may have a rare Web browser that doesn't support this feature. If this is your case, you may have to use different, specialized software programs to reach FTP, Gopher, Telnet, and newsgroup resources.

We treated email addresses a little differently. You may be able to enter an email address in your Web browser. (Just type **mailto:** followed by the email address.) But most businesspeople seem to prefer using the more full-featured programs designed specifically for email. So we give you the email address in the format you'd use in your everyday email program.

Keep in mind that many of the Internet addresses you type are case sensitive. If you see an address like **Accounting.scrooge&marley.co.uk/EMP/BobC** be sure you enter it *exactly* as written, with a capital "A," capitals for "EMP," and "BobC" just as written. If you don't enter characters in the correct case, many programs won't recognize the address and you'll be stuck in the Information Highway's version of the breakdown lane.

What Types of Resources Are Included?

Well, *free* resources, of course.

But seriously, we tried to focus on the Internet resources that businesspeople are most comfortable using. That means the World Wide Web and email, plus small quantities of newsgroups, FTP resources (mostly software programs you can use), Gopher sites, and a couple of difficult-to-use and ugly-looking Telnet resources.

Here are quick rundowns of the different types of business resources we include in this book and the pros and cons of each.

World Wide Web

News flash! The Internet and the World Wide Web are *not* the same!

The World Wide Web (called Web or WWW for short) is only *part* of the Internet. But it is the fastest-growing part of the Internet, especially for business use. More than 200,000 Web sites provide over twenty million pages of stuff open to the public, and hundreds of thousands of pages are available only to registered subscribers. (Many of those subscriptions are free.)

What makes the Web so fast and easy to use is the concept of *hypertext*, which lets you break through the frustrating barrier of being forced to read a document linearly. Instead, you can follow a seemingly infinite number of threads, change paths, and steer through documents, depending on what information you are interested in finding.

An example of hypertext you're probably familiar with is the help screens used in Microsoft Windows and Macintosh applications. When you read a Windows or Mac help screen, you see words that are underlined and usually in a different color from the other text. By clicking on one of these words, you're

You'll find the World Wide Web site of Dun & Bradstreet Information Services at www.dbisna.com. Click on the illustrations or on any underlined text (these are called hotlinks) and you'll go to the "page" described.

instantly taken to another help screen. In this way, you can find the information you want quickly and easily, saving you from having to pore through pages of superfluous documentation.

The basic concept behind the World Wide Web is no different, except instead of linking documents stored on your computer, it links millions of documents, programs, sound bites, movies, and more stored on tens of thousands of computers around the world.

Using a Web browser, such as Netscape or Internet Navigator, you point and click your way around the Web—the Internet's graphical side, complete with pictures, sound, movies, and more. And you can use your Web browser to reach Gopher sites, FTP sites, and newsgroups as well.

If you subscribe to one of the more popular online services (Prodigy, CompuServe, America Online, NiftyServe, or Europe Online), you already have access to the far corners of the Web. (Heck, most of Microsoft Network *is* the Web.) If you subscribe to one of these services, check its help area for more information.

Email

Electronic mail (*email*) is the lowest common denominator of the Internet. If you can send and receive email, you already have access to a huge amount of information on the Net. We've included dozens of email addresses throughout this book that can provide you lots of free stuff.

You'll also find addresses for subscribing to online magazines, newsletters, and gossip on your favorite topics. Caution: email is *addictive*; before you know it, you'll spend more time reading your mail than eating or sleeping.

A lot of the email addresses in *FREE Business $TUFF From the Internet* are for *mailing lists*, sort of online clubs you join to discuss your favorite subjects. Usually when you subscribe, you'll be sent information about the mailing list and its rules, Frequently Asked Questions and answers about the list (*FAQs*), and instructions on how to cancel your subscription. Be sure to save this file on your computer in case you ever want to unsubscribe. It may seem like a waste of disk space now, but it'll save you a lot of headaches later—like when you come back from vacation and find 300 email messages waiting for you in your mailbox.

Newsgroups

The Internet hosts more than 15,000 newsgroups. While some newsgroups are news-only, and some are repositories of *binaries,* (pictures or software programs), most are ongoing discussions about a specific topic. Newsgroups are often great places to ask questions and get answers from experts.

Newsgroups are similar to email discussion groups, but you'll find a couple of key differences. First, any message you send to an email discussion group will be seen only by subscribers to that group, and any message you post to a newsgroup can be seen by almost all Internet users in the whole world. Email is more private. Newsgroups are totally public.

Second, instead of receiving all messages as email discussion subscribers do, when you read a newsgroup you can pick and choose only the messages you want to read. When you enter a newsgroup, you get a list of messages. For each message, you can see its subject and usually (depending on what brand of software you use) the name or email address of the person who posted it. You only read the messages that interest you.

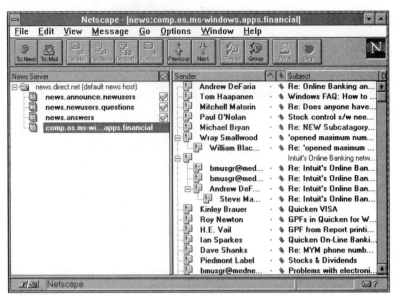

Newsgroups give you a menu of messages. Just pick the message you want and you can read it. You can also reply to other people's messages, and post messages and questions of your own. This is the news:comp.os.ms-windows.apps.financial newsgroup.

Because newsgroups are more public than email discussion groups, they are more vulnerable to becoming clogged with irrelevant emotional rants or spam. If a newsgroup is *moderated*, this is less of a problem. For these groups, someone screens all messages before they are posted to the group, weeding out messages that are inappropriate.

Each newsgroup has its own set of rules, contained in its FAQ. To avoid getting flamed with hate mail, before you post in any newsgroup, read its FAQ and at least fifty or sixty of its messages.

What's All This Fuss about Spam?

On the Internet, spam (with a lower-case "s") doesn't mean meat in a can. It is the equivalent of unwanted telephone solicitation on newsgroups and, less often, in email discussion groups.

Basically, Internet spam means unsolicited advertising in an inappropriate place. Some people have a rather loose definition of spam and describe real spam as being posted or emailed to a large number of places at once. Others

have a more restrictive definition and describe spam as one advertisement posted to one place. Also, the advertisement must have nothing to do with the topic of the place it was posted.

The name "spam" comes from a comedy routine by Monty Python's Flying Circus. In the routine, every single dish in a restaurant includes Spam, no matter how inappropriate. One menu item is "Lobster thermidor *aux crevettes* with mornay sauce garnished with truffle paté, brandy, and fried egg on top, and Spam."

Inappropriate spam on newsgroups can swell to the point where 60 percent or more of all messages on the group are spam. This crowds out the good message traffic and makes it very difficult for readers to get anything of value from the group.

You don't actually want to send unsolicited advertising to newsgroups or to email discussion groups. Email lists will kick you out. Newsgroups can prevent your entire company from ever posting to that newsgroup again. Irate readers of both kinds of groups can flood you with angry hate mail (called *flames*), and program their modems to jam your phone and fax lines. Even worse, you'll make your Internet prospects and customers hate you, which is not a good way to build sales growth. Over the long haul, it doesn't pay to release any messages with spam.

FTP: File Transfer Protocol

File Transfer Protocol (*FTP*) is a way to copy programs and files stored on computers all over the Net. This book contains lots of business applications, spreadsheets, and other software that you can download by FTP.

Many FTP sites—and all of the ones in this book—offer files through *anonymous FTP*, which means anyone can access them. Simply type **anonymous** if you're asked to provide a user name, then your email address if you're asked for a password. (That may seem a little strange, but it works.)

Most Web browsers let you download FTP files by default—provided the FTP site lets you log on as **anonymous**, which means that everybody on the Internet has unrestricted access to the files stored at this site.

Keep in mind that there are millions of other people on the Internet using FTP, and traffic jams sometimes occur when lots of people try to reach the same site

```
Netscape - [Directory of /pub/winworld]
 File   Edit   View   Go   Bookmarks   Options   Directory   Window   Help

 What's New!  What's Cool!  Handbook   Net Search   Net Directory   Software     N

   addressbook/           Thu Feb 08 01:19:00 1996 Directory
   aporia/                Thu Feb 08 01:10:00 1996 Directory
   asciitbl/              Thu Feb 08 02:17:00 1996 Directory
   atm/                   Thu Feb 08 02:29:00 1996 Directory
   autosave/              Thu Feb 08 02:19:00 1996 Directory
   backup/                Thu Feb 08 02:19:00 1996 Directory
   bible/                 Thu Feb 08 02:05:00 1996 Directory
   calculat/              Thu Feb 08 02:07:00 1996 Directory
   calendar/              Thu Feb 08 02:05:00 1996 Directory
   capture/               Thu Feb 08 01:23:00 1996 Directory
   chem/                  Thu Feb 08 01:31:00 1996 Directory
   cica simtel/           Thu Feb 08 01:38:00 1996 Directory
   clipboard/             Thu Feb 08 02:19:00 1996 Directory
   clock/                 Thu Feb 08 02:07:00 1996 Directory
   comm/                  Thu Feb 08 02:08:00 1996 Directory
   compress/              Thu Feb 08 01:10:00 1996 Directory
   convert/               Thu Feb 08 02:23:00 1996 Directory

 Document Done
```

FTP shows you nothing but lists of directories and files. Click on any directory to open it. Click on any file to copy it to your computer. As you can see from this directory of the Winworld software archive at ftp://ftp.csusm.edu/pub/winworld, the lack of any description makes FTP more puzzling to navigate.

at once. Occasionally—especially during peak hours—you'll get an error message saying there are too many people trying to reach the site, and to try again later. This is the Internet's equivalent of a busy signal. Be patient, try later, and don't get frustrated.

Also, pay attention when you *do* connect. Several FTP sites have *mirrors* (identical sites located at different places around the world) you can access that may be closer to where you work, which are often listed when you first enter a site. The closer the site, the faster you'll be able to reach it and grab your files.

Gopher

Gopher is a menu-based system that lets you browse through collections of information and databases on the Net. Once you find what you want, retrieving Gopher documents is as easy as pointing and clicking.

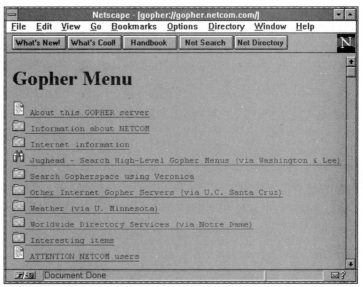

Gopher sites give you a little more description than FTP sites, but not nearly as much as the Web. This Gopher server located at gopher://gopher.netcom.com lets you open directories, read text files, and use search engines.

Telnet

Telnet lets a person on one computer travel over the Internet to a remote computer, log onto it, and run software on it as if you were sitting at it. This sounds cool, but to do this Telnet uses a lowest-common-denominator approach to computing: just text, no pictures, no bells, and no whistles. Many businesspeople who use Macs or Windows (or even DOS) have a hard time struggling through Telnet. Even so, Telnet is the only way you can reach some Internet business resources.

How to Uncompress Free Software

To move things as quickly as possible over the Net, most software programs that you copy from the Internet are compressed to make them smaller. The smaller version is easier and much faster to copy. After you download a compressed file, you need to uncompress it before you install and run it.

If you use a PC, you can use either PKUnzip or Winzip for Windows to uncompress *zipped* files. You will know if a PC file is zipped because it will end with **.zip**. If your file ends with **.exe**, it is a *self-extracting* file, requiring no uncompression program. Just put the **.exe** program in an empty temporary directory and run the program from the Windows Program Manager or, in Win95, the Explorer. Either program is available for free at many sites around the Internet, including:

- **PKUnzip for DOS:** ftp://igc.net/pub/igc/viewers/pkunzip.exe
- **Winzip for Windows:** ftp://oak.oakland.edu/simtel/win3/archiver/ wz60wn16.exe
- **Winzip for Windows 95:** ftp://ftp.outer.net/winzip/winzip95.exe

If you use a Macintosh, uncompressing files is a bit more complex, mostly because the Mac uses several different compression schemes. We highly recommend that you purchase a copy of StuffIt Deluxe, because this commercial package can uncompress virtually all formats, including **.zip** files. The shareware version of StuffIt is much more limited.

Most files in Macintosh archives are stored in a format called BinHex. You can easily identify these files because their file names end with **.hqx**. StuffIt Deluxe can automatically decode BinHexed files, and so can Compact Pro.

Even after you decode a BinHexed file, you might still need to uncompress it. If a Mac file name ends with **.cpt**, it was compressed by Compact Pro. Both StuffIt Deluxe and Compact Pro can uncompress these files. If the file ends with **.sit**, it was compressed by some version of StuffIt, so you'll need StuffIt to uncompress the file. The newer your version of StuffIt, the more likely you'll be able to uncompress the file.

If, after you decode a BinHexed file, your resulting file ends with **.sea**, you're in good shape. This is a self-extracting archive created by StuffIt or Compact Pro. All you need to do is double-click on the file to uncompress it.

Here's where to find the uncompression and decode software for your Mac:

- BinHex: This is the most popular program for unBinHexing encoded files.
  Web: mrcnext.cso.uiuc.edu/~deej/index.html
  FTP: ftp://ftp.sunet.se/pub/mac/info-mac/cmp
- StuffIt Lite: This is the shareware version of StuffIt. It's BinHexed, so you'll need to download BinHex first, so you can decode StuffIt.
  Web: www.aladdinsys.com

FTP: ftp://ftp.204.147.235.101/pub

FTP: ftp://ftp.sunet.se/pub/mac/info-mac/cmp

- Compact Pro: Use this program to uncompress Compact Pro **.cpt** files.

  FTP: ftp://ftp.sunet.se/pub/mac/info-mac/s\cmp

- If you have StuffIt Lite, you can also use the cpt.sit converter to convert **.cpt** files to **.sit** files.

  Web: www.aladdinsys.com

Support Your Local Shareware Programmer

FREE Business $TUFF From the Internet is jammed with tons of programs for you to download, all of which are free to try out. And while many of them are free to keep (*freeware*), many others are *shareware*, a marketing concept which lets you try before you buy. If you don't like the program, delete it and pay nothing. If you like it, send in the registration fee.

Shareware costs nothing—zippo—*unless* you decide to keep it. This try-be-fore-you-buy approach to distribution is a great deal, and not one you're likely to find with most other kinds of merchants.

Basically, it's the honor system at work here, so play fair. Send a little something to keep 'em working on more great programs. And once you've registered your software, many programmers send you an upgraded version of the program with extras not included in the shareware version. Look for registration information when you load the program.

Feed a Cold, Starve a Virus

As Dennis Miller of *Saturday Night Live* fame so aptly put it, "When you link up with another computer, you link up with every other computer that that computer has ever linked up with."

While most of the files you can download off the Net have already been scanned for computer viruses at the site where the files are stored, practice safe computing by using your own virus checker to make sure anything you download has not been tampered with. The odds are extremely slim that you'll be a victim, but if you're one of the unlucky few, you could be in for major headaches—from weird messages flashing on your screen to having your hard drive reformatted. Take the extra time to protect your hard drive. Before you run any program you download, scan it with your virus checker.

Get 'Em While They're Hot

Experienced Net surfers know that three words never used to describe the Net are *concrete, stagnant*, or *static*. Web pages that are here today may very well be gone tomorrow—only to be back the next day with an entirely new look and feel. While this makes for the occasional frustration, it's also part of what makes the Net so up-to-the-minute. Like surfing the Pacific, when you surf the Net no two rides are the same.

Keep these points in mind as you browse this book. We've checked and re-checked Net resources, but don't be surprised if your computer screen doesn't match the pictures shown in this book—or if a resource isn't even available. Many of the resources are constantly updated, improved, and even given complete facelifts. The ease of making changes is actually one of the advantages to online publishing. If something is not right, it's usually easy to fix.

Find Lost Sites with the URL-Stripping Trick

When you try an Internet address and it doesn't work, someone may have moved your resource to another spot on the same site, or given it a new name. This happens often to Web addresses. Here's a trick used by Internet search pros that often turns up such relocated resources.

Let's say that you want an article that tells you how to reduce your office heating expenses from:

www.scrooge&marley.co.uk\pub\lowcost\heating.html

You enter the address in your Web browser and instead of your article you get the dreaded Error 404, telling you that your resource couldn't be found. Calm down! Stop pinching your eyes together! Try this instead. Just delete the last slash and everything to its right:

www.scrooge&marley.co.uk\pub\lowcost

You should get a directory of file names—unless someone renamed the **lowcost** directory to something else. In that case, you'll get another Error 404. If so, repeat the procedure and try again:

www.scrooge&marley.co.uk\pub

This will get you the **pub** directory. Maybe here you'll find that the **lowcost** directory has been renamed **lesscost** and that your file **heating.html** is now named **lesscoal.html**. If you didn't find anything at the **\pub** level, you could take that away and look one level farther down. Based on our experience, in more than half the cases you can find a missing resource by stripping its URL.

Another Neat Trick

And here's another neat trick: Our publisher, Coriolis Group Books, was nice enough to lend us space on its Web server. We'll post any address changes, deletions, and other interesting Net info at this site, on a weekly basis or as time permits. Go to **www.coriolis.com/freebiz** to reach updates and changes.

If you find changes that our Web page doesn't yet list, please send one of us email and let us know:

Pat Vincent   Vince Emery
pjvincent@coriolis.com   vince@emery.com

And if you like this book, you may want to take a peek at our other books. Vince wrote *How to Grow Your Business on the Internet*.

Pat wrote the original *FREE $TUFF From the Internet*, plus *FREE $TUFF From the World Wide Web, Way More! FREE $TUFF From the Internet, FREE $TUFF For Windows 95, FREE $TUFF For Sports Nuts, and FREE $TUFF From the Internet, 2nd Edition*. Pat also was part of the team that wrote *Web EXplorer Pocket Companion*.

FREE $TUFF

Boss (to department head): How many people work in your office?

Department head: About half of them, sir.

Gyles Brandreth

How to Find Business Stuff on the Internet

The first problem most businesspeople have with the Internet is getting connected. After they get connected, the second problem is, "How do I use this (adjective of your choice) software?"

As soon as they use the software, the third problem rears its ugly head. It can be more frustrating than the other two, and for many people, it never goes away: "How the heck can anybody find stuff on the Internet?"

This chapter has the ambitious goal of helping you find *anything* on the Internet. (Or at least, anything *free*. We are tightwads, after all.) Pat and I especially concentrate on finding the kind of stuff that growing businesses need.

Most of this book gives you the lowdown on resources for specific areas of your business, such as your accounting or marketing operations. If you want something for your marketing needs, you can turn first to the *Marketing, Advertising, and Publicity* chapter. Useful as it is, sometimes you won't find what you need there. Next, check the index of this book. If that doesn't help, this chapter and your computer should help you find what you need.

Before you search online, make a plan. Ask yourself, "What exactly am I looking for?" or "How will I know when I have what I need?" Then, most importantly, ask, "What *type of Internet tool* is most likely to have what I need?" This is *the* crucial question when it comes to finding stuff on the Internet.

There are big differences between the types of information you can reach with the different Internet tools. The World Wide Web, email, Gopher, FTP, Telnet, newsgroups, and email lists all carry different information (though they do overlap). And for the most effective results, you'll want to use different search tools depending on which part of the Internet has the information you want.

This chapter is organized to help you do just that. If you want someone's email address, the first section tells you where to go, and what the differences are between the search tools you can use.

After that first section (oddly enough, called "How to Find Someone's Email Address"), you'll see sections on "How to Find Companies and Domain Names," and two sections on Gophers, FTP, and the World Wide Web. One covers *searchers* (also called "search engines"), where you type in a name, word, or phrase so the Web site brings you information on whatever you typed. The other covers *directories*, or lists of files or hotlinks that you scroll down or page through.

Much of your business research on the Net will involve tracking down a specific company, whether by name or by what the company does. Our section on "How to find businesses and business resources" should be a big help to you here.

We follow with sections on email lists, Usenet newsgroups, and "Telnet and Bulletin Board Systems" (BBSes). A word of caution about BBSes might help. Many businesspeople with little online experience think that most of the Internet is BBSes, or even that BBSes *are* the Internet. This is not true. Even worse, some people confuse Internet resources with BBSes, and think that newsgroups are bulletin board systems, or that email discussion groups are, or even that Web pages are all electronic bulletin boards. Don't fall into this trap. People who confuse BBSes and the Net make strategic planning blunders, have difficulty finding stuff on the Net, and (even worse) sound clue-impaired at office parties. Read our "Telnet Sites and Bulletin Board Systems" section for further enlightenment on this topic.

We wrap this chapter up with "How to Find Free Fax Servers" (maybe you weren't looking for them, but they can save you money just the same), and "When all else fails, ask." This last section is our equivalent of "In case of emergency, break glass." You'll find resources where you can ask your toughest questions to real human beings. And even better, you'll get answers.

As a newbie on the Net, you might feel, as one businessman said, that you are "trying to find a diamond in all the dirt." We hope this chapter helps you shovel less dirt and find better-grade diamonds.

While you dig, keep your eyes open for unexpected bonuses. One of the great advantages of the Internet is that, while you look for one thing, you can find something else more valuable.

Searching on the Net is full of surprises. It's often like looking for a needle in a haystack and finding the farmer's daughter.

How to Find Someone's Email Address

Four11 ☆☆☆☆

One of the authors of this book has three different email addresses (and the split personalities to match!). We used him as the guinea pig to test all email address finders on the Net. Some address finders actually found none of his addresses. (You won't see any of those in this book.) Most found just one. Only Four11 found two.

Anyone can use Four11's basic search, but you can register for free to use its improved search, which lets you search by city, state, and country, as well as search by the high school or college someone attended. Four11 can also find people by their *old, expired* email addresses, which is a cool trick. When you register, you can enter your name in Four11's Group Connection feature to find old friends. Four11 won't sell your email address or name to anyone.

There are only two drawbacks to this great service. First, it does not work with all Web browsers. Second, when you register, Four11 gives you a password which (since you use it nowhere else) you will never remember. But don't let that keep it from being your first stop to look up email addresses.

How
World Wide Web

Where
www.four11.com

RES-Links People ☆☆☆☆

This site is not a search tool itself, but it is the most complete directory we found of people-finding tools on the Net. It is fairly up-to-date, and gives clear descriptions of the resources it lists. Not only can you find people's email addresses, you can also acquire names for addresses you have already. Use other resources listed here to find domains and IP addresses. RES-Links also lists phone directories on the Internet, plus ways to look up area codes and postal ZIP codes anywhere in the world.

How
World Wide Web

Where
www.cam.org/~intsci/people.html

Internet Address Finder ☆☆☆

The Address Finder found one of our three test email addresses, with an unexpected bonus. It also listed the correct postal address and provided a hot link to our test name's personal home page. This site gives you unbeatable flexibility in how you find information about a person. You search by last name, with options to narrow your search according to a person's first name, organization, and domain. The Address Finder lets you use wild cards, so if you know the first letter in someone's name (Let's pretend it's "R"), you can type "r*". You can also do reverse searches: Enter a person's email address and find out the person's name and where he or she works. Cool.

How

World Wide Web

Where

www.iaf.net

Knowbot Information Service ☆☆☆

In our email road test, Knowbot found one of our three test email addresses. To reduce the number of visits you must make for finding a person's email address, Knowbot provides one-stop shopping for several resources. At this one site, you can search the InterNIC White Pages, MCImail database, RIPE's European White Pages, Latin American InterNIC, X.500, and others for email addresses and postal addresses. Knowbot does not work with all browsers.

How

World Wide Web

Where

info.cnri.reston.va.us/kis.html

OKRA net.citizen Directory ☆☆☆

OKRA is a disgusting vegetable that oozes slime. I don't know why someone named this address-finder after it, except that okra is easier to spell than ruta-baga. OKRA found one email address in our test. OKRA pulls addresses from a database of everyone who has ever posted a message to an Internet newsgroup, plus (this is something no other site does) addresses of employees from companies' Finger servers. (Maybe it's called OKRA because okra slime sticks to your fingers when you eat it.)

How

World Wide Web

Where

okra.ucr.edu/okra

LookUp ☆☆☆

LookUp's free search found one of our three test email addresses. The free LookUp service is pretty good. It also offers advanced searches for a subscription fee, which the tightwads who wrote this book refuse to even think of paying.

FREE Business $TUFF from the Internet

How

World Wide Web

Where

www.lookup.com/search.html

The Postmaster Trick ☆☆☆

This isn't a resource, but it's a useful trick: how do you find a person's email address when you know only his or her company address? Just send email to **postmaster@address**—but insert the company's address in place of the word "address." For example, if you know Bob Cratchit works for the firm of Scrooge & Marley and the company's address is **scrooge&marley.com**, to find Bob's address you can send a message to **postmaster@scrooge&marley.com**. Your message should reach the person in charge of the company's email. Just ask politely for the email address of Bob Cratchit. Remember to say "Thank you." Most companies' postmasters will take the time to send you a message that includes the address you want.

How

Email

Where

postmaster@whatever.the.person's.company.address.might.be

How to Find Companies and Domain Names

InterNIC Whois ☆☆☆

InterNIC stands for the Internet Network Information Center. It is the registration center for all domain names in North America, and its database of domains is the most up-to-the-minute in the world. That gives InterNIC Whois an edge in finding company information, and in finding people.

Whois is simple to use. Just type your search term and press Enter or Return. If you enter a domain name, you will receive contact details for that domain. If you enter a word or a name, you will receive something quite different: a list of all possible domains, companies, and personal email addresses that contain a match with your search term.

How

World Wide Web

Where

rs.internic.net/cgi-bin/whois

Netfind ☆☆☆

Netfind searches for company names, domain names, and city/state/province information—not people. If you like this book, then you'll like this site, because it's free, fast, and easy, with an occasional burst of humor.

How

World Wide Web

Where

ibc.wustl.edu/domain_form.html

Searchers for Gopher, FTP, and Web Stuff

Yahoo ☆☆☆☆☆

Yahoo is the first place to look for almost anything. It's fast, it's easy, and it gives you what you need most of the time. Yahoo takes a different tactic than most other search engines on the Net. Other searchers send software robots out to scoop up millions of Internet resources. Yahoo hand-picks a smaller number of sites (Web, Gopher, FTP, Internet Relay Chat, some newsgroups, and some email lists) and then Yahoo's small army of professional indexers (human ones!)

Search Yahoo for "accounting" and here's the top of the list Yahoo brings to you.

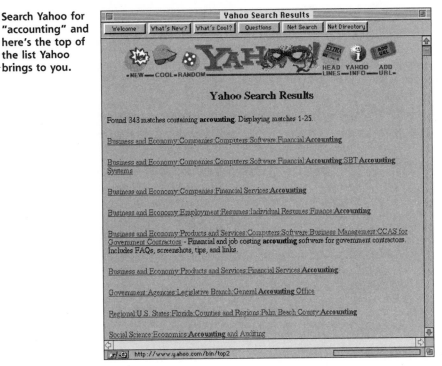

describe and index them. To summarize, Yahoo gives you quality results rather than quantity. Besides, its name is fun and it has the easiest-to-remember URL on the Net!

Some Net search sites add a directory as a sideshow. Yahoo's directories are the bigtop. Many businesspeople use only Yahoo's search engine and never discover its immensely valuable directories. Yahoo arranges them by subject. Its "Business and Economy" directory alone contains more than 10,000 sites, with lengthy subdirectories on business schools, consortia, electronic commerce, jobs, marketing, investments, and many other topics. Yahoo also offers a "What's New" directory. Browsing Yahoo's directories is one of the most rewarding time investments on the Net. It is impossible not to depart with unexpected new resources and information.

This handful of listings from Yahoo's "Electronic Commerce" subdirectory hints at the wealth of useful business info in the Yahoo directories.

Yahoo – Business and Economy:Electronic Commerce

Welcome | What's New? | What's Cool? | Questions | Net Search | Net Directory

- FAST Broker, The - a prototype automated procurement service being developed by the FAST Project at the University of Southern California
- Houston Commerce - Center for Houston business and commerce. Host of Houston Minority Business Council and Host of Houston business community
- International Cyber Commercial Center - Multinational / multilingual world wide Cyber Commercial Center
- Internet Business Information Registry - A non-profit organization that maintains company information on firms.
- Internet Commerce Study - A study regarding Internet commerce -- the first in a series of comprehensive studies from The Toner Group.
- Internet Commerce Testbed
- Law of Electronic Commerce - The legal aspects of doing business without paper. Topics include electronic signatures, computer evidence and tax records of electronic transactions.
- Marketing in Computer-mediated Environments (Paper) - reports the empirical surveying of 290 commercial WWW sites with a view to determining the credence given to different marketing theories by WWW site owners and ultimately to empirically demonstrate the existence of hypermarketing.
- Marketing in Computer-Mediated Environments - Owen Graduate School of Management - Vanderbilt.
- MegaWeb, Inc.
- Meridian Communications - Internet 'storefronts' including lottery purchases, resturants and other business and entertainment related information and services.
- MidAtlantic Electronic Commerce Network
- NAFTA Related EDI and Electronic Commerce
- NetBill Electronic Commerce Project - designing the protocols and software to support charging for network-based goods and services delivered over the Internet.
- Netcheck Commerce Bureau
- Private Capital Markets Directory
- Project 2000 - Research Program on Marketing in Computer-Mediated Environments
- Skeleton Development Corp - The Skeleton Storefront Kit and Skeleton Mall Kit provide extensive shopping functionality for new or existing WWW sites. On-Line Shopping Made Simple!
- Smart Card Cyber Show
- Tenders Electronic Daily - lets you search within public tenders (open contracts) - online service for companies worldwide.
- TITAN - freely available secure order processing system for the Internet. For the purchaser download it FREE and send orders to any of your desired suppliers.
- Versatile Virtual Vending

How

World Wide Web

Where

www.yahoo.com

28

One of Yahoo's great hidden resources is its directory of search engines. After you do a Yahoo search, scroll down to the bottom of the page that contains your search results. You'll see the names of whatever searchers are currently hot, and the word "More." Click on "More" for a whole catalog of neatly described Net searchers.

Alta Vista ☆☆☆☆☆

Robert Seideman says Alta Vista may be the "best search engine on the Web." We'd be hard-pressed to disagree. To demonstrate the heavy firepower and lightning speed of Digital's Alpha computers, this site searches the *complete text*—that's for *all* the pages, not just the home page "front doors"—of millions of Web sites and most newsgroup messages. Alta Vista searches this vast mine of data and returns your findings with amazing speed, especially considering how much dirt it must plow to find your diamonds. A search here will always find several sites not found by other searchers. Not sometimes—*always*.

Search Alta Vista for "trade" and this is the tip of the iceberg you'll get back. Note the humongous number of times Alta Vista found this word in its database.

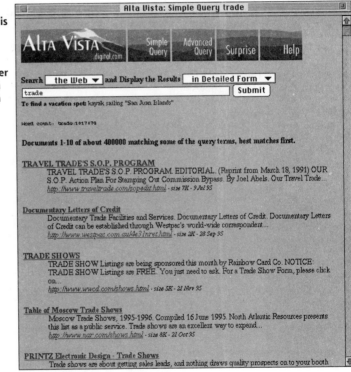

The downside is that Alta Vista is a bit sloppy about matching your search criteria, and will usually return "hits" that have little to do with your topic. "Kinda close" is how Alta Vista matches what you key into your computer.

Even so, Alta Vista makes a far more complete search than any other searcher. It is best at searching Web sites, and InfoSeek beats it at searching newsgroups. Check out Alta Vista's "Advanced Query" features. They let you specify a date range (the only Web searcher that does) and several other parameters. If you do serious digging for Net information, Alta Vista is your power shovel.

How

World Wide Web

Where

altavista.digital.com

Lycos ☆☆☆☆☆

In addition to Web sites, Lycos lets you find stuff on some Gopher servers and some FTP servers. Lycos actually searches *more* Web sites than Alta Vista— millions more. But where Alta Vista scoops up the complete text of all pages, Lycos often indexes only home pages. And where Alta Vista searches each page's complete text, Lycos creates a clever *Reader's Digest* condensed version of each page, with its title, URL, opening lines, and most important words

This search for "trade" shows how Lycos can give you sample text from sites that match your criteria.

Lycos search: trade

Location: http://twelve.srv.lycos.com/cgi-bin/pursuit?query=trade&matchmode=and&minscore=.9&ma

Lycos search: trade

Lycos Feb 14, 1996 catalog, 19,347,216 unique URLs

Found 22758 documents matching at least one search term.
Printing only the first 1 documents with at least scores of 0.900.

Found 256 matching words (number of documents): trade (22758), trademarks (11959), ...

1) Index of /tradetlk/

Ranking: 1.0000

Words matched in page: tradetlk

Outline: Index of /tradetlk/

Abstract: Name Last modified Size Description Parent Directory audionet.gif 30-Aug-95 16:02 6K cassette.gif 14-Jan-96 18:42 5K kustas1.gif 10-Jan-96 15:39 10K mainbann.gif 10-Jan-96 15:50 10K money.gif 20-Sep-95 00:52 1K trade1.gif 14-Jan-96 18:28 5K trade1.ram 28-Nov-95 22:04 1K trade10.ram 20-Nov-95 18:11 1K trade11.ram 20-Nov-95 23:22 1K trade12.ram 20-Nov-95 23:08 1K trade2.ram 28-Nov-95 22:13 1K trade3.ram 28-Nov-95 22:15 1K trade4.ram 28-Nov-95 22:17 1K trade5.ram 28-Nov-95 22:18 1K trade6.ram 20-Nov-95 15:04 1K trade7.ram 20-Nov-95 15:58 1K trade8.ram 20-Nov-95 16:42 1K trade9.ram 20-Nov-95 17:27 1K tradetlk.htm 14-Jan-96 18:22 6K trbann.gif 10-Jan-96 15:21 8K trbann2.gif 10-Jan-96 15:24 8K trbanner *http://www.audionet.com/tradetlk/ (4k) 24-Jan-96*

Refine search: trade   Search Formless

How to Find Business Stuff on the Internet

and phrases. Lycos also gives you a more flexible search mechanism than most sites; for instance, you can search for part of a phrase.

Lycos often finds resources that other Web searchers miss. It gives you results sorted with your closest matches first, and not-so-exact matches afterwards, which saves considerable time. For a treat, check out the Lycos directory of the 250 most popular sites on the Net.

How

World Wide Web

Where

www.lycos.com

InfoSeek ☆☆☆☆☆

As search engines mature, each develops its own personality. Yahoo is straight-forward. Alta Vista is awe-inspiring. Lycos is clever. InfoSeek is a nimble juggler.

InfoSeek delivers so much and does it so well that thousands of people actually *pay* for its services. (That's a dirty word in *this* book.) Infoseek has two levels. There is a free level and a pay-for level—and you can get a free sample of the pay-for goodies.

First, the free version. InfoSeek has the third-largest inventory of Web pages of all the search engines. It also searches newsgroups—the best on the Net at this—and is your best spot for searching newsgroup FAQs. As a comparison, when InfoSeek searches the same newsgroups as SIFT, InfoSeek brings back hits—good ones—that SIFT misses. Part of this is due to InfoSeek's extremely agile search mechanism. It gives you many ways to pinpoint the information you want. For instance, it lets you specify that several words (such as a person's name) are to be treated as one phrase, so you can search for resources that match "Charles Dickens" rather than the mismatches you would get from searching for "Charles" and "Dickens."

Clever as the dickens, I'd say.

It also lets you ask questions, such as, "What law firms handle antitrust cases?" Like Lycos, InfoSeek gives you search results with the best-matching documents on top of the list. On its own, the free version of InfoSeek is good enough to be one of the busiest sites on the Net.

31

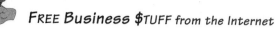

The paid version, called InfoSeek Professional, is even better. It lets you search more resources:

- Gopher, FTP
- Computer magazine articles
- Newswires
- Hoover's Company Profiles
- Medical journals
- Movie reviews
- Cambridge Scientific Abstracts
- And more

You can ask InfoSeek questions like "What law firms handle antitrust cases?" and get an answer.

It also lets you build complicated custom searches and store them so you can rerun them later against newer data. InfoSeek makes a free trial available of InfoSeek Professional. You can have a $15 credit to use InfoSeek Professional for one month or 100 searches, whichever comes first. Read the Web site for instructions on how to get your free sample.

How

World Wide Web

Where

www.infoseek.com

Internet Sleuth ☆☆☆☆

The thick fog on Baker Street could not conceal Holmes' satisfaction at having so rapidly solved the Internet mystery. Observing my puzzled countenance, he spoke, "Well, Watson?"

"How did you gather so much information in so short a time?" I asked. "You must have visited dozens of Internet sites."

"Hundreds," corrected Holmes. "This search required several highly specialized and somewhat obscure search engines. But my secret must be obvious; I went to one site which allowed me to use many."

"But Holmes, I've never heard of such a thing," I replied.

"I employed a trick taught to me by an old Internet scout from the 49th Grenadier's Regiment. It's called the Internet Sleuth, and lets you use more than 400 Net resources—search engines and directories, primarily—at a single Web site. Rather clever, really. So you see, Watson, I was able to employ Yahoo, Alta Vista, Lycos, Open Text, and Veronica, plus the more specialized search tools, such as the APL Quote Server, which I used to retrieve stock quotes. Perhaps what most pleases my personal sensibilities is that this site is as logically organized as a Vulcan's pointed ears."

"What, pray tell, is a Vulcan?" I asked.

"Never mind," responded Holmes, "but it intrigues me to speculate on the profitable uses to which a business could employ the Internet Sleuth." Holmes then ruminated on the contents available in the directory on the Sleuth's home page, where one could examine sections such as:

- Business
- Business Directories
- Companies
- Economics

- Employment
- Finance
- Legal
- Trade and Industry

"An impressive gathering," Holmes continued, "made all the more useful by the Sleuth's apt descriptions of the tools which it presents. One slightly misleading aspect troubles me; when one searches the Sleuth's own search form near the top of its home page, one doesn't search the *contents* of the tools featured on the site, but the Sleuth's *descriptions* of them. But that is a minor flaw, since all other search forms at this site are the ones that 'deliver the goods,' as our roguish acquaintances would say. Now come along, Watson. Mrs. Hudson expects us for dinner."

How

World Wide Web

Where

www.intbc.com/sleuth

 A competing site, **All-in-One Internet Search** uses the same idea as Internet Sleuth. All-in-One's advantage over the Sleuth is that it is trilingual—available in English, French, and Pig Latin. (Really!) Sleuth is better organized and lacks All-in-One's annoying, garish design.

English: www.albany.net/allinone
French: www.media-prisme.ca/all/all1srch.html
Pig Latin: voyager.cns.ohio.edu/^jrantane/cgi/pig.cgi?www.albany.net/allinone

Trade Wave Galaxy ☆☆☆☆

Galaxy searches a huge quantity of Web, Gopher, and Telnet resources to find stuff that other sites can't. Although you can find more Gopher information with Veronica (see below) and more Telnet sites with Hytelnet (see below), Galaxy is the best Web site to search Gopher and Telnet without actually having to use Gopher and Telnet (which are not as easy to use as the Web). It lets you specify more criteria than most search sites, so your results are closer to what you want. Galaxy also offers one of the best sets of directories—especially for business resources—on the Web.

Galaxy indexes resources that other searchers miss. This is the top of a search for "accounting" on Galaxy.

```
┌─────────────────────────────────────────────────────────────┐
│ ▤▤        Searching the TradeWave Galaxy             ▤▤ │
├─────────────────────────────────────────────────────────────┤
│ Galaxy Pages - for "accounting." 18 documents found.      ▲ │
│                                                             │
│   • Accounting (Financial Aspects) - Score: 1000 Size: 4475 │
│   • Financial (General Products and Services) - Score: 360 Size: 21197 │
│   • Software (Computers) - Score: 160 Size: 57609           │
│   • Financial Aspects (Business Administration) - Score: 160 Size: 4813 │
│   • Business Administration (Business and Commerce) - Score: 80 Size: 6604 │
│   • Finance (Consumer Products and Services) - Score: 80 Size: 4806 │
│   • Horses (Leisure and Recreation) - Score: 40 Size: 4822 │
│   • Reading (Leisure and Recreation) - Score: 40 Size: 32509 │
│   • US - Agencies (Government Agencies) - Score: 40 Size: 13187 │
│   • Transportation (Engineering and Technology) - Score: 40 Size: 11538 │
│   • Security (Computer Technology) - Score: 40 Size: 6127   │
│   • Arizona (US States) - Score: 40 Size: 3806             │
│   • Investment Sources (Business and Commerce) - Score: 40 Size: 9296 │
│   • Employment (General Products and Services) - Score: 40 Size: 18715 │
│   • Education (General Products and Services) - Score: 40 Size: 5619 │
│   • Internet Services (General Products and Services) - Score: 40 Size: 78497 │
│   • PC (Software) - Score: 40 Size: 13684                  │
│   • Clothing and Accessories (Consumer Products and Services) - Score: 40 Size: 9868 │
│   ─────────────────────────────────────────────────────   │
│                                                             │
│ World Wide Web Documents - for "accounting." 20 documents, 1026 more qualifying matches │
│ remain. (You can use boolean phrases to refine your search.) │
│                                                             │
│ 1. Accounting / MIS System Selector- Score: 1000 - Size: 27944 │
│                                                             │
│ Excerpt: So . . . Where to from Here? How to Chooses SystemHave YouOUTGROWNYour │
│ People?Unbiased Comparisonof 120 Systems Why SpendMore?Can YOUGUESSthe │
│ MYSTERYSystem?Free Demo The Accounting Library Inexpensive Systems Less Than 300 Do You │
│ Needa Real MIS? Thumbs Down Suggest Improvements Trade NameCross ReferenceThumbs UP I │
│ like This Site We Also Provide Access to The Accounting Library Unbiased Comparison ... │
│                                                             │
│ Frequent Words: 61:account 53:softwar 24:busi 18:client 17:server 13:window 13:manag 12:seri │
│ 12:price 9:comput 9:associ 8:solution 8:pro 7:plu 7:champion 6:vigil 6:intern 6:trade 6:name 6:mi ▼ │
└─────────────────────────────────────────────────────────────┘
```

How

World Wide Web

Where

galaxy.einet.net/search.html

Open Text ☆☆☆☆

With the Internet so decentralized, growing so fast, and covering so many *types* of resources (Web, Gopher, FTP, newsgroups, and so on), no search tool can cover all of them. That is why several of these Net search engines are able to find stuff that the others miss. None can find everything. All find different pieces of the same puzzle. Open Text does better than most. It searches a large archive of more than a million Web pages, Gophers, some newsgroups, and FTP *documents*. This last item is a big deal, because everything else that searches FTP servers indexes only the *names* of FTP files, but Open Text lets you search their *contents*. So just like we said above, Open Text finds stuff that everybody else misses. It's also fast and quite easy to use.

After searching for "trade" with the Open Text search engine, this is the beginning results

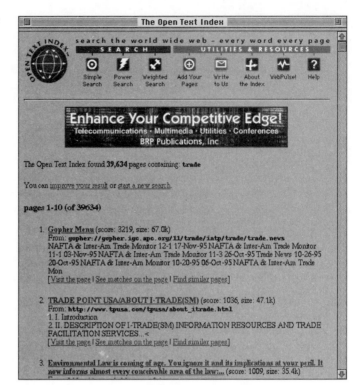

How

World Wide Web

Where

www.opentext.com/omw/f-omw.html

Savvy Search ☆☆☆

Overwhelmed by the hundreds of Internet search engines? Wish you could go to one place, type once, and search several engines at the same time? Well, rub that old lamp, and—poof!—Savvy Search will grant your wish. Savvy Search harnesses the magic powers of the Web to spread your search over several Web search engines.

Not only that, but Savvy Search gives you homepage guidance in your choice of 14 languages:

- English
- Spanish
- French

- Italian
- German
- Dutch
- Norwegian
- Korean
- Russian
- Finnish
- Esperanto (!)
- Swedish
- Danish
- Japanese

It not only lets you search Web sites such as the free version of InfoSeek, but also FTP sites, newsgroups, the Internet Movie Database, and *Roget's Thesaurus*. The drawbacks are that Savvy Search is slow (because you don't get your response back until Savvy receives the slowest response to your search, repackages it, and resends it to you) and your results often have little to do with your topic (because you can't use each site's unique controls to pinpoint your search). But, hey, you got your wish.

Savvy Search searches other Web servers, so it finds lots of stuff, but most searches, like this one for "accounting," bring you off-topic hits.

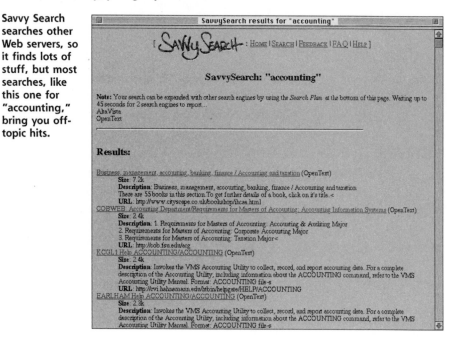

Now be careful—you have only two wishes left.

How

World Wide Web

Where

www.cs.colostate.edu/~dreiling/smartform.html

Archie ☆☆☆

Archie does only one thing, but does it well. If you know the name of a file (perhaps a text document like **huckfinn.txt** or a software program like **wrdprfct.zip**), and you know your file is available on an FTP server but you don't know where, then Archie is the tool for you. Type in your file name and Archie will search most of the FTP sites in the world and tell you all the sites where you can find your file. You don't need to use FTP. This site runs Archie from your Web browser, which makes it much easier to use. For the fastest response, use the Archie Web server closest to you.

How

World Wide Web

Where

U.S.: http://hoohoo.ncsa.uiuc.edu/archie.html

Ireland: www.ucc.ie/cgi-bin/archie

Another Web-ized version of Archie offers more search choices. It is called **ArchiePlex**. Use the Archieplex server nearest you.

U.S.: www.lerc.nasa.gov/archiplex

U.K.: pubweb.nexor.co.uk/public/archie/archiplex/archieplex.html

Australia: www.telstra.com.au/services/archieplex/archieplex.html

Snoopie ☆☆☆

Snoopie searches its own database of almost 6 million FTP files (documents and software programs) and directory names. Snoopie is a very fast searcher. It gives you a list of links to the matching files and directories it finds. Each link shows the size and name of the matching resource. When we searched the same topic with Snoopie and Archie, we discovered that Snoopie dug up more hits.

How

World Wide Web

Where

www.snoopie com

FTP Search ☆☆☆

Our third FTP search tool is plainly named FTP Search, but don't let its mundane name mislead you. Our searches of FTP using this tool repeatedly found the most matches of all FTP tools we tested. Not only that, but FTP Search gives you the most information about its findings: size, date created, type, and other handy data. Its name might be unimaginative, but FTP Search gets the job done with a flourish.

How

World Wide Web

Where

ftpsearch.unit.no/ftpsearch

Veronica ☆☆☆

To a businessperson whose first experience of the Internet was the World Wide Web, going back to Gopher is like time travel to the nineteenth century. The Web flashes in your face, but Gopher seems, quaint, refined, and polite, like a character in a Jane Austen novel. Nobody shouts on Gopher.

Gophers are dying out, but valuable business information is still available on Gopher servers. If you are serious about finding something stored on a Gopher server, try Veronica. It searches 99 percent of the world's Gophers, and also finds some information on Web sites, newsgroup archives, and Telnet sites.

Veronica gives you two ways to find stuff. If you choose "Simplified Veronica: find directory titles" you will browse through a series of menus until you find the one you need. Find it faster by choosing "Simplified Veronica: find ALL gopher types." This leads you to a fast search engine. Veronica searches for words in titles. Type in your keyword(s), and you'll quickly receive a list of all directory titles and document names that contain your keyword. Then, just like the Web, click on the name you want and Gopher will take you there.

How

Gopher

Where

gopher://veronica.scs.unr.edu:70/11/veronica

 Both Internet Sleuth and All-in-One Internet Search offer Veronica access from the Web. If you are unfamiliar with Gopher, one of these Web sites may be easier, but Veronica is faster when you use its Gopher incarnation.

Jughead is another, less-useful Gopher search tool that you will rarely need. Jughead is Veronica turned inside-out. Use Veronica when you have an idea what you want but don't know where to find it. Use Jughead when you are at a specific Gopher server and you want to find information. Most often, a Jughead indexes only menu names for the specific computer where that Jughead lives. There is one Jughead database that contains links to all Gophers. You'll find it at Washington & Lee University:

gopher://liberty.uc.wlu.edu:70/11/gophers/other

Directories for Gopher, FTP, and Web Stuff

RES-Links All-in-One Resource Page ☆☆☆☆

Can't find it? Go here. RES-Links is a wonderful Web directory devoted to one thing: Where to find stuff on the Net. Not only does RES-Links give you hot links to all major search engines, directories, how-to-do-it guides and other tools, but it carefully and clearly *explains the differences between them.*

On your initial visit to RES-Links, first read its page of instructions. RES-Links is organized differently from other directories. Once you understand the logic behind them, you'll find RES-Links' categories and subcategories more useful than plain old alphabetical lists. The instructions include a glossary which explains seemingly tiny distinctions in Net tools that make the difference between your results being bullish or bull you-know-what. If you skip this short glossary, you won't know if a resource can deliver what you need or hang you out to dry.

Then jump to the main RES-Links directories and wail! They'll make finding stuff a lot easier and a lot faster for you.

How

World Wide Web

Where

www.cam.org/~intsci

NCSA What's New Page ☆☆☆☆

Whatever industry you work in, you'll have a tough time visiting this page without finding something new and interesting for your business. The NCSA What's New Page is the number one spot to announce a new World Wide Web site. Every Monday through Friday the contents of this page are replaced with a brand new directory of more than 100 just-opened sites. The top sites of the week are listed first on the page, followed by hot links and descriptions of that day's other new sites.

Invest three to four hours per week on this site for two or three weeks and you'll have a better overview of what's happening on the Net than many Internet pros. You'll probably spot competitors, new Net tools, and maybe a new sales prospect. There are so many sites here that you should ignore the ones of little interest. Besides the current day's world premieres, you can also browse archives of old "What's New" pages by year, month, and date. Unfortunately, these archives are not searchable.

Even without the archives, this will be a rewarding site for your business. You'll find more treasures here than if Bill Gates held a garage sale.

How

World Wide Web

Where

www.ncsa.uiuc.edu/SDG/Software/Mosaic/Docs/whats-new.html

FedWorld ☆☆☆☆

First introduced on the Internet in 1992, FedWorld was implemented to help make it easier for you and me, Joe and Jane Q. Public, to access the many mountains of government documents made available each year. Originally linked to about 50 government bulletin boards, FedWorld has grown into an enormous clearinghouse of government information, with links to over 130 federal agencies and more than 10,000 files.

In addition to links to government Telnet and FTP sites, FedWorld includes hundreds of links to agencies and documents on nearly any conceivable subject. From aeronautics and business to transportation and urban technology, you'll find something useful at FedWorld.

Where

www.fedworld.gov

Links

Federal jobs, by region or state, updated five times per week

Department of Commerce

Bureau of Exports Administration

Import Administration (monitors antidumping and countervailing duty laws)

Foreign Trade Zone Board and Statutory Imports Program

SEC libraries, with *SEC News Digest* back issues

Rule of Law Donor Database (organizations in "New Independent States" cross-referenced and listed by countries in **index.wp5** file)

CALS Computer Aided Acquisitions and Logistics Support

Big Emerging Markets Handbook, a free book from NTIS

Just how much documentation can one government produce?

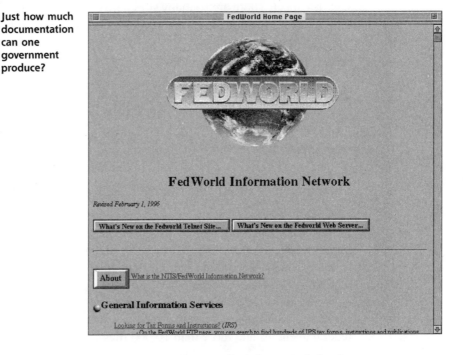

If FedWorld absolutely, positively can't find the U.S. federal government resource you want, take a poke at the **Federal Web Locator** at:

www.law.vill.edu/fed-agency/fedwebloc.html

Argus Clearinghouse ☆☆☆

Hey—this directory is a guide to *directories*! What a great idea. Not only does Argus give you directories available on Web sites, Gophers, newsgroups, and mailing lists, it also tells what's useful (or not) about them. It gives you different ways to look at data—alphabetically, by Net tool, or by subject.

Under its "Business and Employment" heading, you'll find about thirty different topics. Each topic includes clear descriptions, specially written for Argus by a specialist on that subject.

A sample of the information that the Argus Clearinghouse puts at the fingertips of cyberpreneurs.

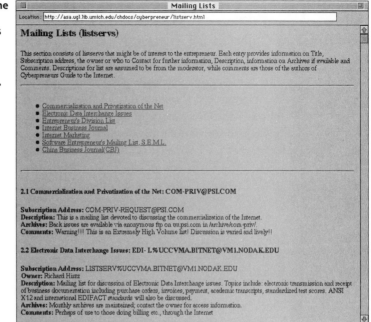

How

World Wide Web

Where

www.lib.umich.edu/chouse

ONLINE WORLD ☆☆☆☆

Online World isn't really a directory. It's a good book on how to use the Internet, available in print and on the World Wide Web. It tells you how to use the Net and other online networks (especially CompuServe). It's useful, although it goes into more technical detail than most businesspeople will need.

So what is this book doing here listed under directories? Funny you should ask. The book's author, a man with the literally odd name of Odd de Presno, describes many useful Net resources. In this Web book, all those resources are hotlinks, just like the other Net directories. Especially see de Presno's chapter on finding stuff, "Looking for a Needle in a Bottle of Hay." His book also includes several solid chapters on how businesspeople can apply the Net.

How

World Wide Web

Where

login.eunet.no/~presno/bok/i.html

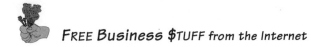

How to Find Businesses and Business Resources

THE BUSINESS GUIDE TO THE INTERNET ☆☆☆☆☆

The previous two sections of this chapter showed you several search sites and directories you can use to find resources of general interest, including some for businesses. (For instance, Yahoo and Trade Wave Galaxy are both good general resources with great directories of business resources.) This section gives you some tools specifically for finding businesses, and more importantly, resources for businesses. This is an important distinction. Directories of companies, for instance, mostly consist of enterprises that serve consumers. Mrs. Fields' Cookies is a company, but will its products and services help you grow your business? Maybe your waistline. Anyhow, this section gives you both: ways to find all kinds of businesses, and ways to find resources specifically for businesspeople.

All of this schpiel is a way to preface an exceptional resource, *The Business Guide to the Internet,* for you and your business. This is a very good free book. In print, it would be hundreds of pages. Its author, Sam Sternberg, gives his book away as an inducement to get you to pay to subscribe to his electronic newsletter. This is one of the ten best books on Internet business. It has short sections on how to apply the Internet to every aspect of your business, followed by listings and descriptions of hundreds and hundreds of Internet resources useful for businesses. There is very useful stuff here for any business even thinking about using the Net.

This Web site features two tables of contents for the book, a brief one and a longer, very detailed list of contents. Note that you cannot read the book itself on the Web, but you can download it to have your own copy. You have two choices: You can either download the entire book with FTP in one big 1.2-megabyte file, or you can use Gopher to copy it in smaller chunks.

How

World Wide Web plus either FTP or Gopher (see above)

Where

www.helsinki.fi/~lsaarine/ssbusg.html

Thomas Register of American Manufacturers ☆☆☆☆☆

This is one of the best business resources on the Net. The Thomas Register Supplier Finder searches through the gigantic Thomas database of hundreds of thousands of U.S. manufacturers by either product (52,000 categories) or by company name. You can narrow your search by geographic parameters. The listings retrieved include company name, contact information, and product lines manufactured. You must register to use this valuable service, but it's free. However, the registration screen has problems accepting some email addresses.

As a test, we searched for "cassette shells" (an obscure product). Thomas couldn't find a manufacturer for that term. We tried "audio cassettes" as a second choice. Thomas responded with a list of 113 manufacturers. Several seemed to have nothing to do with cassettes, but most did, and some manufacturers of shells. If you stump the Web directory and can't find a manufacturer, just fill out a Web form describing what you want. Thomas staffers will research for you for free and respond by fax or email. Now that's service!

If you are a U.S. manufacturer, this site offers another benefit. You can publicize your products by listing your company and what you have to offer, for free. Just fill out a Web form. Your description will be featured in the print version of the Thomas directory and its CD-ROM counterpart, which are used heavily by tens of thousands of purchasing agents.

The Thomas site also features "How to Buy It," short outlines of what to look for when you buy different kinds of business software—manufacturing software, for instance, or inventory software.

How

World Wide Web

Where

www.thomasregister.com/home.html

Hoover's Company Profiles ☆☆☆☆☆

Hoover's provides high-quality stuff for businesses. The star of the show is Hoover's MasterList Plus database, where you can get free capsule profiles of almost 10,000 U.S. corporations. You can search Hoover's MasterList by company name, ticker symbol, location, or sales. The cool thing about these capsule profiles is that each one has hotlinks to that company's SEC filings, stock chart, and (if there is one) Web site. You can't do that with a printed directory.

Move over one page to **www.hoovers.com/bizreg.html** to use Hoover's Corporate Web Register. It has no search engine, but you can scan this directory of a couple of thousand companies with Web sites. Click on the one you want to visit.

There's so much more here to see, you could almost call it Hooverland. You'll find profiles of major industries. "Biz Buzz" gives you the past week's business news. "Biz Book Bestsellers" delivers the scoop on this week's 25 best-selling business books. (I hope that's not a you-know-what scoop.) There are several other columns and features here, all adding up to make Hoover's Dam useful for most businesses. (Well, I *almost* made it through this whole review without including that obvious pun.)

How
World Wide Web

Where
www.hoovers.com

If you'd like free access to Hoover's extremely informative, full-length profiles of corporations, go to **www.pathfinder.com**. You'll find complete profiles on 400 of the largest U.S. businesses.

A Business Researcher's Interests ☆☆☆☆

Mr. Malhotra built this catalog of Internet sites for businesses mainly to serve his own individual needs, but put it on the Web to share with you, me, and other interested businesspeople. He lists more than 1,000 hand-picked resources. This site is especially rich in sites useful for Information Systems managers in businesses. Other high points include many articles on electronic commerce, resources for Web design, "Emergent Organizational Forms & Virtual Organizations," which has useful information for businesses that use the Net as part of their core strategies, and "India Business & Technology." This last section gives you hotlinks to hundreds of business, Internet, and computing resources in India, including news sources and a searchable directory of fax numbers.

About the only drawback to this site is that the resources and links, although carefully selected and organized, have no descriptions. In many cases, you must visit them to figure out why Malhotra chose them.

How
World Wide Web

Where
www.pitt.edu/~malhotra/interest.html

Institute of Management and Administration (IOMA) ☆☆☆☆

IOMA lists most major Internet sites for business, including resources for finance, investment, import/export, and credit management. It jams together hundreds of links with absolutely no descriptions. Some people prefer this approach. Others feel like IOMA throws them into a sea of resources without a compass. Blub!

This site also includes sample articles from dozens of IOMA's business newsletters, ranging in worth from valuable to ho-hum. Sample topics include:

- "Explaining the Odds of Equity Investing to Participants"
- "10 Principles That Ensure Successful Department Reengineering"
- "Fifth Annual Accounting Firm Survey"
- "Bank of America Pinpoints 8 Proposals to Enhance Company Cash Flow"
- "CFOs Suggest Best Practices to Improve Purchasing Function"

Other articles cover human resources management, business law, purchasing, and the construction business.

How

World Wide Web

Where

ioma.com/ioma

CommerceNet ☆☆☆☆

This nonprofit organization is in many ways the center of business on the Internet. Its goal: Make the Net more usable for business and industry. CommerceNet coordinates efforts of its member companies to solve the most vexing problems of businesses on the Net. You have two reasons to visit the CommerceNet site—first, to find out about the organization and what it is doing, and second, to use the many reference resources at this site.

The busiest parts of CommerceNet are its working groups. The Catalog and Directories Working Group handles putting large catalogs on the Net. There is a Collaborative Design, Engineering, and Manufacturing Working Group (called CALS for short), a Payment Services Working Group, an EDI (Electronic Data Interchange) Working Group, and others. The goals and projects of these groups will impact almost all businesses in the next few years.

CommerceNet also provides information on how your business can get connected to the Net (and what to look for in an Internet service provider). If your business has its own Web site, we highly recommend that you read "Understanding the Effectiveness of Your WWW Site: Measurement Methods and

Technology," available here for free. You can also find out about CommerceNet affiliates in Canada, Japan, and other countries.

CommerceNet's directories are arranged in five sections. **Companies and Organizations** contains the Minority Business and Professional Directory (which is searchable and browsable), Hoover's Bay Area 500 (capsule profiles of the 500 largest businesses in the San Francisco Bay Area; does not give Web or email addresses), Internet Consultants (a good, searchable directory), and Internet Access Providers. This last section is searchable by name, capability, or geographic location, but it's woefully incomplete. The geographic location search is weak; it lists providers *located in* your city, not those that *serve* it. This area also gives you hotlinks to the **AT&T Directory of Company 800 Numbers** and Open Market's directory of online commercial sites.

Skip CommerceNet's **Products and Services** section; there's little helpful information here. **Location and Transportation Resources** gives you links to local San Francisco Bay Area resources, the Web site Hotels and Travel on the Net, U.S. State Government Servers, and a U.S. Gazetteer. **Individuals, Groups, and Associations** provides links to the Small Business Advancement National Center, the SBA, and Software Forum, the excellent organization for software company managers formerly called Software Entrepreneur's Forum. **News, Information, and Events** gives you links to online newspapers, newsletters, and trade journals.

CommerceNet also contains a good link called Glossary of Net Terms, and the archives of the technically-oriented **sepp-talk** email discussion group. SEPP is a payment protocol. When credit cards and debit cards are physically absent (as they are for Internet sales), SEPP provides a standard way to process electronic payments.

How

World Wide Web

Where

www.commerce.net

WWW Yellow Pages ☆☆☆

No power-lunch yuppie who has survived the drug-induced '60s would dare claim that cyberspace is a paragon of organization and sensibility—in fact, navigating the Web sometimes seems like a supreme hallucination. It's a great place to go browsing if you've got a lot of time to kill, but if you're looking for something in particular, the Web can quickly seem like a demon bent on hiding the proverbial cyberneedle in a virtual haystack.

That's why you'll appreciate sites like this one at the University of Houston's College of Business Administration. They've gathered all the known Web business sites and compiled a comprehensive listing of links to businesses on the Web.

From the megabuck conglomerates to the doing-business-in-the-garage types, they're all here—or at least almost all. Business is booming in cyberspace, and moving forward at a pace even Michael Eisner would find tough to keep up with. But this site, organized by category, is updated regularly, and makes it easy for you to keep abreast of business sites on the Web. Just check in from time to time to see who has hung up their shingle.

How

World Wide Web

Where

www.cba.uh.edu/ylowpges/ylowpges.html

Open Market's Commercial Sites Index ☆☆☆

Hunting for a business someplace on the Web? Try this site's catalog of 25,000 businesses that have commercial sites on the Web. They all have a paragraph or so of description. You can use Open Market's search engine or browse through the directory alphabetically by name. While you're here, take a peek at Open Market's What's New page. It changes daily, and usually has some interesting new Net businesses.

How

World Wide Web

Where

www.directory.net

Professionals Online ☆☆☆

What you have here are brief directories of some online resources for business professionals. If Godzilla-size directories overwhelm you, try this site's smaller lists of business, finance, accounting, legal, and computing links. You can also use Professional Online's informative job-hunting section. Most listings have short, helpful descriptions.

How

World Wide Web

Where

www.prosonline.com

Information Innovation ☆☆☆

You'll find lots of information here, some of it excellent. This would be a five-star site if only its owners organized it better and kept it more up-to-date. (On my last visit, its What's New page hadn't been updated in *more than a year!*)

Even so, you can make use of the Dictionary of Web Terms, read interviews with cyberbusinessmen (no women yet), read book reviews on Net biz books, and use the site's extensive directories of Net business resources. This site is especially good at pointing out European business resources on the Net. Just remember, it's not as up-to-date as it could be.

How

World Wide Web

Where

www.euro.net/innovation

How to Find Email Lists

Liszt Directory of Email Discussion Groups ☆☆☆☆

Anyone with email can create a small list, and with a small computer and a little software one person can create many lists. Because email lists are so easy to create, they are incredibly decentralized. As a result, email lists are often very hard to find.

This punnily named site lets you search a database of 25,000 email discussion groups. If you want to make Liszt jump through hoops, it can run complicated searches for you. It examines only group names, group email addresses, and incredibly short descriptions. It tells you where to go to get more information on each group, but does *not* tell you where to find FAQs or archives. Note also that Liszt does not search Mailbase email lists. (See below for Mailbase.)

Liszt's software checks every week to make sure each list is still active and that Liszt's information is still up-to-date. Frequent updating and the large size of Liszt's database, make it an excellent place to find discussion groups on topics that affect your business and your own job.

Top of the results from running a simple Liszt search for free email discussion groups with the word "trade" in their names or descriptions.

Email discussion groups are the main course, but there is more. Liszt will also search newsgroups for you—not all of them, but more than 13,000 newsgroups. Not bad for dessert.

How

World Wide Web

Where

www.liszt.com

Mailbase ☆☆☆

Though it houses only 500 or so email discussion groups based in the U.K., Mailbase does a better job of presenting information about its lists than the two resources above. You can search names and descriptions. Mailbase not only presents you with the names and short descriptions of each list that meets your criteria, but also hotlinks you to a detailed description, your list's FAQ, its archive, and step-by-step instructions on how to describe. For icing on the cake, Mailbase lets you browse an alphabetical directory of its discussion groups.

The beginning of the results page created by searching for U.K. email discussion groups with the word "trade" in their names and descriptions.

Search Results

| Welcome | What's New? | What's Cool? | Questions | Net Search | Net Directory |

Search Results

Your search on *"trade"* returned 4 result(s)

Results are *relevance ranked* by WAIS, with 'most relevant' first and take the form of the name of the list (which is a link to that list's Home Page) followed by the description:

- int-trade-research: Information on the development of an International Trade Research Programme Proposal. This will be considered for funding by the ESRCs Research Programmes Board.

- industrial-relations-research: A forum for academic discussion on industrial relations broadly conceived. It covers current research, methods, results and theories on employment relations, collective relationships, trade unions, HRM & employment law.

- nukop-economy: nukop-economy offers regular updates of new economic related UK government publications and a forum to discuss matters arising from them. Keywords: economic activity; industry; inflation; policy; public spending; taxation; trade; unemployment.

- trade-unions-he: The list is for members of trade unions recognised in UK higher education to discuss issues and topics of concern. It is intended to help overcome the distance between the different unions in the sector.

Separate multiple searchterms with *and* and *or* where appropriate. (Where multiple searchterms are used without boolean operators, the default is *or*.) Search terms may be terminated with a wild card (*) and *cannot contain punctuation*. All searches are case insensitive.

Enter search term(s) : [   ]

How
World Wide Web

Where
www.mailbase.ac.uk/lists

Tile.net Lists ☆☆☆

Tile.net's Web site was designed to show off its Tile software for creating Web sites. The attraction here is not necessarily a mammoth number of email lists, but the creative ways in which you can get to them. Click on the word "search" for a search engine, but before you do, feast your eyes on Tile.net's lists of lists. The "Most popular" category shows names, short descriptions, and numbers of subscribers for lists with 1,000 or more subscribers. (The email version of David Letterman's Top Ten List is number one.) You can also track down email lists by subject, by name, by sponsoring organization, and by country. A very good (fun!) way to find useful business lists.

How
World Wide Web

Where
tile.net/lists

SRI's List of Lists ☆☆☆

This is a handmade database of email discussion groups, not as complete as some others, but carefully compiled and worth searching.

How

World Wide Web

Where

catalog.com/vivian/interest-group-search.html

Top of the page showing the results of searching SRI's List of Lists for "accounting."

```
▤             Result of your List of Lists Search             ▣

Result of search for "accounting":


List Name: AECM-L@LOYOLA.EDU
Subscription Address: MAILSERV@LOYOLA.EDU
Owner: E. Barry Rice
Description:

     AECM stands for "Accounting Education using Computers and Multimedia". This
     list/interest group provides a forum for discussions of all hardware and software which
     can be useful in any way for accounting education at the college/university level.
     Hardware includes all platforms. Software includes spreadsheets and related templates,
     practice sets, multimedia authoring and presentation packages, data base programs, tax
     packages, instructor-developed applications, etc. Loyola College in Maryland, which
     has an AACSB-accredited accounting program, serves as the host to the list which was
     established in February, 1994. This list was conceived to bring together accounting
     faculty, authors, developers, publishers and anyone else with an interest in using
     computers and multimedia in accounting education. Subscribers are encouraged to ask
     questions, share ideas and information, and discuss the good and bad experiences they
     have had with various educational accounting software and hardware products.
     Possible topics include: computer applications in managerial/systems/tax; AECC
     curriculum revisions and computer-based pedagogical approaches to support these
     changes; notable educational accounting software and hardware, as well as inferior
     products one should avoid; Information about related conferences, workshops and
     seminars; discussion of articles, books, and notes which subscribers have found
     stimulating and worthwhile; "What's the best software to use for my [blank] course?";
     "In what direction is educational accounting software evolving?"; and "How can I get
     [product] to do [function]?".


List Name: ASACNET
Subscription Address: LISTSERV@PDOMAIN.UWINDSOR.CA
Owner: Andrew Templer (Windsor)
Last Update: 9/4/95
Description:

     ASACNET is an open, unmoderated discussion list for everyone interested in business
     and management from a Canadian perspective. The group was formed for college and
```

Inter-Links ☆☆☆

This site lets you search a collection of 5,900 email lists that run on Listserv software. What makes this site so great? Well, not only can you search discussion group names and short descriptions, but you can also search a longer, more detailed description. You can also search by the list's email address (if you know the address you can find out about the list), and by the name of the person who is the list owner. As you can see from the illustration, Inter-Links shows you long descriptions, which helps you decide which lists meet your business' needs and which ones don't.

Inter-Links' long descriptions save you time by helping you hunt for the right email discussion groups.

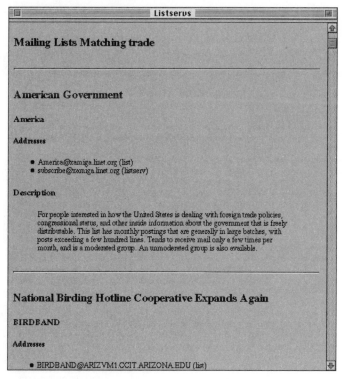

How

World Wide Web

Where

www.nova.edu/Inter-Links/cgi-bin/lists

NEW-LIST ☆☆☆

Want to find out what lists have been newly born? This email list sends you birth announcements of new arrivals as they happen, both the latest discussion groups and new announcement services. Many are computer-related or discuss academic subjects, but more and more are useful for businesspeople. This is a low-volume moderated list, with no spam, so you'll receive only a few messages per week.

Sample announcements:

HTML: HTML Page Creation Assistance List
STEAM-LIST: Industrial Steam Equipment
COMMODIT-E-JOURNAL: Forum for Futures Traders

CONSULT-L: Software Consultants Forum

INVENTORS: Meeting Place for Inventors

How

Email

Where

listserv@vml.nodak.edu

Message

subscribe NEW-LIST Yourfirstname Yourlastname

You can also read these same announcements in the **bit.listserv.new-list** newsgroup.

Sample Announcement of a New Discussion Group

Subject: NEW: STEAM-LIST—Industrial Steam Equipment

STEAM-LIST on listproc@mcfeeley.cc.utexas.edu Industrial Steam Equipment

The STEAM-LIST is intended for discussion of steam generators, piping, and equipment. Boilers, boiler feed pumps, water treatment, corrosion and scaling, valves, PRVs, traps, turbines, flow metering, heating coils, condensate pumps, district heating, system modeling, that sort of stuff. Practical discussions, rather than theoretical or academic ones, are the intent of this list.

To subscribe to the list, send the request

subscribe STEAM-LIST YourFirstName YourLastName

in the body of a mail message to: listproc@mcfeeley.cc.utexas.edu

For example: subscribe steam-list James Watt

The list processor will reject requests that do not contain a personal name, for example, "Jane Doe." Do ☆not☆ include the word "subscribe" in the subject line of the message.

Owner: Miles Abernathy < miles@mail.utexas.edu >

How to Find Usenet Newsgroups

Stanford Netnews Filtering Service ☆☆☆☆

Out of the thousands of Internet newsgroups, how can you find out whether one mentions your product, your company, or your competitor? If you're a big

55

corporation, you can afford to do what Intel does and hire four people to monitor newsgroups. If not, you can go to this valuable free site.

You can do two things here. First, you can search today's newsgroup postings (a mass of text equal to about half of the *Encyclopedia Britannica*) for any names, phrases, numbers, or keywords.

Second, you can use the famous Stanford Information Filtering Tool, called SIFT for short, to be your electronic clipping service. Type in a list of words or phrases, and SIFT will search for them every day. Then, it will build a custom Web page for you, so that, the next time you return, you can read all the messages for topics you requested.

Note that SIFT does not search *all* newsgroups. It inspects only those that begin with these prefixes:

alt.	de. (German)	info.	sci.
ba.	es. (Spanish)	misc.	soc.
comp.	fr. (French)	news.	talk.
dc.	gnu.	rec.	vmsnet.

Pat and I conducted head-to-head comparison tests of SIFT and InfoSeek. We had them both search the same day's groups for the same topics. InfoSeek actually found a few more articles—but, hey, SIFT is free!

How

World Wide Web

Where

www.sift.stanford.edu

Usenet Newsgroups: Resources ☆☆☆☆

Yes, this site *does* show you how to find the newsgroups that help your business. But even better, you can go here to retrieve information about newsgroups and how they work. If you want to use newsgroups for your business on a serious level (more than reading and occasionally posting), visit this site. You'll find everything from basics for beginners through advanced topics for advanced users. There are four guides to creating your company's own newsgroups, and instructions on how to moderate a newsgroup. (We like moderators and anyone else who fights spam.)

How

World Wide Web

Where

scwww.ucs.indiana.edu/NetRsc/usenet.html

Newsgroup Search Engines at a Glance

Confused about the different parts of newsgroups and which resource lets you find what? Run your peepers over our handy comparison chart. In addition to the six resources profiled here, note that other sites are specifically dedicated to either FAQs or newsgroup archives.

Search by:	SIFT	InfoCenter Launch Pad	DejaNews	InfoSeek (free search)	Tile.net	Alta Vista
Newsgroup names		•			•	
Descriptions		•			•	
Moderator names		•				
Contents of FAQs		•		•		
Contents of current messages	•		•	•		•
Contents of archived past messages			•	•		•
"Subject:" of messages	•		•	•		•
Senders' names	•		•	•		•
Dates of message			•			•

Usenet InfoCenter Launch Pad ☆☆☆

You have two resources here. First, a good search engine (that does not work with all browsers) finds groups by newsgroup name, by moderator name, or by description. It also searches the contents of newsgroup FAQs. (But it does *not* search the actual contents of posted messages.)

Second, a directory arranged by those funny prefixes at the front of newsgroup names (such as **alt.** and **biz.**); newsgroup pros call them *hierarchies*. You start with top-level hierarchies and work your way down until you find the newsgroup you want. While handy, the Launch Pad list of top-level hierarchies is not at all complete.

How

World Wide Web

Where

sunsite.unc.edu/usenet-b/home.html

DejaNews Research Service ☆☆☆

DejaNews is a useful resource, once you ignore its hype-heavy home page. You can search its database of newsgroups and postings by the contents of a message, the name of an author who posted the message, the contents of the "Subject" line near the top of each message, and the date a message was posted. DejaNews says it does not search all newsgroups, claiming to skip the **soc.**, **talk.**, and **binaries** groups, and, astonishingly, the valuable **alt.** groups. That's what DejaNews says, but in our tests, it did find messages in some of the **alt.** groups. One great thing about this service is that it stores messages for a long time, up to a year for some groups. That's really valuable when you do in-depth research.

How
World Wide Web

Where
www.dejanews.com

Tile.net Index of Newsgroups ☆☆☆

This site lists *all* newsgroup hierarchies worldwide in a giant directory. It's the most complete catalog of newsgroups—even the obscure ones—we could find anywhere on the Net. Even better, this is the only place that actually *defines* those puzzling prefixes at the beginning of newsgroup names. Sure, everybody knows that groups beginning with **comp.** are about computing, but can you figure out what newsgroups cover when they begin with these prefixes? ("Moses! Take out your tablets. Number from one to ten. This is a pop quiz!")

1. relcom. _____   6. sat. _____
2. gtb. _____   7. hsv. _____
3. stl. _____   8. sdnet. _____
4. pbx. _____   9. chv. _____
5. dungeon. _____   10. adass. _____

This site also contains a searchable database of newsgroups, so you can find a group by subject or by part of its name. Marketers, take note: For some groups, this database shows a group's actual number of readers, its average number of messages per day, the percentage of Internet sites that receive the group, and the percentage of crossposting in the group.

How
World Wide Web

Where

tile.net/news

> **Answers**
> 1. Russia
> 2. Not Great Britain, but Gothenberg, Sweden.
> 3. St. Louis, Missouri.
> 4. Not a switchboard, but Pittsburgh, Pennsylvania.
> 5. Doom computer games.
> 6. Not a weekend day, but San Antonio, Texas.
> 7. Huntsville, Alabama.
> 8. San Diego.
> 9. Charlottesville, Virginia.
> 10. Not blue jean ads, but astronomical data archiving systems and software. No, really!

Usenet FAQs Archive☆☆☆☆

Most newsgroups have FAQs (Frequently Asked Questions) documents. A FAQ contains information about the group itself and what it covers, and many a FAQ contains a good introduction to the subject or subjects that the group discusses—in the best cases, the equivalent of a small guidebook. Sometimes it seems that everybody on the Net pesters you to read a particular FAQ. Okay, but where do you find it?

Well, look no further. This is where you go to find newsgroup FAQs. (Unfortunately, there is no equivalent FAQ treasure trove for email discussion groups. Their FAQs are scattered all over the globe.)

You can search this archive by newsgroup names, by archive names, by newsgroup subjects, and by keywords. Note that you cannot search the FAQ documents themselves. Directories let you look up newsgroups alphabetically by subject or by name.

How

World Wide Web

Where

www.cis.ohio-state.edu/hypertext/faq/usenet/FAQ-List.html

Most newsgroup FAQs are also posted to the newsgroup **news.answers** periodically.

Consultation of the French Newsgroups ☆☆☆

This site—which is only in French—reproduces all French newsgroups (from France—no *Quebecois* here) so people who can't otherwise reach French groups can read their messages on the Web. You can only *read* messages here. You cannot post to the groups or reply to the messages you read. This is useful for francophiles whose local providers do not carry the group. The newsgroup carrying job opportunities can be especially useful, because French businesses post openings both in and out of France. (One job posting asked for an English-speaking writer to work in Luxembourg, but our book deadlines kept us from applying. Darn!)

How

World Wide Web

Where

prof.inria.fr/~pierre/news.html

You'll find a good guide to French newsgroups, their archives, and their FAQs at "Les groupes Usenet fr.*" on the Web at:

www.fr.net/new-fr

Find Telnet Sites & Bulletin Board Systems

Hytelnet ☆☆☆

Telnet is one of the most primitive and puzzling tools on the Internet, but there are many resources that you can't access any other way. Telnet lets you use someone else's computer from a distance; therefore, it had to be primitive so it could work on any system. Hytelnet is the database of Telnet sites, and Trade Web Galaxy has added a friendly Web face to Hytelnet to make it easier to use.

First, you can search the database part of Hytelnet while you're still on the Web. Search for a resource name. Point and click on it and follow the instructions onscreen. You'll go directly to your resource. Once you are in the resource, the familiar Web look is gone and you're on your own, but at least Galaxy helped you get to this point.

How

World Wide Web

Where

galaxy.einet.net/hytelnet/START.TXT.html

Select BBSes on the Internet ☆☆☆

Bulletin Board Systems (BBSes for short) are not part of the Internet. They are online worlds like no other. However, you can reach hundreds of them from the Internet via Telnet. This site has by far the largest catalog of BBSes on the Net. The main pages list BBS names and whether you can reach them by Telnet (and for some, by the World Wide Web), but it gives *no descriptions*. You can't tell which BBSes are for business, which are for programmers, and which are recreational.

Never fear! Go to another page at this site (**www.cris.com/~mark/sbi.lst**) to find descriptions. Be warned: This is a 250 K text file. But you can find information about free BBSes for different businesses, such as Appraisal Profession Online for appraisers and Dental-X-Change for dental professionals.

How

World Wide Web

Where

dkeep.com/sbi.ht

How to Find Free Fax Servers

Internet Fax Server ☆☆☆☆☆

You might find this hard to believe, but you can use the Internet to send faxes all over the world for free. This Internet service has been around for years, but it's amazing how few businesspeople know about it.

This was the first Internet fax server, and it's still the biggest. You can send a fax from anywhere in the world (wherever you go) to fifteen countries:

- Australia
- Canada
- U.S.
- Greece
- Croatia
- Denmark
- Germany
- Hong Kong
- Italy

- Korea
- New Zealand
- Portugal
- Sweden
- Taiwan
- U.K.

In some countries, free faxes can reach only certain area codes. Before you fax, check the "coverage list" at this Web site to see if this service can reach your destination.

Is there a catch? Of course. First, you have to type your message into the forms provided on this Web server, so you can't use graphics or your company letter-head. Second, the cover sheet for your fax will have a small advertising message at the bottom (but no ad will appear on the page with your message).

With every fax you send, you'll get a receipt via email showing that your fax was delivered. Whether you're faxing across the state or around the world, the Internet Fax Server is a real money saver. There are servers in the U.S. and the U.K., so you can use whichever is closest to you.

How

World Wide Web

Where

U.S.: www.tpc.int/faxsend.html

U.K.: www.balliol.ox.ac.uk/fax/faxsend.html

IBAG Faxes ☆☆☆

IBAG lets you send a fax free from anywhere in the world to any fax machine in the Phoenix, Arizona area. Sponsored by the Internet Business Access Group, this fax server lets you cut text from any Windows software and paste it in your message. You'll receive a delivery receipt via email.

How

World Wide Web

Where

www.ibag.com/fax.html

FaxMail ☆☆☆

Send faxes for free to any city in New Zealand. There are a couple of limits. Your fax can only be one page of up to 40 lines of text, and the bottom will include up to 10 lines of advertising. For each fax you send, you will receive a delivery receipt through email.

How

World Wide Web

Where

www.actrix.gen.nz/biz/faxmail/faxmail.htm

Free Fax FAQ ☆☆☆

This helpful Web pages gives you complete instructions for sending free faxes via email to Sweden, Quebec, Kuwait, New Zealand, Canada, and the U.S. There are also instructions for using the Net to send faxes anywhere in the world for much less than the cost of an international call.

How

World Wide Web

Where

www.northcoast.com/savetz/fax-faq.html

Universal Access Web Fax ☆☆☆

This service turns the previous ones inside-out. Instead of using the Internet to deliver faxes, this one uses fax machines to deliver the Internet. You can surf the Web without a computer! Universal Access Web Fax delivers Web pages— pictures and all—to your fax machine. No Internet connection is needed. It will even play Web sound files over your phone. This is a free service, but you do have to pay for a phone call to Southern California.

How

World Wide Web

Where

www.datawave.net

You don't need a Web browser to find out about the Universal Access Web Fax service. You can also retrieve information about it by fax. Call 805-730-7777 from the handset of your fax machine.

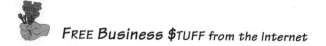

When All Else Fails, Ask

news.newusers.questions Newsgroup ☆☆☆
bit.listserv.help-net Newsgroup ☆☆☆☆

An the old story goes, a father watched his son trying to move a large rock to build a fort. The little boy pushed and shoved for quite a while until, sweating and dirty, he quit. "I give up," he told his dad. "I tried everything I could."

"No, you didn't," said his father. "You didn't ask me for help."

These two newsgroups are places you can ask for help, too. You can ask questions and you'll receive answers. The first of these two groups is the busiest. As well as how-to questions, it gets lots of messages from people looking for penpals. The second generates a lower number of messages. It is mirrored with the HELP-NET email discussion group, and is moderated and spam-free.

Sample topics from **news.newusers.questions**: Hello, send me email anyone; How to Get Overseas Business Connections Through the Internet?; Help with newsgroups; *chi puo darmi una lista di news server Italiani pubblici*?; I blew 3 grand for the system, somebody please just say hi; Siemens PEB2056 integrated circuit; Where to test posts?; How to Chat.

Sample topics from **bit.listserv.help-net**: Eudora problem; Printing from Netscape 2.0 mail; listserv subscription problem; mouse hangs during Netscape connection; Does this exist?; Files with a ☆.GZ; International jobs sites?; Publicizing a home page?; How do I find online college courses?; Need address; Coffee prices in stock market.

How

Newsgroups

Where

news.newusers.questions
bit.listserv.help-net

Help Desk on the Internet

We haven't assigned a rating of stars to the Help Desk on the Internet because it was too new to review. This Web site has mighty, noble ambitions. Visit Help Desk, and enter any questions you have on Internet topics, PC hardware, and software. Leave your email address, and the folks here will get back to you via email. They have even included a way for you to indicate if your question is urgent or not. If this site is well-managed, it can be a tremendous resource for puzzled businesspeople all over the world.

How

World Wide Web

Where

www.webmart.com/the_helpdesk.html

bit.listserv.buslib-l Business Librarians Newsgroup ☆☆☆☆☆

When you can't find the business information you need, it's time to turn to the business information-finding resource. This newsgroup (and its counterpart, the buslib-l email discussion group) is for professional business librarians. These librarians are very helpful at answering business questions. Don't ask "How do I...?" questions here. This newsgroup answers "Where can I find...?" questions. And don't ask obvious questions. Use this newsgroup only after you've already tried looking in other places and failed to find something. When you can't find what you need by searching Alta Vista, try here. This spam-free group is moderated, and is one of the most valuable business resources on the Net so don't abuse it.

Sample topics: 21 CFR part 54?; biographical info on Fujio Mitarai?; Antimony prices; Australian Recordkeeping Guidelines; Library Software; Corporation Home Pages; Q: American Airline Industry in the 1960s: Archival Sources?; Q: radio and television advertising rates?

How

Newsgroup

Where

bit.listserv.buslib-l

FREE $TUFF

I don't want any yes-men
around me. I want everybody
to tell me the truth even if it
costs them their jobs.

Samuel Goldwyn

Business News

On the Net, you can find hundreds of good sources of business news specific to your industry and covering any place or places in the world you do business.

Obviously, we couldn't list all those hundreds of business news sources in one chapter. Instead, we provided you with some of the best overall business news sources and, to give you an idea of what you can get, a sampling of sources that are more specific to certain places and industries. We topped everything off with the best directories we could find that quickly help you uncover the best news sources for your own business.

Did we mention that they're all free? Several top-notch publications that charge big bucks for print editions give you the same information online for free. In fact, by itself the money you save on subscriptions can pay for this book many times over.

A time-saving note: You'll find a zillion magazines and newspapers on the Net. Many of them give you very little or no useful information. They just tell you how to spend your money by subscribing to their publication. For example, a site called Electronic Newsstand (**www.enews.com/business.html**) has dozens of business magazines. Each magazine provides one—count it, one—article and no more. One article is not a good enough reason to repeatedly visit a site. All the sites we cover in this chapter provide you enough news that you'll be sure to visit them again and again.

A High Wire Act

ClariNet ☆☆☆☆☆

ClariNet delivers thousands of business news stories to your desktop every day. You can read ClariNet stories on newsgroups with Netscape and with most other Web browsers.

These are read-only newsgroups. ClariNet gives you stories from Reuters, Associated Press, and NewsBytes, press releases from BizWire, and market reports on high-tech stocks from ClariNet's own TechWire. (It also provides good coverage of sports, but that's a topic for another book.) Stories are sorted by topic. (See our guide below.)

For news about the Internet, ClariNet provides you with *Matrix News,* the respected monthly journal by John Quarterman and Smoot Carl-Mitchell. *Matrix News* normally costs $25 per year, but you can get it free from ClariNet.

And you get something far better than news: sales leads! ClariNet gives you a free subscription to *Commerce Business Daily* , which consists of no news, just "wanna buy" announcements from the U.S. government and NATO. In addition to sales leads from around the world, *CBD* announces seminars and open houses that show you how to sell to government agencies. (You can also receive *Commerce Business Daily* via email for $199 a year, or via the Web for $350 a year. Not from this book!)

ClariNet is great, but for some people, there is a catch. You can read ClariNet newsgroups only if your Internet access provider subscribes to them, and if your software is set up correctly. Some providers subscribe to only a subset of ClariNet; their customers don't receive all the groups, only a portion of them.

ClariNet also has a Web site at **www.clari.net** which provides a list of more than 400 newsgroups. A warning: ClariNet's Web site descriptions of its groups are not always accurate.

How

Newsgroups

Where

For addresses, see the sidebar below.

---

148 ClariNet Business News Sources

Matrix News:
news:clari.tw.new_media.matrix_news—Monthly newsletter about the Internet and other networks; this newsgroup is empty between issues

Sales leads from *Commerce Business Daily:*
news:clari.biz.industry.automotive.cbd—Vehicles and vehicle parts
news:clari.biz.industry.construction.cbd.acquisition—Facilities management and maintenance services
news:clari.biz.industry.construction.cbd.architect + eng—Architectural and engineering services
news:clari.biz.industry.construction.cbd.hardware—Hardware
news:clari.biz.industry.construction.cbd.maintenance—New buildings and structures and maintenance of existing ones
news:clari.biz.industry.construction.cbd.misc—Constructing buildings, tunnels, and other structures
news:clari.biz.industry.construction.cbd.supplies—Construction tools and supplies
news:clari.biz.industry.food.cbd—Food and agricultural products
news:clari.biz.industry.health.cbd—Medical, dental, and veterinary supplies, products and services; includes job opportunities
news:clari.biz.industry.household.cbd—Furniture, food preparation equipment, lockers, floor polishers, toilet paper, and other items
news:clari.biz.industry.information.cbd—Information supplies and services: printing, photo equipment, film/video production, documentation, training, teachers, and job opportunities
news:clari.biz.industry.machinery.cbd.components—Machinery parts
news:clari.biz.industry.machinery.cbd.engines—Engines and accessories
news:clari.biz.industry.machinery.cbd.misc—Machinery
news:clari.biz.industry.metals + mining.cbd—Metals and related items and services

news:clari.biz.industry.misc.cbd.electric—Lighting, power equipment, and security equipment
news:clari.biz.industry.misc.cdb.equip_maint—Equipment maintenance, repair, and rebuilding
news:clari.biz.industry.misc.cbd.equip_services—Equipment leasing and maintenance
news:clari.biz.industry.misc.cbd.housekeeping—Housekeeping supplies and services
news:clari.biz.industry.misc.cbd.lab_supplies—Lab supplies and equipment
news:clari.biz.industry.misc.cbd.management—Various professional services
news:clari.biz.industry.misc.cbd.misc_services—Various professional services
news:clari.biz.industry.misc.cbd.misc_supplies—Miscellaneous supplies and equipment
news:clari.biz.industry.misc.cbd.research—Research project contracts
news:clari.biz.industry.misc.cbd.studies—Research and analysis project contracts
news:clari.biz.industry.textiles.cbd—Textiles and clothing
news:clari.biz.industry.transportation.cbd—Ship repair
news:clari.biz.industry.travel+leisure.cbd—Transportation and lodging
news:clari.tw.aerospace.cbd.components—Aircraft components
news:clari.tw.aerospace.cbd.misc—Miscellaneous aerospace products, supplies, and services
news:clari.tw.chemicals.cbd—Chemical and fuels contracts
news:clari.tw.computers.cbd—Computing and telecommunications hardware, software, and services
news:clari.tw.defense.cbd—Weapons and miscellaneous items used by defense agencies
news:clari.tw.electronics.cbd—Electrical and electronic equipment and parts
news:clari.tw.telecom.cbd—A catchall category: everything from construction of airfield controls to electrical hardware to evaporative coolers; little to do with Telecom

Daily business news:
news:clari.biz.briefs—Short summaries of today's top business stories, posted hourly
news:clari.biz.currencies.misc—World currencies and interest rates
news:clari.biz.currencies.us_dollar—U.S. dollar and interest rates
news:clari.biz.earnings—Corporate earnings, profits, losses, and dividends
news:clari.biz.earnings.releases—Press releases on the above
news:clari.biz.economy.usa—News about U.S. economy, including statistical indicators
news:clari.biz.economy.world—News and statistical indicators on non-U.S. economies
news:clari.biz.features—Longer, more detailed stories on specific business issues
news:clari.biz.front_page—Top five business stories of the day
news:clari.biz.headlines—Top business news, summarized and updated several times daily
news:clari.biz.industry.agriculture—Agriculture, fishing, and forestry business news
news:clari.biz.industry.agriculture.releases—Press releases on the above
news:clari.biz.industry.automotive—News on automotive manufacturing, rental, and retail industries
news:clari.biz.industry.automotive.releases—Press releases about automotive companies
news:clari.biz.industry.aviation—News about airports, airlines, and regulatory agencies
news:clari.biz.industry.aviation.releases—Press releases about the above
news:clari.biz.industry.banking—News about financial institutions
news:clari.biz.industry.banking.releases—Press releases about financial institutions
news:clari.biz.industry.conglomerates—News about holding companies and conglomerates
news:clari.biz.industry.energy—News about energy sources, companies, and prices for all energy sources except nuclear
news:clari.biz.industry.energy.releases—Press releases about the above
news:clari.biz.industry.food—News about the food industry (except restaurants, agriculture, and fishing, which are covered in other groups)
news:clari.biz.industry.food.releases—Press releases about the food industry
news:clari.biz.industry.food.retail.releases—Press releases from restaurants and markets
news:clari.biz.industry.health.care—Health care business news (except pharmaceuticals and medical devices)
news:clari.biz.industry.health.care.releases—Health care and medical press releases
news:clari.biz.industry.health.pharma—News about the pharmaceutical and medical device industries
news:clari.biz.industry.health.pharma.releases—Press releases on pharmaceuticals and medical devices
news:clari.biz.industry.household—News about companies in the furniture and household supply businesses
news:clari.biz.industry.insurance—News about the insurance industry
news:clari.biz.industry.insurance.releases—Press releases from non-health care insurance providers

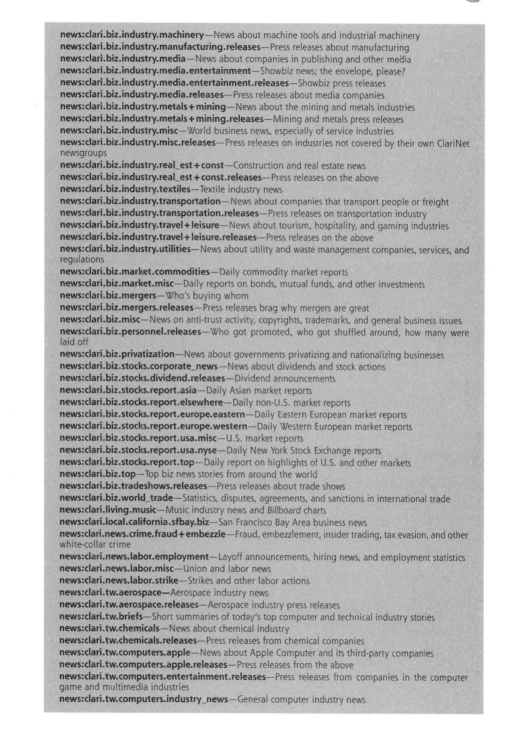

news:clari.biz.industry.machinery—News about machine tools and industrial machinery
news:clari.biz.industry.manufacturing.releases—Press releases about manufacturing
news:clari.biz.industry.media—News about companies in publishing and other media
news:clari.biz.industry.media.entertainment—Showbiz news; the envelope, please?
news:clari.biz.industry.media.entertainment.releases—Showbiz press releases
news:clari.biz.industry.media.releases—Press releases about media companies
news:clari.biz.industry.metals+mining—News about the mining and metals industries
news:clari.biz.industry.metals+mining.releases—Mining and metals press releases
news:clari.biz.industry.misc—World business news, especially of service industries
news:clari.biz.industry.misc.releases—Press releases on industries not covered by their own ClariNet newsgroups
news:clari.biz.industry.real_est+const—Construction and real estate news
news:clari.biz.industry.real_est+const.releases—Press releases on the above
news:clari.biz.industry.textiles—Textile industry news
news:clari.biz.industry.transportation—News about companies that transport people or freight
news:clari.biz.industry.transportation.releases—Press releases on transportation industry
news:clari.biz.industry.travel+leisure—News about tourism, hospitality, and gaming industries
news:clari.biz.industry.travel+leisure.releases—Press releases on the above
news:clari.biz.industry.utilities—News about utility and waste management companies, services, and regulations
news:clari.biz.market.commodities—Daily commodity market reports
news:clari.biz.market.misc—Daily reports on bonds, mutual funds, and other investments
news:clari.biz.mergers—Who's buying whom
news:clari.biz.mergers.releases—Press releases brag why mergers are great
news:clari.biz.misc—News on anti-trust activity, copyrights, trademarks, and general business issues
news:clari.biz.personnel.releases—Who got promoted, who got shuffled around, how many were laid off
news:clari.biz.privatization—News about governments privatizing and nationalizing businesses
news:clari.biz.stocks.corporate_news—News about dividends and stock actions
news:clari.biz.stocks.dividend.releases—Dividend announcements
news:clari.biz.stocks.report.asia—Daily Asian market reports
news:clari.biz.stocks.report.elsewhere—Daily non-U.S. market reports
news:clari.biz.stocks.report.europe.eastern—Daily Eastern European market reports
news:clari.biz.stocks.report.europe.western—Daily Western European market reports
news:clari.biz.stocks.report.usa.misc—U.S. market reports
news:clari.biz.stocks.report.usa.nyse—Daily New York Stock Exchange reports
news:clari.biz.stocks.report.top—Daily report on highlights of U.S. and other markets
news:clari.biz.top—Top biz news stories from around the world
news:clari.biz.tradeshows.releases—Press releases about trade shows
news:clari.biz.world_trade—Statistics, disputes, agreements, and sanctions in international trade
news:clari.living.music—Music industry news and *Billboard* charts
news:clari.local.california.sfbay.biz—San Francisco Bay Area business news
news:clari.news.crime.fraud+embezzle—Fraud, embezzlement, insider trading, tax evasion, and other white-collar crime
news:clari.news.labor.employment—Layoff announcements, hiring news, and employment statistics
news:clari.news.labor.misc—Union and labor news
news:clari.news.labor.strike—Strikes and other labor actions
news:clari.tw.aerospace—Aerospace industry news
news:clari.tw.aerospace.releases—Aerospace industry press releases
news:clari.tw.briefs—Short summaries of today's top computer and technical industry stories
news:clari.tw.chemicals—News about chemical industry
news:clari.tw.chemicals.releases—Press releases from chemical companies
news:clari.tw.computers.apple—News about Apple Computer and its third-party companies
news:clari.tw.computers.apple.releases—Press releases from the above
news:clari.tw.computers.entertainment.releases—Press releases from companies in the computer game and multimedia industries
news:clari.tw.computers.industry_news—General computer industry news

news:clari.tw.computers.misc—Miscellaneous computer industry news
news:clari.tw.computers.networking—Industry news about computer networking, including the Internet
news:clari.tw.computers.networking.releases—Press releases about the above
news:clari.tw.computers.pc.hardware—News relating to Intel-based PCs
news:clari.tw.computers.pc.hardware.releases—Press releases about Intel-based PCs
news:clari.tw.computers.pc.software—Mostly Windows software news
news:clari.tw.computers.pc.software.releases—Press releases mostly about Windows software
news:clari.tw.computers.peripherals.releases—Press releases from companies that make computer peripherals
news:clari.tw.computers.releases—Miscellaneous computer industry press releases
news:clari.tw.computers.unix—News about all 31 flavors of Unix
news:clari.tw.computers.unix.releases—Press releases about the Unix industry
news:clari.tw.defense—News about defense contractors and the defense industry
news:clari.tw.electronics—News about manufacturers of electronics products
news:clari.tw.electronics.releases—Electronics industry press releases
news:clari.tw.features—Feature-length stories about technical industries
news:clari.tw.new_media—News about online services, the Internet, and multimedia
news:clari.tw.new_media.online.releases—Press releases about the above
news:clari.tw.nuclear—Nuclear power and nuclear weapons industries
news:clari.tw.stocks—Daily TechWire stock reports on computer and high-tech stocks, including rarely-covered low-volume technology stocks
news:clari.tw.telecom.misc—News about cable, network, satellite and other non-phone telecommunications companies
news:clari.tw.telecom.phone_service—News about phone companies and long-distance providers
news:clari.tw.telecom.releases—Telecom press releases
news:clari.tw.top—Top stories on computer and high-tech companies
news:clari.world.americas.canada.biz—Business news about Canada
news:clari.world.asia.china.biz—Business news about China
news:clari.world.asia.japan.biz—Business news about Japan
news:clari.world.europe.british_isles.uk.biz—Business news about the U.K.
news:clari.world.europe.france.biz—Business news about France and Monaco
news:clari.world.europe.germany.biz—Business news about Germany

If You Don't Like the News, Make Your Own

CRAYON: Create Your Own Newspaper ☆☆☆☆

CRAYON lets you design your own custom Web page that links to your choices of Internet news sources. You store your custom news page on your computer. Then you can either reach it any time you want by *bookmarking* it, or use your news page as your *home page*, so you have today's news at your fingertips every time you start your Web browser.

CRAYON lets you choose what you link to, and presents your links in sections patterned after those of traditional newspapers: local news, world news, weather, business, technology, arts and entertainment, sports, new Web sites, even comics and columns. You can choose which sections you want, and in which order. For each section, you can either choose which news sources you want from a menu provided by CRAYON, or enter the URLs for any additional sources not listed on the menu.

The World As We Know It

Published by <u>CRAYON</u> - " " - Number 161092 - **FREE**

Flip to: --<u>World News</u>----<u>U.S. News</u>----<u>Regional and Local News</u>----<u>Information and Technology</u>
<u>Report</u>----<u>New and Cool Web Sites</u>----<u>The Tabloid Page</u>--

---

Read all of World News

> *The Electronic Telegraph* (London)
> Financial Times of London

<u>~ Flip to top ~</u>

Read all of U.S. News

> <u>TIME</u> Daily News Summary

CRAYON lets you create your own Web page of news sources and any other Web spots you want to check every day. Here's a simple sample we created in less than ten minutes. (We can click a mouse pretty quickly.)

CRAYON gives you an excellent selection to choose from in its World News section: CNN World News, *Electronic Telegraph*, *Financial Times*, and dozens of news providers from Canada, Israel, Australia, Ireland, Russia, Japan, China, Korea, India, Singapore, New Zealand, and other countries. CRAYON's selection of business news sources is limited, however. You might want to jot down the names and URLs of your favorite business news spots so you can enter them in the space CRAYON provides.

When you're done, remember to save the news page you've created!

How

World Wide Web

Where

crayon.net

How to Bookmark Your Newspaper or Make It Your Home Page

Assuming you use Netscape as your Web browser (most businesspeople on the Net do), here are step-by-step instructions on how to bookmark the CRAYON newspaper you've just created, and how to make it your home page. When you create and save your newspaper, Netscape will suggest that you name the file that holds it **mypaper.cgi**. You can, of course, change that to any name you wish. Before you start the steps below, you need to find your **mypaper.cgi** file on your hard disk.

To make your newspaper home page the first thing you see whenever you start Netscape:

1. With Netscape running, pull down the Netscape *Options* menu.
2. Select *Appearance*.
3. Select *General Preferences*.
4. Under *Browser Starts with*, click on the button for *Home Page Location* and enter the name and location of **mypaper.cgi** or whatever you have called it. If you put **mypaper.cgi** under your **netscape** directory, you only need to type the file name.
5. From the *Options* menu, select *Save Options*.

To bookmark your newspaper so you can open it any time:

1. With Netscape running, go to your **mypaper.cgi** file or whatever you have named it.
2. Pull down the *Bookmarks* menu.
3. Select *Add Bookmark*.
4. Anytime you want your paper, pull down your *Bookmarks* menu and click on its name.

Financial Times for Those with Little Time

Financial Times ☆☆☆☆

One of the planet's best business print publications, the *Financial Times* gives you this spiffy Web version. (We're willing to bet this is the first time "spiffy" has been applied to *FT*.) It's a condensed version of the print publication, perfect for the busy businessperson. This site receives fresh news daily. (Not just weekdays, but seven days a week.)

You get the day's top story, and the top story from Europe, Asia/Pacific, and the Americas, plus the most significant technology story. The best part is "News in Brief," summaries of today's most important 15 to 20 stories, with a global perspective instead of a U.S.-only point of view. You'll also find stock market indexes and a U.K. budget archive.

How

World Wide Web

THE FINANCIAL TIMES GROUP

Highlights from Today's FT | News in Brief | World Stock Market Indices

Contacting the FT | FT-IT Recruitment | FT Information

FT Share Price Service

News in Brief gives you today's most important 15 to 20 stories from the FINANCIAL TIMES. It's a fast way for a busy person to get just the news that matters. (Vince bookmarked it.)

Where

For the fastest response, use the site closest to you:

U.S.: www.usa.ft.com

U.K.: www.ft.com

Internet's Guide to Periodical Literature

Uncover ☆☆☆☆

Remember looking stuff up in your high school library in a set of green volumes called *Reader's Guide to Periodical Literature*? Uncover is the Internet version of the *Reader's Guide*, only instead of letting you find articles in a couple of hundred magazines like the *Guide*, Uncover lets you search through 17,000 different periodicals from all around the world!

They include more than 2,000 business publications, from *ABA Banking Journal* to *Ajia Torendo* (*Asian Trends*). You'll find publications on every other business topic you can imagine (and many you can't—did you know there is a trade journal for people who sell Christmas trees?), from the local to the global, and in several languages. Uncover adds more than 5,000 articles to its database every day.

Besides this free search service, Uncover also provides a free email alert service called Reveal. When a new issue of a periodical carries an article on the topics or people that interest you, Reveal sends you an email message to let you know. To use Reveal, you simply fill out a profile describing what topics interest you.

Uncover will also fax to you almost any article you'd like, but it charges for faxes (you know how we feel about that).

Uncover is a valuable service, but be aware of its weak spots. First of all, its Web site describes its services, but to actually use them it pops you into a plodding Telnet session. This makes Uncover difficult to use at first. Secondly, its indexing is not complete. In several test searches we made, Uncover only provides *some* of the articles in publications. (For instance, Uncover indexes *PC World,* but misses Vince's "Top Web Sites for Online Business" on page 277 of the October 1995 issue. For shame!) Indexing by *subject* is nowhere near as thorough as your old library's *Reader's Guide,* so Uncover misses articles. To compensate, you'll need to be creative and search under multiple topics.

Even with those drawbacks, though, Uncover and Reveal are great tools both for research and to find news on crucial business topics.

How

World Wide Web

Where

www.carl.org/uncover/unchome.html

Is There Anything Good on TV?

Journal Graphics ☆☆

Say you just found out your competitor's chairman was asked incriminating questions on the evening news 10 years ago. Wouldn't you want to know if he was asked questions such as, "When did you stop beating your employees?"

Go to Journal Graphics to find out. This is similar to Uncover. (In fact, this Net site is run by the same organization.) The difference is that Journal Graphics is a kind of *Reader's Guide to Television and Radio.* This is a database of more than 80,000 broadcast news show episodes from PBS, ABC, CBS, CNN, and National Public Radio, from 1981 to the present. You can find episodes by topic, by show name, by broadcast date, by host, and by guests. Searching is free, and you can get a printed transcript for a fee.

Now pass the popcorn, please.

How

Telnet

Where

telnet://pac.carl.org

Once you get in, choose "Open Access Databases."
Then choose "Journal Graphics Online."

Directories of News I

Compilation of News Sites ☆☆☆☆☆

For businesspeople, this directory of news sources on the Net is extremely useful. First, you'll find a large *quantity* of links for business news. Investors will find many good publications. Second, you'll find that the informative *descriptions* of the links are useful. There are many directories of Internet publications and news resources, but hardly any give you more guidance than site names. Some of the descriptions here come from the sites themselves, and suffer from hyperbole and fluff, but many are useful evaluations, apparently written by Webmaster Jonathan Meir himself.

Third, it's timely. Out of all the news directories we checked, this one almost always has *new resources first*. Fourth, Meir keeps his links well-maintained. His directory suffers from less *"dead links disease"* than most others in this field. Visit Meir's site to compile your list of news URLs before you build your own newspaper at CRAYON.

How

World Wide Web

Where

www-leland.stanford.edu/~jmaier/inetnews.htm

Directories of News II

Newslink ☆☆☆☆

Newslink gives you more links to Internet versions of print and broadcast news sources than any other spot on the Net. You'll find a large number of business publications here. Newslink covers publications from all over, and is especially good at listing less well-known periodicals, such as college papers and

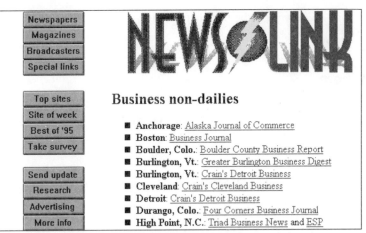

A handful of the many business news sources from around the planet collected by Newslink.

local publications. It's not much on describing resources; you'll only find naked links, and will have to investigate on your own. Newslink requires you to register before you use it, but it is free and well worth the registration.

How

World Wide Web

Where

www.newslink.org

Directories of News III

The Daily News—Just the Links ☆☆☆

Gerben Vos compiled this directory of nearly 300 sources of daily news on the Net. His directory is especially strong at listing news sources outside the U.S., giving you several publications other directories miss. Publications are listed by continent, then alphabetically by countries within a continent. Links are stark naked—no descriptions or evaluations, just countries and publication names. Note that this site gives you just daily news sources. You'll find no weeklies or monthlies here.

How

World Wide Web

Where

www.cs.vu.nl/~gerben/news.html

Directories of News IV

Omnivore ☆☆☆

If you're hungry for news and will eat everything, here's a good place to find electronic versions of print and broadcast news. News sources at Omnivore are categorized by Regional, Subjects, Weather, Magazines, and Other Sources. All categories give you business news sources except Weather. Some links here have short descriptions. Most don't. You'll find a few things here that other directories missed. Just don't say "Oh, wow" with your mouth full.

How

World Wide Web

Where

way.net/omnivore/index.html

They're Free, but What Are They?

Newsletter Library ☆☆☆

This site claims to offer more than 11,000 newsletters that you can get for free. You can get good business newsletters for free here, but you can't find out how many the Newsletter Library offers, or for that matter, *which* newsletters it offers. You don't get to pick newsletters by name.

What you acquire here are a list of hundreds of *overall topics*. Many are business topics. You choose the topics that interest you. The Newsletter Library forwards your name and address to publishers with newsletters on your topics, and the publishers send sample issues to you. The Library charges publishers for your name, and there is no quality control over what you receive.

Our tests of this site generated print newsletters ranging from junky advertising brochures, to free single-copy samples of expensive professional newsletters, to free subscriptions of good trade newsletters. Our tip: The first time you use this site, be selective and choose between one and three topics. See how you like what you get before you decide to select more.

How

World Wide Web

Where

pub.savvy.com

Stay A-"Head" of the Competition

HeadsUp ☆☆☆

To not only succeed but to excel in business, you need every advantage you can get. Part of gaining that advantage is knowing more about your market *and* your competition than the other guy. HeadsUp is a personalized, interactive news service delivered daily to your Internet address. Based on your personal profile, HeadsUp scans over 12,000 articles a day from more than 300 domestic and international sources and delivers you the news that interests you most each morning. Use it for 30 days for free to track competitors, identify sales opportunities, uncover partnerships, evaluate vendors, monitor industry trends, and stay on top of the market.

How

Email

Where

headsup@enews.com

Message

Information on a free trial subscription

No Downside to Upside

Upside ☆☆☆☆

These guys are supposed to be greedy venture capitalists, but on the Internet, they give away the store! This is a great spot for managers and investors in high-tech companies. *Upside* is one of two leading monthly magazines that cover technology investing and venture capitalism. (The other is *Red Herring*.) You'll find *all* of the feature stories and columns of the current issue of *Upside* on its Web site—even the cartoons. The insightful investigative reporting is excellent. And you'll find a searchable archive of back issues. And you can receive a free subscription to the print version!

You'll also find a directory of industry conferences, a directory of links to Web sites with information for high-tech businesses (not much here, but *Upside* does link to its archrival *Red Herring*), a short list of industry associations, stock prices for high-tech companies (live, but with a 15-minute delay), and a "Book of Lists" with financial and stock information on high-tech corporations. The stereotype of selfish capitalist pigs is shattered. It's enough to make Karl Marx weep.

How
World Wide Web

Where
www.upside.com

Preview of Coming Attractions

THE ECONOMIST ☆☆

When we poked and prodded the site of this distinguished weekly business magazine, we were most impressed by its section called "surveys." "Surveys" has no resemblance to the dictionary definition of a survey. Instead, "surveys" supplies in-depth reports on trends of an important industry. You'll find a good report on Internet business, and an excellent one on the telecommunications industries, showing how the Internet will change pricing to a flat-fee model from the current long-distance per-call/per-mile scheme.

The only other interesting part of this site was *The Economist Review*, monthly book and CD-ROM reviews. But this section is not enough to make this site a worthwhile source of business news. Although, *The Economist* promises to add articles from its magazine. Perhaps by the time you visit this site it will have more information.

How
World Wide Web

Where
www.economist.com

Whaddya Call Text Versions of Sound Bites?

CNN Financial Network ☆☆☆

Not for behind-the-curve browsers, CNNfn is a flashy site with many little tidbits of business news: market reports, company earnings, short stories on business and biz-related issues. Don't go here for in-depth information. This is strictly an overview spot. One extra touch: At the end of a story, links take you to Web sites that relate to the story. CNNfn's "Resource Center" gives you directories of small business resources and other business stuff.

You'll find good stock and investment news at this site. Besides market closing figures from 44 world stock and commodities exchanges, you can get U.S.

FREE Business $TUFF from the Internet

market figures updates every three minutes: actives, gainers, losers, and alerts for volume, highs, and lows. There's a quote search (prices are delayed 15 minutes) for stocks, mutual funds, and money market funds. Commodity quotes are delayed 20 minutes. You'll also find a glossary of business terms, a directory of exchanges on the Web, and a guide to free products and bargains. (Free? They're playing our song!)

How

World Wide Web

Where

www.cnnfn.com

More Pictures Than the Louvre

USA TODAY ☆☆☆☆

The Web version of *USA Today* gives you a better selection of business stories than most other Net sources. *USA Today* covers a wider variety of topics than other news sites, and it reports on more subjects. Some stories here have more depth than the print version of *USA Today*. Investors will appreciate free stock quotes, updated every 15 minutes on seven stocks of your choice, plus market summaries and reports on mutual funds and money markets.

The downside to this site is that it's a "muscle site." It chokes your line with so many large graphics files that if you don't have a 56 K or faster Net connection, you'll reach retirement age before some of its pages download.

Not for the bandwidth-impaired, the graphics-heavy USA TODAY site gives you more U.S. business stories than most other Net sources.

How

World Wide Web

Where

www.usatoday.com

Think Globally, Act Locally

U.K. Today ☆☆☆

This online newspaper is published every weekday, and gives you breezy coverage of British national news, with not much business reporting. *U.K. Today* is special, because it links with 22 local papers in England and Ireland to give you the best local coverage of U.K. business on the Net.

How

World Wide Web

Where

www.kdtech.co.uk/uktoday/index.html

It's Goodish, Old Chap, but a Bit Short

ELECTRONIC TELEGRAPH ☆☆☆ .

This Web version of the *London Daily Telegraph* provides the best coverage of British national news on the Net. It's published every weekday, and features a good selection of business stories. The stories drawbacks are that they tend to be rather short and lack the depth of its print versions. You have to register to read the *Electronic Telegraph*, but it's free. Go to "City" for business news.

How

World Wide Web

Where

www.telegraph.co.uk

Could They Call It G'Day Today?

AUSTRALIA DAILY NEWS ☆☆☆

Absolutely the best coverage of Australian daily news on the Net, this electronic newspaper provides few pictures—it's almost all text. It provides quick synopses of Australian stories. If you want news from other countries, go to another Web site. This one is Oz all the way. You won't find too much here in the way of business stories, but you will find all key bits on Australian politics, and of course Oz sports.

How

World Wide Web

Where

www.com.au/aaa/Real_News.html

The Philippines' Business Beat

BUSINESS WORLD ☆☆☆

What you get here is a very good—if a little too graphics-heavy—business daily for the Philippines. A good blend of stories and analyses give you a rundown on today's issues and important government contracts. Investors will appreciate quotes from the Philippine Stock Exchange and mutual funds.

If you do business with or in the Philippines, you'll want to add BUSINESS WORLD to your bookmark list.

How

World Wide Web

Where

bizworld.globe.com.ph

A Singaporean Smorgasbord of Scoops

Singapore Press Holdings ☆☆☆

If you want business news from Singapore, Thailand, or the People's Republic of China, step right up. Singapore Press Holdings gives you a smorgasbord of publications in English and Chinese. From this one page, you can reach:

- *Business Times*—Singapore's business newspaper. The complete newspaper is updated daily on the Net by noon (Singapore time, of course). Investors will want the information from *BT Stock Watch* and SIMEX, the Singapore International Monetary Exchange. You'll get realtime data from SIMEX, including the most active contracts, options, and price quotes.
- *Business Day*—Thailand's business daily gives you short, to-the-point news stories and the *Industrial Purchasing Guide*, a searchable database of businesses and industries in Thailand.
- *Lianhe Zaobao*—Chinese-language publication
- *New Paper*—Singapore consumer newspaper
- *BT Business Directory*—Searchable directory of Singaporean companies
- *Guangzhou Ribao*—Chinese-language news from Canton
- *Computer Times Online*—Covers local high tech
- *Straits Times Interactive*
- *Shipping Times*
- *BT Asian Golf Review*—At last, we get to the important stuff!

How

World Wide Web

Where

www.asia1.com

Chinese Newsletter Platter

CHINA NEWS DIGEST ☆☆☆

China News Digest can be valuable if you do business with Chinese firms or are a Chinese business student. At this site, you get a menu of six different newsletters about business in the People's Republic of China and Taiwan. All the newsletters contain good short articles on general news, business, and economics. And each contains different stories from the others. You can read the newsletters at this Web site or subscribe to them by email.

- *CND-Global*—The mother ship *CND* publication features articles written by volunteers covering news from China and Taiwan. It's published daily.
- *Hua Xia Wen Zhai*—Published in Chinese every Friday, this newsletter's own home page is located at **www.cnd.org/HXWZ**.
- *China Inet Newsletter*—Covers high tech, the Internet, and telecommunications in China.
- *CND-U.S. Regional, CND-Canada Regional,* and *CND-Europe/Pacific*—These three newsletters cover news for Chinese students and scholars abroad, and include job opportunities.

How

World Wide Web

Where

www.cnd.org/CND-Global

High-Powered Management Tips

EPRI JOURNAL ☆☆☆

Each issue of this publication contains three or four articles (from the utility industry's point of view) for business managers on topics such as "The Maintenance Revolution," "Environmental Technology for Small Businesses," "Lighting the Office Environment," "Customer Value Deployment: Turning Information into Action," and "Grabbing a Lane on the Information Superhighway." Most are good general management stories.

This site is the home of the Electric Power Research Institute. *EPRI Journal* also provides EPRI's *Executive Newsline*, a newsletter strictly for utility managers.

How

World Wide Web

Where

www.epri.com

Computer News for Canada

Plesman Publications ☆☆☆

This publisher provides a generous selection of complete stories from each issue of six different Canadian computer business publications. This is a good site for Canadian high-tech firms and retailers, or businesses trying to crack the Canadian market.

Publications include:

- *Computer & Entertainment Retailing*—Monthly newspaper for Canadian retailers of technology products
- *Computing Canada* - Biweekly newspaper for corporate information systems and telecommunications professionals
- *Technology in Government*—Monthly publication for Canadian government professionals
- *Computer Dealer News*—Biweekly news for computer resellers in Canada
- *Direction Informatique*—Monthly French-language newspaper for information and telecommunications professionals and computer resellers in Quebec
- *Sourcerer*—A searchable online database of products, manufacturers, services, and catalogs for Canadian computer dealers

How

World Wide Web

Where

www.plesman.com

The Business of High Tech I

TechWeb ☆☆☆

The CMP stable of high-tech and computing magazines that live at this Web site:

- *Communications Week*
- *Computer Reseller News*
- *Computer Retail Week*
- *Electronic Buyers' News*
- *Electronic Engineering Times*
- *Home PC*
- *Informatiques*
- *Information Week*
- *Interactive Age*
- *Max*
- *NetGuide*
- *Network Computing*
- *OEM Magazine*

- *VARBusiness*
- *Windows Magazine*

CMP provides some good information at this site, but yer gonna hafta dig for it. Bring a big shovel; even at ISDN speeds, the graphics here would choke a T. Rex. The amount of information varies from magazine to magazine. (There seems to be no cross-publication cooperation here.) Some just reproduce one or two articles from the current issue. Others give you a generous serving of articles plus news not carried in the print publications.

Two of the best magazines are the Internet magazine *NetGuide*, which gives you Net.Daily, a batch of news stories about the Net served fresh daily at 9 A.M. every weekday, and *Interactive Age*. TechWeb gives you today's *New York Times* stories about the Net, plus two other departments of daily Net business news. You can read 'em at this site for free, or pay $120 per year (Gasp! Choke! Cough!) to have them delivered via email. For that price, it's worth waiting for the large graphics to download.

How

World Wide Web

Where

techweb.cmp.com/techweb

The Business of High Tech II

ZDNet ☆☆☆

Well, the graphics aren't as overwhelming at ZDNet as they were at TechWeb. This site is also better-organized, and you'll find more information at ZDNet. The Ziff-Davis magazines include:

- *PC Magazine*
- *PC Week*
- *PC Computing*
- *Computer Shopper*
- *Windows Sources*
- *MacUser*
- *MacWeek*
- *Interactive Week*
- *Computer Life*

- *Family PC*
- *Computer Gaming World*
- *Internet Life*

This Web site provides you an overall cross-magazine index, so you don't have to hop from magazine to magazine. The ZDNet home page gives you index tabs so you can find information from several publications at one place. The tabs cover "News," "Products," "Macintosh," "At Home," and "Internet." Unfortunately, the tabs only reach some of the material on each topic, but at least they give you a place to start.

Internet businesses might want to bookmark *Interactive Week*'s section on today's news, which gives you more interesting stories than its competitor *Interactive Age*. You still have to dig for it, though.

How

World Wide Web

Where

www.zdnet.com

Where to Find More Business News

First, check out the directories in this chapter. They will lead you to more business news sources than even Evelyn Wood could speed-read. (Evelyn didn't have to wait for download time.)

Second, go to *The Business Guide to the Internet* in the previous chapter of this book. This site contains a very good chapter entitled "News Sources and In-Company News Services" that you will find helpful in your quest for news.

Third, try looking in the index of this book under **newsletters** for a variety of business publications scattered throughout this book.

FREE $TUFF

There are three kinds of death in this world. There is heart death. There is brain death. And there is being off the network.

Guy Almes

Tools for Internet-Based Businesses

More than 300,000 businesses use the Internet, but not all of them use it for marketing. Many use the Net just for email, or for operations uses, or for collaborative work projects. This chapter is for those people who use the Net to generate profits.

The resources in this chapter will help you in some essential areas that are interrelated. (Or on the Net, intertangled.) You'll find tools and information here to help you get connected, to build your Web site, to make it work, and to sell stuff on the Net.

You'll find several resources to help you with the ticklish area of payment processing—how can you get paid in cyberspace? Let me count the ways. On the other hand, maybe not. There are just too many variations. But let us steer you toward the places that can help you choose what resources are best for your company.

As well as marketing and nontechnical information, this chapter has a hefty number of technical resources. In fact, more than any other chapter in this book. Although we wrote *FREE Business $TUFF From the Internet* for nontechnical businessfolks, you will need to absorb *some* technical information to manage using the Net effectively. If not, you'll wind up having technical people make decisions based on technical factors that should be based on business factors.

We'll use easy-to-understand terms as much as we can, so hang in there. After all, this is for your own profit.

Free and Cheap Web Space, Anyone?

Budget Web Index ☆☆☆☆☆

Our kind of people! These folks give you free directories of free and cheap places that can run your Web site. You'll find two lists at this site. One list gives you places that will lease you low-cost ($20 per month or less) Web space. The other one gives you low-cost virtual hosts that charge $50 per month or less. The companies are listed in no apparent order, but this is still a cost-cutting site you must visit before your start your Web site. These comparison charts make it a snap to narrow your search to the companies that are right for you. Remember that your cheapest alternative may not always be your best, so check references before you sign a lease. And never prepay for a year in advance; if anything goes wrong, you'll be stuck.

Provider	Setup	Rate	Space	Add. Space	Email	Note
Netmar, Inc.	$15	$15	1 MB	~$6/MB	staff@netmar.com	①②③④⑤⑥⑦⑩
A & Z Consulting	$25	$10	10 MB	$0.2/MB	info@azc.com	②③⑥⑧⑨
DataRealm Internet Services, LLC	free	$2	1 MB	$2/MB	info@mail.serve.com	②③④⑧⑨
webdomain webspace service	$149.95	$20	5 MB	$7.5/MB	info@webdomain.com	①②③⑥⑧⑪
Instant Technologies, Ltd.	$10	$20	1 MB	$1.50/MB	webmaster@instantech.com	①②
pair Networks (FTP)	$5	$4.95	5 MB	$0.50/MB	info@pair.com	⑥⑧⑨
pair Networks	$10	$9.95	5 MB	$0.50/MB	info@pair.com	⑥⑧⑨

Here's the top of the Budget Web Index's list of low-cost Web space providers. Note under "Setup" and "Rate" that some, under certain conditions, are free.

How

World Wide Web

Where

budgetweb.com/budgetweb/

These budget options may not offer enough firepower for your business. For a catalog of higher-priced options for leasing a Web server, visit the Leasing a Server page at **http://union.ncsa.uiuc.edu/HyperNews/get/www/ leasing.html**. The descriptions of vendors here are written by the vendors themselves, so take 'em with a grain of salt.

Making a List, Checking It Twice

The List of Internet Access Providers ☆☆☆☆☆

Whether you're a huge conglomerate or a one-person tabletop startup, before you cruise the Net, you have to get an Internet Access Provider so you have a connection. Where can you find one? Right here. This is the most complete directory of Internet access providers anyplace on the planet. (Which makes it a shoo-in for the rest of the solar system as well. Although, there aren't many provider directories among the asteroids.)

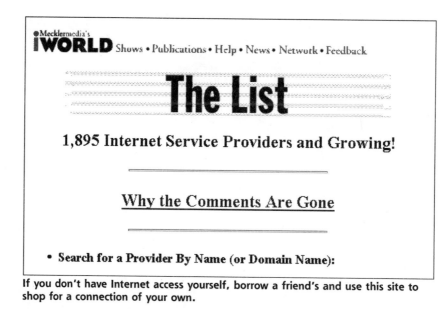

If you don't have Internet access yourself, borrow a friend's and use this site to shop for a connection of your own.

You can look up providers by country or area code served. You can search for a specific provider by its company name or its domain name. For each provider, this directory lists contact information, areas served, services provided, and fees. You have nearly 2,000 providers to choose from. That could be overwhelming, but the tools and information at this site will let you quickly narrow them down to a more workable list of semifinalists.

How

World Wide Web

Where

thelist.com

Don't Get Funny about My Money

WWW-Buyinfo Email Discussion Group ☆☆☆☆

Are you planning to receive (or spend) payments on the Web via credit cards or digital cash? This good email discussion group covers funds transfer via the Web, especially credit cards and digital money. It delivers a low volume of good information, with no spam. Subjects of past messages include: Online copy of IPAY draft charter; Not quite ready for prime time (see sidebar); IETF commerce-related working group forming; CyberCash security; New Telecom Resource Available; FV Demonstrates Fatal Flaw in Software Encryption of Credit Cards. (This last one was somewhat exaggerated.)

Although messages are delivered by email, you subscribe at the Web page listed below. It includes archives of past messages, which you can search by date, author, thread, or subject. This page also includes *lots* of links to Net stuff about electronic commerce and credit cards.

How

World Wide Web

Where

www.research.att.com/www-buyinfo

Not Quite Ready for Prime-time...

David Fox (david@kweb.com)
Mon, 1 Jan 1996 08:27:56 -0800

Happy New Year all,

In preparation for a series of presentations in Jakarta mid-January, I have spent the past couple of days working through the four major transaction systems. I've approached the exercise as a new consumer and thought you might be interested in the outcome.

1a. CYBERCASH. < www.cybercash.com >
Downloaded the most recent Mac client and it installed OK. Appears to have been cleaned up since the Windows client I set up earlier this year and all-in-all functions just fine.

I was surprised to see less than two dozen places < http://www.cybercash.com/merchants/merchant_list.html > to shop with my new wallet. Oh well, time to line the Virtual Vineyards coffers once again.

Like FedEx, it's a site that shows the technology can work.

Trouble was, my first card bounced (a second one did clear). I called their 800 number and left a message. VV's Robert Olsen called me back today (better than Netscape - see below) and explained in detail how the problem was at the acquiring bank end. I think we all know about the issues back in the rooms run by men in white coats.... Seems this time their system was down for maintenance, and they just reject the card. Now, this doesn't happen to the big guys like Lands End. They have special arrangements to keep 'em up all the time. Oh well....

1a. CompuServe Wallet < www.compuserve.com >
As with CheckFree (see below), the CompuServe Wallet is a licensed version of CyberCash wallet system. Well, at least it is supposed to be. It was

advertised a few months ago - I have a flyer in hand and there is a link to CompuServe's page from the CyberCash home page. Only trouble was, I couldn't find anything whatsoever about the CompuServe Wallet. Maybe I was looking in the wrong places? I've sent off a couple of emails, but no response yet.

Using Digital's new <altavista.digital.com> search engine I did locate a home page at <dub-www-svc-10.compuserve.com/wallet/welcome2.html>.

1b. CheckFree Wallet <www.mc2-csr.com/GiftLink/>

CheckFree put together a Christmas special under the banner of GiftLink. Attractive home page. Narrow product offering but at least a few "name brands".

2. DIGICASH/Mark Twain Ecash <www.marktwain.com>

I established a real account in October ("monopoly money" trial started a year ago) and paper work has been sitting in the in-tray since then. Yes. The paper work. You need to set up an account by downloading many pages, mailing it off and awaiting their snail mail reply. I downloaded the client software successfully and began the installation process. I thought my Mac had hung mid-way through, restarted and went through the same process. Third time round, memory of the beta sprang forth - it takes time to crunch the numbers. Three minutes plus on an 040 machine. Would have been nice to have received a warning message....

Then I went to spend some new digital dollars using the Digicash merchant page, only to be rejected by three shops in a row. Ahh, brainwave, these guys probably aren't set up to take the real Ecash, they're all still in beta land. (No wonder, MT charges $250 just to establish an account and takes a couple of $% from consumers to convert $-e-cash then the same back out to merchants.)

So I went to Mark Twain's page to look for merchants. Too bad. Their server was unreachable and remains so 36 hours later. I like the idea of Ecash. I really do. But man alive it's hard work. And I thought computers were meant to make life easier. This definitely isn't ready for my father or my sister.

3. FIRST VIRTUAL

Set up a new account (got to build the mileage on that United card). Yes, it isn't a 2 second process, but then again, it's not that tough either. It will be better when we don't have to wait 2 hours to establish an account. Something about instant gratification. Looking through the InfoHaus merchant list, and once again I found it hard to spend my money. There's some weird stuff out there. At least the FV system worked without a hitch.

4a. SECURE CREDIT CARD: Netscape General Store < home.mcom.com/es-capes/galleria.html >

Thought I might take advantage of Netscape's offer of all '96 updates for a $17.00 fee. This has been on offer for a couple of months, and today was the last day. Made my selection and landed in the "General Store." I was greeted by the following:

"The Netscape General Store is temporarily closed for inventory. Please check back later.

We're sorry for any inconvenience this may have caused. If you wish, you can return to Netscape's home page."

Are these guys for real??? Sheeez@! Can you imagine a major retail store or mail order catalog advertising a special offer, then closing the store on the final day of the "sale". The day after maybe...but on the last day!

Even worse, there was no one I could email, no one I could call and not even a form in which I could leave a message like: "I want to buy, please let me know when I can...." I did leave a voicemail which will probably be answered on Tuesday, I guess.

4b. NETSCAPE GALLERIA < home.mcom.com/escapes/galleria.html >

Free listing service offered by Netscape to licensees of their server prod-ucts. It's interesting to review relatively small number of "commerce en-abled" sites. Take a look.

So there you have it. All around I'd give my day an E for Effort. Flame me if you will, tell me to get off the soap box if you must. But I have to say that collectively, we have to do better if we want the Internet to be used as a preferred place/method of purchase. The net works 24 hours a day, 7 days a week, 366 days a year (at least this year). We need to establish systems and a mindset that supports our work in this environment.

So, just in case any of you are worried all this online shopping stuff moved so fast in 95, and now you've maybe missed the boat - I'd say the ship is still in the dock and they're still rounding up the crew!

Happy sailing.
Regards,
David Fox

```
+ ---------------------------------------------------------- +
| KnowledgeWeb, Inc. |
| Publishers of The Computer Events Directory |
| 9 Laurel Place, #7 San Rafael CA 94901 USA |
| Tel/Fax: 415 485 5508 email: david@kweb.com www.kweb.com |
+ ---------------------------------------------------------- +
```

How Do Dollars Fit through Those Little Wires?

Thomas Ho's Favorite Electronic Commerce Resources ★★★★★

If you want to receive online payments, and you have more questions than can be solved by just plugging in the Netscape Commerce Server, go here to answer your questions. You'll find an intelligently assembled collection of links, with short but helpful descriptions of most. Resources are categorized as "background," "Electronic Commerce examples," "innovative solutions to common problems" (a great spot to learn about online ordering, gaining visibility on the Net, and dealing with blacklists), "information resources," and "related areas." Pull up a chair and invest an afternoon in a thorough exploration of this site. Mr. Ho has done your research for you.

How

World Wide Web

Where

www.engr.iupui.edu/~ho/interests/commenu.html

Or Even Worse, Quarters and Nickels?

Network Payments and Digital Cash ★★★★

An enormous collection of links on the subject. This site is overwhelming at first, but the helpful descriptions of links will give you your bearings. Skip the uninformative introduction page. Everything else at this site is solid information.

How

World Wide Web

Where

ganges.cs.tcd.ie/mepierce/project.html

Where to Promote Your Web Site

A1 Index ★★★★★

EPage FAQ: How to Announce Your New Web Site ★★★★

Pointers to Pointers ★★★★

Web Site Promotion Services ★★★★

Webstep Top 100 ★★★★

Postmaster ☆☆☆
Netpost ☆☆
Webster Group International ☆☆
WebPost ☆☆

When Jaclyn Easton researched her book *Shopping on the Internet and Beyond*, she personally interviewed nearly 3,000 online merchants. She estimates that out of all the companies selling stuff on the Internet, *about 85 percent are not meeting their sales goals*. This jives with a recent survey that estimates that *75 percent of Internet merchants are losing money*. For every winner like PC Travel ($20 million in 1995 sales), there are many losers.

A key difference is that losers saw *Field of Dreams* too many times. They believe "If you build it, they will come." They are dead wrong. If you want people to come to your Web site or subscribe to your email newsletter, you must promote, promote, promote. If you have a printed catalog, you must work to get people to read it. The same is true of your Internet presence.

The nine sites here all specialize in one specific—but important—aspect of that promotional effort. These sites all give you information and/or tools to help you spread the word on the Internet.

Much as it pains us to say it, this is one area where you might be better off shelling out your hard-earned cash. To promote your site on the Net for free you will either have to spend many hours of work, or you will have to restrict yourself to the auto-submit sites listed here, which have severe limitations. In this important area, don't leap at the first free opportunity you see. Browse all nine of these sites before you jump in and start something you may regret.

A cautionary reminder: Please remember that the star ratings provided in this book rate only a company's *free stuff*, and not the quality of its *paid services*. There can be an ocean of difference between the two. For instance, based on what we hear, the top three companies generating results for paid promotions of Web sites are Webster Group International, Netpost, and Webpromote. But these sites don't give much away for free. (Webpromote gives nothing. So we don't list it.) Don't choose a paid promotional service company based only on its Web site. Always call at least three candidates and talk to their staff (and get references) before you make your choice.

A1 Index gives you a directory of nearly 600 sites where you can publicize your site. Everyone who wants to promote a Web site should read the excellent "Secrets of Submitting Web Page URLs" here. You'll also find a very good directory of "Goodies, Gizmos 'n Gadgets" for your Web site, including clip art, CGI scripts, and design tools.

EPage FAQ gives you instructions and a directory of links to places where you can publicize your site, including several not listed elsewhere. **Pointers to Pointers** auto-submits your URL to more than 100 spots, gives you a list of newsgroups to which you can announce your site, and includes a free *Net-News* newsletter for Internet marketers. **Web Site Promotion Services** gives you a long list of sites where you can publicize your site, and is one of the very few to actually describe the sites (so you know what the heck you are promoting to). **Webstep Top 100** is one of those very few. It gives you a list of 100 places where you can publicize your site, with good short descriptions of each.

Postmaster lets you auto-submit your URL to only 25 sites for free, but is the only one of the auto-submission sites that lets you customize your submission for the different needs of different search engines.

Netpost is worth visiting to read its good explanation of the differences in the results you get between auto-submit engines and personally managed promotion. (Beware of exaggeration here, though—Netpost is far from being "the only" service doing this, as it claims.) **Webster Group International** has a shorter explanation of the same differences in its informative FAQ on marketing your Web site. **WebPost** is an auto-submission site that sends your information to 24 spots.

How

World Wide Web

Where

A1 Index	www.a1co.com/home.html
EPage FAQ	ep.com/faq/webannounce
Pointers to Pointers	www.homecom.com/global/pointers.html
Web Site Promotion Services	www.meh.com/meh
Webstep Top 100	www.mmgco.com/wsrev195.html
Postmaster	www.netcreations.com/postmaster
Netpost	www.netpost.com
Webster Group International	www.wgi.com
WebPost	www.sme.com/webpost

Windows Winners Win with Winzip

Winzip ☆☆☆☆☆

Does your business use the Internet and Microsoft Windows? Then you need Winzip, no ifs, ands, or buts. If the Net is important to your business, you're going to wind up getting software from the Net. Ninety-nine percent of the Windows software you receive will be *zipped*, compressed for faster downloading. It's easy to tell if software has been zipped because the file name ends in **.zip**. You'll need to unzip that software so you can use it on your computer. And Winzip is the fastest, easiest way to unzip any software by a mile and a half. (If you're outside the U.S., the fastest, easiest way by 2.4 kilometers.)

With Winzip, you can look inside a file while it's still zipped up, see what's inside it, and even read text files (like a **readme.txt** file) so you'll know—whether your zipped software is worth unzipping or not. DOS unzipped software makes you feel as clumsy at the keyboard as a drunken kangaroo wearing oven mitts. With Winzip, we're as much in command as Captain Picard at the helm. Engage!

How

World Wide Web

Where

www.winzip.com/winzip

Go Here to Learn How

Net.value ☆☆☆☆

The full title of this on-Web newsletter is *Net.value: the Forum for Web Strategy*. By this newsletter's name, you can tell we're talking strategic use of the Web here. This newsletter is written specifically for businesspeople in a clear and to the point manner.

Each issue gives specific examples of businesses using the Net, and it gives names and detailed numbers, which are in short supply on these topics. You'll find important stories at this site that are covered poorly or not at all elsewhere. A recent article explored the precedent set when the U.S. Department of Transportation (ordinarily an agency we'd think has nothing to do with the Web) fined Virgin Atlantic $14,000 for "failing to disclose the full price of flights advertised on its World Wide Web site." Virgin was fined an additional amount for listing a fare which was no longer available.

A high point of each issue is a short list of Web sites; each site serves as an instructional example of a particular technique or idea in business use of the Web. This may remind you of a famous Web site of the past called "Interesting Business Use of the Net," and with good reason. The co-publisher of *Net.value* is Professor Bob O'Keefe, the same man who created that well-known earlier site. When you want to apply the Net in your business, now you can go to *Net.value* to learn how.

How

World Wide Web

Where

www.owi.com/netvalue

Create Your Own Newsgroup

Newsgroup Creation Instructions ☆☆☆

If there is a newsgroup covering your industry, your products, or a topic that interests your customers, it can be an effective channel for extremely low-key soft-sell publicity efforts. Most newsgroups have rules against posting advertisements or press releases, so blatant sales efforts are out.

But what if there are no newsgroups that reach your prospects? You can create one of your own, and it costs nothing to start. If your company is active enough, you might want to create more than one. Digital Equipment Corp., for example, is covered by discussion newsgroups about its products, but also runs "read-only" newsgroups where it posts press releases and newsletters. Digital finds newsgroups effective for publicity and for customer support.

As with any promotional project, distribution is all-important. Not all Internet service providers carry only a subset of the 15,000 or more newsgroups. The most widely-distributed newsgroups are those beginning with **comp.** (computers), **misc.**, **news.** (newsgroups about newsgroups), **rec.** (recreational), **sci.** (science), **soc.** (social and cultural), and **talk.** These so-called "big seven" hierarchies are distributed worldwide. To start a big seven newsgroup (any group beginning with the prefixes above), you must have a subject not duplicated by any other newsgroup, and you must go through a voting procedure to have your proposed group accepted.

It is easier to start a newsgroup in other, less widely-distributed hierarchies, such as **alt.** or **biz.** Anyone can propose a group beginning with these prefixes.

To get distribution, your group only needs to avoid having serious objections against its topic. For many businesses, *local* newsgroups will be most effective. These can be national (**us.** for the U.S., **can.** for Canada, **uk.** for the U.K., **aus.** for Australia), specific to your state or province, or even for your city (**nyc.** for New York City). Local newsgroups are easy to start. Sponsoring one can generate goodwill among Internet users in your area.

Once started, a newsgroup requires little effort from you to maintain, other than to feed it information—unless you decide to moderate your group, the only effective way to keep it from clogging with spam. The information you need to start is listed below. See you in the newsgroups!

How

World Wide Web

Where

Usenet Newsgroup Creation Companion
www.cis.ohio-state.edu/hypertext/faq/usenet/usenet/creating-newsgroups/helper/faq.html

How to Create a New Usenet Group
www.cis.ohio-state.edu/hypertext/faq/usenet/usenet/creating-newsgroups/part1/faq.html

Guidelines on Usenet Newsgroup Names
www.cis.ohio-state.edu/hypertext/faq/usenet/usenet/creating-newsgroups/naming/part1/faq.html

So You Want to Create an alt. Newsgroup?
www.math.psu.edu/barr/alt-creation-guide.html

biz. Newsgroups FAQ
www.cis.ohio-state.edu/hypertext/faq/usenet/biz-config-faq/faq.html

How to Create an aus. Newsgroup
129.78.151.1/danny/usenet/aus.net.news/archive/june-195/0046.html

Neither Rain, nor Spam, nor Dead of Night...

List-Managers Email Discussion Group ☆☆☆

The World Wide Web is only part of the Net, and it certainly can't do everything for you. Electronic mailing lists are one of the most effective ways for companies to make regular contact with prospects, to support customers, to disseminate company news, and to conduct collaborative research projects with workers who are geographically dispersed, or perhaps work for different companies.

Email lists are tricky to run. This email discussion group is a great place for list managers to ask questions and get answers. This is not a technical list. (For technical questions, go to lists for your individual software product. See below for examples.)

In addition to discussions, list members have prepared two sources of information that are useful when you start a list. You can get the group's FAQ by emailing to **majordomo@greatcircle.com** with the message **get list-managers software-faq**. It looks at 14 different software packages. Most are Unix software, but it does mention mailing list software for MS-DOS, Mac, NetWare, VM/CMS, and VMS. It also tells you how to run your own list without using mailing list manager software. The second document compares in detail the three most popular software packages: Listserv, Majordomo, and Procmail. You can get it by emailing to the same address with the message **get list-managers software.review**.

How

World Wide Web

Where

majordomo@greatcircle.com

Message

subscribe list-managers

This list discusses all mailing lists, but the most popular mailing list manager software products have discussion groups of their own. For example, if you run your company's lists using the popular Listserv software, email to **listserv@searn.sunet.se** with the message **subscribe lstown-l Yourfirstname Yourlastname**. Users of Majordomo email to **majordomo@greatcircle.com** with the message **subscribe majordomo-users**.

Internet Inside

Intranet Journal ☆☆☆☆

For most medium-to-large companies, the biggest and fastest return on investment from the World Wide Web is not marketing to customers, but from setting up an internal Web server. This is the fastest-growing use of Internet technology. Netscape estimates that more than half of the servers it sells are for Intranets, as these internal nets are called.

This site has a name like a newsletter, but it's not. Instead, what you get here is the best one-stop shopping spot on the Net for retrieving information about

Intranets and how to set up and run your own. The moderated "exchange" this site runs—its own Web-ized version of a newsgroup or email discussion group—is an active, spam-free place for you to ask questions and get answers on running your Intranet. Intranet Journal links with helpful descriptions which connect you to most of the other hot Net spots of Intranet activity, including several papers and articles. Follow the links to Netscape for demos that show actual screens from the Intranets of 3M, EDS, Cushman & Wakefield, and National Semiconductor.

How

World Wide Web

Where

www.brill.com/intranet

Test Drive This Year's Intranet

Intranet Demo ☆☆

So what can you do with an Intranet? If your boss asks that question (or you're wondering yourself), sit down and try one out. This demonstration puts you at the wheel of an Intranet. You enter your name, your company name, and other data. Then you go through fictional pages for your company's departments: sales, marketing, personnel, and engineering. You see what products are in stock and ready to ship. What products have price changes coming up? You look up phone numbers in your company phone directory. This is a good, quick way to actually experience how useful an Intranet can be.

How

World Wide Web

Where

salesnet.opentext.com:8080/welcome.html

Kegel: the Line King (Ouch!) for ISDN

Dan Kegel's ISDN Page ☆☆☆

A so-called "fast" modem line delivers the Net to you at 28.8 bits per second. An ISDN line can be four times as fast, and will seem much faster. Since ISDN is digital, you don't have to wait for the back-and-forth delay between your modem and the Net for every little graphics file. This might sound great to you, but ISDN is tricky to install, especially Home ISDN. Actually, "tricky" isn't the right word. From personal experience, ISDN installation is painful.

Dan Kegel is here to help. If your business even thinks about installing an ISDN connection, visit this site first. It will help you find out what you're getting into and what resources are available. This site also has background information you'll want before you plan your installation, and support sources to help after you've installed your connection.

Kegel provides U.S. resources and many from other countries, especially in Europe. He has arranged the information in sections, from the basics ("What Is ISDN?") to "ISDN Dialtone Providers Worldwide" (Japan has ISDN pay phones!), "ISDN Videoconferencing," using ISDN for studio-quality audio transmission, and ISDN user groups. Not all businesses will use ISDN, but for those that do, this is an outstanding resource.

How

World Wide Web

Where

alumni.caltech.edu/~dank/isdn

For Sears & Roebucks Wannabes

Publishing Product Information on the Web ☆☆☆

Dan Kegel strikes again with this somewhat useful site for those who want to put single products or catalogs on the Web. You'll find a few how-to resources here, but the best section is "Web Providers' Quoted Rates." It lists rates only for providers who quote fees per megabyte (not those that quote fees *per page*, which is a rip-off you should avoid). You'll see a truly astonishing range of prices for identical services. It's a good eye-opener.

How

World Wide Web

Where

alumni.caltech.edu/~dank/webinfo.html

I'm Innocent—I Was Framed!

Frame Relay Resources ☆☆☆

For some businesses (depending mostly on where you are located), a frame relay connection can provide you with Internet access as fast or much faster than ISDN (see the "Line King" above), and for the same price or even less.

106

This directory of frame relay resources is modeled after Dan Kegel's ISDN site. It gives you frame relay dialtone providers, a list of Internet access providers that offer frame relay connections, and other good info. (Like, what is a FRAD, anyway?) Especially look for the generous selection of articles and white papers on frame relay, each described with a clear summary.

How

World Wide Web

Where

www.mot.com/MIMS/ISG/tech/frame-relay/resources.html

I Want the One with a Green Cover

Print Publications on Business Use of the Internet ☆☆☆

Looking for books on how your business can use the Net? This site lists many (not all) of them, and provides links to reviews, and more links to the home pages of books that have them. You can save time by browsing here before you visit your local bookstore. (Our tip: A recent survey shows that books with green covers generate the most greenbacks. No, really. I surveyed Pat, whose six green books pay him royalties. He may have been a *little* biased.)

How

World Wide Web

Where

arganet.tenagra.com/Tenagra/books.html

Quick Read of the Week

INTERACTIVE MEDIA WEEKLY RECAP ☆☆☆

Catherine Kirkman's short weekly newsletter covers how the Internet and multimedia are used by the showbiz, gaming, and high tech industries. The *Recap* covers the news from business and legal perspectives. Most of the stories are press release-type stuff, but Kirkman occasionally reports a good scoop. You can read the *Recap* on this Web site, or sign up here to receive it free via email.

How

World Wide Web

Where

www.organic.com/recap

107

Bedford Falls S&L Should Click on This

Electronic Funds Clearinghouse ☆☆

Those who think that banks will never transfer money online should visit this site and think again. Twenty thousand financial institutions already do, processing literally billions of electronic transactions each week. This site gives you background information on Electronic Funds Transfer (EFT) and the National Automated Clearing House Association (NACHA). Go to the page on "facts and statistics about EFT, ACH, APP, DDP, EDI, EWI, CTX" to get a lengthy introduction to Electronic Funds Transfer, on and off the Net. This site has a useless home page (click on the pyramid to get in), but you'll find good information inside.

How

World Wide Web

Where

www.efunds.com

Cheque This Out

NetCheque ☆☆

NetCheque is a way for Internet merchants to accept checks online from their customers. Unlike most other online check schemes, it does not require merchants to make a hefty cash deposit. In fact, for many merchants, it's free. The best part of NetCheque is actually an add-on called Pay Per View, or PPV for short. PPV lets a merchant answer a request from a Web browser to look at a document with a preview of the document, plus price information and payment options. The customer's browser (Netscape Navigator, and so on) prepares the payment and passes it securely to the merchant. The merchant then sends the full document to the Web browser.

This gives you a secure way to charge per view—that is, charge for each time someone looks at one of your documents. The drawback is that your customer must have matching software, so this system is only practical if you have clients who would do a significant volume of Pay Per View transactions with you. This Unix software was developed by the Information Sciences Institute of the University of Southern California.

ISI also provides two other software packages: NetCash digital money, and Prospero, which sends and retrieves information from the Net. All ISI software programs are free for businesses making $250,000 or less per year selling services, or grossing less than $1,000,000 selling products.

How

World Wide Web

Where

nii-server.isi.edu/info/NetCheque

Parle Vous Online?

Internet/Minitel Story ☆☆☆

With more than 6.5 million Minitel users, France is proportionately the most wired major nation on earth, and has been for several years. Minitel is a $2 billion source of revenue for France Telecom. An astonishing 15 percent of all direct marketing sales in France are made through Minitel. To put that in perspective, in the U.S., sales on the Internet plus America Online and all other online services *together* add up to less than one percent of direct marketing's $58 billion in sales. If U.S. sales rose to the same proportions as those in France, U.S. online sales would be $8.7 billion. Which shows you we Yanks have a long way to go.

Anyhow, if you want to find out about Minitel, this is a good place. It is a little biased—for instance, it grossly exaggerates how Americans feel about France—but it gives you an idea of what's happening in France. That's especially good to know if you have customers, suppliers, or employees in France.

How

World Wide Web

Where

www.reach.com/matrix/meme.html

The Web site for Minitel is **www.minitel.fr**.

Electronic Commerce You Can Bank On

Financial Services Technology Consortium ☆☆☆

This U.S. government agency acts as a center for research and development on interbank technology. Bankers will find information on the Check Image Exchange Project, the Electronic Check Project (developing an all-electronic alternative to paper checks using existing interbank clearing systems), and the Electronic Commerce Project, including a paper on "Payment Methods over the Internet" in Adobe Acrobat format.

There is also a fraud prevention section, so secured that you must have a passport even to read a description of the section. FSTC's "What's New" page includes the home page of SMART F$: the Society for the Management of Advanced Relevant Technologies in the Financial Services.

How

World Wide Web

Where

www.llnl.gov/fstc

In and around Online

SEIDMAN'S ONLINE INSIDER ☆☆☆

This is the newsletter the big boys read—and the big girls, too. If your business is the Internet itself—as an access provider, journalist, content provider, or whatever—this addictive weekly newsletter will keep you abreast of the latest developments, big and small, of companies in the Internet industry such as Netscape and Microsoft, and of all the online services such as CompuServe and Prodigy.

Robert Seidman also keeps a look out for any new studies on Internet demographics. If you want to know what Steve Case, Russ Siegelman, and the other major players in this game say, subscribe to this newsletter. Seidman runs exclusive interviews and statements from them almost every week. Seidman's coverage is insightful on the major issues and covers interesting stories others miss, such as when "AOL deemed 'breast' a vulgar term and then reversed its position after complaints from women who wished to discuss 'breast cancer.'"

The newsletter is delivered by email. You can read the latest issue—and back issues—at this Web site and subscribe to the newsletter. Or read the FYI below to find out how to subscribe by email.

How

World Wide Web

Where

www.clark.net/pub/robert

To subscribe to *Seidman's Online Insider* via email, send email to **listserv@peach.ease.lsoft.com** with the message **subscribe online-l Yourfirstname Yourlastname**.

I Thought iKP Stood for Internet Kitchen Patrol

e-payment Discussion Group ☆☆☆

This email discussion group discusses electronic payment protocols based on cryptography and online authorization, especially the iKP payment protocol. It is a technically-oriented list, so if you think protocols have to do with good manners, you might want to look the other way.

How
World Wide Web

Where
majordomo@cc.bellcore.com

Message
subscribe e-payment

 Don't give your name in your subscription message.

Give Your Business the Internet Advantage

Internet Business Advantage ☆☆☆

How well you succeed in business usually depends on how well you know your competition, not to mention what you know about your market that your competition *doesn't*. More than ever before, success these days depends on information. Many businesses are now logging onto the Internet to get the valuable information they need to stay ahead of the other guys.

The Internet Business Advantage mailing list is a great intro for using cyberspace to help your business. In addition to valuable discussions about how the Internet can help your business succeed, IBA also serves as a daily business newswire, reporting high quality, hard-hitting information about all aspects of online commerce. If you don't subscribe to IBA, you can bet that one of your competitors already subscribes or will soon.

How
Email

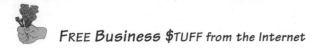

Where

info@wentworth.com

Message

subscribe iba youremail@address

Thou Shalt Not Flame

Internet Code of Conduct ☆☆☆

One of the Internet's strongest appeals also makes it very controversial. For the most part, cyberspace is a free-for-all, with anyone saying, displaying, or downloading anything they want. While this creates a sense of freedom for most of us, all it takes is a small minority to ruin it for everyone.

That's why the Internet Society created the Internet Code of Conduct. This document should be required reading for anyone who ventures into cyberspace. In addition, this site contains a number of valuable documents for anyone who wants to use the Internet to its full potential. Here's a partial listing of documents you can download:

- Ethics and the Internet
- Site Security Handbook
- Guidelines for Management of IP Address Space
- Domain Name System Structure and Delegation
- The Internet Standards Process - Revision 2
- Guidelines for Conduct On and Use of Internet
- NAS Report on Rights and Responsibilities in Networked Communities

How

World Wide Web

Where

www.isoc.org

Much of the information at Internet Code of Conduct is extremely technical.

What's New—I Mean, Where's New?

Net-Happenings ☆☆☆

Do you need to find out what new resources and companies have opened on the Net? Both Pat and Vince rate this newsletter as one of their fave sources of new free stuff on the Net. It consists of nothing but descriptions of new stuff. If you want Net-Happenings delivered to you by email, email to **listserv@lists.internic.nic** with the message **subscribe net-happenings Yourfirstname Yourlastname**. If you feel like the last thing you need is more email cluttering your inbox, you can read *Net-Happenings* as a newsgroup. Instructions to reach this newsgroup are below.

You might find it handy to know that there is a searchable archive of past issues of *Net-Happenings* on the Web at:

www.mid.net/net

How

Newsgroup

Where

comp.internet.net-happenings

 Pat also recommends *Netsurfer Digest*, a more freewheeling source on the Web at **www.netsurf.com/nsd/latest.digest.html** or available by email. Email to **nsdigest-request@netsurf.com** with the message **subscribe nsdigest-text**.

Dear Dr. Internet...

Dr. Internet ☆☆☆

You've read the manuals, you've called the support lines—heck, you've even swung a dead cat over your head at midnight—but you still haven't figured out this Net thing. Who ya gonna call? Dr. Internet, of course. Assuming you've been able to master email—or at least limp your way through it—Dr. Internet could be the divine intervention you've been looking for.

Sort of a cross between Dear Abby, Click and Clack the Car Guys, and that know-it-all at the water cooler, Dr. Internet (really a group of Project Gutenberg volunteers) answers general-interest questions about the Net each month from both newbies and Internet veterans.

How

Email

Where

internet@jg.cso.uiuc.edu

Message

Ask away. The doctor is in.

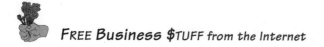

Pay for Overdue Books with Virtual Cash

Webmaster Reference Library ☆☆☆☆

You'll find lots of "how to make and run your Web site" information at the Webmaster Reference Library. You'll find more than 700 links to articles and other Web sites. Links provide helpful descriptions so you know what you're getting into. "Cool Central" is a guide to Web sites that rate Web sites. (Maybe this will spread—we could review reviews of movie reviewers.)

How

World Wide Web

Where

www.webreference.com

Shhh! We're Reading!

Web Developer's Virtual Library ☆☆☆

You might find valuable information at this sprawling, confusing site. Then again, maybe not. Good stuff is located at this site, but you'll have to dig for it, because many links have no descriptions and their names don't provide enough information. Under "Tutorials" you'll find excellent step-by-step lessons on how to add tables, forms, CGI scripts, and Web-searchable databases to your site. The site's FAQ includes a good guide to 15 newsgroups that discuss the Web. Much of the really good stuff is in the "Library." (To go directly to the Library, try **www.stars.com/vlib**.)

How

World Wide Web

Where

www.stars.com

HTML Stands for How To Market Logically

Running an HTML Business ☆☆☆

The HTML Writers Guild is an organization of people who create and run Web sites. This email discussion group talks about the *business* aspects of running a Web site, not the technology. It covers how to word contracts, how to increase traffic, and how to compare different products. A fair amount of the messages are about job opportunities, with people looking to hire both permanent employees and freelancers. It's an active group, without spam, and with a high level of information quality.

How

Email

Where

majordomo@daft.com

Message

subscribe hwg-business youremail@youraddress

 If you want to talk about the technical aspects of HTML and creating Web sites, email to the same address as above. Type in the message **subscribe hwg-basics youremail@youraddress** if you want to talk about starting a Web site. If you want to talk about intermediate-to-advanced technical issues, send the message **subscribe hwg-main youremail@youraddress**.

Masterful Magazine

WEBMASTER MAGAZINE ☆☆☆☆

It calls itself "the executive resource for doing business on the Net." *WebMaster* is a business strategy publication, not a technical publication (although it guides you to technical resources). Its online site has some—not all—that's written for the monthly print publication, plus a lot that appears only online, not in print. You'll find good articles here on using Internet and Intranet technology in almost every aspect of business, including short profiles on how real businesses use this technology.

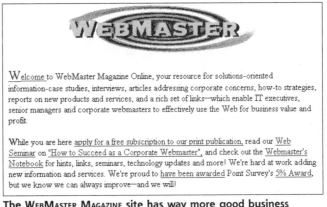

WEBMASTER

Welcome to WebMaster Magazine Online, your resource for solutions-oriented information-case studies, interviews, articles addressing corporate concerns, how-to strategies, reports on new products and services, and a rich set of links—which enable IT executives, senior managers and corporate webmasters to effectively use the Web for business value and profit.

While you are here apply for a free subscription to our print publication, read our Web Seminar on "How to Succeed as a Corporate Webmaster", and check out the Webmaster's Notebook for hints, links, seminars, technology updates and more! We're hard at work adding new information and services. We're proud to have been awarded Point Survey's 5% Award, but we know we can always improve—and we will!

The WEBMASTER MAGAZINE site has way more good business strategy information than its printed counterpart. You can get BOTH versions at this site for free.

Check out *WebMaster*'s repertoire of "Online Web Seminars." These slideshow-like presentations give you a quick education on "How to Succeed as a Corporate Webmaster," "Internal Web Applications," "Intranet," and other topics. In the "Tools and Links for Webmasters" section, you'll find tons of tools, papers, and reports, including a good interview with Elizabeth Osder, "The Vision of an Accomplished Webmaster."

If you like what you see online, you can receive a printed version, too. Just fill out the online form for a free subscription to the printed *WebMaster Magazine*.

How

World Wide Web

Where

www.cio.com/WebMaster/wmhome.html

All the Web That's Fit to Print

WEB WEEK ☆☆☆

The printed version of *Web Week*, actually comes out once a month. But that's okay, because you can read all the articles in the printed version on its Web site, plus a special weekly supplement called *Web Week Wednesday*. You can also wallow through piles of back issues. (Well, they're not really piles because they're online. It's like a virtual attic, but with a search engine.) For answers to questions on running a Web site, check "Ask Dr. Website." You can also find a section here of Web-related job opportunities.

Get both the print version and the online version of WEB WEEK, hot off the press for free. (Except the online version is hot off the server.)

If you like what you see, jump over to the subscription page. Fill out the online form, and if you qualify, you'll get a subscription to the printed version of *Web Week*—for free.

How

World Wide Web

Where

www.iworld.com/ww-online

That Isn't in the Script

Selena's Public Domain CGI Scripts ☆☆☆☆☆

An *electronic shopping cart* lets your customers browse from page to page in your site, selecting items to buy. When a customer goes to your order page, they will see an itemized list with prices of everything he or she selected on your previous pages. Your Web server can't itemize a list with just HTML. You will need a *CGI* script. CGI scripts can be in any computer language. Most are written in Perl, which can run on Windows, Mac, Unix, and other operating systems.

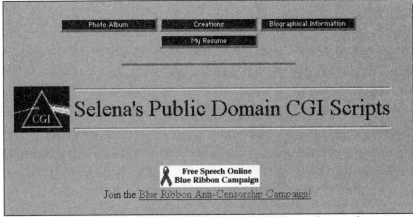

Want your Web site to be able to track customer purchases as they go from page to page? Selena Sol gives you the software for free.

Selena Sol's archive of CGI scripts gives you *three* different electronic cart software programs, plus many additional programs. (You may want to check with your Web page service bureau so you'll know if you can run CGI scripts. Some service bureaus won't let you.)

You'll find programs here to give you a Web site guest book, to create your own message board so visitors can post messages that other visitors can read, to handle membership enrollment, to perform animation, to generate random graphics (so every time someone visits your site, he or she sees a different picture), to authorize passwords, to search for keywords, and more. All of these programs are explained by good descriptions. Links to examples demonstrate many of the scripts, and you'll find links to other script sites.

With Selena's help, you'll shave days off the time it takes to build your Web retail operation.

How

World Wide Web

Where

www.eff.org/~erict/Scripts

 Another CGI script archive is Matt's Script Archive at **worldwidemart.com/scripts**. Before you use any of his programs, be sure to read Matt's FAQ first.

Wizard of the Web

Web Wizard: Duke of URL ☆☆

On the Web, it's better to look good than to feel good, and with Web Wizard, you'll always look *marvelous* (at least your Web pages will). Web Wizard helps you create great looking Web pages in just a few minutes.

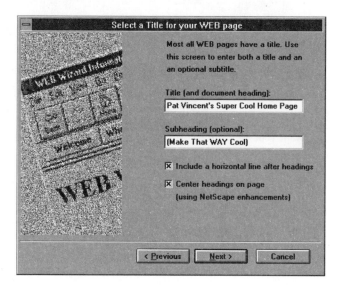

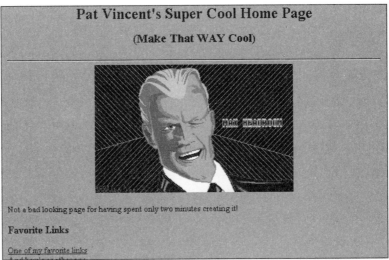

Here's Pat's home page, in case you've wondered what he looked like.

Simply point and click, and your home pages will be the envy of your cyberneighborhood, complete with artwork, graphics, and links to your favorite sites. This software is easy and fast, but it's unable to create complicated or sophisticated Web pages. Besides the Windows version, a Mac version may be available by the time you read this.

How

World Wide Web

Where

www.halcyon.com/artamedia/webwizard

Let's Get Graphic

Interactive Graphics Renderer ☆☆☆

Sure the Web is great because of its ease of use—I mean how hard can it be to point and click? But what really makes the Web, well, the Web, is the graphics. And with the Interactive Graphics Renderer (IGR), jazzing up your Web pages with cool art has never been easier.

This easy-to-use interface for designing customized graphics for your Web pages includes lots of objects, colors, sizes, and other options to help you create great looking Web pages.

At IGR, you can quickly create graphics for your Web pages
that are wild, wacky, and just a little weird—just like the Web.

In addition, IGR includes a limitless supply of artwork for you to create and
modify, and a simple interface for hassle-free downloading.

How

World Wide Web

Where

www.eece.ksu.edu/IGR

This Is a Test

WWW Viewer Test Page ☆☆☆

That new browser you downloaded promises all the bells and most of the
whistles available to make your Web surfing faster and a lot more fun. But you
won't *really* know if it has everything it promises until you access the WWW
Viewer Test Page.

This site acts as sort of a diagnostics tool for your browser. Just click the different buttons available to see if your browser will play QuickTime and MPEG
videos, **.au**, **.aif**, and **.aic** sound files, and more.

How

World Wide Web

Where

www-dsed.llnl.gov/documents/WWWtest.html

Grab a Web and Whack It

GrabNet and WebWhacker ☆☆☆☆

The Forefront Group software company created two utilities for those who spend a *lot* of time on the Net. GrabNet grabs text and pictures from any Web site you visit. You clip the words and graphics you want and put them with site URLs to create an illustrated guide—like graphical bookmarks. It's an excellent bookmark manager.

WebWhacker is a tool for heavy-duty cruisers. You can tell WebWhacker to bring you several sites, go do something else, and come back to visit the sites without waiting (and waiting, and waiting) for stuff to travel to you. WebWhacker stores the sites you want on your computer, ready and waiting for you. You can set it to download huge sites while you sleep and peruse them speedily with your orange juice the next morning.

We highly recommend WebWhacker for all serious Net searchers. Both products are available for Macs, Windows 3.1, and Windows 95.

How

World Wide Web

Where

www.ffg.com

From Word-Processed to Web-Processed

Resources for Converting Documents to HTML ☆☆☆☆

If you build an industrial-strength Web site, you'll have existing documents in WordPerfect, MacWrite, or PageMaker that you'll want to convert into HTML pages for your Web server. This site acts as a central clearing house for converters. Instead of reformatting everything by hand (boring, tedious work), look here to pick up software to do the dirty work for you.

How

World Wide Web

Where

www.w3.org/hypertext/WWW/Tools/Filters/html

Web Creation 101

BEGINNER'S GUIDE TO HTML ☆☆☆

If you want to build your own Web site instead of farming out the work, you'll need to know HyperText Markup Language, called HTML for short. Unlike programming languages, HTML isn't actually all that complicated, so don't get into a dither if you don't know it. In fact, if you can use a word processor, you can probably learn all you need to know about HTML in just a few hours. This site will help, because it gives you step-by-step instructions in the HTML basics. So relax. HTML won't bite.

How

World Wide Web

Where

www.ncsa.uiuc.edu/General/Internet/WWW/HTMLPrimer.html

Paint Me a Rainbow

Paint Shop Pro ☆☆☆

If you don't have an industrial-strength graphics program like Photoshop to design your Web site, don't fret. Paint Shop Pro, a Windows program for creating and changing graphics will handle your retouching and editing, including 20 image filters. It supports more than 30 file formats, including **.gif**, **.jpg**, and all others that are common on the Web.

How

World Wide Web

Where

www.jasc.com/index.html

Sound Advice about Sound

Netscape Sound How-To ☆☆☆

This site will provide sound advice about Netscape sound, and for software to add sound to your Web pages. The instructions on playing sound with your Netscape browser cover Netscape for Windows, and the three software programs are also for Windows.

The first program, Wplayany, is actually an add-on for your browser. It detects and plays most sound files you meet on the Web. Goldwave is a fairly sophisticated

122

sound editing program. WHAM (Waveform Hold And Modify) is for recording and modifying sound to add to your Web page. It reads and writes **.wav** and **.au** files and other formats, and can convert from one format to another. You can open a sound file with WHAM, play the sound, and cut and paste the parts you want to use.

How
World Wide Web

Where
burgoyne.com/vaudio/netsound.html

You Don't Need to Fold Up a Clickable Map

Mapedit ☆☆☆

If you want to have a picture on your Web site where your customers can click on different spots of your picture and be sent to different Web pages, you need to create clickable image maps. These are a MAP file that your Web page presents along with the picture file. Mapedit makes it easy for you to create MAP files. The software comes in Windows, Mac, and Unix versions. Note that you will still need to work with your Web site service bureau to use the MAP with your page.

How
World Wide Web

Where
www.boutell.com/mapedit

Down the Rabbit Hole, Alice Found a Web

Textures and Backgrounds Wonderland ☆☆☆

Don't be put off by this site's garish rainbow home page. You'll find the largest directory of Web page backgrounds and textures at this site, and many are suitable for even the most staid business Web site. Check out the M.C. Escher tiles, and the unique collection from Doc Ozone. Just click and copy to quickly add pizzazz to your own site.

How
World Wide Web

Where
cameo.softwarelabs.com/hotlist/hotlist.htm

Watching the Web

WebWatch for Windows ☆☆☆

The Web is the ultimate "work in progress," and never remains the same even from one hour to the next. On the plus side, that means there's always something new to be discovered; on the downside, there's no guarantee that what you find today will be there tomorrow.

But every obstacle also represents an opportunity—just ask Specter, Inc., makers of WebWatch for Windows. WebWatch helps you keep track of changes in your hotlist and bookmark files, as well as any of your other HTML documents by scanning your documents for links that have changed.

Here today, gone tomorrow. WebWatch will help you
keep track of hyperlinks on the Web.

To download a copy, access this site and click on *WebWatch Product Information*. Next, click on *download the 32 bit version* or *download the 16 bit version* to get your own shareware version.

How

World Wide Web

Where

www.specter.com/users/janos/specter

Download

ww10c_16.zip (92 K)

ww10c_32.zip (132 K)

The 32-bit version works with Windows 95, Windows for Workgroups 3.11, and Windows 3.1 running Win32s; the 16-bit version works with any Windows 3.x version.

Mind Your Own Business

URL-minder ☆☆☆☆

Simply register your favorite Web and Gopher sites with URL-minder, and you'll be notified by email every time they're updated or change locations. In addition, you can even have URL-minder perform searches with your favorite Internet search engine, then notify you whenever the results change. Now you can spend your online time (and money) surfing where no Internaut has gone before, rather than constantly checking sites you've already visited just to see what has changed.

You can use URL-minder to monitor an FTP archive for new files. You can register a Yahoo search with URL-minder and automatically get email whenever something new shows up on your search topic. (This works for other search engines as well.) For your own Web page, you can use URL-minder to add a form on your page so visitors can enter their email address and they will automatically be informed whenever you change that page.

How

World Wide Web

Where

www.netmind.com/url-minder/url-minder.html

Roll Your Own

Design Your Own Web Page Online ☆☆

This page helps you design your own Web page, shows it to you, and emails it to you. You can use this site's graphics or add your own. It claims that anyone can build a page in 15 minutes. We tested this claim and built a page including custom graphics in 9 minutes. This site's one problem is that it gives you many restrictions. Still, if the idea of creating a Web page mystifies you, try this site. In minutes, it will remove any fears you have.

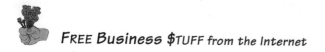

How

World Wide Web

Where

www.virtualrome.com/virtualrome/design/design.html

Don't Count Your Chickens before They Visit

Internet Audit Bureau ☆☆☆

If you have a Web site, you need to know how many people are visiting your site. If your service bureau or company programmers can't give you reports on Web traffic, go to the Internet Audit Bureau.

This free service gives you reports of statistics on the use of your Web pages. IAB reports on *accesses*, which are a more accurate statistic for tracking than *hits* (but not as desirable as reporting on how many unique *people* visit your site). Register at this site, follow the instructions, and place the IAB logo on any page you want the IAB to monitor. Your reports are updated every 48 hours (soon to be daily), and give you the numbers on how many people accessed a page, at what times, and by what kinds of browsers. You can also go here to see reports on the top 25 sites on the Net in different categories, ranked by accesses.

How

World Wide Web

Where

www.internet-audit.com

...Count 'Em WHEN They Visit

AnthoLOGy - Log Analysis ☆☆☆

This page gives techies the clearest possible explanation of five different ways to use your Web server log file to collect page statistics. Marc Hemerik also provides the free software you need, plus a link to Yahoo's directory of Web statistics resources.

How

World Wide Web

Where

elektron.et.tudelft.nl/~mhemerik/antholog.html

VBStat is a good Windows software product that collects statistics from your Web site and produces reports. Get it from **www.city.net/win-http/#vbstat**.

Tip Top Table Tricks

TableMaker ☆☆☆

TableMaker gives you a quick and easy way to create tables in your Web pages. This is a real time-saver for any nontechnical person who wants to add tables of facts, figures, or anything else to a Web page. The version you use on the Web works with all brands of computers.

If you're a Mac-head, you can download a free Macintosh program that lets you do the same thing offline. The Mac version handles lots of data—*big* tables—and can process multiple files and data at one time. Thanks to Sam Choukris, who created this gem.

How

World Wide Web

Where

www.missouri.edu/~c588349/tablemaker.html

Can I Get Matching Drapes with That?

ColorMaker ☆☆☆☆

Sam Choukris strikes again with this easy-to-use tool for picking colors for your Web page background, text, and links. He makes this all possible without having to deal with those annoying hex numbers.

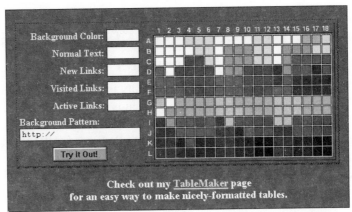

Well, color me wired. This site makes it very easy to colorize your site. Just don't get carried away and become garish unless you sell 60s blacklight posters.

How

World Wide Web

Where

www.missouri.edu/~c588349/colormaker.html

 A good alternative tool for choosing colors in your Web page is the **Thalia Guide** at:
www.sci.kun.nl/cgi-bin-thalia/color/compose

Since CONSUMER REPORTS Doesn't Cover Servers...

Web Servers Comparison ☆☆☆☆

If you decide to run your own Web server on your own in-house computer, this site shows you some alternatives. Paul Hoffman provides side-by-side comparisons of more than 50 different server software programs. The best section is near the very end: 18 free and three shareware servers! Hoffman also directs you to other important sources of information on how to run your Web site.

If you see a different name when you visit, don't panic. Hoffman has promised to change his site's name to something more catchy.

How

World Wide Web

Where

www.proper.com/www/servers-chart.html

Do I Have to Wear Red and Green Glasses?

Adhoc 3D Studio to VRML Converter ☆☆

For most businesses, virtual reality is a bit exotic, like holding your shareholders' meeting on the spinning teacups ride at Disneyland. But if you want to add virtual reality to your Web site, this Windows utility will convert the files you create in Autodesk's 3D Studio to Web-ready VRML files. And remember not to spin around too fast after lunch.

How

World Wide Web

Where

www.best.com/~adhoc/html/vrml.html

Rescues More Webmasters Than Lassie

Hot Dog ☆☆☆☆

This is one of the best HTML editors for creating Web pages—no, wait, it's *two* of the best editors. Hot Dog Standard is great for amateur Web builders, or those just starting out at HTML. Hot Dog Pro has many more features and functions, and is suitable for experienced Web creators building complex sites. Both are well-planned programs with many clever features to make your work easier.

You'll relish the way Hot Dog helps you ketchup with Web work so your site cuts the mustard.

One reality of Web life is that it is easier and less time-consuming to create a Web page than it is to maintain and update one. Hot Dog Pro includes tools to help you with the support you'll need. Both Hot Dogs are Windows software, but their maker promises Unix and Mac Dogs real soon.

When you visit this site to pick up your frankfurters, take time to check out what else it offers. You'll find free clip art here to decorate your Web pages, and a section called "HTML Magic" steers you toward how-to guides for Web creation.

How

World Wide Web

Where

www.sausage.com

Where to Find Way More Free Goodies

Because this book is about business and the Internet, you'll find more free stuff on the topics above throughout this book.

In our last chapter, *Business News*, we gave you a number of good news sources. For example, try the ClariNet read-only newsgroups **clari.tw.computers.networking**, **clari.tw.computers.networking.releases**, **clari.tw.new_media**, and **clari.tw.new_media.online.releases**. ClariNet also gives you a solid newsletter about the Net called *Matrix News*. *Business News* also contains rival trade publications such as *Interactive Age* and *Interactive Week*.

Do you want to know where business is headed on the Internet? For an in-depth outlook on the present and future of Internet business, read the two excellent reports on the Internet and business and on telecommunications provided by *The Economist*'s Web site.

Gonna sell products, services, or ad space on the Net? The chapter *Marketing, Advertising, and Publicity* has more than a dozen resources for you. Especially look at this chapter if you plan to sell advertising space on your Web site. (One survey said that businesses made $43 million in Web ad sales in 1995.) Some spots to check out in this chapter are Advertising World's sections on Web Ad Placement, Media Central's *Interactive Monitor*, the newsletters *Back Channel* and *International Internet Marketing*, *Ad Age*'s forum on Web Statistics, Vidya's Guide to Advertising on the Internet, WebTrack, MouseTracks, and the *Interactive Publishing Alert* site. Don't miss the three email discussion groups: internet-marketing, internet-advertising, and internet-sales.

Our chapter on *Business Law, Trademarks, Copyrights, and Patents* gives you a few handy resources. Besides legally-oriented spots such as the email discussion group on Internet, Computers, and Law, look for general Internet business information in the newsletter *The Quarterly* and in the paper "Developing a Corporate Internet Policy," both provided by the firm of Gray Cary Ware & Freidenrich.

Number-crunchers will find good stuff in our *Accounting and Finance* chapter on Net biz, including the Accounting Professional's Resource Center, the CPA-INET-USE email discussion group, and four newsletters: *Boomer Bulletin*, *Credit Union Tech-Talk*, *Internet Bulletin for CPAs*, and *Double Entries*.

You can also look in the index of this book under the heading **Internet and business** to find dozens more resources to complement this chapter.

As if that wasn't enough, you can also (for free, of course) scope out the Vince's home page for his book *How to Grow Your Business on the Internet* at **www.emery.com/growbook.html.** You'll find the complete text of two chapters of the book—including one covering sales on the Web—plus bonus stuff not included in the print version of his book.

FREE $TUFF

Opportunities are usually
disguised as hard work, so
most people don't recognize
them.

Ann Landers

V.I.P.

Entrepreneurs, Startups, and Home Businesses

On the Internet, no one knows your office is in your basement.

Maybe that's why so many people work at home these days. According to the Telecommuting Advisory Council, 11 million people telecommute. This number has doubled in three years, and the growth rate is increasing. And we're not just talking about telecommuters here. One survey said that half of all new business startups are home-based businesses.

Like Jimmy Durante said, "Everybody wants to get into the act!" Or at least, to get out of those rush hour traffic jams.

For many people who work at home, the factor that makes this possible is the personal computer. Home workers usually use computers more than many office workers. Maybe it's because they're not distracted by hot gossip around the water cooler. In any case, home workers need to keep their computers as well organized as possible, because they depend on their computers more. When your computer shuts down, it can shut your business down with it.

Keeping that in mind, we pay particular attention in this chapter to software tools and utilities that keep your computer secure and well-run, and help you organize your information. We're not talking propeller-head tools that need an MIT genius to run, just dependable utilities for entrepreneurs, teleworkers, and other folks who work at home.

It's a Small Business World after All

Small Business Administration ☆☆☆☆☆

One of the biggest sources—if not *the* biggest source—of information for entrepreneurs and small businesspeople has made a commitment to deliver as much of that information online as possible. You go away from this site a winner.

There is so much at SBA's Web site, we can only give you an idea of what you'll find. Some of the sections of the SBA Web site include:

Shareware Library of Programs to Run a Business—more than 500 shareware and freeware programs for businesses, each with a very short description. You'll find software for customer order management, point-of-sale, bar codes, service call management, manufacturing, inventory, pre-written business letters, and other general business programs as well as industry-specific

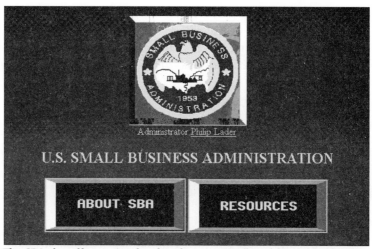

The SBA site offers so much value that on your first visit you should plan to invest at least an hour. Otherwise, you'll miss great free stuff.

programs such as auto repair shop management software, and software for dispatching delivery couriers. Software is sorted into groups for "Starting," "Financing," "Managing," "Marketing," and "Running Your Business."

Commerce Business Daily—today's issue, searchable! Each issue gives you more than 100 sales leads from U.S. government and NATO agencies, arranged by product/service categories. (For more info on *CBD*, see our review of the ClariNet version at the beginning of the *Business News* chapter of this book.) *CBD* normally costs $200 a year to receive online, but you can get it for free at this site.

Starting Your Business—answers to "31 Most-Asked Business Questions," dozens of publications, Small Business Development Centers, regional Business Information Centers, and much more. Be sure to take advantage of SCORE (Service Corps of Retired Executives), which can provide you free training and expert advice for much less than other consultants charge—namely, free!

Financing Your Business—SBA loans, venture capital, surety bonds, *Directory of Small Business Lending Reported by Commercial Banks* (the complete book online), and loan application forms you can download and print.

Expanding Your Business—export assistance for U.S. businesses, small business Technology Transfer Program, and more.

Special Interests—Electronic Commerce and EDI, U.S. Customs Bureau home page, and disaster assistance. The SBA FAQ is hidden in this section.

You'll also find tons of links to other Internet resources for small businesses, unfortunately with no descriptions. There is a good section of links to government procurement resources that explain how you can sell to the U.S. government. Also, the selection of links to resources for businesswomen is a worthwhile visit.

How

World Wide Web

Where

www.sbaonline.sba.gov

If You Want Good Word-of-Mouth

Business Network International ☆☆☆☆☆

Business Network International declares that its "sole purpose is to increase business through a structured system of giving referrals." In 1995, its referrals generated $105 million in business for BNI members in the U.S., Canada, and Europe. It obviously works.

If your business depends on word-of-mouth referrals for sales, this organization (founded by author and businessman Ivan Misner) could be extremely valuable for you. There is no fee to attend meetings, but READ THE FAQ before you decide to join. BNI is not a commitment to be taken lightly.

Besides a description of how BNI works, you'll also find a list of "Business Categories That Have Been Successful," and almost no information under the heading "Other Web Sites for Business Referrals."

How

World Wide Web

Where

www.bninet.com

The High and Lowe of Entrepreneuring

Edward Lowe Foundation ☆☆☆☆

This nonprofit organization is devoted to the support of entrepreneurship, and provides valuable information for Horatio Alger wannabes. One of the best parts is a detailed report from Michigan State University describing what differentiates successful entrepreneurs from those who are not. Based on research into actual practices—what real entrepreneurs actually do—rather than theory, Michigan investigators found six "guiding principles" common to successful entrepreneurs. Those principles and the key actions derived from them are described in *Entrepreneurship and the Future of the American Free Enterprise System*, which you can read at this site. In spite of its grandiose title, the lessons it reveals are useful for businesspeople worldwide.

At this site, you'll also find a somewhat useful searchable bibliographic database of business articles such as: the Library of Congress' *Entrepreneur Reference Guide*, the Library of Congress' *Survey of Nonprofit Business Information Providers* for the U.S., organized by state (for "Nonprofit," read "Free"), and the complete text of the quarterly magazine *Entrepreneurial Edge* (including weekly updates and a searchable archive of past issues). "Business Sources on the Net (BSN) for Small Business and Entrepreneurs" is a goodish Web-ization of Kent State University's Gopher directory of resources. A section called "smallbizNet Pointers" has a tiny list of links.

How

World Wide Web

Where

www.lowe.org

Good Advice for Entrepreneurs

misc.entrepreneurs.moderated Newsgroup ☆☆☆☆

This very active group is *moderated*, so ads are banned, and all you'll find is information—and a lot of it—on topics important to entrepreneurs and small businesses. Full of questions, answers, and advice from graduates of Hard Knocks U., this newsgroup is an excellent resource.

Sample topics: Bounced checks; Experience with SBA Loans?; Export advice; Ideas on a cinnamon roasted almond business; Looking for marketing ideas; Looking for media products; minimalist direct mail vehicle?; Need advice on T-shirt royalties; Need advice on foreign marketing; Startup capital; Visa/MC/AMEX merchant accounts.

How

Newsgroup

Where

news:misc.entrepreneurs.moderated

Sidebar: Visa/MC/AMEX Merchant Accounts

Newsgroups: misc.entrepreneurs.moderated
From: kojola@emi.net (Linda Kojola)
Subject: Re: VISA/MC/AMEX merchant accounts

hr185@ix.netcom.com (Kari Adams) wrote:

> dpdavidoo@aol.com (DPDavidoo) writes:
> > Has anybody out there dealt with Card Service International?
> >
> > I'm a high risk, new start-up mail-order business selling my own
> > invention. Banks either laugh at me or give me that "I'm so sorry" look
> > when I inquire about applying for merchant service status and accepting
> > credit card payments.
> >
> > CSI, while not guaranteeing I'll be accepted, tells me they think I will.
> > Their one-time application fees are higher (for example, $150 versus
> > $50), but they don't laugh at me either.
> >
> > If anybody has had any experience with this company, or can
> > recommend another, please respond.

I have a friend who has a phone order company. She got an account through Card Services and leased its terminal for $49 per month—she signed a 48-month contract. However, after four months Card Services' bank terminated her claiming misrepresentation. She had filled the application out as mail/phone order keyed transactions and she ended up with no account and a terminal she has to pay of the balance.

Those terminals only cost $125-135. The sales agents make their money getting an account opened any way possible, even lies and fraud. Be aware that mail/phone companies pay 4-7 percent retailers pay less than that. If your own bank won't write the account, what makes you think a California bank will take you on and turn you loose? Be careful. I did due diligence before I got merchant processing and I ended up at the National Association of Credit Card Merchants in Boynton Beach, FL—I think their number is 407-737-7500. I don't have to lease a terminal or anything—try them before you sign your life on the dotted line.

[Moderator's Note: Why not add to the contract a clause stipulating that if the bank refuses to honor your charges any more, then the contract nulls and the equipment returns? Remember that *real* contracts are made by both affected parties—not just the biggest.

Furthermore, if you have to pay the balance of the terminal's lease, do you get to keep it? Or do you just hand it back? If so—aren't you being ripped off in a rather obvious way? —SRG]

Find Franchise Facts Fast

Access WWW Franchise Directory ☆☆☆☆

The best spot we could find on the Net for information on franchise businesses, this site includes *IFA's Franchise Opportunities Guide* online, with all the information in the printed directory searchable by category, by name, and by required investment amount. You'll also find a nearly-complete directory of franchise industry associations around the world, including contact information and links to Web pages for those associations that have one.

If you start a franchised business, you may want to bookmark this site because it also contains the home page of F.E.A.T., the Franchise Emergency Action Team. Faster than a speeding bullet, these real-life superheros help franchise business owners in times of emergency. Marvel should make a comic book about 'em. We hope you'll never find cause to call F.E.A.T., but it's reassuring to know they're there if you need them.

How
World Wide Web

Where
www.entremkt.com/access/index.html

Sales Leads and Purchasing Sources

International Small Business Consortium ☆☆☆☆

ISBC, run by volunteers, is a free database matching service for small businesses. Huh? Whazzat mean? Free sales leads and purchasing information, that's what. The ISBC database locates and matches suppliers and buyers with its database. Members are suppliers, buyers, agents, and distributors from around the world. You can list your products in the database for free, and use it for purchasing.

How
World Wide Web

Where
www.isbc.com

Moonlighting by Email

moonlight-l Email Discussion Group ☆☆☆

Here is an email list for you night owls interested in moonlighting from home using your computer. Topics include operating a business on a shoestring, starting up a business, and handling home office issues. In addition, *Moonlight with Your PC*, a free electronic newsletter on the How-Tos of successful moonlighting, is received by this email list once a week.

How

Email

Where

listserv@netcom.com

Message

subscribe moonlight-l

Hey, Remind Me about That

Remind ☆☆☆

Remind is a freeware utility that lets you display reminder messages when you start Windows.

How

FTP

Where

ftp://ftp.csusm.edu/pub/winworld/pim

Download

remind25.zip (57 K)

Daddy, Where Do New Businesses Come From?

National Business Incubation Association ☆☆☆

NBIA is the place where new businesses are born. Or, more accurately, the *places*. This is an organization of venture capitalists, business services providers, and economic development professionals who run business incubators in many countries. Incubators help startups by providing a place where several startups jointly share facilities and services that normally would require a large company's resources. Financial and management assistance is also provided.

This Web site explains the concept of incubators, and gives you an extensive directory of business incubators worldwide. You'll also find a directory of related links. (Sadly, without any descriptions at all. Sigh. Don't these people realize they're on a Web site, not a Gopher?)

How

World Wide Web

Where

ra.cs.ohiou.edu/gopher/dept.servers/aern/homepage/nbia.html

How Much Did You Earn while Reading This?

SalaryMeter, Client Biller, and Tracker ☆☆☆

Here are a couple of programs that, when used together, complement each other nicely. **SalaryMeter** displays the amount of money you're earning while you work (or play, but that'll be our little secret). Now you'll know not only how much *time* you wasted competing in the big office DOOM competition, but you'll instantly know how much *money* you made while you were doing it.

Once you've totaled things up, it's time to pass the buck—or bill—to the patron with the deepest pockets. **Client Biller and Tracker**, an easy-to-use program for keeping track of your clientele, makes it easy for you to bill customers for all your hard labor.

How

World Wide Web

Where

www.acs.oakland.edu/oak/SimTel/win3/finance.html

Download

Client Biller and Tracker: cbill13.zip
SalaryMeter: salry101.zip

Who's the Boss? You Are!

Entrepreneurs on the Web ☆☆☆

The entrepreneurial spirit is alive and thrashing on the Web. If you're one of the little fish, you'll want to check out the tons of resources available to help you succeed and make a splash in the big pond.

Entrepreneurs on the Web provides lots of useful business information, gathered specifically with adventurous venturers in mind.

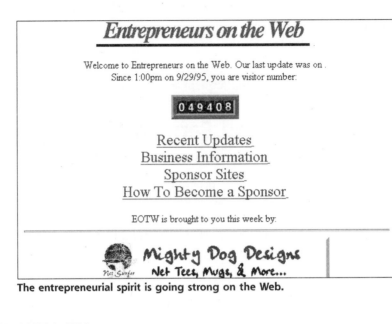

Entrepreneurs on the Web

Welcome to Entrepreneurs on the Web. Our last update was on .
Since 1:00pm on 9/29/95, you are visitor number:

049408

Recent Updates
Business Information
Sponsor Sites
How To Become a Sponsor

EOTW is brought to you this week by:

Mighty Dog Designs
Net Surfer   Net Tees, Mugs, & More...

The entrepreneurial spirit is going strong on the Web.

How

World Wide Web

Where

sashimi.wwa.com/~notime/eotw/EOTW.html

Know the SCOR

Small Corporate Offering Registration (SCOR) ☆☆☆

One of the biggest hurdles that growing businesses have to overcome is the need to raise capital. But new or growing companies have a difficult time gaining access to the stock markets. And unless you're rich, or if Aunt Barbara leaves you the family fortune in her will, or if you've somehow managed to attract the attention of an investment banker, you and your company are dead in the water.

But now there's help for small businesses on the upswing. The Small Corporate Offering Registration (SCOR) provides a new avenue to help small companies raise up to $1 million without having to find an investment banker or expensive securities law firm. Shares issued are freely tradable, and the registration forms are designed for companies, attorneys, and accountants who are not necessarily specialists in securities regulation. Find out if your company is eligible.

How

World Wide Web

Where

www.scor-net.com

Links

List of states allowing SCOR offerings

Qualifications to use SCOR

Complete copy of Form U-7 with instructions

List of Required Exhibits

Financial Statements Requirements

Pacific Stock Exchange Listing Requirements for SCOR Companies

Help Instead of Interruptions

MCI Small Biz Center ☆☆☆

The most interesting original information provided at this site is a winners list of the Positive Performer Awards for small businesses, hosted by *Inc.* magazine and MCI. Most of the value of this site comes from a good directory of links (with helpful descriptions) to resources on the Net. You'll find some of the best sites on business financing and hiring, plus government agencies, professional associations, and news sources. Unlike MCI's other marketing efforts, this Web site won't interrupt your dinner.

How

World Wide Web

Where

www.mci.com/SmallBiz

Hands Off!

Winworld Security Collection ☆☆☆

Computers have become such a common fixture in the home these days, families that used to fight over the bathroom now argue about whose turn it is to get online. But how do you keep the kids from fooling around where they don't belong? When you find out, let me know.

I haven't seen any security programs that are 100-percent foolproof, but here are a few programs that try to solve the problem. These programs enable you to lock others out from different areas of Windows, lock your terminal, and create passwords to keep little hands off.

How

FTP

Where

ftp://ftp.csusm.edu/pub/winworld/guard

Download

chastity.zip (51 K)

lock.zip (11 K)

metz-lck.zip (218 K)

seclau.zip (42 K)

Software Developers Click Here for Profits

Software Forum ☆☆☆☆

If you are in the software business, you may find the Software Forum the most profitable site on the Net. Originally called Software Entrepreneurs Forum, this nonprofit organization is devoted to the business side of the software game. It gives you access to resources no other place can match: insights from hundreds of experts who have each built multi-million dollar software companies. No matter what your question, you'll get answers at this site from seasoned industry pros.

At the Software Forum Web site, you can tap that huge reservoir of experience by joining an email discussion group or two. You have more than a dozen to choose from, categorized according to hot industry topics. (The sidebar below gives you a catalog of topics.) Remember that the pros on these groups discuss business how-tos, not programming issues. You'll participate in discussions via email, but you must visit this Web site to subscribe.

While you visit, poke around at some of this site's other offerings. You'll find news about software technology, computer and communications technology, business management, industry legal issues, finance, software marketing, and, of course, software sales. You can read articles from the group's newsletter *Forum*, and follow links to online resources for entrepreneurs.

With the Software Forum's help, who knows, maybe you'll be the next Bill Gates. Just don't put as many TVs in your custom house as Bill put in his mansion, okay?

How

World Wide Web

Where

sf.interserve.com

Discussion Groups for Software Entrepreneurs

At the Software Forum Web site, you can subscribe to these email discussion groups:

winsig	Windows programs
bizsig	Business
cssig	Client/server programs and systems
macsig	OpenDoc/Macintosh programs
mktsig	Marketing software
mmsig	Multimedia applications and titles
netsig	Internet
opensig	Unix programs and systems
vbsig	Visual Basic
webtalk	Web site administrators and editors
netsales	Network sales and marketing
netinf	Network infrastructure
scycle	Sales cycle automation
comeeff	Marketing communication effectiveness

Consulted by Consultants

alt.computer.consultants Newsgroup ☆☆☆

If your business is consulting about computers, software, or any aspect of computing, you have your own newsgroup. Look past the ads from headhunters and get-rich-quick garbage and you'll find some real consultants helping each other with important issues. You'll also find inquiries from companies looking to hire contract programmers.

How

Newsgroup

Where

news:alt.computer.consultants

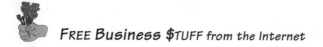

Essential Software

Essential Home Inventory ☆☆☆

If your house or business is burglarized or destroyed, the last thing you want to think about is listing everything that needs to be replaced on an insurance form. That's where Essential Home Inventory can help.

Essential Home Inventory is an easy-to-use shareware program to help you "intelligently" manage your personal and household inventory. Both flexible and fast, Essential Home Inventory is perfect for not only cataloging and managing your household and business items, but also for generating insurance reports and estate plans.

```
┌─────────────────────────────────────────────────────────────┐
│ ─|            Essential Home Inventory (untitled)        |▼|▲|│
│ File  Edit  Find  Options  Help                              │
│ ┌──┐┌──┐┌──┐┌──┐ ┌─Record Contents:──────────────────────┐  │
│ │  ││  ││  ││  │ │         Default [                    ]  │  │
│ └──┘└──┘└──┘└──┘ │         Default [                    ]  │  │
│ Text Picture Statistics Clipboard │ Default [            ]  │  │
│                  │         Default [                    ]  │  │
│ ┌─File Information:─┐ │     Default [                    ]  │  │
│ │                  │ │     Default [                    ]  │  │
│ │ Template:        │ │     Default [                    ]  │  │
│ │                  │ │     Default [                    ]  │  │
│ │ Number of Records:│ │    Default [                    ]  │  │
│ │                  │ │     Default [                    ]  │  │
│ │ This Record:     │ │     Default [                    ]  │  │
│ └──────────────────┘ │     Default [                  ]▼]  │  │
│ ┌─┐┌───────────┐┌─┐  └────────────────────────────────────┘  │
│ │◄││           ││►│         Price [        ]                 │
│ └─┘└───────────┘└─┘         Value [        ]                 │
│ ┌──────────────────┐                                         │
│ │  Add a New Record │   Addendum Name [            ]         │
│ └──────────────────┘                                         │
│ ┌──────────────────┐                                         │
│ │ Delete This Record │                                       │
│ └──────────────────┘                                         │
│  Essential Home Inventory Test Drive 1.0                     │
│        Copyright © 1993  Alston Software Labs                 │
└─────────────────────────────────────────────────────────────┘
```

Did you remember to include the kitchen sink?

How

FTP

Where

ftp://ftp.csusm.edu/pub/winworld/database

Download

ehi10.zip (105 K)

Once you've created an inventory list, be sure to store it someplace safe in case your home or business is destroyed.

The "E" in "Email" Stands for "Entrepreneur"

Entrepreneurship Division Network ☆☆☆

This email discussion group is a mixed bag. You'll find good answers to business questions here, and no spam, but you'll also find too-lengthy announcements for conferences, and academics who supply theories that seem to have no relevance for making money.

Sample topics: Business startup; Hawaii entrepreneurs; cybernetic coffeehouses; mentor and protégé; Journal call for papers; Conference announcement; utility auditing; Case/research possibility; Case Studies for Pilot Project in Russia; Small business and Internet.

How

World Wide Web

Where

listserv@ksuvm.ksu.edu

Message

subscribe entrep-l Yourfirstname Yourlastname

 You'll find an archive of past messages at **gopher://ursus.jun.alaska.edu:70/11/lists**. Unfortunately, it is not kept up-to-date.

Not a Shred of Evidence

Terminator ☆☆☆

You don't need that file any more, so simply delete it and it's gone, right? Not exactly. You actually haven't deleted *anything*; you've simply told your computer that the space is available for storing other files. This system works great if you have to undelete something, but it really stinks if you're trying to get rid of sensitive or confidential data.

Short of removing your hard drive and whacking it with a hammer, there's no guarantee that what you delete today won't end up in somebody else's hands tomorrow. Unless, of course, you *terminate* it. The Terminator file deletion utility is similar to an electronic shredder that makes recovering deleted documents virtually impossible. Rumor has it that this is the same program Ollie North uses for shredding all his electronic documents. Not only does it slice, dice, frappé, and shred your documents, it also makes julienne fries. By the way, this is a Windows program; sorry, but it's not available for Mac users.

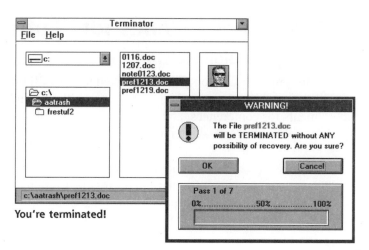

You're terminated!

How

FTP

Where

ftp://gatekeeper.dec.com/pub/micro/msdos/win3/desktop

Download

term20.zip (38 K)

 The documentation included with Terminator warns you that once you delete a file with this program, it's gone for good. And they ain't kidding. Use this utility with caution.

No Fluff, Just Good Stuff

WEB MARKETING TODAY ☆☆☆

Got a Web site of your own? Or thinking about one? Here's a biweekly newsletter for small businesses that market on the Web. Each issue is short—perfect for the small business owner in a hurry—and gives good, basic information on marketing specifically as it applies on the Web. You can read each issue on the Web site or subscribe here to have it delivered by email. At the Web site, you can also read articles from past issues.

How

World Wide Web

Where

www.wilsonweb.com/rfwilson/wmt

The Number You Have Dialed...

Quik Dialer ☆☆☆

When speed dialers were introduced, they were supposed to be valuable business tools for contacting clients, as well as valuable safety tools for quickly calling help. Sounds good, but the only time I use mine is to call up my favorite radio station and Domino's Pizza Hot Line. In fact, I think I could have a pizza delivered faster than it would take me to figure out how to speed-dial the fire department.

But here's an easy-to-use shareware modem speed dialer with some different features. Quik Dialer, which works with your modem, lets you store hundreds of phone numbers in its online Rolodex, and you can even sort them by importance. Plus, dialing is as easy as pointing and clicking, and it'll redial until you connect.

How

FTP

Where

ftp://ftp.csusm.edu/pub/winworld/dialer

Download

qdlr204.zip (212 K)

4 Chaps 4U

How to Succeed in Your Home Business ☆☆☆

Toronto Dominion Bank sponsored the Web-ization of four chapters from this good book on home businesses: "Quiz: How Entrepreneurial Are You?," "Developing Your Business Plan," "10 Commandments of Running Your Home Business," and "Basic Truths about Client Service."

How

World Wide Web

Where

www.tdbank.ca/tdbank/succeed.index.html

Once upon a Time...

Online Time Recorder ☆☆☆

Online Time Recorder makes it easy for you to keep track of the time you spend online. You can track per-minute charges, free time, extended usage, or any other time charges to help you stay within your service's monthly allowance, as well as to compare your service's monthly bill.

And with a built-in log file, Online Time Recorder will keep track of who's online, the date and time of each session, the amount of time spent in each section of the service, and the total time for each online session. You can even use it to record the time spent working on business projects to help you tally your client's bill.

How

FTP

Where

ftp://ftp.csusm.edu/pub/winworld/time

Download

oltime10.zip (42 K)

Business by Email

Biz-Wire Email Discussion Group ☆☆☆

Biz-Wire is a mailing list addressing issues that involve business and the creation of businesses. All aspects of commercial endeavors are welcome, as are announcements and press releases. (But be careful—this is a moderated list, so hold off on that spam.) This list is designed to encourage commercial development of all aspects of business.

How

Email

Where

listserv@ais.net

Message

subscribe BIZ-WIRE Yourfirstname Yourlastname

C'mon, Clean Up Your Desktop!

Disktop Management Utilities ☆☆☆

Remember when you first got that computer? You felt as though the amount of disk space available was limitless. Fat chance. Next thing you knew, those hundreds of megabytes of free space were filled up with spreadsheet programs, flight simulators, and bitmaps of supermodels Niki Taylor and Audrey Taflinger.

Now it feels like half your RAM called in sick this morning and you wonder why you keep getting all those error messages.

Hmm. You need some assistance in the disk management department and this site can help. Within this large collection of Windows utilities are disk compression and file locating programs, utilities to display the amount of disk space available, programs to copy and format disks in the background, and other disk management utilities.

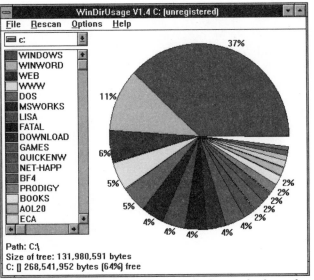

WinDirUsage, a shareware utility that displays a pie chart of your disk space usage, is one of several disk management utilities you can download at this site.

How

World Wide Web

Where

www.acs.oakland.edu/oak/simtel/win3/diskutil.html

Download

Find a file:	epwffv1.zip
WinFree	wfree101.zip
Windows Disk Space Usage	windru14.zip
Win Disk Copy	wndc111.zip

There's No Office Like Home

HIRING SOMEONE TO WORK IN YOUR HOME ☆☆☆

If you're thinking of hiring your first employee for your home-based business, get a copy of this free booklet from the Consumer Information Center. *Hiring Someone to Work in Your Home* is four pages of helpful tips to keep you from breaking any of the federal laws set up to protect your in-home employees. There's helpful tax and payroll advice, descriptions of which services are exempt (no, you don't have to withhold taxes for your in-home baby-sitter), and steps to take when hiring an employee.

How

World Wide Web

Where

www.gsa.gov/staff/pa/cic/other/o-employ.htm

Download

Hiring Someone to Work in Your Home

 The page says it costs fifty cents, but it's really free.

Stick with It

NoteZ ☆☆☆

These days, sticky notes are as much a fixture of modern offices as basketball pools and antacid tablets. Employees seemingly would not be able to function

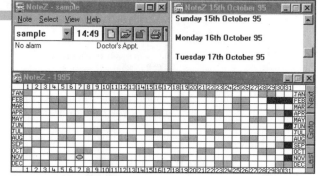
Are you taking NoteZ?

without them. Well, the modern office just became even *more* modern with NoteZ software for Windows 95.

This online version of the popular Post-It notes you'll find splattered all over office cubicles worldwide, combines the convenience of sticky reminders with the power of a personal information manager. Simply click on a date, then key in your reminder, and your virtual note is pasted to your computer screen. NoteZ even has an alarm you can set that's guaranteed to drive co-workers crazy—that alone makes it worth the price of registration.

How

World Wide Web

Where

download.netex.net/w95/windows95/utils

Download

ntz31n.zip (125 K)

Logging in the Hours

Time Logger ☆☆☆

The only thing better than billing a customer for all your hard work is getting paid by a customer for doing all that hard work (then again, maybe it's spending that hard-earned moola). Make sure the paperwork doesn't get bogged down in disputes over how many hours you worked and on what projects. A Windows 95 program named Time Logger lets you track—to the minute—how you spent your time, giving you some valuable leverage when questions arise.

Start using Time Logger before you start logging in the hours.

Simply fill in the information about what you did and when you did it (you can even use Time Logger's stopwatch to keep track of this automatically), and Time Logger creates a list of time records. And Time Logger lets you display any number of fields (such as client, project, duration, and so on).

You can even print reports that document your work, including the time record, summaries, subtotals, and more. Plus, Time Logger's automatic invoice printing makes sticking it to—er, billing—clients easier than ever.

How

FTP

Where

ftp://oak.oakland.edu/pub3/simtel-nt/pim

Download

tldemo32.zip (947 K)

Cutting Corners

Hot Corners ☆☆☆

Office employees who work on sensitive data (like payrolls, organization charts, basketball pools, and so on) are usually required to close documents and lock up their computers each time they leave their desks, even for a minute.

With Hot Corners software for Windows 95, you can quickly turn your screen saver on or off by positioning the cursor in a corner of your desktop that you choose. If your screen saver is password-protected, and you have to leave your desk, place your cursor on a corner of the screen you've defined. Hot Corners activates your screen saver within one second. Then, you deactivate it when you return by placing the cursor on another predefined corner.

How

FTP

Where

ftp://ftp.zdnet.com/zdi/software

Download

hotc.zip (14 K)

Does Your Business Sell Products?

Hi, Finance ☆☆☆☆

This great program helps you answer tough questions: How much should I mark up prices on a product? How many do I need to sell to break even? What's the most cost-effective quantity of items I should order? Hi, Finance is a breeze to use. For instance, when you're figuring out how many pieces you need to sell to break even, you enter your rent and other fixed costs, your cost per unit, and your selling price. Hi, Finance then computes how many pieces you need to sell before you show a profit, and shows you a graph of your profits after you break-even. Use it to figure out "what-if" questions—if your rent goes up, or your costs go down.

It calculates and charts Economic Order Quantities so you can figure out what's the best quantity of an item to buy, taking into account what it costs you to store the item, what it costs you each time you place an order, and your yearly demand for the product. Hi, Finance also calculates the best markup and profit margins on items. It also tracks your investment, monitors personal finances, and calculates loan-related info. If you've ever wondered how much of a product you must sell and at what price to make a profit, Hi, Finance is a tool for you.

How

FTP

Where

ftp://ftp.pcmag.ziff.com/pccomp/960209

Download

hifin.zip

Move the Work Instead of the Worker

Telecommuting, Teleworking, & Alternative Officing ☆☆☆☆

Not only does the Internet enable more people to work at home, it also helps you keep track of that growth, and the rapidly-accumulating wisdom on how to telecommute—and how not to! Updated monthly, this rich Web site links you to more information on telecommuting than any other spot on the Net.

You'll find a good FAQ on telecommuting at this site, and links to many publications and newsletters on this subject from the U.S., Canada, Britain, Ireland,

and Japan. The huge directory of resources is divided into global geographic regions: North America, Europe, Middle East, Africa, and Asia-Pacific (includes Australia).

How

World Wide Web

Where

www.gilgordon.com

Radio Traffic Jam Reports Make Me Smile

Telecommuting Advisory Council ☆☆☆

A solid source of information, the Telecommuting Advisory Council gives you articles on Telecommuting plus links to dozens of resources on the subject. Check out this site's section on "News Stories" for the latest technology for teleworkers, especially fast, cheap cable modems, which the Council monitors for you.

If you can't find the information you need with your Web browser, fire up your email software. You can email the Council and ask questions. But don't ask questions such as, "What is the capital of Assyria?" The Council will only answer questions on telecommuting and teleworkers. (Besides, we already know the capital of Assyria. It's "A.")

How

World Wide Web

Where

www.telecommute.org

Because Modems Get Better Mileage Than Cars

remote-work Email Discussion Group ☆☆☆

Telecommuting is still foreign to some businesses. This email discussion group helps smooth the edges, both by answering questions of teleworkers and by helping managers figure out how to plan and launch telecommuting programs, and how to improve the programs once they get them up and running. Well, not exactly running, because the whole idea is that workers don't have to run from place to place. Maybe up and online?

How

Email

Where

remote-work-request@unify.com

Message

subscribe remote-work

This group also provides telecommuting publications over the Net. For Smart Valley's telecommuting guide (a 100 K file), email to the same address with the message **get remote-work telecmmtng_guide.txt**. The thick book *Telecommuting Centers and Related Concepts* is a 1994 survey of all telecommuting centers worldwide and what makes 'em work (there's a business opportunity here). You'll receive the body of the report separately from its table of contents and executive summary. To receive the contents and summary (40 K), email to the above address with the message **get remote-work telecntr.header + execsummary.txt**. For the body of this book (a modem-choking 520 K), send the message **get remote-work telecntr.txt**.

Pac Bell Wrote the Book on It

TELECOMMUTING RESOURCES GUIDE ☆☆☆☆

This book by Pacific Bell is a very good how-to guide both for teleworkers and for company managers. It starts with the basics. Then it covers how to select the people to telecommute, how to start a telecommuting program, business issues, job duties for a telecommuting project manager, and how to manage telecommuters. A section for teleworkers covers how to adjust to telecommuting, how to motivate yourself, how to structure your work day, and family considerations. A technology section covers the subject from the point of view of both the company and the home worker.

Several appendixes give you the paperwork you need. Forms help you in evaluating a project, choosing workers, choosing managers, evaluating workers, scheduling, analyzing cost/benefit ratios, monitoring security, and more.

You can read the *Telecommuting Resources Guide* on the Web, or download a copy in Adobe Acrobat format to view at your leisure (and to print all those forms).

How

World Wide Web

Where

www.pacbell.com/Lib/TCGuide/index.html

Pacific Bell also makes another helpful book available for its customers who use ISDN. You can read the *Pacific Bell ISDN User's Guide* on the Web at

www.pacbell.com/Products/SDS-ISDN/Book

Where to Find More Entrepreneurial Gems

Heck, we've spread 'em all over this book! Doesn't a small business do marketing like any other business? So read our chapter on *Marketing, Advertising, and Publicity*. Likewise, read any of the other chapters in this book that relate to a function your business performs. We made a special effort to include good resources for small businesses throughout this book.

It also won't hurt you to browse this book's index. Look under **startup resources**.

FREE $TUFF

The codfish lays 10,000 eggs,
The homely hen just one.
The codfish never cackles
To tell you that she's done.
And so we scorn the codfish,
And the homely hen we prize.
Which demonstrates to you and me
That it pays to advertise.

Toronto Globe

Marketing, Advertising, and Publicity

Whether your business is software or kumquats, if you don't get your products or services to the right prospects you will have no sales. Without sales, no income. Without income, you'll have to eat your own kumquats, which at least tastes better than floppy disks.

"Nothing except the mint can make money without advertising," Thomas Macaulay observed. Fortunately for your business, you can get a lot of free help with your advertising, publicity, and other marketing efforts from dozens of Internet resources.

Marketing, advertising, and publicity companies are swarming over the Internet thicker than ants at Godiva Chocolates' company picnic. One recent survey found that for every five businesses actually selling products or services on the Web, there are seven companies trying to sell marketing and advertising services!

This marketing overload can be great for you. Increased competition means that marketing and ad companies are giving away an enormous amount of information, publications, software, and services in a frantic attempt to get the attention of your business. Not all that stuff is useful. In fact, this chapter probably had the worst ratio of diamonds to dirt of any chapter in this book.

But we still found plenty of winners. So pull up your laptop and cash in!

All Internet Marketing is Direct Marketing

DM News Online Edition ☆☆☆☆☆

This is a tool to increase your sales, make no bones about it. *DM News*, the weekly newspaper of direct marketing, brings you an online counterpart that's updated *daily*. This is not a newspaper for the creative side of advertising, but for people who handle the business side of direct marketing. And in case you think your business doesn't use direct marketing, think again. All customer loyalty programs are direct marketing and all telephone sales are direct marketing. And, especially, *all Internet marketing is direct marketing*.

It looks like this site puts the entire print version of *DM News* at your fingertips, and then some. You'll find very good coverage of Internet marketing, top reporting on direct mail and catalog sales, stories on catalog marketing, database marketing, infomercials, home shopping, mailing lists, and the best coverage of international direct marketing anyplace (This is not an empty claim. Vince researched, and *DM News* beat everything else in a walk.).

Lead Stories, March 12, 1996

Paper Direct to Consolidate with Sister Catalogers

Paper Direct Inc., a division of Shoreview, MN-based Deluxe Corp., has announced plans to close its headquarters in Secaucus, NJ, and lay off more than 400 workers. A catalog marketer of specialty stationery and business products, Paper Direct had sales of approximately $100 million last year. The company's operations are to be consolidated with sister direct marketing units in Colorado and Minnesota over the next 18 months. According to Stuart Alexander, vice president of corporate relations at Deluxe, the consolidation of Paper Direct is part of a larger reorganization that has combined more than 15 separate businesses into two distinct units: Deluxe Financial Services, a $1.2 billion provider of check printing and electronic funds transfer operations; and Deluxe Direct, which comprises consumer and business-to-business direct marketers with combined sales of roughly $700 million. Current Inc. is the largest direct marketing unit.

Click here for more direct marketing news than anyplace else on the Net.

Besides the stories, you'll find a good selection of job opportunities, a directory of suppliers and resources, news about direct marketing ad agencies, and a calendar of events. If you qualify, you can even receive a free subscription to the print version of *DM News*.

How

World Wide Web

Where

www.dmnews.com

Planet of the Clio Creatures

Advertising World ☆☆☆☆

Well, Advertising World isn't really a planet, but it does cover the earth. This is the biggest list we could find of advertising stuff on the Net—hundreds of sites carefully arranged in dozens of categories. Most links have short, helpful descriptions.

Here are some of Advertising World's categories, each of which sprouts a subdirectory of its own:

- Account Planning
- Advertisers

FREE Business $TUFF from the Internet

- Advertising Agencies
- Associations
- Books on Advertising
- Coupons (you won't believe how many Net coupon sites you'll find)
- Creative Design & Copy
- Demographic/Economic Information
- Direct Marketing
- Job Hunting
- Media Planning and Buying
- Point of Purchase
- Print Production
- Product Placement
- Public Relations
- Sales Promotions
- Software for Advertising
- Sports Sponsorship
- Web Ad Placement

Whew! And those are less than half of what you'll find here. Good luck, pack your phaser, and we hope you make it back alive.

How

World Wide Web

Where

www.utexas.edu/coc/adv/world

Use the Right Tool for the Right Job

MARKETING TOOLS ☆☆☆☆

If any high-tech tool can help you market your business, this good magazine will cover it. Articles tell you how to apply the Internet, databases, psychographics, integrated marketing, and such seemingly unsophisticated tools as Caller ID on phones.

You can read the complete contents of each issue online, including columns (Database/Direct, Business to Business, Geodemographics, New Tools, Marketing Research, and People Patterns) and regular departments (book reviews,

162

**Let the MARKETING TOOLS magazine's Web site
put some high-tech muscle into your marketing.**

direct marketing software, tools for sales force automation). To top it off, this whole Web site has a built-in search engine so you can search for anything on it. Any serious marketer who wants to get ahead had better plug into *Marketing Tools*.

How

World Wide Web

Where

www.marketingtools.com/mt-current/default.htm

IN MEDIAS RES

Media Central ☆☆☆☆

From the time Homer wrote about Achilles and the Trojan War, every great epic has started *in medias res*, in the middle of things. And that's how you'll feel at Media Central, in the middle of things. In the middle of the media, in fact. (Would this be *in medias media*?)

An almost overwhelming amount of coverage on the media is available at Media Central.

For starters, you can receive the newsletter *Media Central Digest* for free via email, or read it here at the Web site. Each week it gives you an update on the newest Web resources for media and marketing pros.

This site also gives you the top news stories affecting the media (mostly in the U.S.) updated every weekday. Fascinating stuff, if you're interested in media.

But the heart of Media Central is its online library of articles and columns from Cowles/SIMBA publications, which covers the media business. Here you can read articles from the latest issues (plus back issues) of:

- *Interactive Monitor*—Covering online media and marketing
- *Direct*—Covering direct marketing and "precision retailing"
- *News Digest*—Daily news stories about media and marketing
- *Cowles/SIMBA Media Daily*
- *DIRECT Newsline*
- *Inside Media*
- *CableWorld*—Weekly covering cable and other TV businesses
- *Catalog Age*—Weekly bible of the catalog sales industry
- *Directory World*—Weekly news for the Yellow Pages biz
- *On Demand*

You'll find more information at "Site Source." It is a mediocre directory of links and reviews of Web sites. Its best part is probably the winners list of the Golden Link Awards for Web site creativity. You can browse the *Catalog Age 100*, the 100 biggest catalog publishers, and the *Folio 500*, the largest magazine publishers. A section called "Forums" gives mildly diverting email discussions of direct marketing, magazines, new media, and other topics.

A connection to SimbaNet lets you receive free hard copies of the newsletters *Electronic Information Report, Multimedia Business Report*, and *News Inc.*, which covers the newspaper business. Register for free to use SIMBA's searchable online SimbaNet archives.

Media Central could be less time-consuming to navigate, but it's a tremendously valuable resource whether you're a Rupert Murdoch wannabe or dream of being the next Hal Riney.

How
World Wide Web

Where
www.mediacentral.com

A Grade-AAAA Resource

BACK CHANNEL ☆☆☆☆

The American Association of Advertising Agencies publishes *Back Channel*, a useful quarterly newsletter on interactive advertising and marketing. It covers Internet advertising, advertising on CD-ROMs, and anything else new under the sun. (Or under the Sun, if that's the brand of computer you use.)

This site gives you the current issue and past issues, plus some extras. Sections include:

- Pointers—New online resources with short descriptions
- Chat Room—Not a place for online chat, but single-paragraph industry articles
- One on One—Good interviews with interactive marketers, including Peter Kruger on using interactive fiction techniques on the Web, and Tim Gibbons on CareerMosaic
- InterADtivity—Medium-length profiles of interactive advertisements on Web sites, CDs, and other media
- Home Page—Somewhat insightful editorials

- Interactive Discussion Groups—Skip this dead, unused section
- AAAALinks—Includes AAAA's nominations for the top 20 Internet advertising resources and AAAA's newsletter, *Washington Scene,* describing what new stunts Uncle Sam's regulators have in store for the ad game

How

World Wide Web

Where

www.commercepark.com/AAAA/bc.html

Set Your Browser on "Stun"

COMMUNICATION ARTS ☆☆☆☆

If you watch someone play a great game of tennis, you'll probably be inspired to play better in your next game. For years, *Communication Arts* magazine has provided the same kind of inspiration for advertising, multimedia, copywriting, and design professionals. *CA* (as pros call it) stunningly showcases the best work in the business. *CA*'s Web site does the same, and in addition provides information and resources for communication professionals.

CA carefully crafted its exhibits of design, photography, and illustration to avoid overloading your modem and jamming your browser. When you look at an exhibit, you'll see the text accompanied with small thumbnails of the pictures. You download only the full-sized graphics that you want to see, instead of wasting your time waiting for images that don't interest you. Just click on a thumbnail to see its larger version.

In addition to online exhibits of stunning work, the *CA* site gives you five databases: one gives you articles and columns from the past ten years of the magazine, and the other catalogs people and firms whose work was in *CA* during the last two years. A third database provides book reviews from the last five years. The fourth is a U.S. database of professional clubs and organizations. The fifth is a database of U.S. graphic arts service bureaus.

In addition, you'll find good columns on design issues, legal matters, and technology. Good articles on how to find a job in communication fields accompany a list of job opportunities. *CA* also provides an excellent list of more than 150 carefully chosen Web resources with short descriptions.

How

World Wide Web

Where

www.commarts.com

Treasure Chest of Type Fonts

Winworld Postscript Type Fonts ☆☆☆☆

Whether you advertise in print, on TV, or on the Web, you're gonna need type fonts. If you use type and Windows, this site will make you feel as if Ed McMahon, Bob Barker, and Vanna White gave you all their prizes at once.

You'll find nearly 150 Postscript fonts at this site. Some are shareware, but many are completely free. You'll find type for non-Roman languages (Arabic, Russian, Greek), special-purpose fonts like Adobe's Cheq or the *TV Guide*-like Channels, as well as dozens of more "normal" typefaces. (Normal? Should we call Karloff Halloween normal?) And don't forget Davy's Dingbats and Davy's Other Dingbats.

This Greek font and Adobe's Cheq font for chess games are two of many free fonts in this treasure chest of type.

If you have problems loading any of these, read the instructions in "How to Convert Fonts for Use with Adobe Type Manager," which you will also find at this site.

How

World Wide Web

Where

www.csusm.edu/cwis/winworld.atm.html

Catalog of Winworld Fonts

To save time when you're looking for a specific font, here's a quick-reference guide to Winworld's collection of type fonts.

Font	File Name	File Size (in thousands)
"How to Convert Fonts for Use with Adobe Type Manager"	wfn2atm.zip	2
36 fonts: Bodoni (3 weights), Boecklin, Brush Script, Caligula, Agate (3 wts.), Baskerville (3 wts.), Becker, Blippo, Cooper Black, Coronet, Engraver Light, Eurostile, Friz Quadrata (2 wts.), Futura Poster Light, Eras (6 wts.), Garamond Medium Italic, Old Town (3 wts.), Park Avenue, Slogan, Goudy Oldstyle (3 wts.). Check readme.txt for installation instructions.	36psfnts.zip	1,380 (Yep, it's huge. You can get most of these fonts in smaller separate files as well.)
Adobe Cheq (see illustration)	chessfon.zip	187
Alfred Drake (Arabic-like)	alfdrake.zip	36
Allard (looks like Barnum)	joeperry.zip	32
Aneirin	aneirin.zip	19
Ann Stone Dropcap Woodcut	annstone.zip	47
Apollo	apollo.zip	27
Arabic (Persian, Urdu)	baghdadz.zip	47
Baskerville	baskrvil.zip	134
Black Forest	blackfor.zip	85
Bodidly Bold	bodidly.zip	101
Bone Black	boneblak.zip	69
Brushstroke Paint Brush	brushstr.zip	104
Capri	capri.zip	21
Carrick Caps	carrickc.zip	66
Cartwright (like Adobe Ponderosa)	cartwrig.zip	63
Casual Script	duncan.zip	53
Channels (This font prints TV listings. You can print station numbers in little hollow TV screens or reversed out of solid TV screens. It also includes cable network symbols (CNN, HBO, and so on), ratings stars, a "Stereo" symbol, and MPAA movie ratings.)	channels.zip	49
Chisled Rechtman Script	rechtman.zip	31
Classic Heavy Light	classhvy.zip	29
Comics Cartoon	comics.zip	42
Crillee (*Star Trek*-like)	crillee.zip	156
Cunei (cuneiform-like)	cunei.zip	17
Davy's Dingbats	davyding.zip	577
Davy's Other Dingbats	davysoth.zip	86
Dolmen	dolmen.zip	24
Dragonwick	dragonwi.zip	92
Eglantine	eglatl.zip	21
Eileen's Medium and Zodiac Regular	eimzr.zip	19
English-Russian Architect	erarc201.zip	55
English-Russian Courier	erco201.zip	56
Friz Quadrata	frquad.zip	69
Genoa (looks like Venice)	genoa.zip	238
Goodfellow	goodtl.zip	23
Grauman	grauman.zip	44
Greek fonts	grk_font.zip	117
Handwritten Cursive	msbrooks.zip	35
Harting (like a typewriter running out of ribbon)	hartin.zip	78
Heather handwriting script	heather.zip	31
Heraldry	heratl.zip	29
Hunt Speedball (a Mac font included by mistake)	hspdball.zip	47
Ian Bent Dropcap Art Nouveau	iab.zip	39
Igloo Laser	igloolas.zip	72
Judas (like Adobe Ironwood)	judas.zip	68
Juliet	juliet.zip	29
Karkode (based on Goudy Oldstyle)	karkode.zip	255
Karloff Halloween	karloff.zip	25
Kavaler Kursive Bold	kkursive.zip	35

Font	File Name	File Size (in thousands)
Kelly Ann Gothic	klyanngt.zip	78
Kelly Brown Cursive	kellybro.zip	29
Kelmscott	kelmscott.zip	25
Krt Russel	krtrussl.zip	27
Laura McCrary	lmccrary.zip	40
Lauren Script Cursive	laurnscr.zip	32
Lefty Casual	leftycas.zip	79
Lintsec Stensil	lintsec.zip	22
LoopDeLoop (like Beeline)	loopdelo.zip	65
LSC Script	lscs.zip	26
Luxembourg	luxembrg.zip	15
Manzanita (like Victorian wood type)	manzanit.zip	74
Mazama (based on MGB Patrician)	mazama.zip	72
Mesozoic Gothic (based on Publicity Gothic)	mesozic.zip	215
Muriel	muriel.zip	177
Oswald Black	oswald.zip	61
Paris Metro	parismet.zip	50
Perry Gothic	perrygot.zip	33
Polo Semi Script	polosems.zip	71
Prospero	prsprotl.zip	82
Rhyolite Vertical (based on Huxley Vertical)	rhyolite.zip	33
Romeo Old Style Serif	romeo.zip	31
Roost Heavy	roosthea.zip	136
Rudels	rudelsbe.zip	79
Salter	salter.zip	28
Secret Code and Unsecret Code	secretco.zip	85
Shalom Oldstyle	shalold.zip	24
Shalom Script	shaloscr.zip	25
Sharktooth	sharktoo.zip	85
Showboat	showboat.zip	165
Spooky Plain	spooky.zip	44
Sumdumgoi Oriental (Note the pun.)	sumdumgo.zip	33
Taranis	taranis.zip	31
TechPhonetic International Phonetic Alphabet	techphon.zip	75
Tempo	tempofon.zip	259
Tribeca	tribeca.zip	97
Upper East Side	uppereas.zip	110
Upper West Side	upperwes.zip	252
Varah Caps	varahcap.zip	235
Victoria's Secret Handwriting	v-secret.zip	28
Viking	viking.zip	32
Walrod Initials	walrodin.zip	25
Western Style Poster	westslnt.zip	70
Windsor	windsord.zip	133
Zaleski Caps	zalescap.zip	61

Where in the World Can You Market?

INTERNATIONAL INTERNET MARKETING ☆☆☆☆

Erik Granered put parts of his master's thesis on the Net. His site is worth your time if your business can use information from any of these sections:

- Theoretical Foundations of International Internet Marketing—Covers relationship marketing via the Net. One of the most thoughtful analyses of Net marketing anywhere

- International Internet Demographics
- Cross-Cultural Internet Communication—Will make you think about important differences in the way people from other countries communicate. Good for Net marketers who export already or want to in the future
- World Wide Web User Profiles by Geographic Region
- Additional resources for international Internet marketing
- Bibliography (Well, darn. He didn't list any of Pat's or Vince's books. Maybe this isn't such a great site after all.)

How

World Wide Web

Where

www.clark.net/pub/granered/iim.html

B2B 4U

Business to Business Marketing Exchange ☆☆☆☆

Do you do b2b? Business-to-business marketing, that is. If so, you'll want to wallow in this Web site. Provided by the Business to Business Special Interest Group of the American Marketing Association, this site gives you current information about events, research, publications, job opportunities (not many when we looked), and a resume bank (empty when we looked).

You'll also find good links (unfortunately without descriptions) of places to find Internet consultants, very good descriptions of email discussion groups on marketing, and articles. Most are good, but ignore "Knowledge Navigation for the Everyday Manager." It's completely obsolete.

The real jewel at this site is an entire book, *Business Marketing: A Selected and Annotated Bibliography for Practicing Marketers* by David A. Reid and Richard E. Plank. If you want to know more about almost any topic in marketing, look here to find out where you need to go for in-depth info.

Reid and Plank give you more than 1,100 references to informative books and printed writings from 1978-1989. Each one was selected for its usefulness to business marketing managers and is carefully described. No theory. Just practical stuff you can put to work. Be sure to read the "Preface" first to understand the authors' description codes. Then look up the references you need by finding the chapter that covers the subject you want.

Some chapter titles: Business Marketing and Marketing Management; Marketing Intelligence; Buyer Behavior and Purchasing Management; Marketing Planning and Strategy; Advertising and Sales Promotion; Sales Management and Personal Selling; Product Management and Development; Industrial Services; Pricing; Distribution; Special Markets (government/industrial sales, international marketing); JIT and Manufacturing Technology; Strategic Alliances.

How

World Wide Web

Where

www.btob.wfu.edu/b2b.html

"Ya Gotta Know Your Territory"

AMERICAN DEMOGRAPHICS ☆☆☆

The first rule of marketing is to understand your prospect, and *American Demographics* magazine helps market researchers do just that. Its Web site gives you the complete text of very good articles analyzing trends and markets, plus the magazine's columns (Demographic Forecasts, Trend Cop, Checkout Line, and New Frontiers).

You can also read "America's Hottest Markets," which reveals the best metropolitan areas for seventeen categories of household spending. Here you can download the data tables used to create this report so you can do a little analysis of your own. Data tables are available in your choice of dBase format or Lotus 1-2-3. If you get the data tables, also download the **.txt** file next to them. The text file explains where everything is located in your data tables.

How

World Wide Web

Where

www.marketingtools.com/ad_current/default.htm

This Could Be Your Big Break

Global Internet News Agency ☆☆☆

This service for Internet businesses states its mission as providing a place for "finding, publishing, and promoting people and businesses on the Internet." It's a good resource for publicists looking to promote Internet businesses. The best part is "Technology News Tips." Look here for information requests from dozens of reporters from around the world. Reporters post their needs about business and the Net. You read their messages; if your business knows something about a reporter's topic, you can contact the writer directly. This could be your big PR break.

The Global Internet News Agency also distributes daily press releases from several companies dealing with Internet businesses. If you like to stay on top of things, you can sign up for a free email service to receive summaries of today's Internet news releases.

How
World Wide Web

Where
www.gina.com

Life, Liberty, and the Pursuit of Advertising

AMERICAN ADVERTISING FEDERATION GOVERNMENT REPORT ☆☆☆

This free quarterly newsletter, published by the American Advertising Federation (betcha could tell that by the newsletter's name), reports on all enacted and proposed U.S. legislation that affects the ad game. Not only does it give you news from the Feds, but it also reports on legislative news for all fifty states. The information at this site is brief and to the point.

How
World Wide Web

Where
www.aaf.org/pub/aaf/govtreport.html

Information, Please

ProfNet ☆☆☆☆

You can look at ProfNet as a resource to help PR people obtain their clients' publicity from journalists and authors looking for information. If you look at ProfNet the other way, it is a great tool for journalists and authors who need fast access to expert sources. ProfNet is an association of more than 1,000 public information professionals. If you need information for a project, send email to ProfNet and you'll find someone who's an expert on your topic. It's free for you to search for experts.

How

Email

Where

profnet@sunysb.edu

Message

In your message, state:

- Your news organization or publisher
- Describe your project
- Describe what information you want
- Describe what kind of expertise you seek
- Your deadline
- How to reply to you

Spot That Trend

NUMBERS NEWS ☆☆☆

This newsletter promises "timely news on market trends." It delivers short, condensed versions of new research reports—the kind that usually cost $500-$2,500 each—on market trends, demographics, and consumer and business habits. Each issue summarizes about a dozen research reports. You can read the entire current issue of *Numbers News* and past issues on this Web site. You can also use a search page to search the entire site.

How

World Wide Web

Where

www.marketingtools.com/tnn_current.default.htm

Throw the E-book at 'Em

ASI Market Research ☆☆☆

This magnet site for market researchers provides free papers in Adobe Acrobat format ("Advertising's Role in Managing Brand Equity," "Measuring Brand Equity: Some Real Data," "Secrets of Related Recall" [which make a commercial great], and others), links to market research organizations, and links to other market research sites.

But the best part may be the *Internet Market Research/Advertising/Entertainment Industry Email Directory.* You can receive this directory for free if you work in one of the three industries it covers. The only catch is that you must sign up and give your name and email address to be included in future versions. Your listing is also free.

How

World Wide Web

Where

www.asiresearch.com

Confessions of an Advertising Man

ADVERTISING AGE ☆☆☆

This slow-to-download, graphics-heavy site reflects the state of advertising itself: it's a mixed bag of the worthwhile and the useless. You'll find today's latest advertising news (check "Daily Deadline" for the hottest stuff, fresh daily), articles from the print magazine, a good section covering "Interactive Media and Marketing" (including the Net), and discussion groups that *Ad Age* calls "Forums."

AD AGE's "Daily Deadline" gives you today's advertising news free, what's new in Internet marketing, and the latest debates on Web statistics.

Most of these forums have hardly any messages posted, and the posted messages are often useless for professionals—unless pro and con arguments about the Energizer Bunny stimulate your intellect. Postings are unedited; spam thrives. There is one exception: the forum on **Web Statistics** is the best by far, with informed discussion on all aspects of Web site customer tracking, and postings from some of the top names in the industry. There are fast changes taking place in the types of stats that advertisers want to see before they'll pay to advertise on your site. If Web stats are your bread and butter, you'll find this forum a great way to keep on top the latest gyrations.

How

World Wide Web

Where

www.adage.com

A Free Guide to Free Advertising

Vidya's Guide to Advertising on the Internet ☆☆☆

If you advertise on the Internet, want to sell advertising on your Net site, or just want to promote your Web page, make a beeline to Vidya's site. Vidya has an "Internet Advertising Library" with links to papers and directories, but the prime draws are the two directories he compiled.

One is a list of free sites where you can advertise. This goes beyond the usual "free Web site publicity submission" guides you'll find on the Web. Vidya's guide has several less-common variations, and actually lists places that you can promote products as well as Web sites.

His second directory of "Purchasable Ad Space" lists sites where you can buy advertising. (Yeah, I know, in this book, we don't like to pay for anything. But, hey, *window-shopping* is free. And so is Vidya's helpful guide.) For each site, you'll find the site owner, average hits (a misleading form of measurement), cost to advertise, and options.

How

World Wide Web

Where

www.vidya.com/add-lib

Net Marketing by Email

internet-marketing Email Discussion Group ☆☆☆☆

This discussion group on using the Internet for marketing generates a lot of activity—about 150 messages each week. It's a moderated list, so you won't waste too much time avoiding spam This site is also a good place to find an-swers to your questions on this topic and to keep up-to-date with important new stuff coming down the pike. (In the field of Internet marketing, new stuff seems to come every other day.)

You can subscribe via email, as explained below, or visit the group's Web site at **ww.popco.com/hyper/internet-marketing**. On the Web, you can subscribe and dig up past messages discussing the topic of your choice. The archive of past messages has a handy search engine.

Sample topics: Needing strategy advice; REQ: Global Usage & Site Stats; Internet classifieds; Creating an Online Dating Service; Net Demographics; Help needed to convince skeptic; Internet in Slovenia; One to One Marketing and the Web; Route-based search engine for retail shopping; Sponsorship & Advertising Costs; France Telecom/Spanish Telefonica; Best Web Ads of 95; 2nd Survey of Net Business Results; Does anyone really read Internet classifieds?

How
Email

Where
imsub@popco.com

Message
subscribe internet-marketing Yourfirstname Yourlastname

Net Advertising by Email

internet-advertising Email Discussion Group ☆☆☆

Internet Advertising is an email discussion group that provides a forum for business people who are interested in learning new ways to advertise on the Internet.

How
Email

Where
listserv@netcom.com

Message
subscribe internet-advertising youremail@address

Net Sales by Email

internet-sales Email Discussion Group ☆☆☆☆

If you actually *sell* your company's products or services over the Net, join this discussion group. It covers anything related to the actual sales (as differentiated from mere marketing) of stuff online: credit card processing, international shipping, order form design, and a bunch of stuff you won't think of until you read about it at this site. Then you'll go, "Yeah, I've got that same problem," and discover the solutions suggested by more than 1,300 subscribers in 45 countries.

You won't suffer from the clutter of too many email messages jamming your inbox. Instead, the list moderator edits out spam and most rants, and sends you one large email message each day. At this Web site for internet-sales, you can read the group's FAQ, browse archives of past messages, and best of all, subscribe.

How
World Wide Web

Where
www.mmgco.com/isales.htm

On the Right Track for Net Ads I

WebTrack ☆☆☆

Advertisers and advertisees on the World Wide Web can make use of the information provided at this site. WebTrack studies advertising on the Web, and provides two good free resources to give you an idea of the value of the services they charge for.

WebTrack's ad space locator is a guide to places on the Net that charge for advertising. When we checked, it didn't list as many as other space-finding sites—but still, we didn't know that Condom Country sells advertising!

A more complete list is WebTrack's database of advertisers, containing 2,500 companies with advertising budgets of $500,000 or more. You'll find:

- Alphabetical listings of the major advertisers which have Web sites
- All companies that spend more than $500,000 whether they have Web sites or not
- Weekly listing of new advertiser sites and changes to existing sites

WebTrack also gives you a free sample of its newsletter on Web advertising, *InterAd Monthly*. This is an extremely good newsletter, but it costs $200 a year to subscribe. You have to register to look at the free sample issue. When we did, the sample was way more than half a year old. WebTrack's other free services are worthwhile, but a Mesozoic-era newsletter isn't worth registering for, even when it's free.

How

World Wide Web

Where

www.webtrack.com

On the Right Track for Net Ads II

INTERACTIVE PUBLISHING ALERT ☆☆☆

Online advertisers and advertisees are the subjects of this site, offered by Rosalind Resnick for her authoritative newsletter of the same name.

You can search the Online Advertising Index, a database of advertisers and sites that sell online ad space (or should that be space-time?). You can search the Online Advertising Index by site name, keyword, ad rates, traffic volume (measured here only in hits per day), and current advertiser names. Resnick's database covers not only the World Wide Web, but also Prodigy, CompuServe, America Online, Microsoft Network, email advertising, and the mysterious "Other." (Hmmm...Minitel, perhaps?)

For lagniappe, take a peek at the "IPA 50" lists of the top fifty online publications, or sign up for a free announcement list about Resnick's newsletter, Web site, and other projects.

How

World Wide Web

Where

www.netcreations.com/ipa

Smile when You Say That, Mouster

MouseTracks ☆☆☆

"It is universally agreed that the Internet is the hottest new medium since the invention of stone tablets, or at least since *Melrose Place*." Ya gotta like a business Web site with a sense of humor like MouseTracks, especially when it also provides you with good info for marketing both online and offline. Look under the education section for a complete sample issue of Kluwer's *Marketing Letter*. Other MouseTracks highlights include:

- Hall of Malls—Directory of Internet malls around the world
- Nuts & Bolts—Guide to sites with instructions on how to market and sell on the Net. Look here for a list of image archives—lots of free clip art for Web pages
- List of Marketing Lists—Directory of Net marketers
- MetaMarket—Directory of firms selling services to other companies' marketers
- New Medium—Directory of online publications that cover marketing or business

How

World Wide Web

Where

nsns.com/MouseTracks

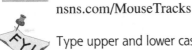

Type upper and lower case exactly as listed under "Where" or you'll get nowhere.

How-to Tips from the Pros

Information Industries Board ☆☆☆

The IIB is an agency of the government of Queensland, Australia. Its goal is to grow high-tech exports by Queensland businesses. To encourage this, the IIB distributes "how-to" information that can be very useful to many marketers in any country.

This page takes you to information generated from IIB seminars. Look for two by Phil Scanlan. The first, "Marketing on the Internet," gives practical instructions on the topic, good for small businesses and entrepreneurs.

The second, "Launching Your Product in the U.S.A.," is for people who market and sell computer software. This information is mostly in outline format, and some pages have very little information, but others are very helpful.

A high point is "Q&A about Dealers and Distributors," which provides a brutally frank report of the difficulties and costs (naming names and giving actual numbers) of selling PC software through U.S. retail and wholesale channels, written by someone who's done it. By itself, this page packs enough punch to make the IIB site highly recommended for anyone who plans to market software in the U.S.

How

World Wide Web

Where

www.iib.qld.gov.au/publish/seminar/index.htm

Deep in the Heart of Tex-Ads

Texas Educational Center for Advertising Software ☆☆☆

A two-question quiz: Does your job involve media planning or media buying? If so, does your Web browser use Java? (Netscape and several others do.)

If you answered "yes" to both questions, the Texas Educational Center for Advertising Software would like to give you free Java software for your job. The most elaborate is the TEC Media Planner. It's a good media planning system with planning tools, databanks of audiences for different advertisers on different media (including Web sites), and estimation tools.

Want to test your training wheels on something simpler? Check out the free TECAS Media Reach/Frequency Generator, another Java software program free at this site.

How

World Wide Web

Where

uts.cc.utexas.edu/~tecas

Hey, I Wish I'd Thought of That!

Paramind ☆☆☆☆

When it comes to brainstorming, most of us end up discussing the weekend's Big Game rather than creating new ways to build better mouse traps. Paramind can help you brainstorm new ideas. A unique brainstorming program, Paramind helps you get your ideas on paper, expand them, and even to create new, fresh ideas.

Equipped with a database of 200 related word chains that you can expand *ad infinitum*, Paramind works as a kind of free-association program to help spark your thought process, changing your 40-watt ideas into floodlight-level business plans.

Where

www.acs.oakland.edu/oak/SimTel/win3/educate.html

Download

paramd15.zip

The Media Circus Is in Town

The Media List ☆☆☆☆

Whether you want to send email to the *Anchorage Daily News* to complain about grizzly bears in your garbage cans or to *Macworld* about bugs in your programs, The Media List is your one-stop directory for email addresses to major and minor media outlets.

You'll find hundreds of PR contacts for newspapers, magazines, TV and radio stations, and other media venues you can reach electronically. Be sure to include your name, snail-mail address, and phone number if you want a publication to print your press release. To paraphrase Hemingway, the joy is not in griping, it's in having griped.

How

World Wide Web

Where

www.islandnet.com/~deathnet/media_email.html

If you'd rather receive the list and updates automatically via email, write to **majordomo@world.std.com** with the message **subscribe medialist**.

Media with a British Flavour

U.K. Media Internet Directory ☆☆☆☆

If you want to reach anyone in the U.K. media, visit this directory. It lists contacts for TV, radio, newspapers, and magazines, as well as freelancers and ad agencies. To give you an idea of how wonderfully obsessive these chaps are about including everything, under the category "Radio" you'll find National Radio, Local Radio, Student Radio, RSL Radio, Hospital (!) Radio, Radio Magazines, and Radio Services.

For each publication or station, the directory gives you contact names (usually more than one), email addresses, and hotlinks to Web sites when they exist. The listings at this site are much more complete than the ones in the Media List. They are quite useful.

How

World Wide Web

Where

www.whatson.com/ukmedia

Read ADNEWS before It's Printed

ADNEWS Online ☆☆☆

Every weekday, this site gives you the *full text* of each issue of *Adnews'* daily publication covering the Canadian advertising industry. Not only that, this Web site gets each issue 12 hours before the hardcopy version comes out! You've heard of *Meet the Press*. Here you can beat the press.

You'll also find a searchable database of back issues, links to advertising and marketing resources (especially Canadian ones), and feature stories from *Adnews'* monthly publication. And as a bonus, this site includes *Chinese Canadian Marketing Update*, monthly news on marketing to the Chinese residents of Canada.

How

World Wide Web

Where

www.io.org/~adnews

Fair Dinkum for Media Types

Australian Media Facilities Directory ☆☆☆

G'day, mate. Are you looking to shoot a spot down beyond the billabong? Have a go at this site before you get your monkey up. It's a black book of Aussie creative agencies and talent, and seems to list every jimmy and sheila in the biz. It even shows samples of their work. (For voice-over talent, you can *listen* to the samples.) If you're in the media industry and not listed yourself, make a visit. It's the Dinkum oil that you can list your business for free.

How

World Wide Web

Where

www.amfd.com.au/AMFD/advertis.htm

Targeting Your Market

MKTSEG Market Segments Discussion Group ☆☆☆

As markets become more and more fragmented, this once-specialized aspect of marketing grows more and more prominent. You can subscribe to this list if you want to discuss marketing and advertising to targeted segments, such as lifestyle segments, or special interest segments. In other words, if you use demographics to define your marketing targets, this site will discuss how to reach 'em. Topics include creative, media, and research issues, as well as database marketing and direct marketing.

So how come I can't find any way to reach my target market of left-handed *Star Trek* fans who smoke illegal Cuban cigars and don't watch Comedy Central?

How

Email

Where

listserv@mail.telmar.com

Message

subscribe mktseg youremail@address

Where High-Tech Marketing Gurus Hang Out

HTMARCOM—High Tech Marketing Communications ☆☆☆☆

If your business markets any kind of high-tech product or service, you'll find the information and discussions in HTMARCOM extremely rewarding. This email discussion group is moderated (and quite well-moderated, we might add) by high-tech marketing specialist Kim Bayne. Besides lots of "how-to" and "where-can-I-find" information, you'll find many job opportunities at this site. (This group calls them "job leads.")

Bayne also maintains a Web site for this group. Look there for a searchable archive of past messages and a FAQ which is very good (except it doesn't mention the archive).

183

Sample topics: DISCUSS Tech Support as Marketing Info Source; DISCUSS Bulk Mail Outsourcing; DISCUSS Managing a Product Giveaway; DISCUSS Marketing to User Groups; INFO REQ Boilerplate RFP Web Design; DISCUSS Direct Mail to Canada; INFO REQ Sources for Direct Mail/DIrect Response Lists; DISCUSS Dir Mail—Best time of year to mail B to B; DISCUSS Marketing Software; DISCUSS Product Review Guidelines; JOB LEAD PR Guru Wanted—Colorado Springs

How

World Wide Web

Where

htmarcom-request@wolfbayne.com

Message

SUBSCRIBE HTMARCOM

More Email Than You Can Eat

Marketing Lists on the Internet ☆☆☆

HTMARCOM's Kim Bayne compiled this directory of more than 50—count 'em, 50—email discussion groups covering PR, advertising, market research, and related topics. As well as healthy, active lists, Bayne also discusses the dead ones. Info on dead discussion groups are better than aspirin when you frustrate yourself trying to subscribe or find to a discontinued email list. ("Oh, *that's* why I couldn't find that list!")

Most marketers browsing through Bayne's directory will find one or two lists that sound promising. Although useful, the directory doesn't provide descriptions of most lists, or FAQ or archive locations. Short descriptions would make it more helpful, as would information on how many people subscribe to lists, and some kind of volume indicators, such as messages per week.

How

World Wide Web

Where

www.bayne.com/wolfbayne/htmarcom/mktglist.html

Tell Ed McMahon We Said "Hi"

Direct Marketing World ☆☆☆

This site provides a resume bank for direct marketers and a list of job opportunities. You'll also find a calendar of direct marketing conferences and seminars.

But the good stuff at Direct Marketing World is in a section called "Library." Go here to find articles from the newsletters *The Catalog Marketer* and *Non-Store Market Report*. Other articles are not part of newsletters, such as "Direct Mail and the Dynamics of Response" (on direct marketing response-enhancement techniques) and the too-simple-to-be-useful "Learning to Sell in Cyberspace."

The best thing in "Library" is the *Direct Mail Guide*. The *Guide* has almost, but not quite enough, information to be a book. It's a how-to guide to the basics of using direct mail lists, clearly explaining the most important information. It contains ten chapters and a good glossary.

To give you an idea of what it covers, here are titles for 6 chapters in the *Direct Mail Guide*:

- Evaluating a List
- What Is a List Broker?
- Testing a Mailing List
- Analyzing Test Results
- The In-House List
- List Management and Maintenance

How

World Wide Web

Where

mainsail.com/dmworld.html

Type, DTP Sites, and a Puzzle

EatArt ☆☆☆

We can't figure out what the name of this site means, but it's for desktop publishers and designers. Maybe they can figure it out. EatArt gives you a quick list of sites for desktop publishers with good descriptions. A second list hooks up typeface lovers to type archives on the Net: Internet Font Archive, Mac Font Archives, Online Type Museum, and others. (Maybe this site is made by a guy named Art....)

How

World Wide Web

Where

www.utexas.edu/coc/adv/creative/art.html

Attack of the PageMaker People

PageMaker Discussion Group ☆☆☆

If you use PageMaker to create your ads and marketing communications, join this discussion group. You'll get extremely knowledgeable help with any PageMaker questions, bug alerts, and free macros and software add-ons. One is a housekeeping script for PageMaker for Windows that saves megabytes of wasted disk space. The group has an archive of help files for both PC and Mac PageMaker people. (Somehow, that didn't sound quite right.)

You can subscribe by email, as described below. The email list has a mirrored newsgroup, **news:bit.listserv.pagemaker**. Any message posted to the list will show up on the newsgroup, and vice versa.

How

Email

Where

listserv@indycms.iupui.edu

Message

SUB PAGMAKR Yourfirstname Yourlastname

The Power of the Prepress

comp.publish.prepress Newsgroup ☆☆☆

This good newsgroup is tightly focused on getting graphics and text ready to go to press. Some subscribers have considerable technical expertise, which they kindly share with those in need of help.

Sample topics: Dot Gain of Photoshop vs. Press; Color Central (Mac) and 100 Mbps Ethernet?; Q: Custom screens from FreeHand or Illustrator?; Scanning photos; Agfa A1 imagesetters?; Halftone screen frequency HP LJ 5MP; Low volume book printing?; Problems Quark/FreeHand output; Finding fonts; What good are 72 dpi photos?; Online Digital Content; PS preview utilities; Mac PS fonts to Sun/Solaris.

How

Newsgroup

Where

news:comp.publish.prepress

And Ink Smells Like Money

Printing Industries of Northern California ☆☆☆

One of the Kersten Brothers, two guys with a large poster company, once described what a printing press sounded like to him as it printed their posters. The noise it made was "Dollarfifty, dollarfifty, dollarfifty, dollarfifty." You can only guess how much profit each poster made.

We hope your printing sounds as profitable. In any case, if you are a print designer or a person who buys printing, you might find it profitable to visit the Web site of PINC, Printing Industries of Northern California. Parts of this site are most useful for people in Northern California, but some of the best parts are useful worldwide.

Our fave is the Print Advice Hotline. Ask any question on printing, and a PINC expert will research your question and email your answer back. This site also contains all the information in the book *Print Buyer's Guide*. Check out the reference info on printing trade customs, and an excellent section on preparing desktop publishing jobs for printing. You'll find this information in the "Print Buyer's Reference," a section which covers print buying basics. It tells how to buy printing and explains different printing processes, paper grades, paper weights (no, not the glass kind, smartaleck), and binding and finishing.

You'll find useful checklists to eliminate the "Oh, I forgot one thing" syndrome when preparing specs, approving art, and approving electronic art. You can also use PINC's directory of printers, binders, and related firms in Northern California. The job opportunities listed at this site are local to the PINC area, and mostly for people who work in printing plants, but jobs for administrators and print buyers are also sometimes available.

How

World Wide Web

Where

www.pincnet.com

Your Link to Wired Ink

PrintersLink ☆☆☆

Wanna send your print jobs to the best/cheapest/fastest printers around the world without actually going there? You can send your print jobs electronically, for free over the Internet. PrintersLink links you with digital printing services worldwide that can receive, process, and move into production print files sent over the Net from anywhere you may be. Read the helpful FAQ for more info.

Now, who was that French philosopher who said, "I ink, therefore I am"?

How

World Wide Web

Where

www.abcdprint.com/-link/p-link1.htm

Where to Find More Marketing and Ad/Pub Stuff

Marketing research devotees will uncover several sites with demographic data in the chapter *A Free Lunch for Economists*, many with datasets preformatted for you to use in spreadsheets.

If you are an advertiser or a seller of advertising space, a very good reference site is the "Advertising Law Internet Site" at the beginning of our chapter on *Business Law*. You might call the Ad Law site a kind of "how to advertise and not get sued" guide. Scattered throughout this same chapter are good spots with information on copyrights, trademarks, and trade dress (when someone copies your look and feel).

The chapter for *Sales Reps and Road Warriors* goes more into the sales end of business, and some good resources that straddle the line are in our chapter on *Tools for Internet-Based Businesses*.

188

If your business markets imports or exports, you might want to browse the *Doing Business Internationally* chapter. And you'll find more marketing info in the index under the "marketing resources" heading.

After you've exhausted the marketing possibilities of this book, visit Yahoo, which we describe in Chapter 2. You can try the Yahoo search engine, but before you do that, we recommend paging through Yahoo's very good Marketing directory. You'll find it under Yahoo's main Business directory. Trade Wave Galaxy is another resource described in Chapter 2 that has a good Marketing directory.

FREE $TUFF

Everyone lives by selling something.

Robert Louis Stevenson

Sales Reps and Road Warriors

Some people claim that another occupation is the oldest profession, but we know otherwise. Before the first transaction of the oldest profession could take place, somebody had to find a prospect, negotiate, and close the deal. Therefore, the oldest profession has to be sales.

We're talking live sales here, face-to-face or on the phone, performed by live sales professionals. Some people get carried away and claim that all sales will eventually happen on the Net, but we know they're wrong. Sales is the eternal profession. As long as there are human beings, sales reps will be selling. Of course, the sharp ones will *use* the Internet as a tool to help them sell. Sharp sales reps never pass up a good tool, and the Net certainly falls under that category.

Another couple of traits that salespeople have in common—at least, the top ones do—is that they love to be organized but they hate paperwork. If that applies to you, you'll be delighted to know that we've included a few software tools that can help you in those areas.

Sales reps also travel more than most people. So we've included the best business travel resources we could find (and we found quite a few of them) in this chapter. Business travelers have different needs than "civilian" travelers. My Aunt Rosie often flies to Minnesota to visit her siblings, but she doesn't worry about missing email messages, dying laptop batteries, or appropriate places to take a client to lunch.

So whether you're a sales pro or a frequent flyer from one of the "lesser" professions, put down the phone for a few minutes and you'll be sure to find some free goodies in this chapter. We certainly don't expect to hear any resistance to our prices.

Your Sales Leads Are in the Email

BidCast ☆☆☆☆

This company will actually email sales leads to you for free! And we're not talking low-grade bingo card leads at this site, but high-grade prospects with funds at hand.

BidCast searches for government procurement announcements, compares them to the products and services your company sells, and sends you all that match.

BidCast scours the Net for sales leads and sends you the ones that want the kinds of products or services your company sells.

You might receive invitations to bid from international (NATO), national, state, county, and municipal government organizations. Bid information and contact names are included so you can follow up on your leads. This is all part of BidCast's free basic service.

You might also give the purchasing folks in your company a nudge about BidCast, because they can post your company's own invitations to bid here for free. This site also gives you a medium-length page of links to related Net resources, some with descriptions.

Selling to government agencies is quite different from selling to "real-world" customers. Not all sales organizations want to pursue government customers. But if yours does, BidCast could be your free ticket to higher sales.

How

World Wide Web

Where

www.bidcast.com

Stick Out Your Tongue and Say "Yes"

Sales Doctor ☆☆☆

Sales strategy consultant Brian Azar hosts this resource for sales pros, with his free monthly newsletter, *The Azar Alternative*, and strategy information on

topics like "The Power Close." Azar's framework for effective selling shows how you can view yourself as a "sales doctor" and help your client by diagnosing what causes your client's pain. Just be sure your client has "medical coverage"—a budget—and can afford your cure.

Check Azar's writings at this site, but skip "The Sales Asylum" cartoon slideshow. It's cute, but useless. The rest of this Web site, however, gives you some worthwhile sales techniques.

How

World Wide Web

Where

www.salesdoctor.com

Uncle Sam Buys Here

Acq Web ☆☆☆

If you sell to U.S. government agencies, you need the information at this site. You'll find a lot of it: more than one gigabyte of information on federal agency and Department of Defense purchasing regulations and procedures.

If you're selling, Uncle Sam is buying. Acq Web is where you go to find out about selling to Uncle Sam.

The problem is, this site is not well-organized. It gives you an overwhelming amount of information (most heavy with government and military jargon), but it is hard to know where to start. Go to the "Index" to find stuff. One clear step-by-step summary would be worth more than all the slow graphics that pack this site. This site is evolving, and may be much more understandable and navigable by the time you visit it. And if you sell to Uncle Sam, you should visit Acq Web, because it has more information on governmental sales than anyplace else on the Net.

How

World Wide Web

Where

www.acq.osd.mil

Developing Your Inner Ham

Edward Tufte on Public Speaking ☆☆☆

As a sales pro, one of the best parts of your job is that you can give demos and make presentations. At least, it's one of the best parts if you're a natural ham, which describes most sales reps. It's so easy to learn to *love* public speaking!

Anyhow, this Web page gives you noted author Edward Tufte's thoughts on how to be an effective public speaker. It's presented in an outline form, so it's a quick read, and is certainly worth your time. You may not agree with everything Tufte recommends here, but you are certain to gain new good techniques from this page.

How

World Wide Web

Where

www.cs.washington.edu/homes/comer/tufte.html

The Business of Business Cards

Rockford and BusinessCards ☆☆☆

For many sales reps, business cards are their most important weapons. At this site, there are two software programs, one for your own cards and one to help keep track of other people's cards. **Rockford** is an easy-to-use shareware program to help you design and print business cards.

While you're at this site, be sure to download a copy of **BusinessCards for Windows** to help you organize and keep track of your contacts' business cards.

How
World Wide Web

Where
www.csusm.edu/cwis/winworld/pim.html

Download
BusinessCards: bcr220.zip (185 kilobytes)

Rockford 3.5:   rckfrd35.zip (208 kilobytes)

 Note that Rockford also requires the Visual Basic Runtime Module, which you can download from the Visual page at this site.

It's in the Cards

Cognitive Business Card Reader ☆☆☆

Cuneiform developed this handy business card reader. Cognitive BCR reads your scanned business cards, then enters the name, address, phone number—and any other information you want included—directly into a database.

Cognitive BCR is Windows 95 software that automatically recognizes card fields, such as name, address, and telephone and fax numbers, then creates a database of your contacts automatically. It even saves an image of each business card, which you can view with the click of a button. There's also an instant card search and retrieval option, drag-and-drop editing, and much more.

How
World Wide Web

Where
www.well.com/user/ctc/bcr.exe

Download
bcr.exe (1.3 megabytes)

 Of course, Cognitive Business Card Reader requires that you have a scanner.

We're behind Schedule!

Almanac ☆☆☆

Good help is indeed hard to find, especially around the office. But help doesn't always have to be in the form of a living, breathing paycheck-gobbling employee.

Good software can also do the trick. Almanac is one of the best personal information managers (PIMs) I've seen, and it'll give most personal secretaries serious inferiority complexes. (Well, some of 'em.)

This handy PIM includes a calendar, daily scheduler, the all-important to-do list, a phonebook, an easy-to-use note-writing feature, and more. There's even a selection of sounds you can attach to your reminders. Now, if it could just make coffee....

How

FTP

Where

ftp://ftp.cdrom.com/.22/cica/winnt/misc

Download

alt35b.zip (466 K)

If you have trouble getting into this site, you can download Almanac on the Web at:

www.cris.com/ ~ randybrg/pims.html

Nice Chatting with You

WinChat ☆☆☆

Remember all that business time lost at the water cooler chatting with your co-workers? Talk about a waste of valuable work time—not to mention breath. But now computers—those way cool tools of efficiency—have even made your Monday morning chat sessions more efficient. Here's a handy Win95 utility that moves those chat sessions away from the water cooler and onto the LAN where they belong.

WinChat lets you communicate with anyone hooked up to your office network. Just click "Dial" and specify the computer name of the person you want to chat with, then type away. You can even type your message before you connect. Now *that's* productive!

How

FTP

Where

ftp://ftp.microsoft.com/Softlib/MSLFILES

Download

chat.exe (45 K)

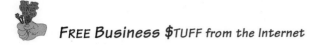

Conquer Your Calendar Confusion

Calendar Collection ☆☆☆

When it comes to organizing your office, the first step is to get out from under the clutter. Let your computer take some of the load off your desk by installing one of these calendar programs.

I won't promise that you'll never miss another appointment or meeting, but these calendars will help take some of the burden off of your tracking efforts. Try out a few of these calendars to find out which one is best for you. Some of the features of the different programs include automatic reminders, day planners, weekly schedulers, and other bells and whistles to help you get the office organized.

How

World Wide Web

Where

www.acs.oakland.edu/oak/simtel/win3/calendar.html

Download

Visual Calendar Planner (885 K):	3dvcp401.zip
Calendar/Reminder (178 K):	am_cr41.zip
Daywatch (238 K):	dw4win10.zip
Employee weekly scheduler (359 K):	sew200.zip

Gooood Morning, Internauts!

Good Morning, Thinkers! ☆☆☆

Here's the perfect Net site for any sales rep whose synapses are misfiring like an engine in need of a tune-up. Kind of the online equivalent of a good cup of java, Good Morning, Thinkers! is billed as a wake-up service for your brain.

Each Monday morning, this automated mailing list emails you a short, light-hearted message designed to wake you up, pump you up, and keep you up through the long week. Now if you can just keep your eyelids up long enough to read it....

How

Email

Where

majordomo@thinksmart.com

Message

subscribe Wake-Up_Brain

Attention Frequent Flyers

WinFly for Windows ☆☆☆☆

Keeping track of your frequent flyer miles may sometimes seem like more trouble than it's worth—until you get that free trip to Hawaii. Hmm, maybe it wasn't that much trouble after all.

Now with WinFly for Windows, tracking your miles has never been easier. WinFly tracks and updates your frequent flyer mileage for most major airlines, including TWA, American, and Delta, and even lets you keep track of mileage you've already redeemed.

How

FTP

Where

ftp://gatekeeper.dec.com/pub/micro/msdos/win3/misc

Download

winfly.zip (120 K)

The Bible of Air Travel

AIR TRAVELER'S HANDBOOK ☆☆☆☆

All but the most experienced frequent flyers will pick up new tricks from this online resource. What began as the Frequently Asked Questions list of the newsgroup **rec.travel.air** has grown into the equivalent of a 470-page book covering every aspect of air travel. Assembled by Mark Kantrowitz, the *Air Traveler's Handbook* tells how to get reduced airfares (mostly for U.S. domestic flights) by creative use of stopovers, circle flights, and other tricks.

It explains the differences between fare classes and service classes, and special fare categories. It tells you how to get refunds, how to take advantage of fare wars, and how to use unusual techniques with travel agents. It also warns you about travel scams. It covers baggage, safety, pregnant passengers, and, of course, frequent flyer programs.

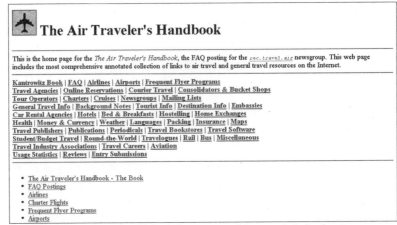

The Air Traveler's Handbook

This is the home page for the *The Air Traveler's Handbook*, the FAQ posting for the *rec.travel.air* newsgroup. This web page includes the most comprehensive annotated collection of links to air travel and general travel resources on the Internet.

Kantrowitz Book | FAQ | Airlines | Airports | Frequent Flyer Programs
Travel Agencies | Online Reservations | Courier Travel | Consolidators & Bucket Shops
Tour Operators | Charters | Cruises | Newsgroups | Mailing Lists
General Travel Info | Background Notes | Tourist Info | Destination Info | Embassies
Car Rental Agencies | Hotels | Bed & Breakfasts | Hostelling | Home Exchanges
Health | Money & Currency | Weather | Languages | Packing | Insurance | Maps
Travel Publishers | Publications | Periodicals | Travel Bookstores | Travel Software
Student/Budget Travel | Round-the-World | Travelogues | Rail | Bus | Miscellaneous
Travel Industry Associations | Travel Careers | Aviation
Usage Statistics | Reviews | Entry Submissions

- The Air Traveler's Handbook - The Book
- FAQ Postings
- Airlines
- Charter Flights
- Frequent Flyer Programs
- Airports

Road warriors of the air will find discounts and how-to info in the AIR TRAVELER'S HANDBOOK.

You'll find the book itself at the address below, but it also has a separate home page at **www.cs.cmu.edu/afs/cs/user/mkant/Public/Travel/airfare.html**. Check there for dozens of related links, including links to bucket shops and other providers of steeply-discounted air travel tickets. Happy landings!

How

World Wide Web

Where

www.cis.ohio-state.edu/hypertext/faq/usenet/travel/air/handbook/top.html

Four Biz Travel Resources in One Spot

Getting Around the Planet ☆☆☆☆

This is the travel department of Time-Warner's busy Pathfinder site. Most of it is devoted to consumer travel—you know, places that serve drinks with umbrellas, or noisy spots you can take your kids. Fortunately for us business travelers, if you ignore the frivolous stuff you'll also find four excellent resources for business travelers.

- *Zagat Survey Guidebooks* - These famous guides to hotels and restaurants are online. What makes the *Zagat* guides different from others is that they are written by travelers themselves. Thousands of travelers report every year, and rank and review restaurants and hotels based on their actual experience. For business travelers, the hotel reviews often contain especially good tips.

Most of Pathfinder's Travel site is for consumers, but some is quite handy for business travelers.

- *WebFlyer* - The only site on the Net just for frequent flyers, *WebFlyer* contains reviews of bonus mile programs, pointing out the best deals. It also points out free car rental upgrades and other little-publicized bonuses you get with your frequent flyer membership. You'll find news about changes in award programs, comparisons of different frequent flyer programs, and one article a month from *InsideFlyer* magazine. *WebFlyer* is hard to reach from the Getting Around the Planet home page. To find it, choose "Travel Deals."

- *Planet Profiles* - If you want to research a destination, this online book has the most details about the most destinations of any spot on the Net. It claims to cover 10,000 destinations. (Compare that with second-place City.Net's 2,000 destinations.) It describes many cities not covered by its competitors. One caveat: *Planet Profiles* is not as up-to-date as it could be. For example, in San Francisco it recommends places that have been closed for years.

- *U.S. Golf Digest*- Just in case you need to play golf—for business reasons, of course. We know you wouldn't play golf for fun. Hey, what's that umbrella doing in your drink?

How

World Wide Web

Where

pathfinder.com/Travel

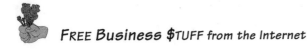

Hotels Are Us

Hotels and Travel on the Net ☆☆☆

This ambitious site wants to give you all the airlines, airports, and hotels any-place in the world that have Web pages. The Commercial Aviation Resource Center (we describe CARC below) lists more airlines and airports. But for information on hotels, this is your best bet on the Net.

How

World Wide Web

Where

www.webscope.com/travel

Before You Travel, Learn Your Territory

City.Net ☆☆☆☆

This is a great place to research any place you intend to visit. City.Net is a huge directory of information on 2,000 destinations worldwide. You can look up any country, U.S. states, Canadian provinces, some counties, and most major cities, and find detailed information about them: weather, attractions, politics, business, and so on.

City.Net is updated daily, so information at this site is more up-to-date than most sites. (Though not perfectly complete—City.Net's list of California counties is missing San Francisco County.) The amount of information varies from destina-tion to destination, but since City.Net links to the major resources on the Net, usu-ally you'll find lots of data. Information is categorized by place. You can find the place you need either by searching or by browsing through a list of countries.

How

World Wide Web

Where

www.city.net

Planet Earth, the Point & Click Version

Virtual Tourist ☆☆☆

What if all the places on Planet Earth were clickable? Imagine being able to click on any continent on the globe and see that continent close-up. Then click on any country in your continent and view that country. Zoom in from any country to view a region. Finally, zoom in to view any city.

Virtual Tourist puts a map-based face on City.Net. Just click on maps to locate City.Net's wealth of information on any spot you want. In addition, Virtual Tourist links to geographically-based Web servers, so when you click on a city you can view a list of the Web servers based in that city.

How

World Wide Web

Where

www.vtourist.com

Fly the Friendly Skies

Commercial Aviation Resource Center ☆☆☆

In the airline industry, there are two things you can always count on: your luggage being lost when you need it the most and fare wars between rival companies. And when one of these wars heats up, the only ones not bloodied are ticket buyers with an eye for a bargain.

Here's a Web site that'll help you keep abreast of events in the air, including links to dozens of major airlines worldwide, and the most links to airports on the Net.

How

World Wide Web

Where

w3.one.net/~flypba/AIRLINES/carc.html

 This site is stuffed with giant (100 K and bigger) graphics that serve no useful purpose. If you have a slow connection, you can kill all the graphics at this site and still reach everything with the thoughtfully-provided text links.

Easing the Travel Travails

Traveler's DataBook ☆☆☆

Long business trips wouldn't be so bad if it weren't for the crummy food, lumpy beds, crowded airports, and jet lag. While the Traveler's DataBook won't make your mattress more comfortable, it might help you sleep a little better.

Travel information is just a mouse-click away.

Designed as a convenient way to access important information needed for business travel, Traveler's DataBook has many unique features for mobile computing professionals, including:

- Toll-free numbers for major airlines, car rental companies, and hotel chains
- Postal abbreviations, area codes, and time zones
- Metric conversions
- Telephone numbers for major credit card companies, traveler's checks, and money wire services
- Telephone numbers for international assistance with physicians or medications
- Telephone numbers for major overnight package delivery couriers
- Telephone numbers for major online sources of information, including Internet access

You can even include personal notes and important personal information, including frequently called numbers, user IDs, priority club numbers, travel expenses, and so on.

How

World Wide Web

Where

www.csusm.edu/cwis/winworld/educate.html

Download

traveldb.zip (98 K)

Have Computer, Will Travel

Road Warrior Outpost ☆☆☆

Every blessing comes with its own curse, and laptop computing is no different. Like a godsend, laptops freed itinerant businesspeople to work on the road, making them more productive and less dependent on the home office. Right. And some of you probably still believe in Santa Claus, too.

Laptop computers can certainly be a blessing, but they also create as many problems as they solve, especially if the user's knowledge goes little past knowing how to turn it on. The Road Warrior Outpost, an Internet resource for portable computer users, contains lots of information and tips that can help.

Look for *Road Warrior News*, a monthly newsletter you can read at this site or receive free via email. You'll also find a good paper on sales force automation, and FAQs on batteries, cellular modems and phones, and upgrading your laptop's hard drive.

How

World Wide Web

Where

warrior.com

Links

Laptop newsgroup

Mac portables newsgroup

Business news

Travel information

PDA: Pretty Darn Amazing

MOBILIS ☆☆☆

This monthly Web magazine is for people who use the most mobile of computers. Not laptops—we're talking PDAs here—Personal Digital Assistants, like the well-known Apple Newton. Until we read *Mobilis*, we didn't know there *was* such a thing as a word processor for these gadgets, which read your handwriting instead of forcing you to use a keyboard. We actually found a flurry of PDA software: Managing Your Money, Lotus Organizer, Microsoft Schedule, databases, and so on. You can even hook them up to bar code readers, so retailers, wholesalers, and manufacturers can have PDAs perform all kinds of clever tricks.

Mobilis reviews the software, reviews the hardware, and interviews the creators of these nimble gadgets. The column "Ask Mrs. PDA" answers questions from readers. The *Mobilis* Web site also contains back issues, a Jargon Index to explain abbreviations and jargon, and an email discussion group for mobile computer and communications users.

How

World Wide Web

Where

www.volksware.com/mobilis

Batteries Are Included

Power Express ☆☆☆

Power Express is famous for having built the world's largest database of batteries. If you use a laptop, you know how frustrating it can be to find information about the often bizarre battery types laptops require. Don't get frustrated—just visit Power Express, where you can search its battery database. Just type in the brand name of your laptop (or any other kind of battery-eating computing device), and get battery information. It's too easy.

While you're at this site, take a peek at the Battery Bible. It provides useful information on how to get longer life from your batteries. And other good tips.

How

World Wide Web

Where

www.powerexpress.com

Take off to PCTravel

PCTravel ☆☆☆

Check out PCTravel to find the lowest fares for airline tickets for over 700 airlines worldwide, and to research flight schedules—all online. You can look up any airline

Getcher red-hot airline tickets at unbeatable prices at PCTravel.

or flight carried by the Apollo Reservation Service. Looking stuff up at PCTravel's site is free, but you must register first.

How

World Wide Web

Where

www.pctravel.com

A Groundhog's View of the World

Subway Navigator ☆☆☆

All aboard for Austria, Hong Kong, Sweden, and all points in between. The URL for this Subway Navigator would be a great one to keep on your laptop computer, especially if you're traveling in a strange land. Nothing is more frustrating or scary than needing directions in a city in which you don't speak the language. Smiling and nodding only goes so far.

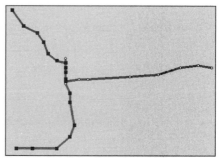
You CAN get there from here, at least according to the Calgary Subway System.

This service will help you find the best route from one metro station to another, in dozens of cities in about 30 countries.

Select the city you want, then click on your departure and destination stations for information on the best route, schedules, approximate travel time, and more. If you're not sure of the names of the stations, you can also choose them from a list.

How

World Wide Web

Where

metro.jussieu.fr:10001/bin/cities/english

Links

Subway lines galore. Just start clicking; you never know where you'll end up.

For the French-language version of this site, go to the same address, and insert the word **french** instead of **english**.

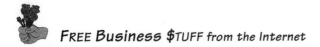

Viva Las Vegas Travel Kit

Travel Bag for Windows ☆☆☆

Before you cash in all your traveler's checks for nickels or practice drawing to an inside straight, you'll want to load this handy freeware program onto your laptop computer. Travel Bag for Windows provides easy access to the most needed travel information—provided your destination is Las Vegas, that is. Just point and click to get:

- Toll-free numbers for airlines and car rentals
- A complete list of major hotel chains
- Las Vegas information and phone numbers
- International travel information
- Local online access numbers in all U.S. cities for CompuServe and America Online

It's rumored that even Wayne Newton makes his travel plans with this handy freeware program.

How

World Wide Web

Where

www.acs.oakland.edu/oak/simtel/win3/entertn.html

Download

tbag20.zip (81 K)

Warnings for Travelers I

U.S. Travel Warnings ☆☆☆

The U.S. Department of State issues Travel Advisories and Consular Information Sheets on other countries, and you'll find them collected at this site. These guides tell you how to avoid dangers—crime, political violence, diseases, environmental hazards—when you're abroad. (It's odd, though, that under "Italy" they don't warn you about Italian hand gestures.)

If you travel internationally on a regular basis, you might like to receive updates as the State Department issues them. You can receive the latest warnings by email by emailing to **travel-advisories-request@stolaf.edu** Leave your message completely blank except for the single word **subscribe**.

How

World Wide Web

Where

www.stolaf.edu/network/travel-advisories.html

Warnings for Travelers II

Travel Advice from FCO Consular Division ☆☆☆

The British government's Foreign and Commonwealth Office issues Travel Advice Notices that are England's counterparts to the U.S. Travel Warnings described above. British advisories are often more up-to-date and more straight-forward than U.S. versions. In addition, the British give you a guide to avoiding crime in Florida, which the U.S. list doesn't cover.

This FCO site also gives you a checklist for travelers—covering the basics—and a good section of "Dos and Don'ts" listed by country.

How

World Wide Web

Where

www.fco.gov.uk/reference/travel_advice/index.html

Don't Drink the Water

International Travelers Clinic ☆☆☆

The greatest risk to international travelers isn't terrorist bombings, kidnappings, or hijackings, it's diarrhea, malaria, and hepatitis (though those afflicted would probably give anything for a terrorist bombing to put them out of their misery). Here's a site that gives you useful information on the health risks that come with traveling abroad and what you can do to minimize your chances of contracting these maladies, for instance:

- Standard food and water precautions can reduce the risk of diarrhea, and antibiotics can rapidly cure it
- Malaria can be prevented by taking malaria medications and using insect repellents to avoid mosquito bites
- The chance of getting Hepatitis A can be reduced by vaccination or an injection of immune serum globulin

- An oral vaccine is now available for protection against typhoid
- Vaccinations against polio, meningitis, and yellow fever are also available

Visit this site to find out more about staying healthy while traveling internationally.

How
World Wide Web

Where
www.intmed.mcw.edu/ITC/Health.html

Links
Travel Medicine Kit

Traveling While Pregnant

Diseases and Immunizations

Environmental Hazards

Motion Sickness

What if Air Travelers Wrote the News?

rec.travel.air Newsgroup ☆☆☆

This newsgroup is where air passengers talk about air travel. Although this is one of the **rec.** newsgroups (supposedly about recreation), more than half of the message traffic on this busy group is from business travelers.

With little spam (mostly from over-enthusiastic travel agents), this site is a good way to keep track of changes in airlines, airports, and frequent-flyer programs. It's also a good place to ask travel questions. Most questions asked at this group are intelligent, and receive well-informed answers. The simple questions about fares and schedules—which any good travel agent could answer—you can just ignore on your way to the good stuff.

These titles, from actual messages posted, give you an idea of the types of information you'll pick up in this lively newsgroup: Aerolineas Argentinas Safety; Easy Sabre online airline information FAQ; Hand Search at Charles de Gaulle Paris; FS: Continental $75 off coupon; British Airways comfort; Montreal airports restructured; No FF seats allocated—what recourse do I have?; Swedes Say Frequent-Flyer Perks Are Bribes; UA mileage wanted; WTB: NYC > Tallahassee.

How

Newsgroup

Where

news:rec.travel.air

 In addition to this travel newsgroup and the one described below, you might check out these for more information:

news:rec.travel.asia

news:rec.travel.europe

news:rec.travel.usa-canada

news:rec.travel.misc

For Sale by Owner: Travel

rec.travel.marketplace Newsgroup☆☆☆

Although most of the messages here discuss recreational travel, this newsgroup is good for business travelers, too. The word "marketplace" in this newsgroup's name indicates that this is a group for buying and selling—in this case, everything related to travel. You can post your wants—like cheap NY to London airfare, or a good hotel in Toronto. Travel agents will respond with their best offers, and veteran travelers will give you hard-bitten recommendations based on experience. You can also sell those nonrefundable tickets you can't use, or sell or trade excess frequent flyer miles.

Here are some titles of actual messages recently posted at this newsgroup. First, a quick guide to some frequently-used abbreviations: FS means For Sale, WTB stands for Want To Buy, and WTT is Want To Trade. The samples: FS: Pittsburgh-SFO Roundtrip $195; Villa for rent in Andalucia; Database of Discounted Cruises; Help...bereavement fees are a joke!; Rome rent; WTB Continental Airlines Business Class Award to Asia; FS:Amtrak SF to NY $150 one way; Barcelona to London by Air?; WTT Delta Miles for United; FS: TWA $100 coupon; FS: Gatwick-Grenada 28 Feb. return 2 wks.

How

Newsgroup

Where

news:rec.travel.marketplace

Eat Well and Stay in Touch

CyberCafe Guide ☆☆☆

Want to pick up and send your email while you're on the road? More than 300 cybercafes now exist around the world. You can drop in to any of these cybercafes and have a good meal seated at a computer that has a T-1 line. (For those of you new to Netdom, T-1 is *really* fast.) Vince swears by cybercafes. He has used the original Cyberia in London (so successful that it's now a chain), Cafe Internet (also in London), Cafe Orbital (in Paris—best pastry of the lot), CyberCafe (NYC), and the Icon Byte Bar & Grill (San Francisco).

Cybercafes give you complete Net access, so you can get your email using Eudora (if you know your IP number), or by using Telnet to reach your Internet access provider. If you're not sure how, that's okay. All cybercafes have a knowledgeable, helpful staff. (In most countries, the staff speaks English, a benefit to us linguistically-impaired Yanks.)

Cybercafes aren't free (depending on the country, $5 or so per half-hour plus your tab), but Mark Dziecielewski's useful directory is. Before you go on a trip, visit Mark's Web site first. Because once you arrive at your destination, you won't find cybercafes under "Internet" in the phone book. And if you ask your hotel staff about cybercafes, you'll probably receive blank stares.

So before you depart, make virtual visits to the cybercafes in your destination city. Jot down addresses, phone numbers, and hours (some are open 24 hours), and you're set. You might want to check with your company's Internet administrator before you leave to get your personal IP address or remote login instructions and a password. If your business is too small to have a system administrator, call your Internet access provider and ask.

And when you get to your destination, remember: It's cheaper to send email than postcards!

How

World Wide Web

Where

www.easynet.co.uk/pages/cafe/ccafe.htm

Where to Find More Sales & Travel Goodies

When you finish with this chapter, go to Chapter 5, *Entrepreneurs, Startups, and Home Businesses*, for several excellent resources for salespeople. Some are aimed at small companies, but some are useful for sales reps and managers of any company, no matter what size.

You might start with the Small Business Administration, which includes good sales software in its SBA Shareware Library. The SBA also gives you *Commerce Business Daily* free, a daily newspaper which contains nothing *but* sales leads. (You'll find a different version of *Commerce Business Daily* provided by ClariNet in Chapter 3.) The SBA will also provide you with expert sales management consultants for free from its SCORE program.

If your business depends on word-of-mouth recommendations for its sales, turn to Business Network International (also in Chapter 5), an organization whose sole purpose is to increase word-of-mouth sales. The International Small Business Consortium can also generate leads. This chapter also describes the software program Hi, Finance, which can help you prepare quotes for prospects.

If you sell computer software, turn immediately to one of the best resources in Chapter 5, Software Forum. The Forum's email discussion groups for software sales managers are extremely valuable. The *VarBusiness* site in Chapter 3 (look it up in the index) is also somewhat useful for software sales.

For a demonstration on how you can use Internet technology to improve the quality of the sales information you receive, try the Intranet demo in Chapter 4, *Tools for Internet-Based Businesses*.

You'll find other useful sales stuff if you turn to the index and look up **sales resources**. If you're a crafty sales strategist, you'll also look up **purchasing resources**, because you know that wherever there's a purchase, there's a sale. For example, if you want to sell to the Australian government, you'll find it helpful to know how their government buys stuff. You can find this info at the Australian Department of Finance site described in Chapter 9.

If you're looking for more travel resources, you'll find more resources in Chapter 12, *Doing Business Internationally*.

FREE $TUFF

With the prices they charge, they ought to call some of those big stores supermarkups.

Robert Orben

For Retailers

You'll find tens of thousands of retailers on the Net, but surprisingly few resources for the retail trade itself. Oh sure, plenty of resources exist for online retailing. We're talking about resources to help retailers run a physical store, those places where you can go in and feel the merchandise. (Or at least touch the plastic wrap around it.)

When you compare Internet resources for retailers to those available in the real world, you'll see quite a contrast. Hundreds of trade publications cover retailing in print. Only a few have dared to experiment with Web sites, shivering as they dip one toe in the water. Among the dozens of top-notch retail industry associations, only a handful say more than "Here's our phone number" on the Net.

Fortunately, several Net sites offer something worthwhile for retailers. Some are useful for retailers overall, no matter what categories of merchandise you might be selling. Others are more specialized, offering a great value for a specialized category of merchants.

If your business is in a retail category served by these sites, you'll find resources here that can help you increase your sales, reduce expenses, and save time. If not, by studying sites of other industry categories, you can pick up tricks that may help in your store—or at least in the creation of your own Web site.

Every Day's a Sale Day at RETEX

RETEX Retail Technology Consortium ☆☆☆☆☆

RETEX is a great way for retailers to save money. How much money? Funny you should ask. The Brookstone chain estimates that RETEX saved it $200 million and cut its credit authorization fees in half. Not bad for starters.

Big savings like that explain why membership in RETEX jumped from 13 retailers to 1,200 in 2 years. RETEX is a cooperative purchasing group, so retailers can gang up and buy high tech products and services at lower prices. Member retailers get discounts on credit, debit, and private label card processing, automation networks, videoconferencing, teleconferencing, telecommunications audits, and other techie stuff.

To become a member, your company must own at least two retail stores, restaurants, or other outlets that sell goods or services. Selling goods online qualifies as one of your stores, which makes that requirement easy to meet. To join,

RETEX is a nonprofit purchasing cooperative that saves member retailers millions on their high-tech purchases.

you also must annually purchase a minimum amount of technology-related products. RETEX has no enrollment fees or annual dues, and you can fill out an application form online. To help you decide, you can read back issues of the *RETEX Quarterly* newsletter.

One caveat: The RETEX home page warns that its over-designed Web site requires at least a 28.8 modem connection. That's no lie—this is a slow site.

How
World Wide Web

Where
www.retex.com

Where Shopkeepers Shop for Info

Retail Info Center ☆☆☆☆

If you're trying to find information on the Net about retailing, make the Retail Info Center your first stop. This combination retailing industry news source and directory of retailing Internet resources is the most complete directory of Net sites for retailers—though it does miss several dozen juicy retailing resources. The Retail Info Center gives you plenty of free information, but some

217

Welcome!

The Retail Info Center is an independently operated, vendor supported, information resource for the Retail Industry.

- New visitors to the RIC should <u>click here</u> for more information about this site.

- The latest additions to the RIC will always be featured in the <u>New</u> section.

- You may <u>Enter</u> the exhibit area here.

- AOL, Compuserve, and Prodigy users may wish to look <u>here</u> for other access methods.

The Retail Info Center gives you retailing industry news and steers you toward other Web sites for retailers.

of its best offerings are restricted to subscribers to *Retail Systems Alert* or members of the Association of Retail Technology Standards.

For instance, the current issue of the monthly newsletter *Retail Systems Alert* is available only to subscribers. But everyone can read back issues of the newsletter going back to 1990. Back issues are not searchable, but you can look through a directory of stories arranged according to subject. *Retail Systems Alerts* covers technology for merchandising, store automation, instore systems, point-of-sale, and replenishment systems, among other topics. *RSA* special reports are also free. They cover topics such as a comparison of QR and ECR, decision support software for retailers, and reengineering for retailers.

Retail Info Center also features a rarely-used "Bulletin Board" section that you can skip. Recent postings were spam. You might want to check out several of the directories for retailers. These are still under construction and vary in usefulness. When we visited, directories included Associations (good), Publications (good), Retailers on the Web (so-so), International (almost nothing), Reference (not much), and Cafe (useless). Links have names but no descriptions, as though created for a Gopher server instead of the World Wide Web.

How

World Wide Web

Where

www.retail-info.com/RICHome.html

We're Number Two—WWWe Try Harder

WWW Virtual Library: Retailing ☆☆☆

The second most complete directory of resources on the Net for retailers is this subdirectory of the WWW Virtual Library. It lists many Web sites that all other retailing directories miss. A lot of the resources here are Web sites useful for merchants who sell over the Net, as opposed to the garden variety of "in-a-store" retailers, but trade shopkeepers will still find plenty to point-and-click about.

How

World Wide Web

Where

www.pncl.co.uk/subs/james/vl/vretail.html

Let's Get Down to Brass Tacks

National Retail Hardware Association ☆☆☆

Hardware and tools seem to be guy things. Some guys love tools, and these guys love to *sell* tools. The top spot on the Net for hardware and home improvement retailers, this site is the joint home (must be a duplex) of the National Retail Hardware Association and the Home Center Institute. They've constructed one of the most informative Web sites built by any retail trade association.

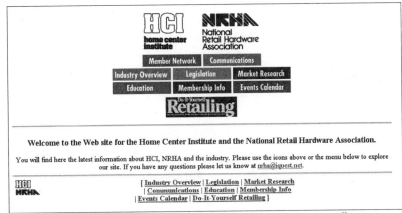

The top spot on the Net for hardware and home improvement retailers.

219

The section called "Industry Overview" provides good reports on hardlines distribution and on the U.S. retail hardware and home improvement market. The "Legislation" department gives you two newsletters: *This Week in Washington*, which is good, and the monthly *Washington Report*, which is even better. Skip "Market Research"; it's just ads. You might want to look at the "Communications" section for association information, or the "Events Calendar." You'll also find the magazine *Do-It-Yourself Retailing* here. It gives you no articles, but the in-depth *Annual Market Measure Report* is yours for free, summing up the events and consequences of the industry's past year.

How

World Wide Web

Where

www.nrha.org

Where's the Best Place to Grow Your Store?

The Future of Retailing ☆☆☆

This detailed analysis shows the hottest U.S. metropolitan areas in the future for restaurants, grocery stores, car dealers, gas stations, furniture stores, hardware stores, shoe stores, clothing stores, and retailers who sell general merchandise.

You can download the numbers for your own analysis. Data covers national projections and individual metropolitan areas for primary retail categories and some secondary categories. You can download the data files in spreadsheet and in **.csv** (comma-delimited) formats. Each file has an accompanying **.txt** text file. Be sure to copy that text file as well, because it tells you where-to-find-what in the data files.

How

World Wide Web

Where

www.marketingtools.com/retail/retail.htm

These Futures Move Slowly

RETAIL FUTURES ☆☆

This Web periodical is published six times a year, reporting on changes which affect the retailing and manufacturing industries. Although some worthwhile

information is presented here; it is sabotaged by a woefully ineffective presentation format that forces you to download a short bit of text (three to five paragraphs), and then wait for the next short bit. Even with an 112 K ISDN connection, we spent far more time waiting than reading. Skip the row of pill-shaped buttons at the top—they are all irrelevant ads for the Web design company responsible for this site.

How

World Wide Web

Where

www.e1.com/RF/RFindex.html

Undoubtedly, the Net's Most Convenient

CONVENIENCE STORE NEWS ONLINE ☆☆☆

When they say "news," they mean it. People in the convenience store industry who use the Create Your Own Newspaper tool (in Chapter 3) will want to include this site for its timely and good news coverage of this business. The news and some other sections of this site, such as the directory of U.S. state-level industry organizations and the retail technology section, are open to anyone who visits this site.

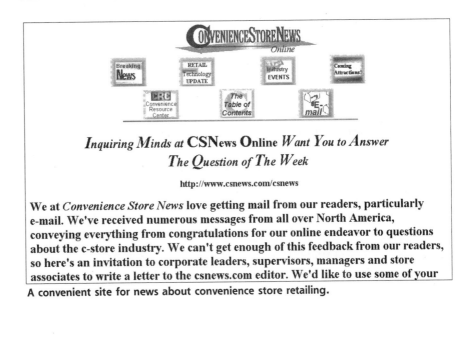

A convenient site for news about convenience store retailing.

However, much of *Convenience Store News Online* is open only to c-store execs and retailers who have registered. (Don't worry, it's still free!) This includes a Convenience Resource Center with a message board, job opportunities, a searchable database of industry suppliers, special purchasing offers, and a chance to participate in industry surveys and see the results. And it's open 24 hours, just like most of the industry it serves.

How

World Wide Web

Where

www.csnews.com

Where Co-op Builds Your Marketing Muscle

Co-op Home Page ☆☆☆

Every retailer worth its salt works to leverage its marketing efforts with cooperative advertising funds (often called *trade allowances*) from its suppliers. Better to have your vendor pay for your advertising and POP than you, right? In 1995, trade promotion spending was estimated to top $33 billion. This Web site is here to help you cash in on your share.

You'll find articles from the *Proclaimer* newsletter covering co-op, and an archive of past issues going back to 1990 that you can read. You'll also find another newsletter, *National Association for Promotional and Advertising Allowances News*, but it doesn't give much info that is useful. You'll find part of one chapter from the book *Co-op Advertising* by Bob Houk (the definitive work on co-op and trade allowances). The excerpt has good stuff on just-in-time manufacturing co-op and new media, and will make you want to read the rest of the book.

The home page of the National Association of Customer Accounting Administrators is within this site, but skip it. It's boring *and* useless. Zzzzz. Instead, check out the job opportunities, the events calendar, the section on legal and regulatory issues, or the links to ad agencies and marketing Web sites.

How

World Wide Web

Where

www.medianet.com/index.html

Fetch My Scissors, It's Planogram Time

Fred Meyer, Inc. Consumer Products Video Images ☆☆☆

Retailer Fred Meyer has built an image library of nearly 175,000 pictures of products. These pix are in the **.tga** graphics format, which can be used with space management software (such as InterSpace, Apollo, or Spaceman) to create planograms. The pictures are also usable in advertising or on Web pages.

Now before you get too excited, we need to let you know that most of Fred Meyer's pictures aren't free. (We can hear you say, "Oh, darn!" from here.) However you can download for free a catalog of them (as a text file) or a huge image database. To avoid killing your modem, the image database is split into 15 large files (in the common **.dbf** database file format), corresponding closely with the merchandise categories that the pictures cover (Food, Drug/Health/Beauty, General Merchandise, Automotive, Housewares, Home Improvement).

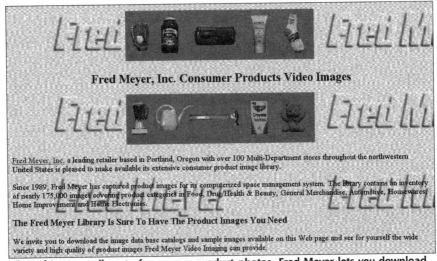

King of Internet clip art of consumer product photos, Fred Meyer lets you download a catalog database here.

This Web site gives you only two free pictures as samples of the other 174,998—but at least one is a teddy bear.

How

World Wide Web

Where

www.teleport.com/~fredpix

223

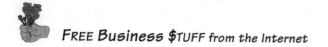

Our Competition Just Bought a WHAT?

RETAIL IT INFORMER ☆☆☆

This Web site serves you daily news articles—mostly covering the U.S., Canada, the U.K., and Australia—about hardware and software for retailers. You'll find out what products are new from vendors, which retailer bought what product (or built it in-house), how much it cost, and what they plan to do with it. *Retail IT Informer* covers Internet retailers as well as physical store retailers, and products include payment systems, credit card processing, point-of-sale, retail inventory, and anything else you can think of (and probably some you can't).

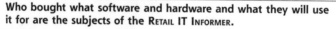

Retail IT INFORMER

A unique news service for professionals in the retail IT sector

- Open Retail IT INFORMER. . .
- Subscription details - plus FREE SUBSCRIPTION to the end of the month
- Closest servers for quickest response times
- IT INFORMER home page
- Please send us your comments!

Who bought what software and hardware and what they will use it for are the subjects of the RETAIL IT INFORMER.

Normally a subscription to the *Retail IT Informer* costs $300 a year, but you can get a free trial subscription that lasts until the end of the month. Our tip: Subscribe right on or after the first of the month so your free trial lasts as many days as possible.

How

World Wide Web

Where

For fastest performance, use the site closest to you:

U.S.:   www.keyway.net/mmp/retail

U.K.:   www.pavilion.co.uk/mmp/retail

For Retailers

A Security Blanket for Your Software

WinU ☆☆☆

These days, more and more retail stores use computers as a selling tool. Customers point and click on screens to learn more about merchandise or to try new software programs.

WinU is a Windows 95 program that lets you decide what software can be used on your computer and what is off limits, which makes it ideal for businesses that want to let the shopping public run certain programs without allowing access to the entire computer. And with WinU, you can set the amount of time someone can use a program before they have to let someone else have a turn. You can even create custom messages warning that their time has almost ended.

Business owners will especially like the File Logging feature, which tracks exactly when and for how long each program was run. Plus WinU lets you use any bitmap as its full-screen background image, so you can even include your company's logo.

How

World Wide Web

Where

www.cris.com/~randybrg/utils.html

Download

win95sec.zip (113 K)

If You Train 'Em You'll Retain 'Em

Reducing Sales Employee Turnover in Retailing ☆☆

This paper by Victoria Seitz discusses the relationship of sales training to reducing turnover, increasing job satisfaction, and increasing performance for retail sales clerks. It's basic, but if you are a new manager in the retail game or have never had a formal education in retail management, it might be profitable for you to take a look.

How

World Wide Web

Where

www.sbaer.uca.edu/docs/proceedings/92swi049.txt

Retail Jobs R Us

Merchandising Technologies ☆☆

You'll find this directory of retailing resources not quite up to snuff compared to the others, but it does give you one thing they lack: job opportunities. It also gives you a few press releases on retail industry news stories.

To start from the top, the first thing you'll notice is that this site has too many graphics on its home page. You can kill all the graphics with your Web browser's handy stop sign and you won't miss a thing. The section on "Space Management Resources" has press releases and a directory of software and hardware contacts.

Go to the "Retailers" section to find jobs. Skip the "Retail Technology Jobs" subsection; it's just one ad for a headhunter. "Retail Sector Jobs" is more promising. It links you with the help wanted pages of retailers' Web sites. Other sections here annoyingly lure you repeatedly to a few pages by listing them several times under different names.

How
World Wide Web

Where
www.merchtech.com

Book Retailers Get Wired, Part I

American Booksellers Association ☆☆☆

Booksellers are one of the most adept of all retail categories at using the Internet. This may surprise you—but only if you don't know that bookstores were some of the first merchants on the Internet, and that book sales generate the second-highest dollar volume of all merchandise categories sold online. (Only software sales are higher.)

With that background, you'll be less astonished to find that the ABA pulls one of the slickest tricks of any trade association online. A member retailer can visit this Web site and log in with a password. Then the member can actually use the Home Page Builder software on the ABA's computer to build a store's own Web pages—without the retailer spending a penny on Web building software!

Book retailers are some of the most sophisticated at using the Internet to market themselves.

The value of the Internet to book retailers becomes plain when you read the ABA's page on "Bookseller Services." When the ABA lists membership benefits, the top spot on the list goes to ABA's Internet directory of member retailers. You can search that directory here, or browse through it alphabetically or by merchandise specialty. You can also look by country. (The organization has members in 30 countries.) You can also read industry news.

How

World Wide Web

Where

www.ambook.org

Book Retailers Get Wired, Part II

Pubnet ☆☆☆

Book retailers are also ahead of the curve when it comes to Electronic Data Interchange, called EDI for short. EDI happens when a retailer's purchase order for merchandise goes directly from the retailer's computer into a vendor's computer. EDI transactions are completely electronic, with no paper version whatsoever. For bookstores, Pubnet (as EDI for books is called) costs less, cuts delivery time, and is more accurate than paper orders. In other industries, EDI can costs tens of thousands of dollars per site to install and take months to set up. Book retailers pay less than $2,000 and set up Pubnet in a few hours.

The Pubnet Web site has links to publisher Web sites, bestseller lists, a searchable database of promotional tours by authors, and a media/publicity database.

227

It also provides booksellers with a list of newly released books, and a directory of links to book industry sites and other EDI sites.

How

World Wide Web

Where

www.pubnet.org

 Cecil Hoge gives a good overview of Pubnet in his book *Electronic Marketing Manual*. You can read that chapter of Hoge's book online at:

www.obs-us.com/obs/german/books/elecmanu/gh212.htm

Book Retailers Get Wired, Part III

Antiquarian Booksellers Association of America ☆☆

"Antiquarian booksellers? Aren't they out-of-touch old geezers who never leave their dusty stores? What are they doing on the Internet?"

They are doing quite nicely, thank you. Categories of merchandise called *search products*—any products customers actively search for—sell well on the Net. An example is baseball cards. Of more than 15,000 newsgroups, the one with the highest message traffic covers buying, selling, and swapping sports cards. Collectible books certainly qualify as search products.

In addition to bringing traffic to their retail stores, ABAA members have the goal—and have made great strides towards achieving it—of making their Web site the number one place in the world—in any medium—for customers to locate their merchandise—rare and collectable books. So successful has the ABAA effort been that the International League of Antiquarian Booksellers has agreed to merge its Internet efforts with the ABAA project, with U.S. retailers at the helm.

Besides acting as a customer magnet (certainly a worthy goal in itself), ABAA also uses its site to disseminate industry information and to recruit new members. Its quarterly *ABAA Newsletter* is available here, plus online research materials, security alerts on stolen books and forgeries, and links to member retailers.

How

World Wide Web

Where

www.clark.net/pub/mharris/newsltr/4-7.html

How Ya Gonna Keep 'Em on the Farm?

Farm Market ☆☆

If you're interested in this growing (literally!) category of non-mall retailing, you might visit this site operated by the National Urban Market Center at Purdue University. It gives a directory of U.S. farmers' markets, with contact information for selling at each, and also a list of related conferences.

How

World Wide Web

Where

newcrop.hort.purdue.edu/farmMarket/farmMarket.html

You might also visit the California Federation of Certified Farmers' Markets at **www.dcn.davis.ca.us/~rmacnear/farmers/info/homepage.html**. Its state-wide listing of markets is more complete than Purdue's and offers a directory of seasonal produce (what's for sale in which month) and a separate buying calendar for fresh produce.

The Littlest Retailers

Open Air Market Net ☆☆☆☆

"A Web guru is someone who has been on the Internet six months longer than you have," says this site. We agree completely. Retailers of all kinds can benefit from reading this site's very good guide, "Tips for designing a market Web site."

We were surprised to find high-tech expertise at a site concerned with low-tech categories of retailing. This Web site is subtitled, "Farmers' Markets, Street Markets, Flea Markets, and Street Vendors," and it covers its subject with gusto. There are lessons here for many types of retailers, not the least of which is the value of enthusiasm, which Open Air Market Net shares about its topic. It's current: updated at least twice a week. It acts as a champion for its customers: it aids vendors looking for help, or just a place to sell merchandise.

A section called "Alerts: Markets in Jeopardy" reports on threatened markets around the world. It has even created its own newsgroup to promote its cause (and itself): **alt.culture.openair-market**. It also provides a directory of market associations, a calendar of conferences, and an email discussion group.

How
World Wide Web

Where
homepage.interaccess.com/~mar/openair.html

Where to Find a Bit More Stuff

For dessert, we'd like to point out that if you want to find out how to retail on the Internet, you could do worse than to sort through the resources in Chapter 4, *Tools for Internet-Based Businesses*.

Many of the resources in our *Marketing, Advertising, and Publicity* chapter are good for retailers. You also might browse Chapter 5, *Entrepreneurs, Startups, and Home Businesses*.

For retail resources in the rest of the book, the index is your best bet. Look under **retail resources**. You may also want to check under **advertising**, **catalogs**, **credit cards**, **customer service resources**, **home shopping**, and **inventory**.

Hope all those help make your cash register ring!

FREE $TUFF

I have no use for bodyguards, but I have a very special use for two highly trained Certified Public Accountants.

Elvis Presley

Accounting and Finance

The best accountants have a passion to organize information and make sure that it is right. So don't let this surprise you: Some of the best-organized and most useful resources on the Internet are accounting and finance resources.

Accountants and finance professionals from all over the world have pooled resources to create extremely valuable Web sites and email discussion groups. Any change in FASB standards, any new government regulation (at least, from governments of major countries), and any new tax policy is communicated worldwide the same day it is issued.

A few words about accounting's email discussion groups: accountants make extensive use of discussion groups (which some people call "email lists"). You'll find 38 groups mentioned in this chapter and another 25 in the following *Tax Reduction* chapter. Many of these groups are tremendously valuable, both as sources where you can receive specialized news quickly and as places where you can ask detailed questions about your work.

In a good group, you'll receive quality answers from pros with first-hand experience. Several accounting discussion groups are available only to qualified professionals, so the level of information exchanged is quite high compared to *open groups,* where anyone can join.

Most accounting and finance groups are *moderated*, meaning that someone takes the time to screen out time-wasters such as spam ads and irrelevant junk messages. These hard-working moderators are like auditors. They make sure that discussion groups have only the proper information from authorized sources. So when you consider subscribing to a group, a well-moderated one can deliver extra value.

Some World Wide Web sites for accounting and finance are equally well-organized. You'll find in this chapter excellent sites for the overall field and for specialized areas. Keep one thing in mind about these Web sites: In their quest for accuracy, these sites change. *A lot.* So when (not if) you look at a Web site from this chapter and you see something significantly different from what we describe, don't fret. Rejoice—you'll have found a resource that's been updated and improved.

Your First Stop for Accounting Treasures

International Accounting Network (Anet) ☆☆☆☆☆

The home page of this Web site makes it look simple. It starts with just a short, clear list. But the best way to put that simple list in perspective is to view it as a balance sheet. Each line item on the Anet home page leads to ledgersful of valuable detail. This site seems to list *every* accounting resource on the Net, but you and I know that Internet sites proliferate more quickly than tax hikes, so that's impossible.

Home Page of ANet - Part of the International Accounting Network

More than you can shake a stick—um, an abacus—at is what you'll find at the Anet Web site. The large amount of unique information at this site and tremendous number of links make Anet one of the top five accounting sites on the Net.

Yet, the folks at Anet make a valiant effort. Some of the information here is low-quality, and some is for academics rather than businesspeople, but if you poke around you'll find things your business needs, plus useful stuff that you'd never even think about. You'll find more than 30 email discussion groups on:

- Accounting topics
- Informative archives of past discussions from those groups
- Hundreds of links to Web sites
- Newsletters (including the American Accounting Association's *Information Systems/Management Advisory Services Section Newsletter*)
- A pitifully small selection of software (Anet's only weakness)

- A contact directory of accounting associations worldwide
- A *searchable* bibliographic database
- Other directories

The home page of the American Accounting Association is located within the Anet site. Whew! It makes me depreciate just to think about it.

How

World Wide Web

Where

anet.scu.edu.au/net

(or)

In the USA: www.rutgers.edu/Accounting/anet/ANetHomePage.html

The Sistine Chapel Ceiling of Accounting Sites

Kaplan's AuditNet Resource List (KARL) ☆☆☆☆☆

This huge catalog of accounting, taxation, investment, and financial resources is not only frequently updated and understandably organized, but—even better—every resource is extensively and intelligently described by James M. Kaplan. KARL includes many, many resources both on the Internet (newsgroups, Web sites, email discussion groups, and so on) and off (such as CompuServe and America Online resources).

There are pointers to hundreds of resources here—so many that you won't have time to look at all of them. But you won't need to, because Kaplan's clear descriptions tell you the difference between resources (such as variations between the *two* email lists for auditors who use ACL software), so you can save time and visit only resources that most closely meet your needs. Kaplan's site is a tremendously useful accomplishment. Bravo!

Rip-off warning: An unscrupulous entrepreneur appears to have copied the KARL list and printed it as a booklet of tax, investment, and accounting resources. The booklet is advertised on financial newsgroups and on CompuServe. The original KARL Web site (and its email version) is more complete, more up-to-date, and (best of all) free. Before you pay for any booklet that sounds like a listing of accounting resources, ask if it's "based on" the AuditNet list.

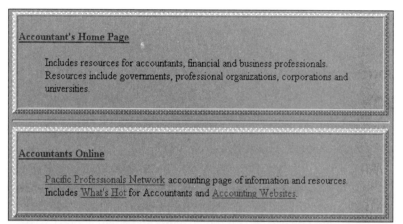

Easily one of the top five resources on the Net for accounting and financial professionals, KARL serves a seemingly inexhaustible banquet of riches.

How

World Wide Web

Where

www.unf.edu/students/jmayer/arl.html

This booklet is also available by email at:

jkaplan@apaccess.org

(Tell Jim Kaplan that Vince and Pat told you to ask for the latest version.)

When the Going Gets Rough, the Pros Go Online

Professionals Online ☆☆☆

If you're overwhelmed by the KARL or Anet directories, try this simpler catalog of accounting resources. This directory of Web sites, organized by profession, includes several categories of interest to accounting people. It is well-organized into subcategories within each profession and gives short descriptions of most resources. Some of the resources listed are duds but some are good.

Look under "Netsearch tools" to find more accounting and finance sites, and under "Biz," "Finance," "Accounting," "Law," "Computers & Technology," and "International." If you need a job, don't miss "Job Opportunities."

How
World Wide Web

Where
www.prosonline.com

bob.cratchit@scrooge&marley.co.uk

Accounting Email Directory ☆☆☆

Looking for the email address of that CPA you met at the virtual money seminar last February? Try this site. It's a directory of names and addresses of
accounting, audit, and financial management pros. You can look people up,
and you can add your own name and email address so people can find you. You
can search by name, geographic location, and industry.

How
World Wide Web

Where
www.unf.edu/misc/jmayer/email/home.html

How to Use the Net for Accountants

Accounting Professional's Resource Center ☆☆☆☆

This site is run by Kent Information Systems. The folks at Kent help accounting and financial pros use computer technology, especially the Internet. You
can sign up here for excellent email discussion groups on accounting topics
and read sample issues of Kent's newsletters. You'll also find Site Seeker, a
quite good, well-organized directory of accounting and taxation resources on
the Net. When I looked, Site Seeker contained resources for the U.S. only. I
hope to see that change soon.

How
World Wide Web

Where
www.kentis.com

Summa the Best Accounting Sites

Summa Project ☆☆☆☆

This vast, searchable directory of worldwide accounting resources is managed
by the Institute of Chartered Accountants in England and Wales. A good deal

of the information here is not available elsewhere. You'll find lots of resources here, including the European mirror site of Anet. (Though Summa refers to Anet by its full name, International Accounting Network. Those Brits are *so* proper.)

How

World Wide Web

Where

www.icaew.org.uk

Accounting in Many Lands

AIntAcc-L International Accounting Email Group ☆☆☆

If you're involved with international or multinational accounting, you'll find useful discussions and announcements on this email discussion group. It's moderated, so there is no spam, although rare, on-topic commercial announcements are permitted. You'll also find some job openings on this quiet, low-volume group. An archive of past messages is available at:

www.scu.edu.au/anet/lists/aintacc-l/index.html

Sample topics: United Kingdom Accounting/Recordkeeping Requirements; The Implications of NAFTA on Accounting; Address of AICPA?/Which FASB to order?; Accounting Profession in Vietnam; Chinese government accounting; Heia Skandinavia!; Accounting Case Studies Experts for Pilot Project in Russia; INSOL International Regional Conference for Asia

How

Email

Where

listproc@scu.edu.au

Message

Help me

Finanz und Deutsche

de.etc.finanz Newsgroup ☆☆☆

For personal and small business finance and accounting in German, try this active group. It covers credit cards, banks, loans, taxes, foreign exchange, and related topics. Besides questions and answers, periodically you'll find reports on these subjects.

Sample topics: Aktuelle Angebote DM-Tagesgelder; Angebot und Machfrage; Betrug durch Banken; Effektivzins/true yield; Upgrade auf Quicken?

How

Newsgroup

Where

news:de.etc.finanz

The Beauty of the Maple Leaf

Chartered Accountants of Canada ☆☆☆

You'll find two high points here. The first is an excellent and thoroughly described list of Web sites dealing with the specialized field of environmental accounting, business, and the environment in general. We're not talking just Canadian environmental resources, but stuff for the whole planet. You'll find resources from (and for) the U.S., the U.K., and elsewhere.

The second high point is a selection of articles from *CAmagazine*. This site also includes abstracts on forthcoming standards, accounting job openings, and, as a *coup de grace*, you can read everything in your choice of English or Française.

How

World Wide Web

Where

www.cica.ca

Forever Young

Ernst & Young Canada ☆☆☆

In addition to promoting E&Y services, this site provides lots of good information on Canadian taxes, analyses of trends and economic statistics, and job openings. You'll also find links to business resources on the Net and stuff for human resources management.

How

World Wide Web

Where

tax.ey.ca/ey

Canadian Accountants, Ay?

Ormsby & Mackan ☆☆☆

If you don't want to wait in long lines at the Revenue Canada Web site (see next chapter), you can pick up Adobe Postscript versions of the 10 most-often-used national Canadian forms here, plus tax forms for Ontario. This site also offers monthly articles on taxes and accounting topics, links to business resources (especially Canadian resources), and a built-in Web search engine.

How

World Wide Web

Where

gold.interlog.com/~fmackan

Accountancy Practice Makes Perfect

CharterNet: Institute of Chartered Accountants in Ireland ☆☆☆

Very good articles from *Accountancy Ireland* magazine make this site worthwhile for working accountants from any country. The articles give you no-nonsense advice on the business of accountancy, with titles such as "Buying or Selling an Accountancy Practice?," "Merging Accountancy Practices," and "The Admission and Retirement of Partners." This site also offers an online library catalog, Irish taxation news, PracticeNET, and links to some Internet accounting resources.

One part needs improvement: a resume bank of ICA members in several countries looking for full- and part-time employment, both permanent and temporary. It's a good idea, but the register charges prospective employers a fee to use it. Unfortunately, that fee discourages employers from using the register to hire ICA members. The remainder of this site is what makes a visit worth your time.

How

World Wide Web

Where

www.icai.ie

FREE Business $TUFF from the Internet

Financial Fair Dinkum

Australian Department of Finance ☆☆☆

Here you can read the full text of the report by ADF's Information Technology Review Group. It makes interesting reading for any Aussie business manager concerned about the impact of technology on business and international trade in Oz in the future. You'll also find employment opportunities, complete government budgets, and (great news if you want to sell to the government) RFQs for upcoming purchases.

How

World Wide Web

Where

www.nla.gov.au/finance

This Dragon Does Accounting

Loyal Dragon Project ☆☆☆

The best site for info on accounting, auditing, and taxation in Hong Kong, this site also has links to PRC resources. You'll find information here on HK Inland Revenue ordinances, accounting standards in HK, and HK venture capitalist, stock, and trust information. Contained within this site are the home pages of the Hong Kong Society of Accountants and the Chartered Association of Certified Accountants.

You'll find links to legal and business resources in Hong Kong and the PRC, but most links just have names and no descriptions. Links are also provided to accounting jobs in Hong Kong. You'll also find a description here of an email discussion group on accounting in Hong Kong.

How

World Wide Web

Where

accounting.greatwall.com.hk

 Information about this group is available by email at:

clement@iohk.com

Mr. Washington Goes to Smith

WAccNet, the Washington Accounting Network ☆☆☆

Useful but not overwhelming, this site provides an email discussion group for accountants in the State of Washington, an FTP site, and links to other Internet accounting resources, tax resources, and Washington State resources.

How

World Wide Web

Where

www.eskimo.com/~earl

How to Grow Your CPA Firm

CPA-MGMT-MRKTG Email Discussion Group ☆☆☆

This is a spam-free, moderated email discussion group on managing, marketing, and growing a CPA firm. In this group, questions from beginners generate some genuinely helpful answers from experienced vets. The group is open to all accounting and taxation professionals, not just CPAs, but subscriptions are restricted only to professionals in the field—neither students nor wannabees need apply. The restricted access keeps the level of usefulness high. You will use email to take part in discussions, but you need World Wide Web access to subscribe to this group.

How

World Wide Web

Where

www.kentis.com/sublist.html

Where Business Is Booming

BOOMER BULLETIN☆☆☆

Is your business booming? Maybe *Boomer Bulletin* can help. CPA Gary Boomer writes this chatty monthly newsletter that tells CPAs how to use computers and technology to improve their practices. If a piece of CPA software makes Windows blow up, you'll read about it here—and with luck, find out how you can work around the bug.

How

World Wide Web

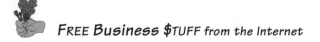

Where

For a free subscription: www.kentis.com/freeboom.html

To read a sample issue: www.kentis.com/BoomerB6_95.html

Accounting Software, Computers, and You

AAccSys-L Accounting Information Systems Group ☆☆☆☆

This moderately active email discussion group talks about *everything* having to do with accounting systems software and hardware. It is moderated, so you won't find spam. What you will find are questions, answers, and conference announcements. An archive of past messages is available at:

www.scu.edu.au/anet/lists/aaccsys-l/index.html

Sample topics: Multicurrency accounting; Longevity of CIO tenure; MS Access or Excel practice sets; entry-level accounting package with job cost; Banking on the Internet; Procurement card policy

How

Email

Where

listproc@scu.edu.au

Message

Help me

Does Your Software Do Windows?

comp.os.ms-windows.apps.financial Newsgroup ☆☆☆☆

This active discussion group on Windows software is only 5 percent spam, but it discusses personal finance software (Quicken, Quickbooks, Money, TurboTax) more than business accounting programs. It's still a good resource, with questions and answers, technical tips, bug reports, user group meeting announcements, and some opinionated rant (but not much).

Sample topics: Best Way to Do a Year-End Closing; Black register headings in Quicken under Win 95; Cost and Profit Center analytical tools; Excel oddity; I don't see how home banking will work; Intuit ExpensAble; MS Money versus Quicken; NASDAQ Level II feeds; Pretax Insurance Premiums; Online banking fees.

How

Newsgroup

Where

news:comp.os.ms-windows.apps.financial

Intuit ExpensAble

From: jbauer@quanta.com (Jon Bauer)
Newsgroups: comp.os.ms-windows.apps.financial
Subject: Intuit ExpensAble.

I've been using Intuit's new expense reporting program for about a week now and have some comments and questions about it. Dunno if anyone here is using it, but thought that this would probably be the best place. (It is a Windows-based financial type of application.)

1. Intuit ExpensAble is pretty well designed, and uses many of the Quicken-type keystrokes in most cases. To scroll up and down in your list of entered expenses, however, they don't allow you to use the page up and page down keys, and it takes a LONG time to scroll through the list using the up and down arrow keys. Why disable page up and page down? Stupid.

2. I am a FULL-time traveler. I mean, 100 percent. The way my T&E works is that I use my company's American Express card as much as possible, which they pay for, and then I need to show my out-of-pocket expenses, which are reimbursed. I can't get ExpensAble to show an expense report of BOTH my company expenses, AND my out-of-pocket expenses. It will only show my out-of-pocket, no matter which report format I choose. Documentation makes no mention of this.

3. I want to add an expense type called "snack"—ExpensAble wants me to link this new type to an existing expense type. Problem is, I don't like any of the existing types. None really suit the expense type of "snack". I guess I could call it "lunch" or "breakfast", but I want to just call it "food!"

Anyone have any positive/negative experiences with this product?

Has anyone really linked this product to their Quicken data?

Basically, if I can't get the expense report to print both my out-of-pocket, AND my company expenses (and I need them to be tallied separately), then the program is junk to me.
- Jon Bauer

jbauer@quanta.com or jbauer@pepsi.com
url: quanta.com/~jbauer

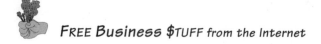

Spreadsheet Fever

comp.app.spreadsheets Newsgroup ☆☆☆☆

Whether you love your spreadsheet or hate it, either emotional extreme means you use it a lot, so this discussion newsgroup might help you. It is an active, high-volume group, with the latest bug reports and news, plus lots of questions and answers. This group is most helpful to new users. Though the group covers all spreadsheets, including mainframe ones, most of the action centers around Excel, Quattro, 1-2-3, and Unix spreadsheets, plus their add-on products. There is little spam here.

Sample topics: Black-Scholes Formula; Condensing in Lotus; Contour Maps Required; Excel Bug; Excel Swap X & Y Axes?; Setting Font for Footers in 1-2-3; Math Bug in Microsoft Excel; Macro Problem; New Bug in Excel; Printing Cell Formulas; SuperCalc DOS & ODI Drivers.

How

Newsgroup

Where

news:comp.apps.spreadsheets

Spam with Accounting Software on the Side

biz.comp.accounting Newsgroup ☆☆☆

This used to be a great discussion newsgroup but is now just a so-so one. The reason: the encroachment of spam. There is still good discussion here about accounting software, but I estimate that 60 percent of the messages posted are spam ads that have nothing to do with this group's topic. This is a dramatic (but sad) example of the need for newsgroups to be moderated.

Sample topics: Accounting—Dairy Industry; Accounting Computer Software Information Wanted; Announcing new accounting package; Anyone heard of Data Pro accounting software?; Federal TSP percent; Macola experience needed; M.Y.O.B. and Simply Accounting; Medical HMO Billing Software; Non-profit accounting; Seeking Database of CPAs; Sub S Corporation Basis Withdrawal.

How

Newsgroup

Where

news:biz.comp.accounting

It's Gonna Cost Me How Much?!

Annual Percentage Rate Program for DOS ☆☆☆

The sticker price doesn't look too bad, and you might be able to squeeze the monthly payments into your budget, but how much is that new car *really* going to cost you? Crunch the numbers and find out with the Annual Percentage Rate Program for DOS.

```
                        DISCLOSURE INFORMATION
                    AMOUNT FINANCED      =       10,000.00
                    FINANCE CHARGE       =          800.00
                    TOTAL OF PAYMENTS    =       10,800.00

   PMT STREAM
     NUMBER            PMT AMOUNT          NO. OF PMTS      PDS - DAYS
   ----------          ----------          -----------      ---------
       1                 300.00                36            1     0




        ANNUAL PERCENTAGE RATE    =      5.0648 %


   VIOLATION     The APR is overstated by:                    2.4352 %


            Do you wish to calculate another APR (y/n/p=print)?    y
```

Read the fine print and don't sign anything until you've run the numbers through this APR calculator.

You'll get a breakdown of the way the monthly payments combined with the accruing interest jack up the total cost. After you've put your eyeballs back into their sockets, maybe you'll realize this isn't such a good deal after all.

The software package also includes a real estate construction financing program, in case you don't want to live in your new car.

How

Gopher

Where

gopher://gopher.ed.gov

Go To

Educational Software

IBM Computers and Compatibles

Download

apr32.zip (121 K)

The files here are compressed, but might not include the **.zip** extension. Not to worry, simply rename the files with **.zip** tacked onto the end (for instance, **calendem.zip**) and they'll unzip fine. There are dozens of other programs stored here, as well. Read the Directory of Contents located at this site for more details.

Go Figure

Judy's TenKey Calculator for Windows ☆☆☆

When it comes to finding great try-before-you-buy business software, you can't go wrong on the Net. And here's the proof: Judy's TenKey, a flexible online calculator, will make your Windows calculator look like an electronic abacus.

Judy's TenKey includes a scrolling tape to record your calculations, which you can save, print, and resize. You can also modify tape entries—causing the tape to recalculate—or reuse previous entries in new calculations. Plus, the display is fully customizable, so you can optimize it to fit your needs.

And it's easy to calculate monthly payments, expected investment growth, inflation adjustment, and more. The scrolling tape feature is perfect for

It all adds up: The Net is the place to find great business software.

statistical calculations, including average values, sums, or even standard deviations (as opposed to your substandard deviations—who says I didn't pay attention in algebra?).

How

FTP

Where

ftp://ftp.csusm.edu/pub/winworld/calculat

Download

10key301.zip (183 K)

This site includes dozens of other calculators of all types, including financial calculators that mimic HP's gadgets. Read the **calculat.ndx** file for more information.

Windows 95 Adds Up

RCALC 2 Calculator for Windows 95 ☆☆☆

When it comes to using many online calculators, I'd prefer counting on my fingers. With a few I've tried, I'd even prefer using my toes. Needless to say, RCALC 2 was a nice surprise and a welcome addition to my shareware collection.

This excellent calculator lets you *hear* the numbers as they're entered. It might take you a few minutes to get the hang of using RCALC, but once you do, you'll never go back to any of the other online calculators you've tried. And even more important, the built-in voice feature will help keep you awake during all that number crunching.

Now you can see the bottom line—and hear it, too.

How

World Wide Web

Where

www.cris.com/~randybrg/utils.html

Download

rvspolish2.zip (332 K)

Whoever Dies with the Most Money Wins

Money Smith 95 Accounting Software ☆☆☆

Money Smith 95 is an update of the award-winning accounting system from Money Smith Systems that harnesses the power of Win95. This full-featured double entry bookkeeping system, financial calculator, and investment tracking system is all rolled into one powerful program. It may be the only financial software package you'll ever need.

Some of Money Smith's features include:

- A double entry bookkeeping system
- A financial calculator
- A graphical toolbar with the most frequent functions
- Fully interactive reports and graphs

247

- Automatic and memorized transactions
- A suite of automatically updated reports and graphs
- Investment support for stocks, mutual funds, and securities
- International currency and date support
- Printer support, including fonts and margins

Money Smith is a lot of financial software that won't cost you a lot of money.

How

FTP

Where

www.nmia.com/pub/monsmith

Download

smith95.zip (343 K)

Medlin in Other Peoples' Business

Medlin Accounting Software ☆☆☆

Simple but functional, these highly-regarded shareware accounting programs are useful for small businesses. Medlin offers a suite of DOS accounting software (GL, A/P, A/R, payroll, and invoicing), and a second family of products for Windows (GL, A/P, and payroll). A Windows A/R program is due in 1996.

How

World Wide Web

Where

community.net/~medlinsw

Better Than a Magic Eight Ball

Computerized Accounting Analysis ☆☆☆

Looking to buy accounting software? This online database looks at the specific needs of your business and makes recommendations based on feedback from thousands of accounting software users. Kinda like *Consumer Reports* for accountants, only it's on the Web.

Expect to spend about twenty minutes filling in the lengthy online questionnaire. (By itself, filling out the questionnaire helps your software search, because as you fill it out, it walks you through an analysis of your needs.) When you are done, the Web site will find software that matches your criteria and return its findings to you. Of course, if you don't like computers, you could always use the Magic Eight Ball (**found.cs.nyu.edu/downing/eightball.html**) to help you decide.

How

World Wide Web

Where

www.accounting.org/acctques.html

So Who Pays for This Web Site, Anyways?

ATechno-L Accounting and Technology Investments ☆☆☆

How do you handle the special accounting needs of technology? This new low-volume, moderated email discussion group covers this topic. Sometimes subscribers drift into how to *apply* technology rather than how to *account* for it. An archive of past messages is available at:

www.scu.edu.au/anet/lists/atechno-l/index.html

Sample topics: Other accounting for technology sites; Integrated IS Chargeback Systems; Electronic commerce and accounting firms; Will Internet help for accounting business?; Transfer Pricing audit.

FREE *Business* $TUFF *from the Internet*

How
Email

Where
listproc@scu.edu.au

Message
Help me

Trying to Find a Diamond in all the Dirt:

name = "David Hardidge"
email = "dahardidge@dttus.com"
subject = "Re: Will Internet help for accounting business?"
inreplyto = "Will Internet help for accounting business?"

As a relative newcomer to the Internet, I am still coming to grips with how big it is. Not just in terms of the number of people, but the resources behind it. Also, coming from commerce, I have not received the same degree of use, or support that our academic friends have had. For me, most of the learning is teaching myself.

Although I work in a large accounting firm, I do work in a small department of 5 people. I have found it easier to explain the Internet as a series of services, rather than one big black box. I think the following will benefit small and large firms:

- Electronic mail—Which expands your current internal communications to outside your organization, including clients and customers, suppliers, and associates. People now put their email addresses on business cards.
- Mailing lists—For example, the ANet lists (of which this is one). Also, refer to Jim Kaplan's AuditNet Resource List.
- World Wide Web—Currently appears in the media more as recreational than business, for example "Cool sites to visit." A few businesses, including accounting firms (e.g. Deloitte) have Web pages, it is still experimental, and a bit of putting up the flag to ensure we are not missed.

Still a few problems with commerce and buying and selling over the Web, but a number of secure systems are starting to appear.

I think the research use of the Web will dramatically increase, and become the future standard research tool. Just as we have moved primarily from paper, to on-line services like Dialog, and I think in the future to the Internet (World Wide Web).

There are definitely weaknesses in determining the quality of material on the Web (like trying to find a diamond in all the dirt). There are also problems with trying to locate the desired information, but search engines and robots are starting to appear, such as Lycos, Webcrawler, and BabyOil.

Today, certainly there are limitations, but I am looking to the future. With the continued growth, well actually, exponential growth, a "critical mass" will soon arrive.

We only have to see how fax machines, personal computers, and mobile phones have come out of nowhere to be an integral part of business. Anybody else have any thoughts?

David Hardidge
David_Hardidge_at_DTT.AU.MELBOURNE@dttus.com
or dhardidge@acslink.net.au
www.deloitte.com.au
www.dttus.com

National Accounting and Auditing Phone: + 61 3 9208 7293
Deloitte Touche Tohmatsu Fax: + 61 3 9208 7001
505 Bourke St
Melbourne, 3000
Australia

How Smart Is Your Software?

AIntSys-L Intelligent and Expert Systems Email Group ☆☆☆

For those extremely computer-literate souls among us who can tell the difference between artificial intelligence and the real thing, here's a worldwide discussion-and-announcements email group. The quantity of messages is low, and most are announcements of conferences, but there is some interesting Q&A in this American Accounting Association group. It is moderated and spam-free. If you're research-inclined, you'll find an archive of past messages is available at:

www.scu.edu.au/anet/lists/aintsys-l/index.html

Sample topics: Object-oriented AI; PAAM Conference; International Meeting on AI in Accounting; Finance and Taxation; Call for Papers on Electronic Commerce; measurement of use; accounting information classification.

How

Email

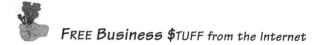
Where

listproc@scu.edu.au

Message

Help me

Accountants and the Net: the True Scoop

CPA-INET-USE Email Discussion Group ☆☆☆☆

In spite of its name, this discussion group is not just for CPAs. However, it is restricted to accounting and tax professionals only. If you are an accounting pro who wants to get the most out of the Internet, this may turn out to be one of the most valuable resources you come across. Discussions here cover every way possible that accountants use the Internet, whether for internal administrative communications or for external client service. People in this group gained insight from actual hands-on experience, and you can leverage their know-how. The group is moderated, so there is no spam. Most subscribers are based in the U.S. You will use email to take part in discussions, but you need World Wide Web access to subscribe.

How

World Wide Web

Where

www.kentis.com/sublist.html

This BULLETIN Just In

INTERNET BULLETIN FOR CPAs ☆☆☆☆

With all the electronic newsletters this book talks about, delivered by email or the World Wide Web, you may say, "Hey! Doesn't anyone *print* anything anymore?" Of course they do. Take the *Internet Bulletin for CPAs*, for example. It is nicely printed and slickly-designed, and it explains how accountants (all accountants, not just CPAs) can use the Internet.

Each issue contains clear instructions on how to use Internet resources, reviews of new Internet software, reviews of new Internet accounting resources, and articles on how to apply the Net in your day-to-day accounting operations. I find this newsletter a valuable tool. It costs $105 a year, but you can get a free sample issue delivered to you by a mailcarrier (remember them?). This site

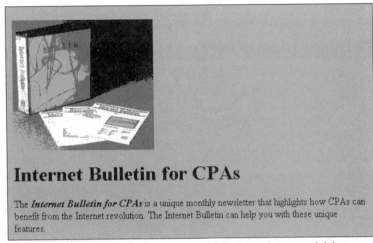

Internet Bulletin for CPAs

The *Internet Bulletin for CPAs* is a unique monthly newsletter that highlights how CPAs can benefit from the Internet revolution. The Internet Bulletin can help you with these unique features.

Get a free copy of this slickly-designed-printed newsletter explaining the Net for accountants.

also has back issues, but the Web-ized back issues aren't complete; they have only tables of contents and a couple of sample stories.

How
World Wide Web

Where
For a free sample copy: www.kentis.com/order.html

To read Web-ized back issues: www.kentis.com/archive/pastib.html

Web Magazines Have No Centerfolds

CAMAGAZINE ☆☆☆☆

You won't find all of this monthly magazine for accountants on the Web, but you will find one major article from each issue (on topics of interest to accountants in every country, such as a good overview of computer fraud), plus a large selection of shorter news items of interest mostly to Canadians. That's only natural, since *CAmagazine* is published by the Canadian Institute of Chartered Accountants. New issues are added at midmonth. You can choose to read in English or en Française.

How
World Wide Web

Where
www.cica.ca/camag/issues/e_issues.htm

FREE Business $TUFF from the Internet

READER'S DIGEST for Accountants

DOUBLE ENTRIES Newsletter ☆☆☆☆

If you want to know what's going on with all the major accounting journals but you don't have time to read them all, read *Double Entries* instead. This short, chatty weekly newsletter gives good coverage of accounting news all over the English-speaking world, especially in the U.K., U.S., Australia, and Canada.

You'll find out about tax changes, new laws, new Internet resources, FASB standards, and summaries of important stories in other journals. Think of it as an electronic *Reader's Digest* for accountants. If you'd like to look at past issues, you'll find a handy archive on the Web at:

www.scu.edu.au/anet/lists/adble-l/index.html

How

Email

Where

listproc@scu.edu.au

Message

Subscribe ADble-L Yourfirstname Yourlastname

You can also subscribe on the World Wide Web, at:

anet.scu.edu.au/anet/lists/adble-l

Observations of Interest

THE MARKET OBSERVER ☆☆☆

This weekly newsletter serves credit union managers, but can also be useful for other financial pros. It covers bond markets, investment, and deposit regulations. Each issue also has brief, to-the-point coverage of interest rate changes and the factors that affect them.

How

World Wide Web

Where

www.lsfu.org/~lai/mobserve/thisweek.htm

More News for Credit Unions

CREDIT UNION TECH-TALK ☆☆☆

This newsletter reports monthly on hardware, software, and technology vendors that serve credit unions. *Credit Union Tech-Talk* is written in a friendly, chatty style, with articles on new products, computer anxiety, and the management skills you need to implement technology. It pays particular attention to home banking. You can read the current issue on the Web, or subscribe and get two issues delivered free.

How

World Wide Web

Where

Current issue: www.icon-stl.net/jsweeney/cu/wra/cuttci.html

Free subscription: www.icon-stl.net/jsweeney/cu/wra/subscribe.html

C.U. Real Soon

Credit Union Land ☆☆☆☆

If you manage a credit union, if you are a customer at a credit union, or if you are considering adding credit union benefits to your employees, this is the place to go. It's the Web center of the credit union universe. Resources include a searchable index of:

Some of the graphics files for Web pages that you can copy from Credit Union Land.

- C.U.s, links to C.U. Web pages
- Email addresses of C.U.s
- Text of applicable federal and state regulations
- Text of NCUA letters
- A mailing list for internal auditors of credit unions
- Industry conferences

There are active job opportunity pages, including a page where you can post any C.U. job openings you may have, and another where you can view job offers—including some for high-caliber positions. You'll also find an online Statement of Financial Accounting Standards #107 (SFAS 107) calculator. Finally, there is a library of .gif graphics files you can copy and put on your Web page.

How
> World Wide Web

Where
> www.culand.com

Willie Sutton's Favorite Web Site

Banking on the WWW ☆☆☆☆☆

Except for Dickens' Dombey & Son, this site seems to have links to every bank on the Net, plus every site for bankers, a lot of resources, and information useful for people in other businesses. In spite of its name, Banking on the WWW includes both Web and non-Web resources. Presented by the Institute of Finance and Banking at the University of Gottingen, most information here is available in your choice of English or German. Things here change often. On my last visit, I found sections named:

- **Guides**—banking directories and resources, most with helpful descriptions
- **Banks of the World**—listed by country; also cyberbanks, investment banks, and offshore banks
- **Supervising and Deposit Insurance**—links to FDIC, recent and historical statistics on U.S. banking, Federal Reserve banks, Federal Reserve Board, banking and bankruptcy
- **Academic Research on Banking**—institutions, seminars, and conferences
- **Banking and Finance in Electronic Media**—links to free and pay-for electronic newsletters. Watch out here, some links are to sites (Wong's Email Quoter, NASDAQ Financial Executive Journal, and Investment Insight) that have been long dead, some for more than a year.
- **Law and Banking**—links to German and U.S. banking laws and German Internet laws
- **Currency Page**—a very good guide to all sites on the Web dealing with currency or exchange rates
- **Finance Page**—some links to resources, but not as rich as other finance sites
- **Money Page**—a good selection of links and information to resources dealing with money and payment systems, including digital money and electronic commerce
- **Miscellaneous**—a very good selection of links with short, clear descriptions, covering a wide range of Net resources

How

World Wide Web

Where

www.wiso.gwdg.de/ifbg/banking.html

Extra, Extra, Read all about It

BANKING & FINANCE IT INFORMER ☆☆☆

This newsletter covers information technology for banking and finance operations, delivering news stories and analyses to your desk every day. A subscription normally costs £200 (or $300) per year, but you can register here and get a free trial subscription that lasts until the end of the month. (Subscribe early in the month so your free sample lasts longer.) The Web site also gives you three or four sample stories.

How

World Wide Web

Where

www.heyway.net/mmp/banking

All the News That's Fit to Account For

ANews-L Email Announcement List ☆☆☆

This "news-only channel" for accountants is run by the folks at Anet. If you subscribe, you will receive a low quantity of good email news messages. Announcements cover new accounting resources on the Internet, conferences, and previews of journal articles. An archive of past messages is available at:

www.scu.edu.au/anet/lists/anews-l/index.html

Sample topics: Australian Accounting Review articles on the Web; ASCPA Australian Accountant articles on the Web; CCH on the Web; New on FinanceNet in November; 8th Annual Conference of Accounting Academics; Call for Papers: 14th International Association of Management Conference; European Business Ethics Conference; Conference on Technological Assaults on Privacy.

How

Email

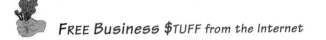 *FREE Business $TUFF from the Internet*

Where

listproc@scu.edu.au

Message

Help me

Where to Find Money

Commercial Finance Online ☆☆☆☆

Looking for money for your business? At this site you'll find a database of commercial banks, investment banks, financial consultants, and venture capitalists.

But wait, there's more! If you need financing, you can list your business finance solicitation or proposal in a searchable database. It's free! This is a great idea, but the search tool available for potential investors is extremely limited. Still, it's an easy, low-cost way for you to tap sources of funding.

But wait, there's still more! This site also offers eight email discussion groups on professional finance topics. All groups except **Asset-Based Lenders** are open to everyone. Discussions are delivered by email, but you need to visit this Web site to subscribe:

- **Factoring**—People who subscribe to this group discuss A/R and invoice factoring and working capital solutions
- **Leasing**—This discussion group covers leasing and lease transactions
- **Investors**—Subscribers discuss making investments in business finance, commercial real estate, stocks, options, and buying and selling businesses
- **Imex**—This group covers import/export financing, letters of credit, and related topics
- **Mergers**—The heavyweight topic here is financing mergers, acquisitions, and leveraged buyouts
- **Venture**—The subscribers to this group discuss venture capitalists, equity transactions, and angles, from both sides of the fence: looking for investors and investments
- **Trade**—Read postings of trade and business opportunities: local, national, or international
- **Asset-Based Lenders**—This discussion group is open only to people who work for asset-based lenders (banks, finance companies, factors, lessors, and so on). Participants discuss business development, credit analysis, collateral examinations, workouts, and related topics from the lender's point of view.

258

Commercial Finance Online also includes a searchable education database But each time I have visited this database, I have never been able to get it to work.

How

World Wide Web

Where

www.cfonline.com

If you want to go directly to the subscription page, visit it at: **www.cfonline.com/cgi-win/cfonline.exe/getlists**

Except Asset-Based Lenders, which has a sign-up page of its own at: **www.cfonline.com/ablform.htm**

You Mean It's Not about Fort Knox?

FinanceNet ☆☆☆

Vice President Al Gore is responsible for this information-packed site. The main attraction is a library of government financial statements and plans, from the U.S., Canadian, U.K., New Zealand, and Australian governments.

You'll also find an Electronic Commerce Page, with information on electronic commerce, electronic purchasing, and EDI resources. There are more than 20 email discussion groups covering different aspects of national, regional, and local government finance and accounting: procurement, payroll, and so on. This site addresses the needs of government financial managers.

It is a good site with lots of easy-to-find information, but it's mostly for government. There is little here for business. An exception is a list of government asset sales, which may lead to bargains for some companies.

How

World Wide Web

Where

www.financenet.gov

If You Do It the Company Way, Part I

MGMT-ACCT Email Discussion Group ☆☆☆

People on this moderated email discussion group discuss management accounting. Subscribers (tax and accounting professionals only) work within companies, almost all within the U.S. The moderator ensures that subscribers are qualified and that the list is spam-free.

Discussions focus mostly on cutting costs and increasing efficiency, but questions, answers, and tips cover other areas as well, such as employee benefits, administrative communications, and reducing order fulfillment lead times. You will use email to take part in discussions, but you must have World Wide Web access to subscribe.

How

World Wide Web

Where

www.kentis.com/sublist.html

If You Do It the Company Way, Part II

AMgtAcc-L Management Accounting Email Group ☆☆☆

On this email discussion group, people from all around the world ask questions and give answers about management accounting. Like the group above, it is moderated and there is no spam here. The volume of messages is low. Most messages are questions and answers, with some announcements and some job openings. For a sneak preview of this discussion group, visit its archive of past messages at:

www.scu.edu.au/anet/lists/amgtacc-l/index.html

Sample topics: Seeking ABM & EVA for financial institution; Decentralization and Management Accounting Systems; Accounting Manuals; Sales returns; Just-in-time; Financial Management Data; CFO position opening; Throughput accounting; Structuration Theory in Management Accounting.

How

Email

Where

listproc@scu.edu.au

Message

Help me

As the World Turns: the Accounting Version

AA-STDS-APP Email Discussion Group ☆☆☆☆

If you'd like to discuss your actual accounting and auditing problems with pros from other companies (and hear their horror stories), but want to remain anonymous, subscribe to this email discussion group. Subscribers hash out real accounting and auditing problems in real companies, with the caveat that the real names of the companies are never, ever used. This is a moderated group, so there is no spam, and you must be an accounting or auditing professional (not a student) to subscribe. You will use email to take part in discussions, but you need World Wide Web access to subscribe.

How

World Wide Web

Where

www.kentis.com/sublist.html

Off the Balance Sheet and On

AFinAcc-L Financial Accounting Email Discussion Group ☆☆☆☆

Subscribers around the world report news, ask questions, and give answers about financial accounting topics. Occasionally, job openings are posted. This is a moderated, spam-free email discussion group. An archive of past messages is available at:

www.scu.edu.au/anet/lists/afinacc-l/index.html

Sample topics: Capitalized interest; Accounting for Acquisitions—Deferred Settlement of Cash; Goodwill for Mining Companies in the U.S.; bar coding; Information—Is it an asset?; German references on stockholder value; Major Upgrade of Aust. Auditing Standards; Accounting Standards in Electronic Format; The Elliot Wave Principle; Off Balance Sheet Debt; Use of Fixed Assets That Have Been Fully Depreciated; Finance Team for Enterprise Restructuring Project—Kazakhstan; Accrual Accounting Statements.

How

Email

Where

listproc@scu.edu.au

Message

Help me

Information—Is It an Asset?

subject = "Re: Information—Is it an asset? (fwd)"
Sender: earl@eskimo.com (Earl Hall)
Subject: Re: Information—Is it an asset?

Andrew Priest [a.priest@cowan.edu.au] wrote in email which I could not tell if it was also posted to the list, but I felt it was worthy of discussion on the list. (I apologize to Andrew if the message was indeed intended for private discussion as I consider it a breach of netiquette to take private email public.)

> In Australia we "ignore" internally generated goodwill! However, given
> that the Australian Taxation Office [ATO] treats this "information" as an asset
> for Capital Gains Tax purposes and that there appears to be some sort of
> market for it, it would appear to be another form of asset and therefore
> should be capitalised, assuming a reasonable probability of future economic
> returns.
>
> Comments?

U. S. taxing authorities recognize internally generated goodwill as an asset on its sale and allow capital gains taxation. With multi-divisional corporations selling divisions almost as a routine business practice, the sale of goodwill is not that unusual.

Market Value Added accounting techniques are able to quantify these "assets." Therefore, there is the existence of something providing a reasonable probability of future economic returns which is reasonably subject to valuation and recognized by taxing authorities as a capital asset, but is ignored for financial accounting.

Similarly, service businesses develop customer lists which have market value, are reasonably subject to valuation and have a reasonable probability of future economic returns, yet these assets are also ignored for financial accounting.

As a practicing CPA, I value my client list on an annual basis because I perceive it as an asset that has value and this information is helpful to know for making decisions as to practice continuation and other matters. Similarly, I have internally developed information in various forms that would have different values if marketed differently and I evaluate that at least annually as part of my internal practice review. I encourage clients to make the same review of off-balance sheet assets because it helps their business make effective use of all of their resources, not just those recognized for financial accounting purposes.

However, knowing and using something as a financial resource and having that financial resource recognized for financial accounting purposes are two different things. There is a widespread suspicion of financial statements that include nontangible assets even if those statements provide a truer picture of an entity's position.

Until this widespread suspicion is overcome, I think that accounting standards setters are probably correct in not recognizing internally generated goodwill in whatever form it comes (goodwill, customer lists, information, technology, human resources, asset appreciation, and so on).

= Earl =

From the Yakima of Washington—Upwind of Radioactive Emissions
earl@eskimo.com—Downwind of Volcanic Emissions
check out www.wolfenet.com/ ~ earl/index.html

This Discussion Group Is a Gas!

AOilAcc-L Extractive Industries Email Discussion Group ☆☆

This highly specialized email discussion group provides a way for accountants in the oil and gas industry (and occasionally, in the mining industry) to swap questions and information with their counterparts around the world. Compared to other accounting email groups, this one generates only a tiny number of messages to and from a small number of subscribers, but those subscribers are intensely interested. This group is moderated, so there is no spam. You can drill for an archive of past messages at:

www.scu.edu.au/anet/lists/aoilacc-l/index.html

Sample topics: Oil and Gas Finance and Accounting; Inquiries about the petroleum industry; Conference and new journal; Petroleum accounting; Pre-production expenditure; Mining accounting and extractive metallurgy; Environmental accounting; Exxon Valdez.

How
Email

Where
listproc@scu.edu.au

Message
Help me

Free Business $TUFF from the Internet

Treasure for Treasurers

Treasury Connection Discussion Group ☆☆☆☆

If you're a treasury management pro, check out this discussion group on global treasury management. As a subscriber, you can post questions, answers, and comments by email. Every Friday, you'll receive a digest of all messages sent by subscribers over the past week, moderated and spam-free.

Sample topics: ACH; CMOs; Mexican Peso exposure; New Tools in Treasury Management; Prompt Payment Act of 1995; Same day funds settlements; Treasury Workstations; Wholesale lockboxes and A/R outsourcing; Yield Curve opportunities.

You can subscribe either by email or on the World Wide Web, but either way you'll receive messages by email. Only subscribers can participate in "Treasury Connection Live," the monthly live online chats with guest treasury experts. You'll receive information on "Treasury Connection Live" when you subscribe to the email discussion group.

How

World Wide Web

Where

www.nationsbank.com/ccm/connect.htm

(or)

majordomo@www.nationsbank.com

Message

Subscribe treasury connection

There is also a Treasury Connection FAQ on the Web at: **www.nationsbank.com/ccm/faq.htm**.

If you want a preview of what you'll receive, visit the group's archive at: **www.nationsbank.com/ccm/archive.htm**.

News and New Web Sites

Harcourt Brace Professional Publishing ☆☆☆

You'll find two attractions at this site. *CPA's Weekly News Update* is a free newsletter published every Monday. It has 6 or more articles covering taxation, accounting, and finance, plus industry-specific stories on topics such as accounting for construction companies. This newsletter is not delivered. You must visit the Web site to read it. You can also browse an archive of past issues.

The second attraction awards the "Top 5 Accounting Web Sites of the Week." Every week, you'll find five new (or almost new) sites by and/or for accountants. There is an archive of Top 5 Sites from past weeks. This is a good way to find useful new resources, but it gives absolutely no descriptions of the winners, just their names. Why did they win? I haven't a clue. Descriptions or comments about winners would add significant value to this site. Even so, this is still a good way to learn what's hot.

How

World Wide Web

Where

www.hbpp.com

Accountants Are the Conscience of Business

AEthics-L Accounting Ethics Discussion Group ☆☆☆

This low-volume email group mostly delivers papers and conference announcements on the subject of Accounting Ethics, but you'll also read some interesting questions and their answers. This is a moderated and spamless group. An archive of past messages is available at:

www.scu.edu.au/anet/lists/aethics-l/index.html

Sample topics: Ethics among Accounting Academics; First World Congress of Business, Economics and Ethics; Auditors & Ethics; AETHICS-L Digest; Insider Trading and the External Auditor.

How

Email

Where

listproc@scu.edu.au

Message

Help me

Auditors Have Questions, We Have Answers

AAudit-L Auditing Discussion Group ☆☆☆

If you've got questions about external or internal audit, this is a good place to get answers. Most of the messages on this medium-volume discussion group are questions and well-informed answers from all over the world. You'll also read conference announcements, some job opportunities, and a few reviews of new books. To perform due diligence before subscribing, audit the archive of past messages at:

www.scu.edu.au/anet/lists/aaudit-l/index.html

Sample topics: Excess & Obsolete Inventory; Job Opportunities in Internal Audit; Add value and performance measures; Cycle Counting Policy and Procedure; IASB Exposure Draft; Collection Agency Review; Need help with EDI question; Public reporting on internal control; Material Inventory Assessments.

How
Email

Where
listproc@scu.edu.au

Message
Help me

A New Internal Audit Broom Sweeps Clean

Columbia University Internal Audit Site ☆☆☆

The internal audit information presented here is intended for Columbia's own departments, but it may be useful for your business. If you have an internal audit staff, they can copy the documents here and modify them for use on your own Intranet. First, there's a questionnaire you can fill out to see how thorough your own internal controls are. Questions have hot links to related topics in the *Guide to Internal Controls*. Columbia's *Guide* is a good starting point to build your own. Especially valuable is Appendix IV, a checklist of crucial internal controls.

How
World Wide Web

Where
www.columbia.edu/cu/ia/index.html

A Book for Auditors

ACTIVITY BASED RISK EVALUATION MODEL OF AUDITING (ABREMA) ☆☆☆

If you audit financial statements, check out this small (more than 100 pages of text) but dense online book. You'll need a background in financial statement auditing to understand and use *ABREMA*, but its information is split into "novice," "intermediate," and "advanced," which makes it easier to comprehend. It is mostly useful in independent auditing of corporate financial statements, and helps auditors concentrate on the activities that are most likely to jeopardize the financial health of a company. Barings' auditors should have read this.

How

World Wide Web

Where

www.efs.mq.edu.au/accg/resources/abrema/index.html

A Neighborhood Pub for Auditors

alt.business.internal-audit Newsgroup ☆☆☆

This helpful newsgroup gets questions and answers from auditors around the world. About 40 percent of the messages are spam, and less than 5 percent are emotional rants. This leaves 55 percent of the messages as good stuff, including a few job opportunities.

Sample topics: Are you in a new Client Server environment?; Audit Seminar Advice; Auditing and Security; Computer Auditor Vacancy; Evaluating Internal Control; Fraud prevention; Help with Encryption Audit; Internal controls for charitable fund-raisers; NAFTA audits of origin.

How

Newsgroup

Where

alt.business.internal-audit

Shhhh—Info System Auditors at Work

INFSEC-L Information Security Discussion Group ☆☆☆

This is a tough email discussion group to join. It's for information security and auditing pros. Prospective subscribers are screened, so only qualified professionals get in. If you audit information systems, check this out. Otherwise, take a powder.

How

Email

Where

listserv@etsuadmn.etsu.edu

Message

SUB-INFSEC-L Yourfirstname Yourlastname

Jobs for Accountants Who've Already Had One

JOBS-ACT Job-finding Email List ☆☆☆☆

Unlike most Internet job-finding services, this one is only for the experienced. It is restricted to seasoned pros in taxation, auditing, accounting, finance, and cash management. It is *not* for students. This spam-free list is moderated, and applicants are screened. Subscribers receive job openings by email. Most (but not all) of the openings listed here are in the U.S. Personnel managers looking for experienced candidates can email to the address below.

To find out about an archive of past job openings, email to the same address below, but with the message: ARCHIVE JOBS-ACT

How

Email

Where

jobs-act@execon.metronet.com

Message

SUBSCRIBE
(Do *not* include your name.)

Testing, Testing...

Accounting Institute Seminars ☆☆☆

Of interest only to U.S. CPA candidates, this site presents computer form answers to the questions on recent CPA exams, instructions on how to take CPA exams, where to apply in each state, and a sample of how AI seminar workbooks teach an issue. This is the only spot I found on the Web that gives instructions on how to apply for a U.S. CPA certificate if you are a foreign citizen.

How

World Wide Web

Where

www.ais-cpa.com

For Students Only

AStdnt-L Accounting Students Discussion Group ☆☆☆

Okay, so some accounting groups say, "Hey, no students!" This email discussions-and-announcements group says, "Yo! Students only!" It provides direct accounting-student-to-accounting-student contact around the world. The low volume of messages is unmoderated, so you can say anything you want, but somehow the spam level stays way low. (It is almost nonexistent.) You can ask questions, get answers to questions, and read announcements like interviews and job openings. If you're into ancient history, dig into the old messages archive (Cough! Cough! Excuse me, virtual dust.) at:

www.scu.edu.au/anet/lists/astdnt-l/index.html

Sample topics: Dollars for doctoral students; ASCPA Survey on Graduate IT Skills; Graduate recruitment—Coopers and Lybrand UK; Graduating Seniors and Interviews; Asset Revaluations; One-Person "Meetings"; accounting question; Accounting Majors; Please help!

How

Email

Where

listproc@scu.edu.au

Message

Help me

Credit Where Credit Is Due

misc.business.credit Discussion Newsgroup ☆☆☆☆

This discussion newsgroup was started in October of 1995 to discuss credit issues affecting businesses. It generates a medium quantity of messages, and miraculously so far has no spam, no rant, and lots of good information from all over the world. If your job involves accounts receivable or granting or getting credit, this is a valuable resource for you. It is especially valuable if your company does business internationally.

Sample topics: Preferences under sec. 547; Aging of receivables; Business & Individual Background Reports; Credit Repair Agencies in Britain; Collectability of Commercial Accounts; Export Insurance; Purchase Orders with different terms; Filing complaints against collection agencies; How does offering prepayment up front work for you?; International collection; Need info on Brazil.

How

Newsgroup

Where

Misc.business.credit

A Credit Manager's Delight

Credit Management Information and Support ☆☆☆☆☆

Here's a rich gathering of information and links to other sources on every aspect of credit management: bankruptcy, business credit, credit reporting agencies, economic information, financial statement analysis, international business credit, Internet industry credit groups, legal information.

Go here for these credit-related email discussion groups:

- **BANKRLAW**—Bankruptcy law
- **CLLA**—Commercial Law League of America, dealing with business bankruptcy and commercial collections
- **CREDIT-MGMT-L**—U.S. and international business credit
- **PETITIONS**—High-profile bankruptcy cases
- **LNET-LLC**—Limited liability companies
- **ROUNDTABLE**—Case-specific discussions of bankruptcy
- **TWN**—An announcement list with bankruptcy news, public notices, and liquidations

Much information on this site is available nowhere else on the Internet. Check out *Bankruptcy Story*, a short, fictional (but true-to-life) story showing bankruptcy from an attorney's point of view. You'll find no flashy graphics here. In fact, you'll find no graphics at all, just tons of useful, well-organized information. The only flaw is that most of this site's links give names only and lack descriptions. Even so, this site is worth a lengthy visit if you work in any of the topics it covers.

How

World Wide Web

Where

www.teleport.com/~richh

Going Down for the Third Time

Internet Bankruptcy Library ☆☆☆☆

The Internet Bankruptcy Library is a very good site if you're involved in bankruptcy, or if you have debtors who are in bankruptcy. It also has useful information for investors about companies going into and out of bankruptcy proceedings. You'll find directories here of conferences, publications, and people in this field, plus lists of public companies in Chapter 11, info on stocks and bonds of companies in bankruptcy, post-reorganization stocks, and current Chapter 11 petitions.

Subscription information is available here on several email discussion groups: BANKRLAW, ROUNDTABLE, CLLA, AIA (see below), STATE, and IWIRC. There are also links to other bankruptcy resources on the Internet from around the world, but mostly in the U.S., Canada, and Russia.

How

World Wide Web

Where

bankrupt.com

Not Jane Fonda's Kind of Workout

TURNAROUNDS & WORKOUTS NEWSWIRE Newsletter ☆☆☆☆

If you're a professional or an investor involved in bankruptcy, insolvency, or reorganizing companies in trouble, get your free subscription to the electronic version of the print newsletter *Turnarounds & Workouts*. This is a supplement to the print version, not a replacement. But it has enough information to be worthwhile on its own.

How

Email

Where

listserve@bankrupt.com

Message

subscribe twn youremail@address

For a list of Frequently Asked Questions about *T&W Newswire*, look on the World Wide Web at:

bankrupt.com/tw.faq.html

If you'd like to look through past issues, go to:

ftp://bankrupt.com/TWN_Archive

I Have No Money, and I Must Count

Association of Insolvency Accountants Group ☆☆☆

This email discussion group is for members of AIA and for nonmembers who are professionals dealing with insolvency. You'll find a medium volume of messages, with some organizational chatter, some good questions and answers, and conference announcements. It is open (anyone can subscribe) and unmoderated.

How

Email

Where

listserve@bankrupt.com

Message

Subscribe aia youremail@address

Where to Find More Accounting and Finance Stuff

I feel like the master of the orphanage in *Oliver Twist*: "What?!! You want *more*?"

If this chapter doesn't make you cry "Enough, already!" just turn to the chapter on *Tax Reduction*. Most resources in that chapter have something to do with accounting and/or finance.

If you're looking specifically for finance resources, turn the pages to the chapter on *More Profitable Investing*. Other finance resources are more suited for startups and entrepreneurs and are included in *Entrepreneurs, Startups and Home Businesses*. Some of the resources in the economists' chapter are kinda finance-related. But that may be stretching things.

There's some international miscellany in the chapter on *Doing Business Internationally*.

If you're looking for IWIRC, the Women's Insolvency & Restructuring Confederation, you'll find it in our *Businesswomen* chapter, along with information on women- and minority-owned banks in the Minority Bank Monitor.

If you still want more, you have three alternatives:

1. Many of the Web sites in this chapter (especially KARL, Anet, and Credit Management Information and Support) are directories that will point you towards hundreds of other resources.
2. Check the index to this book, especially under **accounting resources**, **credit management**, and **financial institutions**.
3. Our chapter on *How to Find Business Stuff on the Internet* can help you find what you want among the tens of thousands of Net resources out there, especially if you are looking for one specific site.

Happy hunting!

FREE $TUFF

The hardest thing in the
world to understand is
the income tax.

Albert Einstein

Tax Reduction

As the saying goes, there are only two things in life we can be sure of: death and taxes. Unfortunately, they don't come in that order.

Help is available from many Internet sites that deal with taxation. Most sites discuss personal income taxes and ignore the avalanche of business income and other taxes that overwhelm your company. Many tax sites are just advertising billboards for tax practitioners. I don't consider "Hi, I do taxes. Hire me." to be a helpful resource.

Even sites run by government tax agencies offer limited information. Some, like the U.K.'s Inland Revenue, seem more interested in making money by selling print publications than in telling you what regulations your business must follow.

Fortunately, a small quantity of truly valuable Internet tax resources do address business needs. Some address the needs of professional tax practitioners. Others are useful for small businesses and entrepreneurs. The good sites listed here provide solid information and will let you know when new additions pop up on the Net.

All the Income Tax That Fits

TaxSites ☆☆☆☆

This site's goal is to list *all* income tax resources on the Net, worldwide. It is an impressive site, with dozens of valuable resources for tax professionals. (Because this site lists *everything*, there is chaff among the wheat.) TaxSites has a built-in search engine, so you can pinpoint specific information without browsing through the whole site. If you browse, the short, clear descriptions of most resources will help you find what you want. Look at the bottom of the home page for a list of important new additions.

How

World Wide Web

Where

www.best.com/~ftmexpat/html/taxsites.html

It's a Small World after All

Tax World ☆☆☆☆

This site's name sounds like an amusement park that I *don't* want to visit. Imagine a park named Witholding Land or a ride called the Tax Forms from Hell. Actually, what you'll find at Tax World is tax information from around the planet. Skip "Downloadable Files." They are mostly uninteresting, old university course material. But check out "Tax Information Sites." The good stuff is here: a tax tools index, city tax resources, state tax resources, U.S. federal tax Net sites, legislative tax resources, and a good section called "International Tax Resources."

How

World Wide Web

Where

omer.cba.neu.edu/home

Tax News from the Web

Tax Analysts ☆☆☆

Tax Analysts is a nonprofit organization that spreads information to tax practitioners, mostly about U.S. taxes. Their Web pages tell how to order publications and databases, and offer two resources for tax professionals.

The first site, *Tax Calendar*, lists government events such as hearings, meetings, seminars, and conferences on taxation. It's useful, but not as complete as it could be. The second resource, *Tax Notes NewsWire*, is updated three times every workday with the latest tax news. If you're biting your nails in suspense about the outcome of a tax hearing or a new government ruling, *Tax Notes NewsWire* could relieve your tension and your damaged cuticles.

How

World Wide Web

Where

www.tax.org

If you'd like to go directly to *Tax Notes NewsWire*, the site you want is at:

www.tax.org/news.htm

The IRS Loses, from TAX NOTES NEWSWIRE

QUERY: Please check out the first story and let me know if you have any strong feelings about this one way or the other. It's one of the few times (if any) in which the Service has lost its seemingly aggressive bid to include as much it can into the category of inventory — at least according to some observers. What do you think?

Computer Manufacturer's Spare-Parts Pool Was Capital Asset, Not Inventory As Urged By IRS.

The Federal Circuit, reversing the Court of Federal Claims, has held that a computer manufacturer properly treated its pool of spare parts as a capital asset, rejecting the Service's determination that the parts constituted inventory.

Apollo Computer Inc., which was succeeded by Hewlett-Packard Co., manufactured and sold computers and computer equipment. Apollo also operated a repair business under several arrangements, including warranties on the computers that it sold to customers. For this repair business, Apollo maintained a pool of "rotable" spare parts—parts that were substituted for original, malfunctioning parts. The malfunctioning parts were usually repairable, so Apollo would repair those parts and place them in the spare-parts pool.

On its tax returns for the years 1983 through 1985, Apollo treated the pool of rotable spare parts as a capital asset, and claimed depreciation and investment tax credits. The IRS disallowed the deductions and credits, asserting that Apollo was required to treat the parts as inventory. The Court of Federal Claims agreed with the IRS, finding that Apollo's repair business was a mix of service and merchandising, and that the rotable spare parts were held for sale to customers in the course of that repair business. (For a summary, see *Tax Notes*, Dec. 19, 1994, p. 1507; for the full text, see 94 *TNT* 243- 5, or *H&D*, Dec. 13, 1994, p. 3131.) Hewlett-Packard filed this appeal.

Senior Circuit Judge Daniel M. Friedman rejected the lower court's finding that Apollo sold its rotable spare parts to customers, concluding that Apollo merely used the parts "to enable it to provide better service, i.e., to avoid the additional computer downtime that the customer would suffer if the malfunctioning part were merely repaired." Further, the court concluded that Apollo's customers did not pay for the replacement parts, but, rather, that Apollo simply factored the depreciation costs of maintaining the spare-parts pool into the total costs of providing the repair service. Judge Friedman cited Honeywell Inc. v. Commissioner, T.C. Memo. 1992-453, 92 *TNT* 164-25, aff'd, 27 F.3d 571, 94 *TNT* 135-16 (8th Cir. 1994), which involved similar facts.

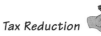

Moreover, the appeals court pointed out that "both Apollo and its customers had the same item before and after the replacement." Thus, the customer did not receive any tangible item that it did not have before the exchange of parts, and Apollo's pool of parts was not reduced (unless a malfunctioning part could not be repaired).

The appeals court also was not persuaded by the lower court's, and the government's, emphasis on the passing of title. "That passage of title may be required for a sale," Judge Friedman wrote, "does not mean that passage of title itself creates a sale." Again, the court emphasized that the volume of parts in the pool was necessary for the operation of Apollo's repair business, and that this volume "did not vary appreciably from the time that the cost [of establishing the pool] was incurred." Because the exchange of parts was not a "sale," the court concluded that the "'sale of merchandise' . . . was not 'an income-producing factor'" in Apollo's repair business. Finally, the court held that the IRS did not properly exercise its discretion in determining that the spare-parts pool constituted inventory.

21 Neighborhood Pubs for Tax Specialists

Tax Analysts Email Discussion Groups ☆☆☆☆

This may sound like one of those hard-sell TV commercials: "But wait—there's more!" In addition to the Tax Analysts World Wide Web site, you can subscribe to the organization's plethora of discussion groups—21 of them, in fact. Think of them as places where you can talk with your peers who work in specific areas of taxation. These are moderated groups, so you don't get any spam (hurray!).

Messages come to you in digest format, so instead of getting a flurry of email messages throughout the week, you get one long message about once a week with all of that week's correspondence combined. Except for the International Group, the content of most groups covers U.S. taxes. Most provide a low quantity of high-quality messages. Valuable information is delivered by news items, questions, and their answers. Just pick your topic or topics from the list below.

Tax accounting	accounting.group@tax.com
Taxes and financial institutions	banking.group@tax.com
Tax-exempt bonds	exemptbond.group@tax.com
Bankruptcy and insolvency	bankruptcy.group@tax.com
Business taxes	biztax.group@tax.com
Criminal violations	criminal.group@tax.com
Employment taxes	employment.group@tax.com

Estate, gift, and trust taxes	estate.group@tax.com
Excise taxes and user fees	excise.group@tax.com
Tax-exempt organizations	exempt.group@tax.com
Farm and ranch taxes	farm.group@tax.com
Individual income taxes	individual.group@tax.com
International taxation	international.group@tax.com
Tax legislation and policy	legpolicy.group@tax.com
Natural resource taxation	resource.group@tax.com
Partnership taxation	partnership.group@tax.com
Pensions, benefits, and ERISA	pension.group@tax.com
IRS practices and procedures	practice.group@tax.com
Real estate taxes	realestate.group@tax.com
S corporations	scorps.group@tax.com
State and local taxes	statetax.group@tax.com

How

Email

Where

The address to the right of any group you wish to join

Message

subscribe youremail@address

 You can find archives of past messages from all Tax Analysts discussion groups (plus background information and how to use them) on the World Wide Web at:

www.tax.org/notes/default.htm

Surf the IRS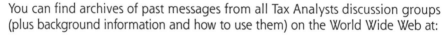

Internal Revenue Service Code ☆☆☆☆

This is way cool for tax dudes and dudettes. Here are two different ways you can surf the IRS. Both sites give you the complete, up-to-date IRS tax codes, and both let you find the section(s) you need by performing interactive online searches. One site gives you more ways to search, the other is easier to use.

How

World Wide Web

Where

For full-text search using *and*, *or*, and *not*:
www.fourmilab.ch/ustax/ustax.html

For simple keyword search:
www.tns.lcs.mit.edu:80/uscode

The Lord Giveth, and the IRS Taketh Away

Internal Revenue Service ☆☆☆

The folks at the IRS run the world's most successful mail-order business. You've really got to hand it to them. I mean, you've *got* to hand it to them. But this IRS Web site could offer more for its customers. The Service does provide some useful information, but it could provide a lot more.

What you'll find here are tax forms and instructions, downloadable in several formats. You'll also find *searchable* online tax forms, so you can type in a key word or phrase and find all of the forms in which it appears. You'll also find tax tables, regulations, and a simple FAQ.

A special page for small businesses details the free print publications and instructional videos you can order. Unfortunately, you can't order them from this Web site. In fact, you can't order print copies of anything here. There is a Help Desk, but it will only help you find the online forms I described above, and the Help Desk takes four or more days to respond to your questions. I'd like to see the IRS use online ordering forms and have a realtime Help Desk for tax questions. For right now, its Web site is useful but limited.

How
World Wide Web

Where
www.irs.ustreas.gov/prod/cover.html

A Tax Board for the Surfboard State

California Franchise Tax Board ☆☆

I know this site holds limited appeal for the rest of the world, but since California businesses account for 25 percent of all commercial domains on the Internet, I thought some of my readers might deal with state income taxes from the former Bear Flag Republic. California receives more tax income than 90 percent of the countries on this planet, but you'd never guess it from this no-frills site. You'll find simple personal and corporate tax information. There is a FAQ on corporate tax, and you can download tax forms in Adobe Acrobat format.

How
World Wide Web

Where
library.ca.gov/California/ftb/html/home.html

281

Revenue Canada Does It Right

Revenue Canada ☆☆☆☆

Out of all the national governments' tax departments on the Net, Canada's is the most useful. I wish other countries would provide some of the tools that Revenue Canada supplies, such as free tables you can download and plug into your software. The tables give you formulas that calculate payroll deductions for Canada Pension Plan, Quebec Pension Plan, unemployment insurance, and income taxes. You'll also find federal tax forms here that you can copy, plus forms for provincial taxes compressed with HTML **readme** files. There are hundreds and hundreds of files here.

RC seems to put *everything* on the Net that was ever printed about Canadian and provincial taxes. You can download brochures, bulletins, Customs notices, *Excise News*, guides (covering income tax, sales tax, Customs duties, and other taxes), memos, press releases, FAQs, regulations (complete text), and even technical publications.

Everything is available in English and *en Française*, except ISO 8859 information which is *en Française* only. The only drawback is that the site is on a Gopher server and not on the World Wide Web. When you visit, be sure to look under the Construction Area for new information.

How

Gopher

Where

gopher://gopher.RevCan.CA:70

Maple Leaf Tax Help, Part I

Deloitte & Touche Canada ☆☆☆

Deloitte & Touche provides useful information on Canadian business and on ways to reduce corporate taxes. Everything is presented both in English and *en Française*. Look for its two newsletters: *TaxBreaks*, with news on Canadian taxes, and *Cross-Border TaxBreaks*, covering Canadian and U.S. tax and Customs issues faced by Canadians who have U.S. investments.

How

World Wide Web

Where

ftn.net/DT

Maple Leaf Tax Help, Part II

can.taxes Discussion Newsgroup ☆☆☆

This active group discusses Canadian tax issues. Most of the discussion is about personal taxes (the non-business kind), but this group is busy enough to generate interesting business tax discussions as well. About 15 percent of the messages here are useless rant, 5 percent spam, and 80 percent good stuff.

Some sample topics:

- Filing tax returns via the Internet
- Canada/U.S. tax info
- Capital Acquisition
- CDN living in U.S.
- Meal per diems

How

Newsgroup

Where

can.taxes

Maple Leaf Tax Help, Part III

KPMG Tax Online ☆☆☆

This site is crammed full of Canadian tax info, in English and *en Française*. You can read copies of the *Canadian Tax Letter* newsletter and search through a database of Canadian tax tips. Investors might want to check some of the tips on taxation of investment income.

How

World Wide Web

Where

www.kpmg.ca

Tax Updates Down Under

Australian Taxation Office ☆☆☆

G'day, mate! This relatively new site doesn't offer a lot of information, but it's a start. You can find the latest ATO press releases here, plus information on

PAYE, PPS, and sales tax. There are links to other Australian tax sites, the Oz Treasury, and Department of Finance.

How

World Wide Web

Where

www.webaustralia.com.au/ato/atohp.htm

A Tale of Two Newsgroups

misc.taxes and misc.taxes.moderated Newsgroups ☆☆☆

This is similar to one of those good news/bad news jokes.

In this case, the bad news is that the **misc.taxes** newsgroup provides some good information, but forces you to slog through spam and a lot of ranting and raving. People mostly discuss individual U.S. taxes here, although there is a tiny amount of corporate discussion.

Sample topics:

- Basis for non-Federal citizenship
- Capital Gains Tax and what should I do?
- Estate Tax Software—Any?
- Flat Tax = no IRS?
- IRS is NOT a U.S. government agency
- Incidence of payroll-deducted taxes
- States with no income tax?
- States with no sales tax?

The good news is that a new newsgroup was created in December 1995, called **misc.taxes.moderated**. The moderator will block the spam (and I hope the rant, too), so good info should be easier to find here.

How

Newsgroup

Where

misc.taxes

misc.taxes.moderated

If you'd like to read the FAQ for **misc.taxes**, you'll find it at:

www.kentlaw.edu/cgi-bin/faq/misc.taxes

There is also an archive of past messages from **misc.taxes** at:

www.kentlaw.edu/cgi-bin/ldn_news/-D+misc.taxes

You're right, that *is* a bizarre URL. You can also receive **misc.taxes** using email. The email version is mirrored to the newsgroup version, so any message posted to either version is copied to the other. The advantage of the email version is that it is semi-moderated. Spam is deleted, but pointless political rants are left intact. To subscribe to the email version, send the message **SUBSCRIBE FedTax-L "Your Real Name in Quotes"** to **listserv@shsu.edu**. A searchable archive of email messages is available at:

gopher://Niord.SHSU.edu/11gopher_root:[_data.fileserv.fedtax-l]

Tax Facts Fast as Flashcraft

TAXDIGEST **Email News** ☆☆☆☆

The facts, only the facts, and nothing but the facts. Well, a little question-and-answer discussions with opinions are mixed in, too. But for the most part, *TaxDigest* is email-delivered news of the latest judicial, legislative, and IRS procedural developments on U.S. income taxes. This is a very valuable resource for U.S. tax professionals.

How
Email

Where
taxdigest@aol.com

Message
Yourfirstname Yourlastname Yourcity Yourstate

 A handy archive of past issues of *TaxDigest* is on the World Wide Web at:

www.unf.edu/misc/jmayer/taxdig.html

Tax Help for Brits, Part I

Tax Net ☆☆☆

A guide to British taxation for beginners, this site provides helpful tips dealing with taxes and self-employment, payroll tax, investments, capital gains, and personal pensions. Tax Net's information covers the basics, but is spread across

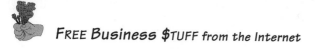

many pages, each with a small-to-medium amount of information, so you'll often have to click-and-wait to find what you need. Ignore the section titled "Great Tax Debate Bulletin Board." It has only a handful of months-old postings. The other parts of Tax Net contain the useful stuff.

How
World Wide Web

Where
www.purple.co.uk/purplet/tax.html

Tax Help for Brits, Part II

United Kingdom Tax Resources ☆☆☆

This is a simple but good guide to sites dealing with any kind of U.K. taxes, from VAT and Inland Revenue to customs and excise. It lists government Web sites, educational sites, and accountancy firms that provide U.K. tax info on the Net. Each site clearly describes what it has to offer.

How
World Wide Web

Where
omer.cba.neu/othersites/UK.html

The Centre of British Taxation

Inland Revenue ☆☆☆

British businesses will discover some useful information here, but Inland should provide more. You'll find a variety of resources for your income tax, corporate tax, capital gains tax, and petroleum tax, and a Self-Assessment Tax Return Consultation Pack that lets you do some of your work online. You'll also find email addresses of tax offices, and PC and Mac versions of tax forms (Adobe Acrobat, anyone?).

The "Open Government Leaflet" is really an FAQ. You'll find answers to frequently asked questions on tax forms and schedules, with some examples. Tantalizingly, you'll find lists of Inland Revenue publications, but Inland has chosen *not* to make them available online. How annoying! You can read about Inland's valuable *Tax Bulletins* here, but you can't get to them. Would another tea party catch Inland's eye?

How

World Wide Web

Where

www.open.gov/uk/inrev/irhome.htm

Where U.S. Tax Pros Hang Out

TAX-PRCT-ISSUES Email Discussion Group ☆☆☆☆

This moderated email discussion group is open only to tax practitioners and taxation accountants. Subscribers discuss actual cases, but no one uses real company names. Because the group is moderated, you won't find any spam here. This group is a valuable resource, but discussions seem to cover only U.S. taxes. You will use email to take part in discussions, but you must have World Wide Web access to subscribe.

How

World Wide Web

Where

www.kentis.com/sublist.html

Tax Talk from All Over

ATax-L Taxation Email Discussion Group ☆☆☆

ATax-L is a low-volume, moderated, and spam-free email discussion group on taxation with a refreshingly non-U.S.-centric slant. An archive of past messages is available at:

www.scu.edu.au/anet/lists/atax-l/index.html

How

Email

Where

listproc@scu.edu.au

Message

help me

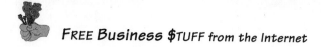

A Tax Tip a Day Keeps the Audit Away

Canadian Tax Tip of the Day ☆☆☆

This advice column gives you quick daily notes about new laws, tips about deductions, and warnings about future changes from the KPMG accounting firm—all delivered to your desktop once a day.

How

Email

Where

majordomo@kpmg.ca

Message

subscribe taxtips

Where to Find More Tax Reduction Stuff

Many of the resources in the *Accounting and Finance* chapter of this book deal with different kinds of taxes, so scrutinize them closely.

Some of the resources in the *Doing Business Internationally* chapter review international taxes. If you're looking specifically for Hong Kong taxation, Loyal Dragon links you to most Hong Kong tax resources, and many Chinese ones as well.

There are a few resources for tax law in the *Business Law* chapter. And as always, if you can't find it in this book, the chapter *How to Find Business Stuff on the Internet* gives you the tools you need to track down other resources that the Net offers.

FREE $TUFF

October is one of the
peculiarly dangerous
months to speculate in
stocks. The others are
July, January, September,
April, November, May,
March, June, December,
August, and February.

Mark Twain

More Profitable
Investing

You'll find literally thousands of Web sites, email discussion groups, and newsgroups on the Internet, all dealing with investing and investment-related topics.

The good news is that instead of having to wait for a monthly newsletter to be typeset, printed, and delivered to you s-l-o-w-l-y via snail mail, you can get decision-making information in minutes—and instead of relying only on information in your city, you can scour the planet from your desktop (or laptop).

The bad news is that many Web sites for investors are clogged with graphics that take forever to download, which is maddening, especially for fast-paced New York investors. (Investors from New York get impatient? Naah, never. Well, maybe sometimes. But only when they're awake.)

Even worse is that you can only find *some* kinds of investment information on the Web, especially if you look only for free information. You'll discover a wealth of market figures, indexes, and statistical information on trends. The Net is lush with broad-brush, overall data and summaries. But when you look for information on individual companies, you'll feel like you're wandering through a desert. Analysts' detailed reports on specific corporations are as uncommon as ice cream factories in Death Valley.

True, a lot of companies announce that they provide reports on the Net. But when you go to their Web sites, usually you find that you pay $295 and they will email the report to you, or that the report is available only to investors who have accounts with that firm. Most brokerages and investment companies have Web sites, but they give you only press releases and useless corporate fluff.

This is not to say you can't find solid investment data, research, analyses, and even good software. It takes digging and time, just like the real world. Fortunately, you've hired Vince & Pat's Free Stuff Excavation Company, and we've mined dozens of glittering investment gems for you.

The Importance of Being EDGAR

EDGAR ☆☆☆☆☆

If you're looking for information on a publicly-traded U.S. corporation or a major mutual fund, let EDGAR do your work. EDGAR stands for Electronic Data Gathering and Retrieval, and is a database of all corporate filings with the U.S. Securities and Exchange Commission since January 1, 1994.

There are two EDGAR sites on the Internet, this one operated by New York University and another operated by the SEC itself. The former is far easier to use, and has a link to its SEC counterpart if you'd like to try it.

You can find a company by its name, ticker symbol, or Zacks symbol. You can use partial names and specify date ranges and the types of information you desire. Check out the "Current Events" section to find prospectuses (prospecti?) and Schedule 13D acquisition reporting. If you want financial ratios, look at 10-Ks. For executive pay (Michael Eisner made *that much?*) and summaries on acquisitions, review DEF14A proxy forms. The13D and 13G schedules tell when one corporation buys 5 percent ownership in another.

Mutual Fund Sector Tracking lets you choose a Zacks industrial sector and track mutuals movement via quarterly filings. If you're really into EDGAR, you can download two big books on it: the merely Incredible Hulk-sized *RR Donelley EDGAR Filing Guide* and the much bigger Godzilla-sized *SEC Filer's Manual*.

You can even download free software to convert EDGAR files to Microsoft Word. Now don't say we never gave you anything.

How

World Wide Web

Where

edgar.stern.nyu.edu/edgar.html

Extra! Extra! Read All about It!

WALL STREET JOURNAL. ☆☆☆☆

No single news source has made as much money for as many investors as *The Wall Street Journal*. Maybe someday the same will be true of its Web site.

You have a couple of different ways to read the *Journal* online. First, you can read what is available at this Web site. Some parts of the paper are free, and some free parts are expanded from the print version. You can read Walt Mossberg's "Personal Technology" column. He covers high-tech for businesspeople in a refreshingly down-to-earth way: "I don't know about you, but it drives me nuts when I go to a home page so crammed with fancy graphics that you can do your taxes in the time it takes to download."

You can also subscribe to your own customized version of the paper, called the *Personal Journal*. Described by the paper as "published for a circulation of one," there is a fee for this online version, but you can try it for two weeks at no charge. It requires you to download free Windows software to use.

How

World Wide Web

Where

www.wsj.com

Ex, Buys, and Videotape

Chicago Mercantile Exchange ☆☆☆

"The Merc" is the biggest futures exchange in the world, and it built a Web site to match. It's stuffed with so much information it will take you hours to navigate. We'll give you an outline guide to some of the high points.

From its home page, "CME News Center" takes you to new investment products, while "What's New" leads to new Web stuff.

Most of the Web site action is under the "Products and Prices" heading. There, "Off the Ticker" gives you flash quotes updated every 10 minutes, currency futures and options prices updated every 10 minutes, and daily settlement prices.

If you want to learn about currency trading, the Merc would like to send you this free introductory video, THE CURRENCY OPPORTUNITY.

You can get Chicago Board of Trade (called CBOT for short—doesn't that sound like a cute *Star Wars* robot?) delayed quotes updated every ten minutes, and closing prices. You'll also find good info from the *CME Daily Information Bulletin*, six days' worth.

If you're a beginner in this territory, head for "The Merc at Work," a clearly written guide that introduces commodity, futures, and currency markets, all described with a welcome touch of humor.

"Growth and Emerging Markets Division" markets futures in currencies, stock indexes, and interest rates for emerging market countries—you know, places we used to call "underdeveloped."

The "Currency Futures" section suffers from too much clip-art-itis. A section on "How to Get Started Trading Currencies" is unbearably irritating, giving you one paragraph per page, which forces you to frequently go to the next page and wait forever for graphics. A "Foreign Currency Aptitude Test" is a good idea, but brought our 112 K ISDN connection to its knees, pleading. We had to give it the Heimlich Maneuver to save it from death by graphixiation. If that sounds bad to you, don't despair—go to the "Currency Futures" section and order the Merc's free videocassette, *The Currency Opportunity*. This video covers the basics for investors considering currency investments for the first time. In a humorous talk show format, guests (including investor Jim Rogers) clearly explain how currency trading works, and how to get started.

"Financial Traders' Homework Page" is a good directory of Internet resources, but would it be too much to ask for descriptions? This is another Gopher directory on the Web. "Livestock Traders' Homework Page" is the best agricultural and livestock directory we found on the Net, even without descriptions.

In the "Education" section, you can order free reports on the January Effect and the Value Effect (two annual cycles that affect prices), and read the complete *CME Rulebook* if you're wondering about the Merc's regulations.

As you can see, you'll find a lot of stuff at the Merc. Pretty impressive for a place founded to sell pork bellies!

How

World Wide Web

Where

www.cme.com

Life Files of the Rich and Famous

Legendary Investor Selections ✩✩✩

Have you ever looked at a self-made success like billionaire investor Warren Buffet and asked yourself, "Gee, how could I find out what stocks he buys, so a little of his savvy could rub off on me?" Well, now you can.

Legendary Investor Selections gives you reports based on the 13F reports filed by famous investors, including Buffet, George Soros, and others. This service gives you daily lists of large stock buys, sales, and holds by managers. Separate reports profile hedge funds, value investors, and growth investors. This service is free, but you must register to use it. No more excuses—now, go out and be an investment success!

How
World Wide Web

Where
worthnet.com/www/13f/index.htm

Stay in Touch

Investor In Touch ✩✩✩✩✩

As we explained in the introduction to this chapter, finding free information on the Internet about individual companies is like searching for water in the Sahara desert. As we crawled over burning sand across this parched wasteland, thirsty for relief, we saw a shimmer on the far horizon. "Just another mirage," we muttered, "or a commissioned brokerage." We dragged ourselves to a hill of dried-out Charles Schwab brochures and gasped in surprise. That was no mirage—it was Investor In Touch!

Now that we've beaten that metaphor to death, we can tell you that Investor In Touch gives you a database of more than 15,000 publicly held companies worldwide that have analyst coverage. Look up your target company and get a description, address, officers, estimated earnings, analyst coverage, research reports (if available), stock quotes, and links to on-Net info. Most of this information comes from *Nelson's Directory of Investment Research.* You'll also find graphs of price action for more than 7,000 companies. Investor In Touch is not only a good resource for investors, it is also useful to look up potential sales prospects and suppliers.

A separate section here gives you a separate directory of corporations with registered investor relations pages. A section called "Research Searches" leads to Andy's Genetic Earnings System, which uses genetic algorithms to find and list companies worldwide with significant estimated changes. Andy's system is worth a look. Investor In Touch also provides a directory of exchanges around the planet. (Didn't we say that was no mirage?)

How

World Wide Web

Where

smokey.money.com/ssnhome.html

Back to the Futures

misc.invest.futures ☆☆☆

This futures trading newsgroup is very active (*lots* of messages posted every day), with about 15 percent spam and ads, but most readers are experienced traders who swap information and answer questions about the field. The pros seem helpful to the newbies here.

Sample topics: Anybody use TAIPAN?; Commodities Industrial Use Report - September; Crack/Energy Spreads; Fruit Outlook Summary; Futures trading system—Help; Gold, silver options? Heating oil/u.l. gasoline spread behavior.

How

Newsgroup

Where

news:misc.invest.futures

Re: Futures Trading System—Help

From: rkhale@richmond.infi.net (Richard Hale)
Newsgroups: misc.invest.futures
Subject: Re: Futures trading system -Help

In article < 44ml1v$khn@bcarh8ab.bnr.ca >, anagaraj@bnr.ca says...

> I would really like to know whether it is possible for a small investor
> to trade in commodities and if so what will be the usual minimal
> investment one has to make to trade in futures/commodities trading.

Depends what you mean by small. If you take the position that losing half your starting capital represents failure (i.e. a need to find a more effective method), I believe that, to trade commodities, you need to have an account of about $25,000. You could stretch down to $20,000 maybe, but then your margin for error is small.

The reason I suggest this account size is so you can trade the "trending" markets like T-Bond and currencies, which is where the money can be made most consistently. To trade stock indexes, $50,000 account would be minimum in my opinion.

However it is possible to have a smaller account (no less that $10,000) and trade wheat, cattle, hogs, etc. A portfolio with a mix of grain, meat, metal, softs would be less risky than trading only one market. If you are interested, email me a request for the method I use to determine adequate margin.

The biggest mistake most traders make is not having adequate capital. This means having a large enough account as well as maintaining adequate reserve margin to prevent "price shocks" (which can jump your stops) from wiping you out (and maybe even making you owe more than your account has).

> I would also like to know whether there are any books I should go through
> to learn the basics in this trade.

These are the books I would recommend reading:

Reminiscences of a Stock Operator, Edwin Lefevre

Winner Take All, William R. Gallacher

The Disciplined Trader, Mark Douglas

By the way, Gallacher's book gives a method for determining market commitments based on capital available. I use a modification of his method for my trading.

Good luck.
Richard Hale

From: minervino@aol.com (Minervino)
Newsgroups: misc.invest.futures
Subject: Re: Futures trading system -Help

Don't call yourself a bonehead — you will only be a bonehead if you listen to those ads!

I encourage you to read all you can about the futures market — how the markets work, how leverage can work for you and against you, money management techniques, etc. If you send me mail to remind me (minervino@aol.com) I will go through my bookshelf and send you some recommendations.

Ninety-five percent of people lose money at this. Of the 5 percent who make money, 95 percent of those people are "professionals" — either people who do it for a living and are good at it or people who work in the pits and scalp profits. From the way you describe your experience at it (nil) you will almost certainly be roadkill for the professionals.

Here are my recommended steps for you:

1. Read everything you can (lots of it will be trash but read it and decide what seems to make sense). At this point you'll be especially dangerous to yourself.

2. Add up your net worth. Multiply it by 5 percent. If the result is less than $10,000, go back to Step #1. (I don't think you should commit more than 5 percent of your net worth to this, if that 5 percent is less than $10,000, you don't have enough to get to step 3.)

3. Buy one contract of whatever you are interested in. At this point you'll know what a tick is worth in that contract, how to avoid taking delivery of 100,000 hogs, etc. Feel what it's like to have your money on the line. Keep reading all you can and talking to people who do it for a living.

4. Hopefully, either concurrently with step 3 or after step 3 you can develop a trading system which you believe will make money and you can stick to. Keep reading all you can and talking to people who do it for a living.

5. Start implementing your system. Keep reading all you can and talking to people who do it for a living. The market will tell you if you should continue to pursue trading or if you should look for another line of work.

I do this for a living managing other people's money. I have been very successful at it. That doesn't mean I have all (or necessarily any) of the answers but I have been where you are. If you decide to throw caution to the wind, trade US T-Bonds...I'll be waiting for your money...

— Jim

The Ups and Downs of Wall Street

Security APL Quote Server ☆☆☆☆

Buy! Buy! Buy! No, wait—Sell! You'd better decide for yourself. But you'd better decide fast. And if you want timely news of the Wall Street roller coaster, you're not going to get it from your afternoon newspaper. Hop on the Web for free electronic quotes and graphs of the Dow Jones Industrial Average and S&P 500.

All information posting is delayed a few minutes to satisfy the SEC. You can even get historical data and graphs of stock performances over the past 25 years.

There are more than a dozen quote servers on the Net, but this one gives you lots of information that its competitors lack. It provides quotes on U.S. and Canadian stocks, money markets, and mutual funds. If you don't know a company's ticker symbol, click on "Ticker Symbols" to look it up. A "Market Watch" page gives indexes updated once every three minutes. You can also request multiple quotes, look up puzzling buzzwords in an indexed glossary, look through a company name database, and follow links to other Web sites' news about your security. The quote server also supports the GET method, so you can bookmark your favorite securities.

How
World Wide Web

Where
www.secapl.com/cgi-bin/qs

Links
Ticker Search

Dow Jones Industrial Average

S&P 500 Index

Security Blanket for Investors

PAWWS ☆☆☆

Investing is a tricky business, and smart investing can be downright nightmarish—assuming you can sleep at all. Luckily, there's help for the newbie who wants to do something more with his/her money than stuff it under his/her mattress—or flush it down the toilet. In addition to its famous quote server (see above), Security APL provides Portfolio Accounting World Wide from Security APL (PAWWS), which gives you many free services (and several that charge those pesky fees) that include a financial library with loads of links to other Web and Internet resources to help you learn as much as you can about investing and the companies on which you are betting.

And if you think you're ready to start investing, but aren't *quite* sure, take the PAWWS Portfolio Management Challenge. This contest gives you the chance

298

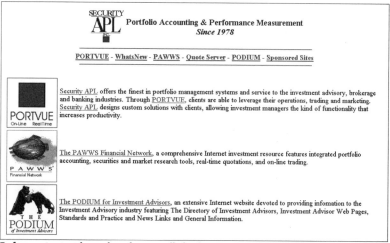

Before you start investing, invest a little time at Security APL—time well spent.

to test your money management skills against competitors from around the world, using (almost) live security prices, at no risk: because it's all play money.

You'll also find a free Web-delivered weekly magazine, *Money Talks*, with analyses from the *New York Times'* Robert Metz and other financial writers. Regular columns cover equities markets, the electric power industry, personal finance, mutual funds, and retail industry investments.

Griffen Financial Services also provides free stock reports and a market outlook as part of PAWWS. And you'll find job opportunities and other free info that we bet you can't wait to get your own pawws on!

How

World Wide Web

Where

www.pawws.com

Links

Industry Classifications

PAWWS Portfolio Management Challenge

Dow Jones Industrial Average

Market Watch

Personal Investment and Tax Information

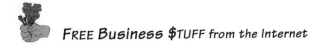

The Feeling Is Mutuals

NETworth ☆☆☆☆

Mutual funds make it simple to get started, simple to make money, and simple to lose your shirt if you're not sure what you're doing. NETworth can help you get up to speed and have you wheeling and dealing like a Rockefeller in no time.

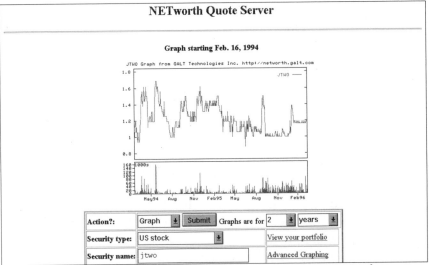

Free stock charts for time intervals you specify. These show the company that owns NATIONAL LAMPOON.

Featuring in-depth information on thousands of mutual funds, NETworth helps you get information straight from the managing companies, including a prospectus and performance figures.

You'll get prices quoted direct from the markets via dedicated S&P real-time data, access to a database featuring information on over 5,000 mutual funds, a comprehensive listing and samples of financial newsletters, and access to question-and-answer forums with some of the industry's most knowledgeable professionals.

In addition, NETworth's Mutual Fund Market Manager offers loads of information on how to pick the best mutual funds to fit your needs. There are also company profiles, fund descriptions, and an option that lets you order more information on the funds you choose.

But wait, there's more! No, not a Ginsu knife. Even better. A free quote server for U.S. and Canadian stocks gives you information and draws graphs for you.

(For an example, see the illustration.) You can browse a directory of publicly-held companies on the Web, and Disclosure, Inc.'s database of public company information. A directory called Insider is one of the best directories anywhere of Internet investment resources. It gives brief descriptions of resources, and often links to key pages *within* a resource, so you don't have to start at some corporate tombstone home page and slog through a bunch of useless filler to get to the spot you want. (It lists *nine* fantasy portfolio games.) The Insider directory even has a search engine of its own.

If you register, you can get yet more free information. You can even build a personal portfolio that you can review instantly when you make return visits. Those who register can receive information at NETworth or have it delivered via email. Ya want fries with that?

How
World Wide Web

Where
www.networth.galt.com

Mining for Moola

The Investor Channel ☆☆☆

If you're ever one of the lucky ones to strike gold on the Internet, make this your first stop. The Investor Channel is the Web's most comprehensive site for tracking investments in the mining industry.

From gold exploration to diamond mining, the Investor Channel has information to assist you with your investment decisions, including company profiles, news releases, the current closing quotes, industry data, and related investment news. You also find a list of recommended "Hot Stocks" from mining and other industries.

How
World Wide Web

Where
www.wimsey.com/xr-cgi-bin/select?/0@/Magnet/mc/cover.html

Links
Newsletters and Newsgroups leads you to the *California Mining Journal* and the *Tandem Capital Report* on mining stocks worldwide.

Invest in Canada

misc.invest.canada ☆☆☆

This is an active group of beginner-to-intermediate investors, mostly swapping questions and answers about individual Canadian companies and specific investments in Canada. Less than 5 percent spam.

Sample topics: 20/20 India Fund; Canadian currency; Gold stocks, year-to-date; GYR, BLJ, MEO End of Day Data; LBG down 30 percent on the news; MPV down on high volume?; Mutual fund info sources; Nova Scotia broker wanted; Regarding Shorts on the Vancouver Exchange.

How

Newsgroup

Where

news:misc.invest.canada

Keep Your Eye on the Canadian Insiders

Canada Stockwatch ☆☆☆

Canada Stockwatch serves a generous smorgasbord of free services for investors who track Canadian companies: VSE/ASE indexes and top traders daily, TSE/NY daily indexes, and daily gold and silver prices for starters. Then it gives you a database where you can look up every Canadian publicly-traded company and find its address, phone number, closing stock price history, price/volume charts, and news bulletins.

But the icing on Canada Stockwatch's cake is the free use of a database of all Insider Trading Reports compiled by the BCSEC since Sept. 1, 1995. You can find out when top execs are buying and selling their own stocks, and use their actions to plan your own purchases and sales.

How

World Wide Web

Where

204.191.227.10

Investing for Mathheads

misc.invest.technical ☆☆☆

This active group for experienced investors concentrates on the numbers, with some company-specific posts. Less than 5 percent spam. A list of Frequently Asked Questions is available at: **fortress.wiwi.uni-frankfurt.de/AG/JWGI/ FAQS/tech-faq.htm**

Sample topics: 5 Dow stocks; At last, a use for Dan Dorfman?; Black-Scholes add-in for Excel; Chart opinions on MNCO and BRBC; Daily Treasury Yield Curve Rates—September; Delta Neutral Trading; Metastock vs. Supercharts— which is better?; Moving Averages; Prechter newbook.

How

Newsgroup

Where

news:misc.invest.technical

Formulas for Wealth

Excel Formula Archive ☆☆☆

This archive gives technical analysts and investors ready-to-use Excel spreadsheets based on the Vidya, CMO, and DMI investment formulas described in Chande's book *The New Technical Trader* and in *Technical Analysis of Stocks & Commodities* magazine.

How

World Wide Web

Where

www.halcyon.com/neal/challenge/archive/excelForumulae.html

Sand in Your Shorts (Short SALES, of Course)

TRADER'S WEEKLY VIEW FROM MALIBU ☆☆☆

From the beaches of Southern California come two free sample issues of *Trader's Weekly View from Malibu*, a newsletter delivered to you by email. It covers stock and bond markets, plus some commodities. Each issue recaps the past week's action and looks forward. It concentrates on technical analysis— just the price action numbers—and on identifying analytical tools for traders to use in these markets. Your two free issues are an appetizer to entice you into buying a paid subscription, which includes updates during the week.

How

Email

Where

daytrade@aol.com

Message

Tell him Vince and Pat sent you and ask for your two free issues.

This Site Teaches Investing, Not Spelling

nVestor ☆☆☆☆

See how much you can make playing $100,000 on the stock market. This free stock market game by the League of American Investors is a real life, realtime simulation. You create your own stock portfolio, learn financial details about real companies, and invest, starting with $100,000 in simulated money invested in twenty companies. You earn an international rank compared with all other players worldwide. Register on this Web site, but you'll play the actual game via email.

Along with the game, when you register you'll receive a free subscription to *Weston's Directory of Free Corporate Reports* to help you dig up background information. Just remember never to spell "investor" the way this game does.

How

World Wide Web

Where

www.investor-net.com

Want Some Hot Investment TIPs?

Telescan TIPnet ☆☆☆

TIPnet is a Telescan database service for investors. TIPnet gives you info on more than 75,000 stocks, mutual funds, bonds, options, futures, commodities, industry groups, and market indexes. Whew! Then it adds historical price and volume information (back to 1973, the Age of Bell-Bottoms) and current online quotes from NYSE, Amex, NASDAQ, Canadian exchanges, and futures and options stuff. TIPnet also provides company reports, business news, and an "Autoflag" for your portfolio.

You can try TIPnet at no charge for thirty days. You have to register; but even though you have to fill in payment information when you do, if you cancel you will not be charged. If you'd like a peek without registering, try the free "guest" logon for a one-shot look at a tiny subset.

How

World Wide Web

Where

www.telescan.com

Stocks, Stocks, and More Stocks

misc.invest.stocks ☆☆☆

If you have questions about an individual company's stock, here is a place to turn. This active group primarily poses questions about specific corporations—and, of course, provides the answers. This group is less than 5 percent spam, and will be helpful for investors of intermediate experience.

Sample topics: 3 point displacement?; A Classic Short Sale Idea; Bearish case: What's your opinion?; Cellcore or Cytogen, any info?; Downloading stock information; Israeli stocks [ELT] Elscint; Lattice Semiconductor—Why so Volatile?; NASDAQ trading policies—Is my broker telling me the truth?; [FJC] Fedders, any followers?

How

Newsgroup

Where

news:misc.invest.stocks

One Graph Is Worth a Thousand Words

The Stock Room ☆☆☆

Free graphs from Jason Martin, a molecular biologist interested in finance, stocks, and the Web. Programs here extract data from quotes of indexes and present it to you in graphical form. The charts created by Martin's software are illuminating, but be warned that the graphs will not display properly for all browsers.

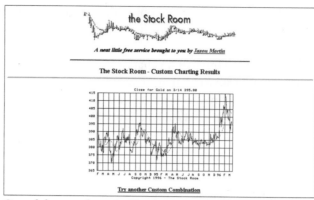

One of dozens of graphs The Stock Room will create for you.

How

World Wide Web

Where

loft-gw.zone.org/jason/custom.html

Invest in Australia

aus.invest ☆☆☆

G'day, mate! Investment Q&A for people from many countries who invest down under, and from Aussie investors themselves. Some of these blokes are tougher than Crocodile Dundee.

Sample topics: Australian index funds; Australian Index Charts; China stocks; Genuine Investors Required; Composite Buyers/QIW and Davids Holdings; Public Stock Data; Solomon Lew Survey Results; Submission to Australian Corporation Laws Simplification Task Force; Tax returns by Internet.

How

Newsgroup

Where

news:aus.invest

LIFFE Is Full of Ups and Downs

LIFFE ☆☆☆

LIFFE is the London International Financial Futures and Options Exchange. You'll find introductory information on derivatives here, and background on

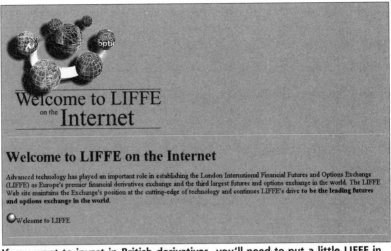

If you want to invest in British derivatives, you'll need to put a little LIFFE in your portfolio.

the U.K. regulatory structure. Corporations investing in derivatives should read *Managing Derivatives Risk: Guidelines for End-Users*. Based on studies of misuse problems (does the name Barings ring a bell?), this report sets down six core principles for managing the risks inherent in derivatives. It also provides information on how to implement the principles in your corporate cash management.

LIFFE online also brings you three quarterly newsletters: *Bond Futures and Options Review, Money Market Futures and Options Review*, and *Equity Products Review*. If you're still hungry for LIFFE, you'll find pages of statistics on more topics than we can list here.

How

World Wide Web

Where

www.liffe.com

Play Footsie with FTSE

Electronic Share Information ☆☆☆

ESI plans to create a stock exchange that is completely online. For the present, ESI offers investors information about shares on the existing London exchange. Register for its free services, and you'll receive:

- Top 400 London stock exchange prices updated eight times daily
- London closing prices for all stocks
- FTSE index updated in realtime
- Free tastes of some of ESI's fee-based services for investors

How

World Wide Web

Where

www.esi.co.uk

Tops on Trusts

Interactive Investor ☆☆☆

This site for investors in U.K. trusts and funds is quite good. Once you've completed its free registration, you can search through information on 1,500 U.K. funds and browse tables with yet more data. Presented by the Association of Unit Trust and Investment Funds, performance tables give you details on every unit trust, investment trust, PEP, and SIB-authorized offshore fund. When OEICs start in England this year, we expect that this site will cover them as well. The Association also gives you a good FAQ on unit trusts, a glossary, and information on 120 Unit Trust management companies. This site provides by far the most detail we found on the Net covering these topics.

How

World Wide Web

Where

www.iii.co.uk

Take Stock in the U. K.

MoneyWorld ☆☆☆

For entry-level information on investing in the U.K., MoneyWorld is your first place to turn. Actually, it covers a bit more than just the U.K. For instance, you can find a stockbroker here for Southern Ireland and the Channel Islands as well.

What you'll find here are good short guides using nontechnical writing to give you the basics on derivatives, unit trusts, OEICs, finance for women, and several other topics. You can also look up data on annuity rates, PEPs, and other investments. Although primarily a personal finance resource, much of MoneyWorld is useful for small businesses as well.

How

World Wide Web

Where

www.moneyworld.co.uk

Training Wheels for Beginners

misc.invest ☆☆☆

This very active group for entry-level investors runs about 10 percent spam, but the rest is questions, answers and useful information. Covers mostly U.S. markets, but also Hong Kong and others. Look here for many free (and valuable) newsletters and announcements of new Web sites for investors.

Sample topics: Looking for an online list of Stock Splits; Buffet's Annual Reports; Chicago/New York Commodity Prices; Delta Neutral Trading; Foreigner wants to open USA account, what is required?; Has anyone read "Investment Biker" by T.J. Rodgers?; Need some advice re living trusts; Holt's Actives Report; Holt's Market Report; Holt's Opt Stock Report; Holt's Volume Report.

How

Newsgroup

Where

news:misc.invest

RiskMetrics: a Jewel of a Tool

J.P. Morgan & Co. ☆☆☆☆

As Yogi was smarter than the average bear, J.P. Morgan seems smarter than the average investment company, if you base your judgment on the excellent free stuff it provides on its Web site.

First you've got your indexes: commodities, currencies, bonds in emergency markets, government bonds. Good material, but (yawn) we've seen them all before. Then you've got the *World Holiday and Time Guide*, useful not only for global investors, but for travelers, multinational purchasers, and international trade mavens.

But the jewel is a tool: RiskMetrics. RiskMetrics is both a software tool and a method you can use to estimate market risk based on the Value-at-Risk approach. You can download everything you need: software (for the Mac, Unix, or Windows), data sets, even a plug-in module with proposed European regulatory changes. Government bonds, money markets, foreign exchange, and equity indexes are covered for 14 countries plus the Ecu, with commodities volatility for eight more countries. You can also download extensive documentation, including a quarterly online newsletter, *RiskMetrics Monitor*. There is an active user group as well.

Now, how many other investment companies would be smart enough to create something like RiskMetrics? These J.P. Morgan people must be pretty bright.

How

World Wide Web

Where

www.jpmorgan.com

Quotes Served with Links on the Side

Lombard Quote Server ☆☆☆

Register first to get free time-delayed market quotes with hotlinks to additional data. Other freebies here include graphs for any time interval that you specify, and "Research Links," a short directory of links, some with descriptions.

How

World Wide Web

Where

www.lombard.com

A Mutuals Clone, Only Better

Mutual Funds Magazine ☆☆☆☆

Here's an online clone of the respected magazine, plus a few twists the print version can't deliver: hotlinks to companies, a searchable online database of funds, a directory of fund companies, and an interactive total return calculator. Did we mention the archive of back issues?

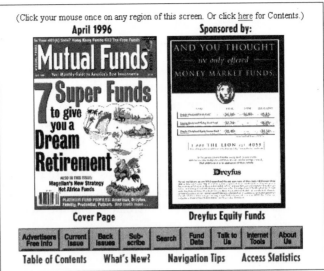

It's not exactly the cover of ROLLING STONE, but for mutuals
managers the cover of MUTUAL FUNDS MAGAZINE can be more
financially rewarding.

How

World Wide Web

Where

www.mfmag.com

Interested in Interest?

Interest & Currency Consultants ☆☆☆

I&CC is an independent consultancy specializing in currencies and interest
rates. (You probably already figured that out from its name.) It makes predictions on medium-term (weeks to months) movements, and gives good summaries of its predictions—and more importantly, the reasoning behind its
forecasts—on its Web page. You can also register to receive one free copy of
an ICC report (normally $20-$52) via fax or email. The free offer is buried, so
follow these instructions. To get your free report, go to the page with the summary of recent publications, scroll to the bottom, and look carefully.

How

World Wide Web

Where

www.xxlink.nl/icc

Read Your Email, Spot a Trend

Financial Economics Network Discussion Groups ☆☆☆

The Financial Economics Network has a Web site at **www.crimson.com/fen** which is useful for economists and some investors, but in addition to that Web site FEN also maintains more than twenty email discussion groups on investment, financial, and economic topics. These are private groups, moderated to block spam. Announcements, questions, and answers more often deal with underlying theory than with the merits of specific investments. Some are decidedly academic in tone. But most of these groups are good sources of information on their topics, and new trends sometimes surface here before being noticed by the more commercial side of the Net.

AFA-BANK	Banking
AFA-INV	Investments
AFA-CORP	Corporate finance
AFA-INT	International finance
AFA-DER	Derivatives
AFA-ACCT	Accounting and finance
AFA-MKTM	Market microstructure
AFA-VCAP	Venture capital
AFA-EMKT	Emerging markets
AFA-SOFT	Financial software
AFA-CFA	Financial analysts
AFA-REA	Real estate
AFA-WA-R	Washington real estate
AFA-LE	Law and economics
AFA-ECMT	Econometrics and finance
AFA-SIV	Small investors
AFA-SBUS	Small business finance
AFA-PERS	Personal finance
AFA-SINV	Social investing
AFA-REG	Regulation
AFA-INS	Insurance

How

Email

Where

Register with either Wayne Marr at **marrm@clemson.clemson.edu** or John Trimble at **trimble@vancouver.wsu.edu**

Message

Your message will be read and processed by one of the two people above, not by a machine. Ask politely to subscribe to the list you want. Give its name as listed above.

Invest in Japan

fj.life.money ☆☆☆

This Japanese-language group generates a moderate volume of questions and answers on personal finance and investing. Look for its excellent FAQs on personal finance topics.

Sample topics: Financial Policy; Foreign stocks; Hong Kong Stocks Summary; How to word "NEARI"; Koutei buai; securities companies; FAQ: Credit Card exchange rate; FAQ: How to get foreign currency; FAQ: MMF.

How
Newsgroup

Where
news:fj.life.money

Invest in Deutschland

de.etc.finanz.boerse ☆☆☆

This active German-language group provides information for German investors, including charts, listings, questions, answers, and some humor. (Such as the claim that in Bank24 Online, the "24" stands for "24 Minuten Wartzeit, bid die Homepage geladen wurde.") I found more coverage of the DAX market here than in any other newsgroup. Almost no spam.

Sample topics: Borsenindices und Fidelityfonds?; Historische Daten DAX; Kurse dt. Investmentfonds; Suche Kurse als WWW-Seiten; VTX: Aktuelle Devisen Kurse Geld; VTX: Investmentfonds-Luxemburg Deutschland; VTX: Investmentfonds.

How
Newsgroup

Where
news:de.etc.finanz.boerse

Time for a Reality Check

Reuters Money Network ☆☆

Reality Online, developers and operators of the nation's leading online personal investment service, runs Reuters Money Network, an online service dedicated to personal investing. It includes a good free quote server for stocks, mutuals, call options, and put options. You can also read ancient back issues of the newsletter *Reality Investor*, containing little information.

How

World Wide Web

Where

www.rol.com

Can I Quote You on That?

Quote.com ☆☆☆

You're only as rich as the bottom line on your portfolio. And it's too late to sell if there's nowhere to go but up. So stay on top of the markets via Quote.com. This company was the pioneer in free quotes on the Net. Register here to get up to five stock, mutual, money market, or commodities quotes per day free. You can also research Quote.com's staggering number of *realtime* indexes, and check out it's good directory of "Other Links for Investors," several with detailed descriptions telling you what makes them so valuable.

Stock quotes and lots of market-related freebies at Quote.com.

How

World Wide Web

Where

www.quote.com

 If you'd like to receive up to five quotes a day via email, send email to **info@quote.com**. For the "Subject:" line of your message type **help**, and for the body of your message type nothing but **help**.

Wrap Music

AMR Publishers ☆☆

This site provides information for people who handle privately managed accounts. You'll find basic information for beginners, a list of top-performing money managers, and two online newsletters. *Managed Money Perspectives* covers managed money for personal investors. *Wrap Fee Advisor* is a monthly newsletter for wrap fee providers, covering news, regulations, and technology (especially new software) in the wrap fee field. There's little on the Net specifically for wrappers. AMR provides welcome relief.

How

World Wide Web

Where

www.secapl.com/AMR

Get Your Portfolio Back in the Black

Personal Finance Center ☆☆☆☆

Wouldn't it be nice to have your own personal investment manager to guide you through the tricky waters of financial investing? Well this is cyberspace, remember, where all your wishes come true.

The Personal Finance Center's "Brain Trust" lets you pick the brain of top investment strategists about your personal finances, and then posts your questions and the experts' replies. They even provide free help in planning or evaluating Internauts' investment portfolios. Previous discussions covered:

- Saving for college
- Finding good financial books
- Investing for retirement

The best thing here may be an online book *Investment Strategies for the 21st Century* by Frank Armstrong. As Armstrong puts it, "I have often stated that the average stockbroker's advice is worth far less than zero. The large brokerage houses are understandably concerned that this perception should not spread." Armstrong's right, and the background he gives will help you see through much of the misinformation stockbrokers spread. His "cans of tuna fish" analogy alone can save you from major losses, as it defuses one of the most common mistakes that small investors make.

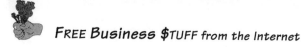

You'll also find investment articles from other Web sites, and a directory of popular investment resources.

How

World Wide Web

Where

gnn.com/meta/finance

Are All Your Eggs in One Nest?

NEST EGG MAGAZINE ☆☆☆☆

Playing the stock market is a tricky business—so tricky it makes playing the wheel in Vegas seem like an exact science. You'll want to hedge your bets as much as possible by getting all the help you can *before* taking the financial plunge into the icy waters of investing.

No rotten eggs in this nest, just good financial advice.

This nest of investment advice gives you several eggs, each with its own sub-set of resources for investors. The best of the nest is probably the Smith Barney Wall Street Watch, with an online IRA calculator, a list of today's ten most-requested stocks on the Web site, a futures research department (commodities reports, a report on how weather will affect agriculture, and other reports), and other departments you must register to enter for free.

Web Finance is a unique online magazine run by *Investment Dealer's Digest*. This is online heaven for people passionately into financial stuff on the Net.

Web Finance covers the financial companies on the Internet, and is not only a valuable resource for investment pros, but also one of the best spots anywhere covering business use of the Internet (in this case, financial and investment businesses). It is the best place to go if you want news of new Web sites for brokers and other industry professionals. Check out its excellent "Gateway Index" directory, aimed at pros and not individual investors.

The nest also gives you the Tradeline Investor Center, with information updated daily on mutual funds and equities, and its namesake *Nest Egg Magazine* for small investors, which is unfortunately not updated frequently.

How

World Wide Web

Where

nestegg.iddis.com

MACRO-INVESTMENT ANALYSIS for a Micro Price

Home Page: Professor William F. Sharpe ☆☆☆☆

Nobel Prize winner William Sharpe is publishing his new book *Macro-investment Analysis* on the Web, free of charge. He posts each new chapter as he finishes it. Sharpe aims this book at investment analysts who help investors choose between different investment vehicles or portfolios. His Web site also includes software that you can download, and a lengthy Dow-Jones interview with Sharpe on style analysis.

How

World Wide Web

Where

ekele.stanford.edu/~wfsharpe

Where to Find More Investment Stuff

Within this book, your first stop should be Chapter 17, *A Free Lunch for Economists*. You'll find that many of the resources in that particular chapter are useful for investors.

Next, go to chapter 9, *Accounting and Finance*. Investing winners here include KARL, Professionals Online, the Loyal Dragon Project, *The Market Observer*, Banking on the WWW (especially check that one out), Money Issues Online,

Commercial Finance Online, Treasury Connection, the Internet Bankruptcy Library, and the newsletter *Turnarounds & Workouts Newswire*.

Several international investment resources are listed in the next chapter, *Doing Business Internationally*, and you'll find some good ones in Chapter 3, *Business News*.

After browsing those chapters, you might like to take a stab at our index. You'll find the biggest list under the heading **investment resources**. You might also want to take a peek at what we list under **agriculture, bonds, capital assets, credit management, economic resources, financial institutions, insider trading, insurance, mergers & acquisitions, real estate,** and the ever-popular **trusts**. If you've been bad, look under **white-collar crime**.

FREE $TUFF

The knowledge of the world
is only to be acquired in the
world, and not in a closet.

Lord Chesterfield

Doing Business
Internationally

We've talked with hundreds of companies that market on the Internet. One thing surprised all of them, from one-person startups to giant conglomerates: the volume of Internet sales they generate from customers in other countries. The Net not only makes international trade possible; the Net actually makes international business hard to avoid. Many U.S. companies are intimidated by this, but only at first. Once they see that international business just takes a little extra paperwork and a little juggling for language differences, the fear turns to eagerness—namely, eagerness to do more.

Whether you want to purchase internationally or sell internationally, and whether you are a vet or a newbie at the international trade game, you'll find plenty of Internet resources to help you start and refine your cross-border operations.

Nearly every company has highly individualized needs in this area, and an Internet resource that's a godsent gift to one business trying to import fabrics from Nepal will seem completely useless to another that wants to sell German machine parts to customers in Saudi Arabia. Take our ratings with a grain of salt in this section, because one company's international bread and butter will look like food scraps to another. The key is to look for resources that might fit your industry and your geographic needs.

This Accent Makes Things Easier to Understand

Accent Software ☆☆☆☆☆

When you buy and sell with businesses in other countries, you can try to do everything in English. But you might find out that you can sell more if you are willing to read and send email in other languages. And you might discover that you can strike better purchasing bargains if you can read Web pages that use non-Roman letters. Maybe you'll even want to put up a Web site in, say, English, French, German, Japanese, and Arabic. Wouldn't it be great if someone came up with software tools that made it easier for you to do all those things? And wouldn't it be even better if you could download all that software from the Internet instead of having to drive to a computer superstore, and wait in line for a pimply 17-year-old to tell you, "If we have something like that, it *might* be over there," indicating 23 aisles of software boxes, each the length of the Santa Monica Freeway?

We thought so, too. That's why the appearance of Accent Software on the scene made us rejoice. It specializes in software products that read eight different character sets, so you can see up to thirty languages displayed in their actual characters instead of uL)98>J#l$(5@, or some other gibberish that looks like Popeye swearing.

Accent also makes a multilingual word processor that performs serviceable automatic translations, but what really gets us "hot and bothered" are Accent's Internet products:

- **Accent Multilingual Mosaic** - A Web browser that supports all languages that use Roman characters (English and most Western European languages), plus Japanese, Arabic, Greek, Hebrew, and Cyrillic (Russian) typefaces. If you've ever visited Japanese Web sites, you'll know what a big difference this can make. It works with any language version of Windows, although sometimes you have to tell the browser what language it's reading.
- **Multilingual Mailpad** - Using any language version of Windows, it allows you to send and read email in 30 languages.
- **Accent Multilingual Publisher** - Builds Web pages in 30 languages.

To save you from hunting for parking spaces, Accent lets you download all these products from the Net. You can try before you buy, with no pesky re-stocking charge. Accent products that you download do have a built-in expira-tion date (like Netscape Navigator); but until they expire, you can try out its products for free.

On its site, Accent also provides an "Accent Resource Center," a directory of multilingual Web sites. It's a so-so list with short descriptions. You'll find oth-ers in this chapter that are more complete. But with software this cool, who cares about a directory?

How
World Wide Web

Where
www.accentsoft.com

Um, Import Means in, Export Means out, Right?

Trade Point USA ☆☆☆☆

This international trade site provides a variety of resources to boost your im-port-export skills. Check out the *I-Trade Export Guide*, a book for companies that want to expand export operations or start exporting. It integrates the U.S.

Department of Commerce's *Basic Guide to Exporting* with new, original material. Most of the *I-Trade Export Guide* is available on the Web.

Another section of this site gives you a searchable database of importers, exporters, and products. A section on doing business under NAFTA includes links to most of the NAFTA how-to information and news available on the Net. Trade Point USA was created for U.S. companies (did the name give you a clue?), but can be useful for traders anywhere.

How

World Wide Web

Where

www.tpusa.com

Think Big

alt.business.import-export ☆☆☆☆

If you like to think big—really big—this newsgroup is for you. For instance, the kind of "big" where you buy your morning orange juice in cargo containers of 100, 55-gallon steel drums. This group receives messages from companies all over the world who are interested in buying and selling products in huge quantities, mostly commodity-type items. One of the most active trading spots on the Net, messages here run about 20 percent spam, with most of the rest being legitimate sales offers. You'll also find a smattering of buyers looking for specific products, and some job offers in the import-export field. Occasionally there are terrific bargains, when someone must sell a shipload of stuff before a tight deadline.

Sample topics: Wtd: Exporters of PC components; FS: light crude oil, Low Cost Ocean Freight; Wanted—Ships for Soap; GSM Phones; Wtd: Au Bullion; Concentrated Orange Juice or Grapefruit Juice; 120,000 Sets of Headphones; Asian Company Looking for Sellable U.S. Products; For Sale, Grade "A" & "E" Sugar; Free listing of suppliers, agents & distributors.

How

Newsgroup

Where

news:alt.business.import-export

Don't Say "Hold the Mayo"

From: dhewes@slip.net (dhewes)
Newsgroups: alt.business.import-export
Subject: Mayonnaise

Proforma Offer	:	Mayonnaise
Price	:	US$ 13.85 per case.
Packaging	:	12 / 32 oz. bottle per case.
Quantity	:	1,300 cases per 20' container.
Terms	:	F.O.B. Factory, City of Industry, CA USA.
Payment	:	Cashier's Check / Wire Transfer prior to loading.
Lead Time	:	Approx. 10 Working Days, Product made Fresh to order.

Contact: Spencer Holeman
Holeman & Associates
Burlingame, CA. USA
Tel: 415-697-4800
Fax: 415-697-4899
email: dhewes@slip.net

A Slow Gold Mine for Exporters

TradePort ☆☆☆☆

TradePort is by far the single most informative Web site for U.S. businesses that desire to export. Actually, other sites may have more information, but TradePort organizes most of it so you can actually find what you need.

TradePort is a very good resource, but suffers from the dreaded diseases overgraphicitis and tinypage-itis.

For instance, it offers a very good FAQ (which it calls Q&A) on exporting, which we highly recommend to anyone new at this game. When a word puzzles you, look it up in the glossary provided. You'll find a great directory of market research for exporters, letting you tap "how do I find customers?" information on this site as well as on others. Included are good directories and guides on product classifications (and why exporters need 'em), legal matters, how to find buyers, shipping (turns out not to be as tricky as you feared), where to obtain financing (best section on this we found anywhere), and how to find what import duty rates are charged by your customers' countries.

All of that said, TradePort does have its limits. Although free, you must register to use it. That's no big deal, because your payoff is so impressive. Worse is the extreme overuse of many, many graphics files. Once you get past the home directory, we recommend that you use your browser's stop sign button to kill all graphics on every subsequent page of this site. You'll still be able to reach 90 percent of the information due to TradePort's thoughtfully-provided text links. Even if you have to reload a page every now and then, that will take far less time than waiting for enough graphics to clog the Mississippi.

Some sections suffer from another problem. For example, "Trade Expert" gives very good information on how to export, but only provides a tiny amount of information on each page — spread across many, many pages. To understand how hard-to-read "Trade Expert" can be, try this. Pick up your copy of *Seven Habits of Highly Effective Nuns* or any other business book you like. Read three or four paragraphs. Now close your book and put it down. Wait a minute or two and pretend you're downloading at $3 an hour. Then pick up your book and read four more paragraphs. Put it down and repeat the cycle until you can't stand it any more. Frustrating? We think so, too. Skip "Trade Expert" unless you've got the patience of Mother Teresa.

TradePort is sponsored by the Department of Commerce and two San Francisco area organizations: the Association of Bay Area Governments and the Bay Area Council. TradePort is supposed to be used only by California businesses. We figure if that old line "On the Internet, no one can tell that you're a dog" is true, no one will be able to tell that you're not from California. That makes TradePort a very good resource for anyone from Nome to Rome.

How

World Wide Web

Where

www.tradeport.org

A Compass for International Traders

Trade Compass ☆☆☆☆

This all-in-one center for importers and exporters provides a lot of information that is difficult to find elsewhere on the Net. You'll discover an active section of sales leads and "wanna buy" notices for wholesale goods, and more sales leads from the United Nations Electronic Trade Opportunity System, and still more sales leads in the form of government bid tenders from around the world. Trade Compass also provides U.S. Customs Container Status information, shipping schedules, tariffs, and many good directories of government information (U.S., U.S. states, and other countries), international trade organizations, trade databases, and many other subjects.

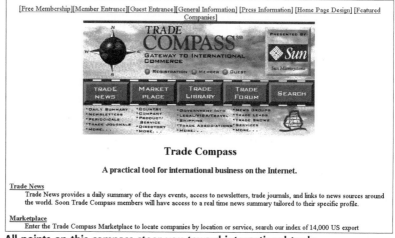

All points on this compass steer you toward international trade.

Trade Compass uses a Web feature called *frames*. If you're new to frames, you'll have a frustrating time getting around. Why? Frames will disable the Back and Forward buttons on your browser. Here's the quick secret to navigating any site with frames. If you use Windows or Unix, move your mouse so your cursor is on the frame in which you would like to go back or forward. Click your *right* mouse button. A popup menu will give you the choices "Back in Frame" or "Forward in Frame." Choose the one you want. If you use a Mac, do the same thing by moving your cursor over the frame. Then hold your mouse button down until you see the menu.

Once you understand frames, Trade Compass is a rich and worthwhile site. You must register to use it, but most of what you'll find here is free.

How

World Wide Web

Where

www.tradecompass.com

Practices Make Perfect

INTERNATIONAL BUSINESS PRACTICES GUIDE ☆☆☆☆

When you export, you not only have to understand how to do business in your own country, you also have to know the business practices of each country where you sell. You'll get confused, and the Department of Commerce has done its part to help—no, not to help you get confused. To help make things clear. The Department of Commerce created this reference book to help you do business in any of 117 nations. It provides country-by-country reviews of legal practices and business operations. For each country, it covers foreign corporations, agents and distributors, joint ventures, import duties, import restrictions, intellectual property rights, taxes (oh, darn), regulatory agencies, and foreign investment rules, plus other topics. It's an excellent reference if your business has plans for doing anything more than ship products overseas, and can be helpful even for that.

How

Gopher

Where

gopher://umslvma.umsl.edu/11/LIBRARY/GOVDOCS/IBPA/IBPG

For Experienced Global Biz Pros Only

Global Interact Network ☆☆☆☆

Global Interact Network can be a valuable information resource if you are an international trade veteran. It is an email discussion group in which experienced pros answer each others' questions about international business issues. Membership is open only to business professionals with a background in international business. Students need not apply. To join, you must agree to share your expertise with other GIN subscribers.

How

Email

Where

ciber@msu.edu

Message

Your email will be read by Mr. Tunga Kiyak, not by a machine. It should include this information:

Family name
First name
Other names
Email address
Home phone
Work phone
Fax
Postal address
Country
Your company or organization name
Areas of expertise
Countries of expertise
Are you an AMA member? Yes or No

How Many Dollars in a Pound's Worth of Yen?

Exchange Rate Calculator Page ☆☆☆

The best exchange rate calculator on the Net, this one computes to and from any currencies on the historical exchange rate for any day you select from 1 January 1990 to yesterday. It also quotes the 75 percent interfractile range when enough prices are available. Olsen & Associates updates rates here daily, while the better-known Koblas Currency Converter is updated only once a week. Currencies can change a great deal in one week—just ask Barings. (Maybe Nick Leeson used Koblas.)

How

World Wide Web

Where

www.olsen.ch/cgi-bin/exmenu

Have You Converted?

Metric Conversions ☆☆☆

The extent of our knowledge of the metric system is that a 10 K race is a little over 6 miles, 90 kilometers per hour rounds out to about 55 miles per hour, and that four liters of beer converts to one heck of a hangover. What more do we need to know?

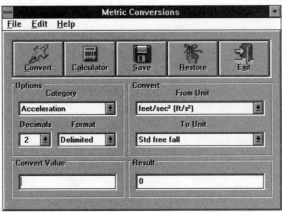

Have you converted?

If Metric Conversions is any judge, we still have a long way to go. This shareware program will help the metrically challenged (like me) convert mass, volume, acceleration, pressure, velocity, and lots more. You'll even receive help converting such non-metric units as fortnights, lunar moons, and horsepower.

How

World Wide Web

Where

www.csusm.edu/cwis/winworld/convert.html

Download

convrt25.zip (72 K)

How Many Centimeters to a Cubit?

Entisofs Units ☆☆☆

If you need industrial-strength conversions, try this oddly-named calculator for Windows. It recognizes standards of measurements and translates them from one format to another. It works with metric, English, ancient, and even more specialized units of measure. The software recognizes their names, abbreviations, and common synonyms. In addition to the Entisofs Units Windows program, you'll get handy add-ins you can plug into Access or Excel if you use those products.

How

World Wide Web

Where

www.csusm.edu/cwis/winworld/calculat.html

Download

esunits1.zip

Do Not Enter

FOREIGN ENTRY REQUIREMENTS ☆☆☆

In some parts of the U.S., getting across the border is as easy as knowing who won the 1949 World Series. It's not that easy in other countries. This 20-page booklet shows you the requirements for getting your feet firmly planted in the soil of many foreign countries. You'll learn what kind of identification is required (even if you don't need a passport), as well as what

> BANGLADESH -- Passport, visa, and onward/return ticket required. Tourist/business visa requires 2 application forms, 2 photos. Business visa also requires company letter. For longer stays and more information consult Embassy of the People's Republic of Bangladesh, 2201 Wisconsin Ave., N.W., Washington, D.C. 20007 (202/342-8373).
>
> BARBADOS -- U.S. citizens traveling directly from the U.S. to Barbados may enter for up to 3 months stay with proof of U.S. citizenship, photo ID and onward/return ticket. Passport required for longer visits and other types of travel. Business visas $25, single-entry and $30 multiple-entry (may require work permit). Departure tax of $25 is paid at airport. Check information with Embassy of Barbados, 2144 Wyoming Ave., N.W., Washington, D.C. 20008 (202/939-9200) or Consulate General in New York (212/867-8435).
>
> BELARUS -- Passport and visa required. Visa requires 1 application form and 1 photo. The visa processing fee is $30 for 7 working days, $60 for next day, and $100 for same day processing. (No charge for official travelers.) Transit visa is required when travelling through Belarus ($20). For additional information contact Embassy of Belarus, Suite 619, 1511 K Street, N.W., Washington, D.C. 20005-1403 (202/638-2954).

A sample from FOREIGN ENTRY REQUIREMENTS, **downloaded from the Consumer Information Center.**

countries require immunization certificates, what you don't want listed on your visa when traveling to certain areas, which countries require proof of funds (presumably in case you need to buy your way out), and much more. There's even a list of embassy and consulate addresses where visas may be obtained along with any special requirements. Oh yeah, I almost forgot: 1949 was the year of the Yankees (who else?).

How

World Wide Web

Where

www.gsa.gov/staff/pa/cic/trav&hob.htm

Although it says it costs fifty cents, you can download it for free.

Wanna Work in the U.S.?

The Visa Maze ☆☆☆

If your business wants to hire an employee from another country, or if you're a non-U.S. citizen but you'd like to work in the States, you can have a tricky time getting the U.S. visa you'll need. This page tells how to get a temp or permanent U.S. visa, with all your alternatives clearly spelled out by attorney Matthew Schulz.

How

World Wide Web

Where

www.schulzlaw.com/%Emschulz/mschulz_mae.html

That's a Fact, Jack

CIA Publications ☆☆☆☆

Produced annually by the good guys at the Central Intelligence Agency for a very exclusive audience of U.S. Government officials (and 20 million of their closest Internet friends), the *CIA World Factbook* contains detailed information on over 250 countries, continents, regions, and territories around the globe. And I do mean detailed. We're talking *minutiae*.

Interested in banking in Bermuda? It's here. How about France? Oui. And never again will you find yourself embarrassingly unprepared on a sales trip in Antarctica. A sampling of the information you'll find here includes:

- Location and size
- Boundaries and terrain
- Climate and natural resources
- Population and birth rate
- Religions and ethnicity
- Government and economy
- Head of state's horoscope and shoe size

So whether you're interested in overthrowing a government or just want to know a little more about a country before doing business in it, check the *Factbook*. It even gives you a wide assortment of world maps in both GIF and JPEG formats.

The *CIA Factbook* isn't the only publication available. Before you visit a country, if you want to understand the local politics you might also read the directory *Heads of State and Cabinet Members of Foreign Governments* so you know the players and their positions.

How

World Wide Web

Where

www.odc.gov/cia/publications/pus.html

Links

Reference Maps

Selected International Environmental Agreements

Weights and Measures

Cross-Reference List of Geographic Names

No Matter Where You Go, There You Live

Living Abroad ☆☆☆

You'll find good excerpts here from the book *Living Abroad*, giving the basics on how to live in another country, with several sections detailing specifics of individual countries. For some countries, you'll also find directories of relocation services, serviced apartments, rental agents, moving companies, and other resources to help you settle in.

How

World Wide Web

Where

www.livingabroad.com

Uncle Sam Helps Kick Out the Jams

International Trade Administration ☆☆☆

The ITA is chock-full of information for both importers and exporters. Check out the "Internet Library" for U.S. import regulations. Other sections give you good instructions on how to export. Find out about U.S. trade missions, which sell U.S. products to buyers in other countries. Trade missions are categorized by industry, such as several trade missions selling U.S. software overseas.

Other sections focus on trade with specific parts of the world, such as the Central & Eastern Europe Business Information Center, mercifully called CEEBIC for short. If you want to buy or sell from this area of Europe, you can review trade leads, browse a searchable archive of U.S. Embassy cables, find details on reconstruction in Bosnia, link to resources in CEEBIC countries themselves, and research CEEBIC job opportunities. (CEEBIC's direct address is **www.itaiep.doc.gov/eebic/ceebic.html**.) You'll find ITA information on opportunities on other parts of our planet as well.

How

World Wide Web

Where

www.ita.doc.gov

We Can't Think of Anything Funny about Carnets

U.S. Council for International Business ☆☆☆

This is the U.S. office of the ATA Carnet Guarantee Chain. If you need an ATA carnet, go to these people. If you export and don't know about carnets, visit this site to see what you're missing. The Council also provides a short directory of links for exporters.

How

World Wide Web

Where

www.uscib.org

A Directory and a Growing Library

International Business and the Internet ☆☆☆

A good directory of resources for international trade is the centerpiece of this site, with good stuff categorized by country or by subject. Don't overlook the small-but-growing IBD Collection, where you'll find research reports and papers on global trade topics.

How

World Wide Web

Where

www.et.byu.edu/~eliasone/main.html

Bug-Eyed over BEMs

Big Emerging Markets (BEMs) ☆☆

When we read science fiction, BEMs stand for Bug-Eyed Monsters, the kind that book-cover paintings show grabbing a screaming damsel in a spacesuit. At this site, however, BEMs are Big Emerging Markets, which means Places You Can Sell Things.

We were wary about this site. Any URL beginning with **www.stat-usa.gov** is a red flag. Stat-USA describes stuff that sounds great, but when you get to its site, you find Uncle Sam with his hand stuck out, expecting you to pay. In this particular case, you'll find Uncle asking you to shell out $45 for a book on BEMs. However, this site provides summaries and samples from the book that are useful by themselves.

The summaries describe key BEMs in Asia, Africa, Europe, Latin America, and the Middle East. For each BEM, you can read about market access and competition, "Big Emerging Sectors," and key economic indicators. There is also a Q&A laden with sales pitches for the book.

How

World Wide Web

Where

www.stat-usa.gov/itabems.html

North America Free Trade Agreement

NAFTA ☆☆

Will NAFTA be an economic boon to thousands of businesses throughout Canada, the U.S., and Mexico—or, as Ross Perot warned, should we start listening for the giant sucking sound of American jobs going south? Read the full text of NAFTA and decide for yourself.

How

World Wide Web

Where

the-tech.mit.edu/Bulletins/nafta.html

Hot Spot for Business with Japan

U.S.-Japan Technology Management Center ☆☆☆☆

The hot spot here is in the "Japan Window" section. The entire *Directory of Japanese Trade and Technology* has been put online! Published by the European Union-Japan Centre, this book can be immensely useful if your company does business with Japan. Chapters include full contact information and lengthy descriptions telling you where to find statistics, economic yearbooks, corporate information, market and industry reports, patent info, information about individuals, business and manufacturers' associations, information brokers, market research firms, English-language magazines, newsletters, and fax services, and much more. It also gives an outline of JETRO activities.

You'll also find news stories in the "What's New" section, including business news and stock results, plus the top news from the big three daily papers: *Asahi, Mainichi,* and *Yomiuri.*

The "X-Guide" gives directories, including a lengthy one on Japanese law, with subdirectories of resources dealing with employment, product liability, and intellectual property. This site also gives you a list of Japanese corporations, a directory of political and government organizations (economics, international trade, industry), and a section on working, studying, living, and traveling in Japan.

How

World Wide Web

Where

fuji.stanford.edu

The Japan That Can Say No

THE JAPAN THAT CAN SAY NO ☆☆☆

This book was a bestseller in Japan, and gained a lot of attention in the U.S. Co-authored by Akio Morita, founder of Sony, and Shintaro Ishihara, a powerful member of Japan's Liberal Democratic Party, this book is an eye-opener on the business philosophy of Japan. It's a great resource for any businessperson who currently does or plans to do business in Japan. Know your market!

How

World Wide Web

Where

www.teleport.com/~richards/JapanNo/index.html

The Japan That Can Say, "We'll Help"

Economic Planning Agency ☆☆☆

"Lotsa good stuff" here for companies planning to do biz with Japan. The Agency has Web-ized the annual *The Economic Survey of Japan*, and also provides white papers, and summaries of Japanese economic performance in Japanese and English. You'll also find:

- Yearbook of the Japanese Investment Council
- Complaints on Japanese market access (with instructions on how to place them)
- Product liability law in Japan
- Charts of the Japanese economy
- Annual Report on National Accounts, downloadable (in English and Japanese) in spreadsheet format

How

World Wide Web

Where

www.epa.go.jp

Nothing Wrong about Hong Kong

Hong Kong Business Directory ☆☆☆

Hong Kong has become a cash machine for companies located around the globe. Exciting and fast-paced, Hong Kong has emerged as a booming manufacturing and exporting mecca.

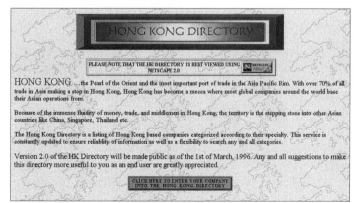

The Hong Kong Business Directory puts you in touch with the Orient's mecca of manufacturing.

The Hong Kong Business Directory can connect you to over *123,000* firms dealing in textiles, clothing, electronics, plastics, tourism, and more on Hong Kong island and the New Territories. Once you've located the companies you want to contact, you can quickly and easily fax them to get more information. Find out why the Pearl of the Orient is also called the Far East's most vibrant commercial center.

How
World Wide Web

Where
www.hkdir.com.hk

Asian Manufacturers and News

Asia Online ☆☆☆

The famed Silk Road that ran from China to Europe a thousand years ago may be closed, but traffic has detoured onto the Information Highway, which has been resurfaced and built for speed just in time for the 21st century. And the mode of transportation has been upgraded from horses and carts to bytes and bits.

Asia Online includes listings of Asian business and information services, online exhibitions, news, and convention schedules. There's even an online shopping mall and travel guide. Sure, it may lack some of the romance and adventure of the original Silk Road, but you'll make the trip a lot faster now.

F.I.S.H. reports live from the Singapore stock exchange.

You'll find here a directory of 1,400 manufacturers, plus procurement announcements, Asian manufacturing news, and industry outlook reports on Asian manufacturing. The directory of Asian corporations is a bust—only a handful of them—but the news directory is better, including the *Asia Business News*, *Nanyang Siang Pau* (the Chinese-language Malaysian paper), and *Financial Interactive Service Hub*, or *FISH* for short. *FISH* gives you live indexes, gainers, and losers from the Singapore stock exchange, including live graphs of intraday indexes. It also provides business news, and a directory with a good set of links (no descriptions) to financial information worldwide.

How

World Wide Web

Where

asia-online.com/index1.html

Help for Doing Business with Asia

See-Chai Lam Centre for International Communication ☆☆

Advances in transportation and telecommunication technology have linked a large part of our society with those of Asia and the Pacific region. The resulting increase in international, intercultural, and interlingual relationships has created a need for professional competence in context-sensitive international communication. Find out more about the business communication skills you need in order to compete in the competitive and emerging Asian markets.

Under "Forum Reports" you'll find papers on cross-cultural business and management. The Centre also provides a "gopher server" with business and marketing resources, and Web links to Japanese and Chinese software archives and Asia-Pacific resources.

How

World Wide Web

Where

hoshi.cic.sfu.ca/index.html

Resources to Do Biz in Europe

Business Monitor ☆☆☆

For a good source of trade information, especially about European countries, meet the Monitor. It provides a variety of information on different international trade topics, some concerning non-European countries such as the U.S. and South Africa, but mostly focusing on Europe. To help you find information quickly, everything on this site is searchable by company name and by topic. You must register to use Business Monitor, but it is free. A few samples of what it covers:

- An employer's guide to Irish employment law
- Legal and tax aspects of corporate investment in Ireland
- Tax and competition laws
- Many one-paragraph summaries of U.K. business topics from KMPG
- English translations of Swiss banking and tax laws
- English translations of French laws, ranging from the full text of regulations to one-paragraph summaries

How

World Wide Web

Where

www.businessmonitor.co.uk

Looking to Do Business in Toronto, Eh?

Canadian Business InfoWorld ☆☆☆

This directory is a useful starting place to do business with Canadian companies. It gives you a directory of Toronto companies, both alphabetically by company name or by type of company (manufacturer, wholesaler, etc.). The directory is also searchable, and offers you a side directory with info on Japanese companies in Ontario.

How

World Wide Web

Where

csclub.uwaterloo.ca/u/nckwan/./html/directory

Note the odd touch in the address above. Yes, it does have two slashes with nothing between them but a dot.

El Mercado Mexicano en el Mundo

Asociation de Industriales del Estado de Mexico ☆☆

This Spanish-language directory gives importers and exporters a way to contact Mexican industries. Companies are categorized according to product types.

How

World Wide Web

Where

telesur.acnet.net/AIEM

If you're interested in Mexican real estate, visit **telesur.acnet.net/DANMAR**.

European Electronic Information Market

Information Market Guide ☆☆

This site provides a gateway to the European electronic information market: software, databases, CD-ROMs, image banks, and so on. It gives you a directory of information products and services available in Europe, with all content available in all nine EU languages. (Let's see, English, French, German, Italian, um... er.... That's funny, I can always remember all Seven Dwarfs.) You can navigate the directory using Common Command Language (CCL) or menus.

Register to get your own password and a manual. To register, send your name and complete postal address to:

ECHO European Commission Host Organisation
B.P. 2373
L-1023 Luxembourg

How

World Wide Web

Where

www2.echo.lu

News from Croatia

Cro-News ☆☆

Millions of Americans have ancestral ties to Croatia, and interest in this region is still strong. Subscribe to this mailing list and you'll receive first-hand accounts of what's happening in Croatia, horrifying though it might be. There are also highly informative and highly charged debates about what can be done to stop the fighting. If you're trying to get a better understanding of the confusing issues surrounding this bloody conflict, this mailing list is a must.

How
Email

Where
cro-news@well.ox.ac.uk

Message
Subscription to Cro-News

Hey ,Boys and Girls, What Time Is It?

WorldClock ☆☆

Worldtime International Clock ☆☆

It's always happy hour somewhere, and with WorldClock, you'll always know the location. The Daylight Position Map is a clock that displays a map of the world showing which areas are currently illuminated by the sun and which areas are dark. It also displays your current local time, as well as Greenwich Mean Time.

Also while you're here, be sure to download a copy of the Worldtime International Clock for Windows, which allows you to customize

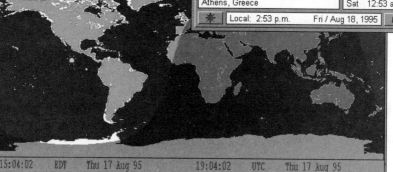

Too much time on my hands.

and show the time of day in up to six cities around the world at the same, um, time.

How

World Wide Web

Where

www.csusm.edu/cwis/winworld/clock

Download

WorldClock	world21.zip	(60 K)
Worldtime International Clock	wtm21d.zip	(83 K)

It's Mac Time!

Mac Map Clock ☆☆
World Clock Lite ☆☆

The Worldtime International Clock that I just described is a Windows-only utility, but Mac users needn't feel left out in the cold. A worldwide clock has long been available for Mac users, and it's built right in. If you haven't discovered this one yet, give it a try. Just open the Map control panel and set your current location. Then, you can click on any point on the map and it will give you the time at that location along with its distance from you in miles or kilometers. And think of all the download time you save.

If you need something more sophisticated, try World Clock Lite. The program automatically displays clocks for up to five cities around the world, and shows you which part of the globe is in daylight and which part is in darkness. It takes only a click to switch to different clocks around the world.

World Clock Lite has a very nice graphical display, and provides many options for customizing its appearance. The author also makes a commercial version available, so if you find this version of the program useful, you might want to order the complete version. In any case, this program is great for frequent travelers. If you have a Power Book, you can load it and use it while you're on the road.

How

FTP

Where

ftp://ftp.sunet.se/pub/mac/info-mac/app

Download

worldclock-lite.hqx (146 K)

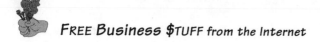

Raise the Flag

WorldFlag ☆☆

The only thing I know *less* about than geometry is world geography. And when it comes to matching flags with their countries, I'd be hard-pressed to identify anything more than the Stars and Stripes—and that's on a relatively lucid day.

But here's a program that could actually make learning the flags of the world (gasp!) *fun*. WorldFlag includes bitmaps and icons of just about every national flag in the world. And in addition to dressing up your documents with these colorful symbols, with just a few clicks of your mouse you can dress up your Program Manager by changing your existing Windows icons to flag icons. Not only will you learn the different flags, but your Windows desktop will start to look like the United Nations.

How

FTP

Where

ftp://gatekeeper.dec.com/pub/micro/msdos/win3/icons

Download

wrldflag.zip (81 K)

 At the risk of sounding too technical, here's how to change an existing icon to a new one: Simply click once on the icon (in your Program Manager window) that you want to change, click on Properties from the File menu, then press Change Icon... from the Program Item Properties window. Type in the wrldflag.dll path in the File Name box (for instance, c:\software\flags\wrldflag.dll), then press OK. Then just select the flag you want and press OK. (All you Mac people out there quit smirking and just be quiet.)

How to Travel & How to Talk

Travlang ☆☆☆☆☆

Travlang provides two related resources in one place, both created to help travelers—especially business travelers—in a hurry. The first half gives you one-click shopping for information on transportation, hotels, rail travel, car rental, maps, telephone numbers, and other on-the-road essentials.

The second half is a language resource specifically for travelers. Do you speak Spanish or Italian? Hey, who doesn't? French? *Oui*. But what about Russian,

Search here for a quick fix when you need to learn any of 24 languages in a hurry, and when you need travel info.

German, Dutch, or Portuguese? Um, well.... If not, check out Travlang. This site acts as your personal online interpreter, with many common—and not so common—languages covered (including Latin, official language of the Vatican—which is a country, even though tiny).

Designed to help globetrotters quickly master the basics of a language, Travlang provides guides to 24 languages. You'll find lessons, lists of common words and phrases with their translations, sound files you can click on to hear the words, and a huge assortment of links to other language resources on the Web. Check out Ergane, free multilingual translating software for Windows.

How

World Wide Web

Where

www.travlang.com

Languages of the World, Unite!

Human Languages Page ☆☆☆

This site is called the Human Languages Page, which I suppose differentiates it from animal, vegetable, and mineral languages. Anyway, this is probably the largest collection of language information on the Web. You'll find links to old standbys like French, Spanish, and German, but you'll also find links to information on languages as obscure or specialized as Esperanto, Lojban, Maori, and more—even Klingon.

You'll find links to online dictionaries and language tutorials, international periodicals (including online newspapers), and language-research information. This site is great for just about anybody who's interested in other languages—from first-time travelers to experienced linguists and language educators. This site was nominated for a 1995 Global News Navigator Best of the Net Award, and deservedly so.

How

World Wide Web

Where

The Human Languages Page has two mirrored sites. For fastest response, use the one closest to you:

U.S.: www.willamette.edu/~tjones/Language-Page.html
U.K.: www.dcs.warwick.ac.uk/~bear/Language-Page.html

This site has home pages in German, Dutch, French, Spanish, Russian, Portuguese, Norwegian, Afrikaans, and other languages. And if you're looking for a language-related job, check here for job opportunities.

You Speak My Language

Foreign Language Resources on the Web ☆☆☆

If the topic of conversation is languages on the Internet, The Foreign Languages on the World Wide Web page has to enter into the discussion. This comprehensive site is a close runner-up to the Human Languages Page in terms of depth, and offers its own unique slant on language information. Where the Human Languages Page covers resources *about* languages, this spot covers resources *in* languages. To be specific, in non-English languages.

Look here for links to language tutorials, literature, and travel information. France is especially well-represented here.

This one is highly recommended for travelers and anybody who's curious about other languages and cultures. The author of this page, Steve Thorne, is very discriminating, so only the best foreign language and cultural links are included here—but that still includes several dozen resources.

How

World Wide Web

Where

www.itp.berkeley.edu/~thorne/HumanResources.html

How to Say "PC" in 150 Languages

MULTILINGUAL PC DIRECTORY ☆☆☆☆

Knowledge is power—or so said the old Saturday-morning *Schoolhouse Rock* commercials—and Knowledge Computing is leading the way in bringing the power of PCs to the world through its innovative multilingual software.

The *Multilingual PC Directory* is the definitive guide to multilingual and foreign language products for IBM PCs and compatibles. It includes details of nearly 400 products for more than 150 languages available in over 70 countries from over 1,000 manufacturers, publishers, and affiliates. If you word process in Portuguese, do spreadsheets in Spanish, or create graphics in Greek, the *Multilingual PC Directory* is definitely for you.

Available in hard copy (for $52.50), Windows Help format (a 610 K download), or on the Web, this source guide includes product and company profiles, computer requirements, and languages supported. Contact information is also covered, including addresses, telephone and fax numbers, and some email addresses.

How
World Wide Web

Where
www.knowledge.co.uk/xxx/mpcdir/

Languages for Mac Users

University of Michigan Language Software ☆☆☆

Here's equal time for Mac users: The University of Michigan's Macintosh archive has arguably the best collection of language-learning software for the Mac. (PC and Unix users might want to stop reading this page before their eyes glaze over.) After each software program's description, we've added in parentheses the decompression software you'll need to unstuff that particular program.

- **Multilingual: Flashworks** - Flash card program for learning foreign languages. Comes with databases for German, Spanish, French, Greek (including PostScript font), and Hebrew (including bitmap font). (BinHex4.0, Compact1.51)

- **Spanish Practice** - Learn Spanish grammar. Requires HyperCard. (BinHex4.0, Compact1.51)

345

FREE Business $TUFF from the Internet

- **Spanish: Aprendemos** - About one thousand Spanish words with English translations. Requires HyperCard 2.0. (BinHex4.0, StuffIt3.50)
- **Spanish Teacher** - Tests your Spanish skills by asking you to translate words. (BinHex4.0, Compact1.51)
- **Korean Han Kit** - This language kit provides you with everything you need to use Korean on your Macintosh. Simply pull down the keyboards menu, choose your favorite keyboard, and begin typing with Han fonts. (BinHex4.0, StuffIt3.50)
- **German: Leger** - Leger is a text editor for large files integrated with a hypertext English-German dictionary. It can use the Apple PlainTalk extension. (BinHex4.0, StuffIt3.50)
- **Thai Tutor1** - Learn the Thai numbering system, and how to pronounce Thai numbers. (BinHex4.0, StuffIt3.50)
- **Thai Tutor2** - Learn the Thai alphabet, and how to pronounce it. (BinHex4.0, StuffIt3.50)

How

World Wide Web

Where

www.umich.edu/~archive/mac/misc/foreignlang

Download

Flashworks	flashworks1.07.cpt.hqx	(452 K)
Spanish Practice	apracticarespanol.cpt.hqx	(72 K)
Aprendemos	aprendemosespanol1.001l.sit.hqx	(238 K)
Spanish Teacher	spanishteacher.cpt.hqx	(38 K)
Korean Han Kit	hankoreankitdemo1.0.sit.hqx	(358 K)
Leger	leger1.01.sit.hqx	(1,909 K)
Thai Tutor1	thaitutor1.1a.sit.hqx	(695 K)
Thai Tutor2	thaitutor2.2.sit.hqx	(1,352 K)

Japanese for Mac Users

University of Michigan Japanese Software ☆☆☆

Businesspeople who use Macs and want to do business using the Japanese language may find these five software programs helpful. After each software program's description, we've added in parentheses the decompression software you'll need to unstuff that particular program.

- **GomTalk** - Resources (cdev, inits, ResEdit templates) that allow users of KanjiTalk (the Japanese operating system) to install System 7.0 on their machines. The manual is in Japanese, btw. (BinHex4.0, Compact1.51)

- **Japanese Prelector** - Study system for students of Japanese, specifically designed to improve the effectiveness of learning vocabulary and Kanji. Also serves as a dictionary, aids students in correct grammar, and assists teachers in arranging and controlling course content. (BinHex4.0, Compact1.51)

- **Mac Japanese Dictionary Lookup** - A lookup program for Jim Breen's Japanese-English and Kanji dictionaries available at monu6.cc.monash.edu.au. Requires KanjiTalk, or System 7.1 with the appropriate Japanese modules. (BinHex4.0, StuffIt3.50)

- **Mac Kanji Converter** - Converts Japanese Kanji codes to/from Shift-JIS, JIS and EUC formats. Also can use Mac, DOS or Unix formatted text. V. 0.93. (BinHex4.0, StuffIt1.51)

- **OpenBook** - Displays Kanji on any Mac, but needs Japanese system software for input of new Kanji words which are all pronounced during practice; v1.02 fixes problems with crashes on newer Macs; requires at least 68020, will run on PowerMac but isn't native. (BinHex4.0, StuffIt3.5)

How

World Wide Web

Where

www.umich.edu/~archive/mac/misc/foreignlang

Download

GomTalk:	gomtalk1.21.cpt.hqx	(92 K)
Japanese Prelector	japaneseprelector1.2.cpt.hqx	(891 K)
Japanese Dictionary Lookup	macjdic1.30.sit.hqx	(202 K)
Mac Kanji Converter	mackc0.93.sit.hqx	(36 K)
OpenBook	openbook1.02.sit.hqx	(2,586 K)

I Think I'm Turning Japanese

Nihongo Sensei ☆☆☆

Here's a program that—believe it or not—makes learning Japanese fun, without making you feel that your tongue has been stepped on by a sumo wrestler. Nihongo Sensei is a Windows program that displays a word in Japanese characters and uses your sound card to say the word simultaneously. In addition to printing quizzes along with your scores and keeping statistics on your progress,

Colors		

Text

yellow

English	Japanese	
white	shiroi	しろい
black	kuroi	くろい
yellow	kiiroi	きいろい
red	akai	あかい
blue	aoi	あおい
gray	haiiro	はいいろ
brown	chairo	ちゃいろ
green	midori	みどり
pink	momoiro	ももいろ
orange	orenji	おれんじ

Update
Save
Delete Problem
Add Problem
Quiz Name...
Clear Scores...
Exit

Somebody email me when you find out what Nihongo Sensei means. I'll be waiting...

Nihongo Sensei lets you input vocabulary words to study. You can even mark especially tricky words you want to concentrate on for repeated practice.

Some of the categories to study are:

- Colors
- At a Hotel
- Greetings
- Relatives

While it would probably take less time to take a slow boat to Tokyo than to download these four programs, the wait will be worth your effort.

How

World Wide Web

Where

www.acs.oakland.edu/oak/simtel/win3/educate.html

Download

japan12a.zip	(277 K)
japan12b.zip	(307 K)
japan12c.zip	(239 K)
japan12d.zip	(54 K)

All four programs are needed to run this program. Download each into a separate directory (like JAPANA, JAPANB, and so on), then unzip each file. Go to the first directory and click on INSTALL.EXE to start the installation. When prompted to insert a new disk, just change the path name to the next directory (JAPANB) and continue the installation.

Here's another language program you can download at this site as well:

mb12.zip   Multi-language learning environment

Win95 Goes Global

Windows 95 Multilanguage Support ☆☆☆

These days, you hardly hear the word *economy* unless it's preceded by the word *global*. So make sure your software is as worldly as your potential market. Whether you're doing business in Bulgaria, writing checks in Czech, or polishing the boss's apple in Polish, you'll want to install Microsoft's multilanguage support utility.

This Windows 95 program lets you write documents in Bulgarian, Belorussian, Czech, Hungarian, Greek, Polish, and several other languages.

How
FTP

Where
ftp://ftp.microsoft.com/Softlib/MSLFILES

Download
lang.exe (1,370 K)

Parle-Vous Francais?

You, Too, Can Learn French ☆☆☆

Jaques Leon, a native of France and current resident in Montreal, Canada, has generously made this interactive Web site available for those who want to learn French in the privacy of their homes; but want a more interactive approach than those found in books or in tape series.

A nice feature of this site is the liberal use of sound file links that you can click on to hear how the lessons should sound. Currently, the sound files are in **.wav** format only, so you'll either need to be running Windows with the MPLAYER sound extension or you'll need to have a sound conversion utility that can convert **.wav** files to a sound format that works on your computer.

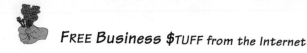
How

World Wide Web

Where

teleglobe.ca/~leo/french.html

Where to Find Way More Goodies

We've packed a lot of free stuff throughout this book that's useful for international trade tycoons. After you pull everything you need from this chapter, you'll probably want to review Chapter 7, *Sales Reps and Road Warriors*. You'll find good resources here for international businesspeople, especially in the second half of the chapter.

Your next stop should be the index of this book. You can use the index two ways to find resources to help you globalize. First, you can look under the heading **international trade resources**. It will lead you to dozens of resources that are scattered throughout the book. (If you have shipping questions, look under **logistics resources**. Or try **travel**.)

Secondly, you can look under headings for countries with which you want to do business. For example, if you want to do business with Canada, look under **Canadian resources**, or under **German resources** to do business with Germany. Businesspeople in Quebec will be pleased to know that we have separate categories for **French-language resources** and **France resources**. You can differentiate between information that's in the French language (and may deal with any country), as opposed to resources (which may be in any language) to help you do business with French companies.

Similarly, you'll find a separate index heading for **Chinese-language resources**, a section that deals with several different countries.

FREE $TUFF

The meek may inherit the earth—
but not its mineral rights.

J. Paul Getty

Business Law, Trademarks, Copyrights, and Patents

Someone once said, "The wheels of commerce are greased with laws." I don't know what that means, but it sounds pretty good.

Actually, I prefer another saying about commerce and law, spoken by Don Corleone in Mario Puzo's novel *The Godfather*: "One lawyer with his briefcase can steal more than a thousand men with guns."

The Internet brings you enough stuff to fill several briefcases, even those accordion-fold expandable types favored by the paper-intensive legal trade. But you can't steal the resources in this chapter, because they're all given away for free.

The Ultimate Law List

THE LEGAL LIST INTERNET DESK REFERENCE ☆☆☆☆☆

The complete text of this book by Erik J. Heels is available on the Web. Heels' extraordinarily comprehensive guide concentrates on U.S. legal resources, with a smattering of resources from other countries (mostly Canada, Australia, and Europe). Heels lists more than a thousand legal resources. He describes each one's sponsoring organization, and often gives a detailed exploration of individual sites. The printed version of this book is well worth its $30 price. The World Wide Web version is free and includes a time-saving search engine, making this site an outstanding value.

> *The Legal List* is the short name of the book *The Legal List, Fall 1995 Internet Desk Reference, Law-Related Resources on the Internet and Elsewhere*. First published in 1992--and now in its seventh edition--*The Legal List* is a consolidated guide to all of the law-related resources available on (and off) the Internet. As of spring 1995, *The Legal List* is being published exclusively by Lawyers Cooperative Publishing.
>
> In addition to being available as a paper-based product, *The Legal List* is available as an ASCII text-only file. The ASCII text-only file can be retrieved via e-mail (from LCP's List Server) and via anonymous FTP (from LCP's anonymous FTP Server). It is also available on Usenet--see the FAQ for details. Also, *The Legal List* is available as a compilation of HTML files via LCP's WWW Server.
>
> - Search *The Legal List*.
> - Browse *The Legal List* HTML via a clickable Summary of Contents.
> - Get *The Legal List* ASCII via LCP's FTP server.
> - Submit information for inclusion in *The Legal List*.
> - Frequently-Asked Questions (FAQ) file for *The Legal List*.

This great guidebook is more than worth its $30 cover price. It's yours for free on the Internet.

How

World Wide Web

Where

www.lcp.com

The Legal List Internet Desk Reference is also available via FTP from **ftp.lcp.com/ pub/LegalList/legallist.txt** (a nearly 400 K file). You can get the textfile by email. Email to **listserv@lcp.com** with the message **subscribe legal-list Yourfirstname Yourlastname**.

It Pays to Advertise (but Don't Get Caught!)

Advertising Law Internet Site ☆☆☆☆

Does your business advertise? Most do. And whether your business advertises on the Internet, on television, in print, or by telephone cold calls, this site has important information for you. (At least, if you have a U.S. business. Because except for links to European ad law resources, everything here is U.S.-only.)

Created by Lewis Rose, an ad law attorney with the firm of Arent Fox, this huge site (approaching 300 pages) gives you original articles, the full text of nearly all (or so it seems) federal laws, regulations, agency rulings, articles about laws that affect advertising, testimony and speeches on the subject, and links to other sites. You'll also find some material on state regulation of advertising. Much of the material here is available nowhere else.

Take advantage of this site's excellent free discussion forum. You can ask questions about laws on advertising and get answers from attorney Rose and other experts in the field. Until I read this forum's messages, I had no idea that rules even existed about the size of disclaimers in print and on TV. But somebody asked, and this forum answered.

To keep you on the top of the latest developments that affect ads on the Internet, Rose includes original material on that topic. Government authorities have levied fines of more than $10,000 on Internet advertisers, you might want to look here for articles on "Policing Cyberspace Advertising," "Potential Liability for Online Service Providers," domain names and trademark law, and other hot topics.

Hot tip: The best way to find your way around this site is to go to the button bar at the bottom and click on INDEX. And if you really like this site, you can

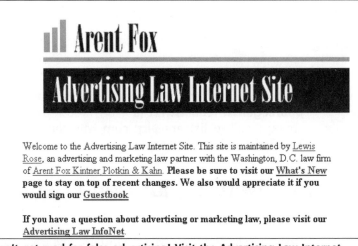

Don't get sued for false advertising! Visit the Advertising Law Internet Site instead.

subscribe to its announcement list. Once a month or so, you'll receive an email message telling you what's new here.

How

World Wide Web

Where

www.webcom.com/~lewrose/home.html

Cornell's Cornucopia of Codes

Legal Information Institute ☆☆☆☆☆

The Legal Information Institute (LII)at Cornell Law School is a one-stop shopping bonanza for law-related stuff. Since its establishment in 1992, the LII has continually strived to find new ways of electronically distributing legal documents. Now, in addition to its regular task of distributing hypertext course supplements to Cornell's lawyers-in-training, the dissemination of legal information via the Internet has become one of its mainstays.

You'll find links to a plethora of law-related sites and texts, including:

• *Cornell Law Review*

• Recent decisions of the New York Court of Appeals

• Searchable hypertext version of the full U.S. Code

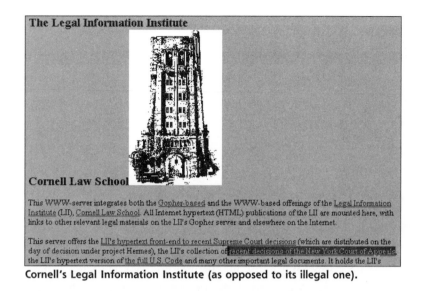

The Legal Information Institute

Cornell Law School

This WWW-server integrates both the Gopher-based and the WWW-based offerings of the Legal Information Institute (LII), Cornell Law School. All Internet hypertext (HTML) publications of the LII are mounted here, with links to other relevant legal materials on the LII's Gopher server and elsewhere on the Internet.

This server offers the LII's hypertext front-end to recent Supreme Court decisions (which are distributed on the day of decision under project Hermes), the LII's collection of recent decisions of the New York Court of Appeals, the LII's hypertext version of the full U.S. Code and many other important legal documents. It holds the LII's

Cornell's Legal Information Institute (as opposed to its illegal one).

- The complete Uniform Commercial Code in searchable hypertext. (The UCC regulates sales, leases, funds transfers, investment securities, and virtually every other aspect of commerce in the U.S. To go straight to the UCC, try **www.law.cornell.edu/topics/commercial.html**.)

- "What LII's Big Ear Has Heard on Law-Related Lists" (the best way to find new Net resources for law)

- Hypertext front-end to recent Supreme Court decisions

- International law

How

World Wide Web

Where

www.law.cornell.edu/

East Is East and WEST's Is Free

WEST'S LEGAL DIRECTORY ☆☆☆

Need to find a lawyer or two? Would 650,000 do? That's how many are listed in *West's Legal Directory*. If you want to look up any attorney in the U.S. or Canada, or any law firm, this is the site for you. Biographical profiles on attorneys include postal address, phone number, court and bar admission years, areas of practice, educational background, and other details.

You can search for attorneys with any specialty in a specific geographic area, or search by name or firm name. You can also use the parameters here to find an old friend or classmate who went on to law school, or to find an attorney for a friend who needs legal services away from home.

How

World Wide Web

Where

www.wld.com

Email Your Lawyer Today

Carswell Canada Legal Directory ☆☆☆

Here you can search through a directory of Canadian attorneys. While an attorney's individual listings are not as detailed as those in *West's Legal Directory*, Carswell does provide two valuable items that *West's* doesn't: each attorney's email address, and for each attorney who has one, a clickable link to the attorney's Web site.

How

World Wide Web

Where

www.carswell.com/LawDir

No Cobwebs on Cyberjournals

Findlaw ☆☆☆☆

Can't find the latest journal with the loophole on a brand-new legal rule that threatens your bread and butter? No time to search through musty stacks of old law publications to find a crucial article that affects your business? Do your searching on the Web instead. Findlaw lets you go to one place to search articles in all the legal journals available on the Net. Many of these journals have articles about business and law. In fact, most of them do.

You can search *Cardozo Arts & Entertainment Law Journal, Cornell Law Review, Intellectual Property Law Journal, Journal of Law and Commerce, Russian Business Law Journal*, and dozens more. To top it off, Findlaw gives you a pretty good directory of links to other Net legal stuff. Much better than digging through those back-issue boxes in the janitor's closet. You know, the ones behind the old unusable mops.

How

World Wide Web

Where

www.findlaw.com

Not Getting Enough Email? Try This

Chicago-Kent's Guide to Legal Resources ☆☆☆☆

You've got a nice searchable guide to Internet legal stuff here. It's not as up-to-date as it could be, but it is well-organized and can lead you to many useful sites.

But the best part about this site is **Legal Lists**, the most complete guide to legal discussion groups anyplace on the Net. Legal Lists, created by Lyonette Louis-Jacques, catalogs and describes more than 400 Internet email lists that handle legal issues, and lists (without describing) more than 80 law-related newsgroups. Dozens of newsgroups discuss business law, including several lists specific to law as it affects certain industries. Ms. Louis-Jacques has done an outstanding job including lists from outside the U.S., especially lists in languages other than English. If legal issues directly affect your business, look here to find a list for you.

How

World Wide Web

Where

www.kentlaw.edu/lawnet/lawlinks.html

Baby, It's Code Outside

California Revenue and Taxation Code ☆☆☆

Actually, you can reach all California State laws here. Revenue and taxes hit businesspeople where they live, but you might someday also have a need to check out laws in one of these areas:

- Unemployment Code
- Commercial Code
- Business and Professions Code
- Corporations Code
- Insurance Code, Financial Code
- Labor Code

You can search through all of this stuff by keyword, or zero in on what you need by type of code.

How

World Wide Web

Where

leginfo.public.ca.gov/calaw.html

Legalese in Black and White

Gama Legal Forms ☆☆☆☆

You've seen enough episodes of *L.A. Law* to know your way around the courtroom. Just fill out the forms and sign the necessary papers, and you'll be able to handle 90 percent of your own legal hassles.

This site includes more than 50 legal forms you can copy. Here are some samples:

- Demand For Arbitration
- Demand For Mediation
- Stockholders' Agreement
- Articles of Incorporation
- Stock Purchase Agreement
- General Consent Agreement
- Independent Contractor Agreement
- General Power of Attorney
- Agreement Settling Boundary Line Dispute
- Authorization To Release Employment Information
- Product Licensing Contract
- Breach Of Contract Notice
- Formal Request For Credit Report
- Freedom of Information Act Request

How

World Wide Web

Where

www.gama.com/forms.htm

For more free legal forms, try **'Lectric Law Library** on the Web at **www.lectlaw.com**. This is certainly the funniest Internet law site, but much of the material here is just legal trivia, amusing but not useful. Go to The Forms Room for more than 70 downloadable forms. If you can stand the screaming all caps letters, you can copy good business law forms from this site.

Serve Yourself Salad Bar and Law Clinic

Nolo Press Self-Help Law Center ☆☆☆

Nolo Press publishes very good do-it-yourself books on legal issues, such as *Patent It Yourself*. This site is mostly a catalog of their books, but you will also find dozens of short articles on legal topics, many covering business law issues. Look under the directory headings Business & Workplace, Intellectual Property, Immigration, and Represent Yourself in Court. Some examples of what you'll find:

- Can You Really Get A Patent without a Lawyer?
- The Easy Way to 'Patent Pending' Status
- When Copying Is OK: the Fair Use Rule
- What Small Businesses Should Know about Trademarks
- Software Development Agreements
- Online Legal Advice: Let the Browser Beware
- Represent Yourself in Court: Is It Really Like Doing Your Own Brain Surgery?

How

World Wide Web

Where

gnn.com/gnn/bus/nolo

Follow the (News) Letter of the Law

Arent Fox Publications ☆☆☆☆

As partners in one of the largest firms in Washington, D.C., Arent, Fox, Kintner, Plotkin, and Kahn are experts in representing governments, international companies and organizations, and trade associations in litigation and arbitration. I'm sure they're well paid for it, too.

But wait, these guys also publish an extensive list of free newsletters you can request online. You can read 'em on the Web, you can get 'em by email, and you can even receive printed copies by postal mail. (Of course, email is fastest.) Sign up on this Web page for the delivery method of your choice. Titles include:

- *Business Bullets*—Real estate and general business law news
- *Communications Counsel*—News of communications law and the communications industry
- *Employment News*—Labor and employment law issues
- *Environmental Law & Toxic Liability*—Environmental law or liability relating to toxic substances or hazardous materials
- *Government Contracts*—Government contracts developments
- *Health Information Systems and Telemedicine*
- *Health Law Trends*
- *Tax Bullets*
- *TIPsheet*—Technology and intellectual property
- *Washington AgLaw Report*—Agricultural law, especially production and marketing
- *Washington International Report*—U.S. trade policy and legislation

How

World Wide Web

Where

www.arentfox.com/publicat.htm

This Library Makes House Calls

U.S. House of Representatives Internet Law Library ☆☆☆

You won't find this valuable law tool on Thomas, the loudly-ballyhooed Web site for the House. Maybe this is just Newt Gingrich's little secret. Created for use by House members, this well-organized site has directories that link to more than 1,600 Internet law resources. And we don't mean just U.S. law. This one connects to online sites with laws from more than 80 countries. This is an especially good place to visit if you are looking for the actual text, from the country of your choice, of a law or a treaty. Resources here are arranged in seven sections. (One for each of the deadly sins? Naw, must be the habits of highly effective people.)

- Federal laws
- State and territorial laws

- Laws of other nations
- Treaties and international law
- Law school library catalogs and services
- Legal profession directories
- Reviews of law books

How

World Wide Web

Where

www.pls.com:8001

The Internet, Legally Speaking

Gray Cary Ware & Freidenrich ☆☆☆

Gray Cary Ware & Freidenrich is a commercial law firm representing many of California's telecommunications, manufacturing, software, banking, and financial institutions. And now it has hung its shingle in cyberspace.

And that's good for you, because the Gray Cary Ware & Freidenrich Web site includes lots of information about doing business on the Internet, protecting yourself legally in cyberspace, and other legal issues—and it won't cost you $200 per hour. In addition, you'll find the full texts of U.S. copyright, trademark, and patent laws, as well as links to other legal resources on the Net.

You'll find many informative articles written by staff experts on business issues, including "For the New Lending Officer: a Primer on Three Key Lending Regulations," "Cooperative Advertising Programs under the Robinson-Patman Act," legislative analyses such as "The Private Securities Litigation Reform Act of 1995," and several articles on trademarks for products, technology, and multimedia.

You can read two good business law newsletters by GCW&F at their site. *U.S./ Mexico Legal Reporter* is a must for any company in either country that trades with the other. It has detailed, in-depth articles that cover topics such as maquiladoras, investment, new Mexican business laws, and customs policies. The second newsletter, simply called *The Quarterly*, features good articles on Internet business and non-Net business law topics. Look for an article on "Developing a (Corporate) Internet Policy", and don't miss *The Quarterly*'s archive of articles from past issues.

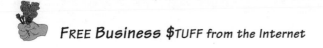

How

World Wide Web

Where

www.gcwf.com

On Top of Law Down Under

Legal Information Index ☆☆☆

This is the best Internet source for Australian law resources. Updated once a week (every Monday morning), it covers contract law in Australia, aboriginal law, Australian aviation regulations, tax law, and all other legal fields. This site pays special attention to the impending government regulation of the Internet in Australia. Most of its hotlinks to other sites include short descriptions. Here's a good idea: At the end of each link listed, this site displays in parentheses what country the resource covers or, if it handles a single Australian province, which province.

How

World Wide Web

Where

spirit.com.au/~dan/law

Expand Your Horizons—Think Globally

International Trade Law Project ☆☆☆

This site has a good deal of useful information on International Trade Law, but it has a way to go before it becomes truly comprehensive. High points include "International Trade Conventions and other trade instruments," which gives you the text of agreements arranged by year (with documents going back to 1883!), a directory of international trade organizations, the "Trade Law Library" (a catalog of hotlinks to related sites), and a section on international trade law materials. A built-in search engine helps you find what you want at this site.

How

World Wide Web

Where

ananse.irv.uit.no/44/trade

There's No Business like Law Business

Business and the Law ☆☆☆

Reinhart, Boerner, Van Deuren, Norris & Rieselbach is one of the many law firms hanging its shingle in cyberspace in recent months. And from what I've seen at this site, it's one of the best—especially for Internauts looking for lots of law-related links and information. Rather than just filling up its Web pages with self-promotional diatribe like many businesses on the Internet, this firm has loads of valuable links to business- and law-related Net pages.

You'll find free stock quotes and daily financial highlights, links to the House of Representatives, FedWorld, the U.S. Patent and Copyright offices, and lots more.

How

World Wide Web

Where

www.rbvdnr.com

Links

Health Care

Labor and Employment

Employee Benefits (includes "How GATT Affects Your Retirement Plans")

Environmental (includes "Federal Law Permits Clean-Up Costs to Be Recovered")

Trusts and Estates

International (includes "Financing Foreign Sales," "Doing Business in the USA: an Introduction for Foreign Investors," "Legal Aspects of Foreign Distribution," "Structuring and Documenting International Mergers and Acquisitions," and more)

The Law of the (Cyber) Land

cmplaw-l Internet, Computers and Law Discussion Group ☆☆☆

Talk about your hot topics. Here's a mailing list that combines the Internet, computers, and law into one comprehensive forum for discussion. You'll find in-depth analyses and hot debates on the still-gray legalities of free speech on the Net, copyright violations, pornography, and many other computer- and Net-related issues. Now if someone would just combine biking, brewing, and books into one mailing list, I'd never have to subscribe to another list again....

How
Email

Where
listserv@nervm.nerdc.ufl.edu

Message
subscribe cmplaw-l Yourfirstname Yourlastname

How to Be a Smart Asset

ARVIC's Guide to Intellectual Property ☆☆☆☆

What if another company stole your business name? Have you protected your-self from such an attack? Can someone copy your trademarks? Your patents and copyrights? And how much money are your trademarks, patents, and copy-rights actually worth?

A survey by ARVIC found that less than 8 percent of businesspeople under-stand the value of intellectual property assets. This good, free book addresses that problem. It is written for accountants and businesspeople, not for lawyers. It provides information on how to protect your intellectual property assets and how to register them in Canada. (While written by and for Canadian businesspeople, most of this book is valuable for businesses in all countries.)

ARVIC's Guide to Intellectual Property includes a good questionnaire that you can fill out to calculate the value of your company's intellectual property. The total may surprise you.

The book also includes 18 forms that you can copy, such as a confidentiality agreement, an employee noncompete agreement, and other forms to protect your intellectual property assets. You'll find worthwhile suggestions in *ARVIC's Guide*. Read and use this helpful information. Don't be ignorant about the value of intellectual property.

How
World Wide Web

Where
www.arvic.com

 This site has a mystery: Who or what is ARVIC? There is no description of ARVIC at this site, no address, no phone number, and no other contact information. There is not even an email address for a Webmaster. Talk about low-key sales techniques!

Smart Stuff about Intellectual Property

misc.int-property Newsgroup ☆☆☆☆☆

This active newsgroup does receive some rants and raves, but most messages are serious ones about copyright, patent, trademark, and trade dress issues. (If you must know, *trade dress* isn't designer clothing but the type of intellectual property violation committed by knock-offs, imitations, and counterfeits.) In this newsgroup, amateur's questions (when sensible) are answered by pros in the field. This is a good resource to ask when your business has intellectual property questions. As a bonus, you'll find hardly any spam here.

Sample topics: A simple(?) question on Fair Use Doctrine?; Abolish Copyright; Determining patent infringement; Knock-off golf course—why trade dress infringement?; Looking for patent search firms; My Thoughts on Copyright Law Changes; Patent Bar Exam applications; Pendency of applications in U.S. PTO.

How

Newsgroup

Where

misc.int-property

One Question Answered by misc.int-property

From: eskargo@nyc.pipeline.com (Eric S. Goldman)
Subject: Re: A simple(?) question on Fair Use Doctrine???

In article < A simple(?) question on Fair Use Doctrine??? >,
Bob Costa < bcosta@investorweb.com > ' wrote:

> How much of a copyrighted work can I quote, before I get in
> trouble with copyright law? Is this a simple answer, like 100
> words or less? Or is it more complex??
> Do I have to attribute any quotes?

There is no simple test in terms of word count for fair use. If you are quoting a song lyric, for example, then there may not be 100 words in the original.

Fair use is a judgment call based on the four factors set forth in the Copyright Act for evaluating such use. This judgment is best made by experienced counsel.

Eric S. Goldman

Copyright Info

LOCIS (Library of Congress Information Server) ☆☆☆

Is that book, magazine story, photo, or software that you want to copy and sell copyrighted or in the public domain and royalty-free? Find out the information you need by using LOCIS—the Library of Congress Information Server. LOCIS contains copyright data and records from 1978 to the present. If it has already been written, sung, or performed, you'll find out about it here. *You can even register your work online.*

One important note, though. Searching LOCIS can be very frustrating if you're a new user. The are many complex commands. Be sure to download and read a copy of the *Guide to Quick Searching LOCIS*.

How

Telnet

Where

locis.loc.gov

Go To

Follow login instructions

 You can search on the Web via a Z3950 gateway (whatever that is). For information, Web over to:

lcweb.loc.gov/z3950

 LOCIS also holds an International Legal Database, with abstracts of all Spanish-speaking and Portuguese-speaking legal publications since 1976, and it also includes some French ones. A Spanish-language legal serials database contains abstracts about laws in Spain, Latin America, and Central America.

Do You Copy?

Copyright Clearance Center Online ☆☆☆

When does a copy become a copyright violation? It depends on who you talk to and, unfortunately, that just might be a very expensive lawyer if somebody sues you for infringement.

Before that happens, check out the Copyright Clearance Center (CCC) to learn about protecting yourself—and your publications—in cyberspace. CCC can help make sure you comply with the U.S. copyright law and show you how to collect payments for your own copyrighted material.

How

World Wide Web

Where

www.copyright.com

Links

Harry Fox Agency for clearing U.S. music copyrights

CANCOPY, Canadian copyright licensing organization

CLA, the U.K. copyright licensing organization

United Nations World Intellectual Property Organization

 Online copyright searching can be easy by accessing the free CCC demo catalogs.

A Patently Good Web Resource

STO Internet Patent Search ☆☆☆

Okay, so you've built a better mouse trap and are ready for a stampede of buyers. But before the world beats a path to your door, make sure somebody else hasn't already built your invention.

The Source Translation & Optimization's (STO) Internet Patent Search System provides Web users a way to perform patent searches, as well as accessing information on the patent process. STO provides free patent information and a free patent search service. Currently, you can retrieve all patent titles since 1970 by class or subclass code, as well as obtaining information on filing fees, archives of articles from the Internet Patent News Service, and the latest info from the IPNS, which is an excellent source for patent-related news bulletins and lists of new patents.

You can determine patent class by using either the Manual of Classification or the Index to Classification. You can also retrieve patent abstracts by using patent numbers, and search for patents issued since the 1800s by using the U.S. Patent and Trademark Office's classification system.

How

World Wide Web

Where

sunsite.unc.edu/patents/intropat.html

Links

U.S. Code Section 35—federal patent laws

Internet Patent News Service

Patent offices in U.K., Brazil, and Hong Kong

Patents and AIDS

U.S. Patents Project at CNIDR ☆☆☆

The nonprofit Center for Networked Information Discovery and Retrieval gives you a zippy, easy-to-use way of browsing the U.S. Patent Classification Database and find patent info going back to the dark ages of 1976. (You remember—bell bottoms.) You can enter words or phrases and receive all patents containing those words. This is much easier than learning the classification schemes.

Another CNIDR database gives you access to a very specialized set of patents. The AIDS Patent Project (at **patents.cnidr.org:80**) lets you search U.S. patents related to Acquired Immune Deficiency Syndrome.

How

World Wide Web

Where

patents.cnidr.org:4242

This Week's New Gizmos

Internet Patent News Service ☆☆☆

Here's a great way to discover new technologies to license, and find out what kinds of techo-creativity other companies are up to. You can get a weekly list of new patents delivered to you free via email. The list includes the titles and numbers of all new patents issued that week by the U.S. Patent and Trademark Office (or the PTO, as patent pros call it), plus instructions on how to obtain complete, detailed information on any patent that tickles your fancy. You'll also receive occasional patent-related news stories. Whether it's a new dingus, a gizmo, or a watchamacallit, you'll find out about it first from this list.

How

Email

Where

patents@world.std.com

Message

Okay, this will take some explaining, so be patient. It's not complicated, you just have a few choices. Most of these email services process your subscriptions with a computer. This one uses a real live human, who will read your message and will need your information in this order:

- Your name
- Your postal address
- Your email address
- Next, describe what kind of patents you want to receive by typing a one-word signal:
  - To receive only mechanical patents: MECHANICAL
  - To receive only chemical patents: CHEMICAL
  - To receive only electronic patents: ELECTRONIC
  - To receive every kind of patent: ALL
- Next describe what format you want to receive:
  - If you want to receive plain text: ASCII
  - Or, if you want a smaller, compressed file: UUZIP
- (optional) Your occupation
- (optional) How you plan to use patent info
- (optional) Tell him Pat and Vince sent you

Okay, Find Me a Perpetual Motion Machine

U.S. Patent and Trademark Office ☆☆☆

You can search here through abstracts of all U.S. patents back into the 1970s, but there are better searches available elsewhere on the Net. The good information at this site are downloadable forms (Patent Application, Patent Copy Sales, Trademark/Service Mark Application), and an excellent catalog of patent and trademark information resources on the Net. This directory is well-organized, lists good resources and, out of all the Net catalogs we've seen, gives you the most helpful descriptions of patent and trademark resources. It will save you a lot of click-and-wait time checking out sites that turn out to be turkeys.

How

World Wide Web

Where

www.uspto.gov

Clearly Canadian

Canadian Intellectual Property Office ☆☆☆

This site provides detailed and thoughtfully written guides to Canadian patents, copyrights, and trademarks, as well as the protection of industrial designs and (a hot area in the intellectual property field these days) integrated circuit topographies. Each guide has an exceptional glossary for defining terms in its field. We only wish CIPO would add forms you could copy, and a free searchable database would be helpful, too.

How

World Wide Web

Where

info.ic.gc.ca/opengov/cipo

Law-ware for Hardware and Software

KuesterLaw Technology Law Resource ☆☆☆☆

The stated intent of this site is to be the most comprehensive technological law site on the Net. And it really perfoms what it claims to do. Whether your company business is software, hardware, wetware (biotech), or any other kind of techware, this site will have information for you. KuesterLaw is especially rich in information on copyright, trademark, and patent information: court decisions, pending laws, U.S. and state laws. (U.S. trademark laws differ from state to state, but you probably know that already.) You'll find original material here covering basic information on patents and trademarks (including how to apply), plus hundreds of links to other resources.

How

World Wide Web

Where

www.kuesterlaw.com

Is Your Software Protected?

LEGAL CARE FOR YOUR SOFTWARE ☆☆☆☆

Legal Care for Your Software, still the industry's defini-tive book on software protection law 10 years after first being published, is now completely revised and the entire book is on the Web. Programmers can obtain practical ad-vice on getting the most for their efforts, as well as learn-ing how to protect their code from software pirates. There are even sample contracts and forms you can copy from the Net and use.

A Step-by-Step Legal Guide for Computer Software Writers, Programmers and Publishers

You've just written the next software bestseller and can't wait to reap the rewards of long hours of hard work. Or, your company needs to hire several programmers to integrate your systems and you want to make sure you're guaranteed satisfactory performance. Before you take the next step, be sure that you've taken proper care to insure your success. Is that contract you signed really a fair return for your efforts? Have you taken the necessary steps to protect that brilliant code, or will the pirated version be out before your own? And if so, do you have recourse? How do you go about making sure that you do?

LEGAL CARE FOR YOUR SOFTWARE, *The Fifth Edition*, is now completely revised and remains the software industry's definitive book explaining software protection law. It shows how to take advantage of it, and offers practical advice for writers and publishers of computer software. It includes tear-out contracts and forms ready to be used or modified.

This book has saved software companies tens of thousands of dollars. It's worth every penny of its $40 price, and is yours free on the Internet.

Written by Daniel Remer and Robert Dunaway, this step-by-step guide is a must-have for any code jockey or multimedia artist looking to score big in software publishing. With plenty of commonsense advice, *Legal Care for Your Software* is arguably the best guide for legally protecting your software. The Web site includes everything in the $40 printed version of the book.

Legal Care for Your Software shows you:

- When and how to use trade secret, copyright, patent, and trademark protection for your software
- Contract nuts and bolts—how to negotiate, write, and agree to contracts that protect both parties and ensure a strong working relationship
- The types of contracts common to software publishing, including work-made-for-hire and royalty agreements
- How to limit your liability when the program is published—protecting not only your program but yourself
- Common sense advice on how to avoid legal hassles before they occur
- How to obtain copyright protection in different countries

How

World Wide Web

Where

www.island.com/LegalCare/welcome.html

Where to Find Way More Goodies

If you've read this whole chapter, then you've found less than half the legal resources in this book. Almost every chapter contains more resources.

In Chapter 2, see Internet Sleuth, IOMA, Professionals Online, and especially FedWorld. For software to make even a regal legal eagle wriggle (say that three times, real fast!), see Chapter 5. You'll find Online Time Recorder, Time Logger (billable hours, anyone?), and SBA's Shareware Library.

If you're in the software biz, see Software Forum. Chapter 9 delivers *Double Entries,* Internet law and banking law, the book *International Business Practices Guide,* "how to get a U.S. visa" at Visa Maze, *Foreign Entry Requirements,* NAFTA, Business Monitor, and Japanese law resources. Our next chapter has a glossary with European legal considerations in buying and selling. Also, take a peek at Electric Ideas Clearinghouse.

You'll find more on harassment and discrimination in Chapter 18. Peruse our index under **legal resources** for even more stuff.

FREE $TUFF

Organized crime in America takes in over forty billion dollars a year. This is quite a profitable sum, especially when one considers that the Mafia spends very little for office supplies.

Woody Allen

Resources to Help You Buy Better Stuff Cheaper

Whether you're in manufacturing, wholesale, or retail, the heart of your business is making a profit on your products. And you know the old saying about making money on products. The whole secret is "Buy high, sell low." (What? We've got it backwards? Well, no wonder we were never successful entrepreneurs!)

Seriously, though, the two verbs in that saying (regardless of the order in which you say them) are "sell" and "buy." One is as important as the other. You can only sell something if you buy it first. Purchasing today is more important than ever, and factors such as intensifying price competition, increasing quality, and ever-tighter, just-in-the-nick-of-time deadlines all exert increasing pressure on the people working hard to make the best buys.

It's no surprise that purchasers are turning to the Net as a way to cut a little slack and create some breathing room. It's also a good way to stay in communication with other purchasing pros.

Here are some good purchasing resources, each one inspected and tested to make sure it can help you in your work. We wouldn't dream of giving you useless purchasing Internet sites (and there are many), or silly ones like the Ferrengi Rules of Acquisition.

What? You actually *want* the Ferengi Rules of Acquisition?

Well, since you asked: **tamu.edu:8000/~jpq0042/index.html**

(Just do us a favor. Don't tell our editor Ron that we slipped that one in, okay?)

A FAST Way to Cut Your Purchasing Costs

FAST Electronic Broker ☆☆☆☆

Would you like to hire a purchasing agent to find new vendors and cut prices? Even better, would you like to hire one absolutely free of charge? FAST Electronic Broker is a nonprofit service that costs nothing to join and charges no monthly annual fees. It gives you an easy way to solicit bids from more vendors, and a means of nailing down favorable prices.

Operated by the Information Sciences Institute at the University of Southern California, FAST is most effective at reducing costs for small quantity purchases. Because it uses email and the World Wide Web to quickly disperse

Companies large and small can take advantage of FAST to find new vendors and reduce costs.

your requests for quotes and to send price quotes back to you, FAST is ideal for handling rush orders. (Bet you guessed that from its name.)

You can use FAST like this. After you register as a member (which is free), you send FAST a request for price quotations using email or a handy-dandy Web page. When FAST gets your RFQ (or your RFP, depending on what purchasing lingo your company prefers to use), it matches your needs with its huge database of vendors and distributors. Then it emails your RFQ to appropriate suppliers. The suppliers email price quotes to FAST, which emails them to you. You compare the price quotes you receive from FAST with any quotes you receive from any other sources, adding (pay close attention, here's the important part) an 8 percent surcharge to the FAST quotes. That surcharge is how FAST recoups its costs. You let FAST know if you want to order from one of the quotes it sent to you. If so, FAST places your order with the vendor (to take advantage of the quantity price breaks FAST earns, like any other purchasing co-op). The vendor ships directly to you. The vendor bills FAST. FAST pays the vendor and bills you. You pay FAST.

FAST has been doing this since 1990. At its Web site, you'll find articles that have been written about this service, papers explaining FAST in more detail, and all the information you need to open your business' own account.

Like those old aspirin commercials used to say, "For FAST, FAST, FAST relief!" Or, better FAST than half-FAST.

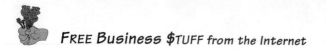

How
> World Wide Web

Where
> info.broker.isi.edu/fas

The Center of the Purchasing Universe

National Association of Purchasing Management ☆☆☆☆

NAPM is without a doubt the leading association of purchasing pros anywhere on our planet. Not because it has 38,000 purchasers as members and 179 affiliated organizations, but because of the value it delivers. Makes sense. NAPM members are the sharpest people around when it comes to getting value for money, so it figures that they would create an organization that gives them big bangs for their bucks. (Besides, NAPM conventions are a lot of fun!)

NAPM's Web site also delivers. If you're a professional purchaser, first things first: Wanna learn how to do your job better and be worth a higher salary? Check out the information on how you can earn certification as a Certified Purchasing Manager. Those pros who go around with the three letters "CPM" after their name have proven know-how in this field. Beginning purchasers (or "purchasing wannabees" as they are more commonly known) can read "A Career in Purchasing."

You can read the latest NAPM Semiannual Economic Forecast here, including seasonal adjustment factors to the Purchasing Managers' Index (PMI) going back to 1992. This forecast projects U.S. manufacturing trends for the next six months.

You can also read the monthly *NAPM Report on Business*, considered by some to be the most reliable near-term economic forecast. It gives you the monthly PMI, with statistics on production, new orders, order backlogs, prices, inventories, employment—as well as which products went up in price last month and which went down. This can be extremely useful information not only for purchasers, but also for investors, economists, and other business planners.

For "how-to-do-it" purchasing information, you can read good articles from NAPM Insights from the last three issues of *Purchasing Today.* You'll usually find helpful stories on how to improve quality, how to purchase internationally, and other hot topics in purchasing biz.

The drawback to the NAPM site is that it's horribly graphics-laden. Our guess is that it was designed by some purchasing newbie who said, "Hey, on our Web server, it's going to cost the same to use giant graphics as little ones. What a bargain! Where's that life-sized photo of the Grand Canyon?" It may cost NAPM no more to use these huge, pointless graphics on its site; but time is money, and it costs NAPM members and prospective members an immense amount of time to wait for them to download. We recommend that you use the stop sign button on your browser to kill all of the graphics on every page except one. If you go to read NAPM Insights articles from *Purchasing Today,* wait for the graphics. You need that 71 K picture. It is the only way to reach the magazine articles. Of all organizations, we were most surprised to see NAPM commit such a wasteful squandering of member resources.

How

World Wide Web

Where

www.napm.org

High Service from High Tech Purchasers

NAPM - Silicon Valley ☆☆☆☆

This local branch of NAPM offers a world-class purchasing site, with completely different contents from its parent organization. The coolest thing happens to be information from a study sponsored by CommerceNet and NAPM on Internet-Based Purchasing. It looks at the demographics, attitudes, and the actual use of the Internet and the World Wide Web for purchasing. Go to the section labeled "Results" to find what this study discovered.

Go to "Purchasing Web of Articles" for about 20 articles on purchasing and EDI basics. "Career Enhancement" gives you job opportunties, and members can use the resume bank here as well. You'll find a list of purchasing software programs, a directory of seminars (including an Internet-based purchasing course), and a section called "Library" that offers a catalog of reference books on purchasing.

You will find two directories of Internet resources for purchasers; but after a closer look, you'll see that they are actually one directory presented two different ways. One gives you resources by category, the other (the "Mother Directory") alphabetically by name. They both provide you with good links to other purchasing sites, but no descriptions of them. Many sites listed are vendors local to Silicon Valley.

For dessert, you can sign up here to join the NAPM - Silicon Valley's email list.

How

World Wide Web

Where

www.catalog.com/napmsv

The Big Easy Gives You the Rules

NAPM - Greater New Orleans ☆☆

The smaller Web site created by New Orleans' NAPM chapter gives you two things we couldn't find at either of the two bigger NAPM sites above. First, you can acquire the complete NAPM "Principles and Standards of Purchasing." Secondly, a small directory of "International Articles," which links to publications on the Net that leads you to articles on buying and selling internationally. You'll also find a couple of links to good purchasing resources.

Now can we go to the Gumbo Shop on Saint Peter's Street and purchase more of the best blackened redfish we've ever eaten? Please?

How

World Wide Web

Where

www.gnofn.org/~napmgno/napmgno.htm

Dutch Treat

Purchasing & Supply Chain Management Resources ☆☆☆☆

Purchasing guru Rob van Stekelenborg created this impressive list, one of the two most complete purchasing resources directories on the Net. This list is longer than the other, but it includes many resources on topics other than purchasing, such as electronic commerce, workflow management, and reengineering. You'll find more links here to articles about purchasing than anywhere else, and (though 95 percent of everything here is in English), also a few resources in Dutch. Just links, no descriptions. And yes, we did scratch our heads trying to figure why van Stekelenborg put some of these here.

How
World Wide Web

Where
www.tue.nl/bdk/PierreBreuls/ipsera/rstindex.htm

The Other Best Purchasing Directory

Purchasing & Materials Management Resources ☆☆☆☆

This directory, prepared by Solutions Consulting Group, is the second of the two most complete directories of purchasing resources on the Internet. This wanders less from its topic than the other. Like its counterpart, this directory gives you just a Gopher-like list of links with no descriptions telling you why they are included, or what to look for on the linked sites.

How
World Wide Web

Where
www.solcon.com/resource.htm

Pssst—Wanna Save Big Money on a Chopper?

Aircraft Shopper ☆☆

Not many businesses buy aircraft, but if yours does, you can save money here. Aircraft Shopper is like a virtual used car lot, but instead of cards, it sells used aircraft. You'll find more than 800 aircraft for sale from more than 100 dealers, brokers, and private parties worldwide. This site is one of the best—if not *the* best—place to save money on used aircraft, on or off the Net. And there is no charge for purchasers to use it. (Of course, you do have to pay for any planes you buy.)

Stuff for sale is arranged into categories: turbojet aircraft, tuboprop aircraft, multi-engine, single engine, helicopters, warbirds (!), float/amphibian, aircraft partnerships (when you want to split costs by sharing with somebody), aircraft wanted, and a directory of aircraft manufacturers.

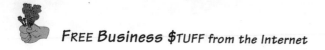

How

World Wide Web

Where

aso.solid.com

Tea and Where to Find Phone Systems

Broadband Telephony Buyer's Guide ☆☆☆

So your company wants to buy telephones? Pull up a chair, settle down. Have some tea, it's good for you. How many telephones will you need? That's a lot of telephones. Is that too many for a party line? Try some cookies. My niece Anna made them. So where do you go to buy that many phones? They don't have that many at the mall. And you're going to want some long wires, and some of those pushbutton things. I keep my old dial phone, it's good enough for me.

You might want to know about this place to buy phones that Anna found. Such an eye for bargains she has! She said it links to more than a thousand vendors of more than five hundred kinds of phone products all over the world. Who needs that many? I remember when we had just one, Ma Bell. That had to be good enough for *all* of us. Anna said this place tells about cables and those funny control boxes with all the lights, and those wireless and cellular phones for those people who talk in their cars when they should be driving. Anna says it tells her where all the service and fix-it companies are, too. It even has a list of the jobs you can get.

She told me about all this just to conclude that working in broadband was not what I thought. I told her that with all the talking on telephones she did as a teenager, it's a good thing now that she can have a few hundred of her own. Have some more tea.

How

World Wide Web

Where

www.indra.com/unicom

P is for Purchase Order

Procurement & Purchasing Glossary ☆☆

Blanket, standing, or otherwise, purchase orders and purchasers generate arcane terminology. This dictionary of purchasing-related words and phrases includes not just definitions, but for many entries also the legal considerations that ensue from using that word or phrase. This glossary also pays special attention to terms and usages common to the bureaucrats from Brussels, paperwork makers for the European Union.

How

World Wide Web

Where

www.europrofile.co.uk/glossary.htm

Buy and Sell the Rights to High Tech

Dual-Use Marketplace ☆☆☆☆

This is an unusual purchasing resource. Most businesses will have no use for it, but the ones that do need Dual-Use Marketplace will find it extremely valuable. It is an electronic shopping mall where companies find new manufacturing technologies and new product ideas. Companies can sell them as well.

This is a place to purchase and sell licenses to use technology. You are not buying the actual hardware itself. You buy only the rights to use a process or a software innovation or an equipment design. Perhaps you'll use it to automate your assembly line. Perhaps you'll incorporate it in a product you sell. You shop by reading descriptions of technologies that are available to license. You can post "want-to-buy" notices for the types of technology you need to acquire. You can also post your partnering opportunities, potential joint ventures, and research collaboration opportunities.

You must register to use Dual-Use Marketplace, but it is free to search and view for technology to license and for companies that would make good partners. It is also free for you to post your needs, or to post technologies you want to sell. This is a good sales resource, so if your company has any rights it could potentially sell, you might want to poke your marketing manager in the ribs (gently) and pass along our review.

How

World Wide Web

Where

www.crimson.com/market

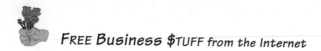

Last One to Leave, Please Turn Out Lights

Electric Ideas Clearinghouse ☆☆

If you want to cut energy costs for a large commercial or industrial business, you might visit this difficult-to-use Telnet site. You'll find more than 1,000 software files, many dealing with reducing energy use. Check the list of most popular software for a quick way to find such gems as life cycle cost calculation spreadsheets, HVAC fine tuning to reduce costs, VFD pump and fan estimation, and other programs to increase energy efficiency and track costs. You'll also find more than fifty discussion groups on energy-related topics ranging from software to regulations to electric vehicles, and a few reports on energy efficiency for businesses.

How

Telnet

Where

telnet://eicbbs.wseo.wa.gov

Workin' on a Supply Chain Gang

Integrated Supply Chain Management Project ☆☆☆

A supply chain is only as strong as its weakest manager. The University of Toronto created this site to explain how to use software and networking to manage the supply chain process. It describes the organization of supply chains from raw materials supplier through manufacturers and distributors to customers.

You'll find a paper "The Integrated Supply Chain Management System" in Postscript format, plus several other papers on information agents, coordination, scheduling, logistics, and resource management. Most of the papers are more theoretical than practical, and will be most useful to large corporations.

How

World Wide Web

Where

www.ie.utoronto.ca/EIL/iscm-descr.html

 To save time when you visit the supply chain Web site, you can kill the useless 75 K graphics file.

Igor the Hunchback Should Have Shopped Here

BiotechNet Buyer's Guide ☆☆

Well, you can't really buy brains here, but you can purchase a lot of lab equipment. BiotechNet has created a database of products in chromatography, electrophoresis, molecular biology, and other essential areas in the biotech industry. You can search for vendors by product, by company name, and by description. If your search retrieves nothing that matches your needs, you are taken to a page where you can browse a directory to find what you do want.

How

World Wide Web

Where

petrified.cic.net/eaton/prod/html.dir/index.html

Large-Lot Buyers Discount Shopping Club

Trade-L ☆☆☆☆

Does your company buy welding rods, Portland cement, dyes, packaging, or container-loads of grain? How about a vegetable oil factory? Software by the pallet-load? Everything we just mentioned has actually been posted for sale on Trade-L, a hybrid email list and Web site. If you purchase items in bulk—especially commodities—Trade-L can be a real moneysaver for you. Think of it as one of those Price Costco discount stores, only online. You never know what you'll find for sale, but it is almost guaranteed to be the biggest size possible, and probably a real bargain.

You can post your "want-to-buy" notices here, too. And Trade-L is free to both buyers and sellers. The quickest way to get an idea of its offerings is to visit the Trade-L Web site, which is updated daily with new listings.

If you like what you see, you'll probably want to subscribe to the email list. Just email to **trade-l-request@intel-trade.com** and make the "Subject:" of your message **SUBSCRIBE** and the body of your message just the single word **SUBSCRIBE**. Postings are moderated, and no spam nor multi-level marketing nonsense is allowed.

How

World Wide Web

Where

www.scbbs.com/~tradewinds

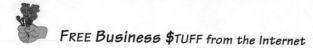
The Information Gateway

Gateway 2000 Email Discussion Group ☆☆

Here's a novel idea: If you want the best information about the products you use or are thinking of buying, talk to the people who are already using them. Nah, too obvious. Still, that's the idea behind the Gateway 2000 mailing list.

Created and maintained by those who use Gateway 2000 products, this list discusses the good, bad, and ugly of the products offered by this computer mail-order giant.

How

Email

Where

gateway2000-request@sei.cmu.edu

Message

subscribe gateway2000

A digest form of this mailing list is also available. See dealer for details, mileage may vary.

Government for Sale

FinanceNet Government Asset Sales ☆☆

Looking for a good plasma arc furnace? Maybe some slightly used metallurgical grade fluorspar? Kyanite? Regardless of what you're buying, there's a good chance the government is selling it.

The FinanceNet Gopher site provides daily listings of government assets for sale, including aircraft parts, office furniture, communications and lab equipment, automated data processing equipment, and more. You'll even find entire buildings for sale, though no monuments (yet).

How

Gopher

Where

gopher://pula.financenet.gov

Go To

Government Asset Sales
Federal

You can also receive a copy of the current daily listing automatically via Internet email by sending a blank email message to **cbd@financenet.gov**.

Buy from Banks

FDIC Asset Sales ☆☆

After the recent savings and loan fire sale, it would be a major understatement to say that the public's confidence in American banking is "shaken." "Beaten to a pulp" is more like it. In fact, more than a few people didn't sleep soundly until they started using their money for mattress stuffing.

The Federal Deposit Insurance Corporation (FDIC) is the independent deposit insurance agency created by Congress to boost public confidence in our banks. You'll find information here on how you can buy FDIC-held assets: bad loans and the collateral for them, including lots of real estate.

How

Gopher

Where

gopher://gopher.fdic.gov

 Investors may also smile to hear that they can get on an email list of notifications of bulk sales of FDIC loans. Email to **listserv@nic.sura.net** with the only message: **subscribe bulksale Yourfirstname Yourlastname**.

Know When to Say When

Express Meter Audit Kit ☆☆☆

How much software do you need? It sounds like a trick question: How much do you got? But rephrase it as "How much software do you want to pay for?"— and the answer is: "As little as possible."

The Express Meter Audit Kit will help you determine how many software licenses your company *really* needs and how many it's paying for that go unused. Produced by the Express System's Software Management Resource Center, the Express Meter Audit Kit, available for free, provides a snapshot of up to 30 days of application usage for any number of users on any type of network, including the Internet. It gives users a no-cost method of assessing how your company could benefit from proper management of its software assets.

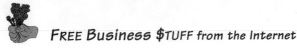

Where

www.express-systems.com/

Links

A Guide to Software Management (online booklet explaining how to audit software use)

Walt Disney's Home Page

Look What's in the Candy Jar

3M Candy Jar ☆☆☆

Next to Velcro, we've got to say that man's greatest accomplishment in the Twentieth Century has been the invention of Post-It Notes. Oh, sure, there was that moon landing thing, but c'mon, how many of us are ever going to be up there collecting moon rocks? Landing on the moon was more of a high-tech, testosterone-pumping barroom bet, but Post-Its, now there is a scientific achievement.

From the same gods who brought you invisible Scotch tape, 3M, here's on online place to go for free samples of their other products, including Post-It Notes. Just fill in the online form (hey, be flattered these giants of industry want to know your name), and pick the product you'd like them to send you, including:

- Post-It popup note samples
- Brochure with sample tape flags, pop-up notes, and Fax Notes
- Post-It recycled paper notes
- Scotchpad carry handle
- Transparency film for Inkjet printers
- Flip-frame transparency protectors

How

World Wide Web

Where

www.mmm.com/market/omc/forms/omcndjar.html

Where to Pluck More Prizes for Purchasers

There are dozens more purchasing resources in this book, in almost every chapter. First, if you are interested in shipping or EDI, read the next chapter on

Logistics and Transportation to find what you need. (If you are not interested in EDI, you should be, because when companies move to EDI, purchasing often becomes the point operation for the whole company.)

One of the best purchasing resources in the entire book is located in Chapter 2, *How to Find Business Stuff on the Internet*. The venerable *Thomas Register of American Manufacturers* has a remarkably useful free Web site where you can research products and vendors. The Thomas site also includes a useful How to Buy It section. As long as you're already in Chapter 2, you might look at some of the purchasing stuff at IOMA, including "CFOs Suggest Best Practices to Improve Purchasing Functions," and under Fedworld peek at CALS, Computer Aided Acquisitions and Logistics Support.

Chapter 3 steers you towards *Electronic Buyers News* and Thailand's *International Purchasing Guide*.

If your company is a small business, you may be especially interested in Chapter 5, *Entrepreneurs, Startups, and Home Businesses*. Check out the International Small Business Consortium as a way to reduce costs. If you plan to buy software, you might look at the SBA Shareware Library as a potential source. And purchasers in companies of all sizes can use the Hi, Finance software to calculate Economic Order Quantities.

Give BidCast a review in Chapter 7 to see if you can send it your RFQs. And if your company is a retailer, RETEX, the Retail Technology Consortium in Chapter 8, might become one of your favorite resources.

If your company needs to buy accounting software, the Computerized Accounting Analysis in Chapter 9, *Accounting and Finance*, can make the process faster and more thorough for you.

If you like the idea of Trade-L, described above in this chapter, you might take a look at a more loosely run counterpart described in Chapter 12, *Doing Business Internationally*. A newsgroup called alt.business.import-export, it works much the same as Trade-L; except with the newsgroup, you need to filter out some spam and irrelevant messages. Chapter 12 gives two more resources to international purchasers, Trade Compass and the *Directory of Japanese Trade & Technologies*.

If all those resources don't sate your hunger and you still want more, look in our spiffy index under the heading **purchasing resources**. (Originally we were gonna call it **great free stuff for buyers**, but decided the more boring heading would be easier to find. So much for the rewards of creative genius.) While you're in the index, look up Industry.Net. It's a good site for industrial purchasers.

FREE $TUFF

Things may come to those who wait,
but only the things left by those
who hustle.

Abraham Lincoln

Logistics and Transportation

389

Oh, you're in logistics. Right, you don't have time to read an introduction. Somehow people who keep track of things and move things from one place to another are always people in a rush.

Hey, sorry for slowing you down. Here's a quick chapter for you. Now we'll shut up and let you get on with it.

Track That Package: FedEx

Federal Express ☆☆☆☆

Does anybody else remember those funny, fast-talking Federal Express commercials? We do, and we miss 'em. You won't find any "fast talking" at the FedEx Web site, but you will find FedEx Ship software for Windows and Macs that you can download. It helps you prepare packages and print airbills so you don't have to fool with typing those messy carbon-paper forms. It also creates a shipping history for you, so you can look up and report on your past shipments.

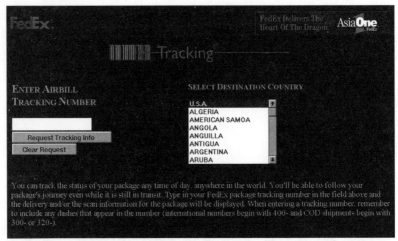

The FedEx package tracking Web page shows you where your package goes every step of the way.

The most-often-used page here is undoubtedly the FedEx package tracking page. Enter an airbill number, and you'll find a history of where your package is or has been, updated every step of the way and literally minute-by-minute.

How
World Wide Web

Where

www.fedex.com

 If you'd like to skip FedEx's intermediate pages with all their time-wasting graphics, you can jump right to its package tracking page at: **www.fedex.com/ track_it.html**

Track That Package: UPS

United Parcel Service ☆☆☆☆

With more than 3 billion parcels and documents delivered annually worldwide, United Parcel Service is the world's largest package distribution company. Now, in addition to its arsenal of over 500 aircraft, 130,000 vehicles and 2,400 facilities spread across 200 countries, they're taking their business into cyberspace.

```
┌─────────────────────────────────────────────────────────────┐
│  PACKAGE TRACKING  ·····························   📦         │
│                                                               │
│  Tracking number: [_____]         │
│                                                               │
│  [   Track this package   ]  [  Clear form and start over  ]  │
│                                                               │
│  Tracking Tips:                                               │
│                                                               │
│  UPS tracking numbers typically are of the following formats: │
│                                                               │
│    • 1Z 999 999 99 9999 999 9                                 │
│    • 9999 9999 999                                            │
│    • T999 9999 999                                            │
│    • D999 9999 999                                            │
│                                                               │
│  Spaces and dashes entered in tracking number will be ignored │
│                                                               │
│  Tracking information availability varies by UPS service selected. Consult the UPS Service Guide or, in the US, call │
│  1-800-PICK-UPS (1-800-742-5877) for more information.        │
└─────────────────────────────────────────────────────────────┘
```

Look up a package with the UPS online Packaging Tracking Web page.

The UPS Web site lets you download software: QuickCost Calculator for Windows (1,085 K), Tracking Software for Windows (261 K), and Tracking Software for Macs. You can also use four online interactive tools to look up UPS shipping information: QuickCost Calculator, UPS Service Mapping, Ground Time In-Transit Estimator, and the ever-popular Packaging Tracking lookup to see if that package you sent has arrived yet.

How

World Wide Web

Where

www.ups.com

The Shipping News

CARGO LETTER ☆☆☆☆

If your company uses several carriers to ship cargo, or if your business is part of the cargo industry itself, do yourself a favor and read *Cargo Letter*. This free newsletter covers all modes of the industry worldwide, with news stories, statistics, and quick, to-the-point analyses. It brings you the good news, but doesn't ignore industry problems. (Until we read *Cargo Letter*, we didn't know the extent of modern piracy at sea. With high-tech gear, sea pirates are now a bigger menace than they were 100 years ago. Could be a nice story idea for Tom Clancy; but for cargo shippers and insurers, pirates are a pain in the aft.)

Each issue gives industry stock prices and ends with new Web links to cargo sites around the planet. You can browse an archive of back issues here as well as the current one. About the only flaw with *Cargo Letter* is that new issues come out at irregular intervals.

How

World Wide Web

Where

www.interpool.com/cargo.htm

Straighten Up That Warehouse

OnTime Warehouse Management System ☆☆☆

If your warehouse is a mess, here's a good, straightforward way to organize the goods. The OnTime Warehouse Management System runs on Windows 3.11 or Windows for WorkGroups. For a warehouse with about 1,000 pallets, OnTime's maker recommends that you have at least a 486 processor with 10 megabytes of free disk space and 16 megabytes of RAM, plus an SVGA monitor or better.

How

World Wide Web

Where

www.coast.net/simtel/simtel/win3/business

Download

whse11a.zip   (2,626 K)

Keep on Trucking

OVERDRIVE **Online** ☆☆☆

Billing itself as the "World Wide Web site for the American trucker," *Overdrive* Online is updated weekly with news, columns, and features from the truckers' magazine, plus a guide to stations and programming for the Overdrive Radio Network, and links to the newsgroups **misc.transport.trucking**, **misc.transport.road**, and **misc.transport.misc**.

Where the rubber meets the information superhighway. (Yeah, we hate that cliche, too.)

Truckers will find several employment-related services here, including employment tips, a trucking employment Q&A column, and job opportunities. Look for the free service to which you can send your resumé to be analyzed, duplicated, and sent via email to employers with vacancies that match your experience.

How

World Wide Web

Where

www.overdriveonline.com

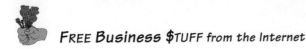

Planes, Trains, and Trucks—No Boats

Transportation Resources ☆☆☆

This enormous directory steers you to Web sites worldwide dealing with ground transportation, air transportation, and transportation overall. Somehow, it overlooks ships, ports, and everything dealing with water. Hydrophobia, perhaps? This directory's special strength is in transport organizations. It lists hundreds of them, including the most complete list of transport academia we've found anywhere.

Its weak spots include not being as up-to-date as it could be—lots of dead links—and, although Transportation Resources overwhelms you with hundreds of links, they are impossible to differentiate because it doesn't give you even the briefest hint of descriptions.

How

World Wide Web

Where

dragon.princeton.edu/~dhb

Planes, Trains, Trucks, AND Boats

Transport Web ☆☆☆

While not providing links to as many resources as the Transportation Resources directory above, Transport Web is more up-to-date and much easier to use. Besides the expected transport corporations and government agencies, you'll find a directory of transport software listing more than a hundred software packages. (Don't get too excited, they're the kind that will cost you money.) Transport Web gives you good pointers to online publications covering transport, and a good list of transport email discussion groups with how-to-subscribe instructions and a description for each one.

Transport Web also provides the most complete catalog anywhere of transport newsgroups. It categorizes them as either "Professional/International," "Recreational," "Alternative," or "Local/National," and provides a short description of each.

How

World Wide Web

Where

www.transportweb.com

Transport Planner's Tool

Linehaul-Backhaul ☆☆☆

This software program for 32-bit Windows (Win95, NT, 32s—which has more flavors, Unix or Windows?) gives you a tool to help design and plan transportation systems. The program itself is 226 K, and to use it you will also need to download the 77 K **scienmfc.dll**, which is available here. If you'd like to experiment with test data to figure out how Linehaul-Backhaul works, copy the 83 K of case data as well.

How

World Wide Web

Where

angelico.marc.gatech.edu/LOGISTIX.HTM#projects

Inventory Tracking

Inventory for DOS ☆☆☆

Still trying to manage your inventory by traditional manual stock-picking techniques? Here's a good way to ease into a more automated approach. This simple little MS-DOS program does a good job of tracking inventory and producing reports based on sales histories. It also produces invoices. By default, it's set up to track auto parts; but you can change the inventory categories and inventory items to anything you want.

How

World Wide Web

Where

www.coast.net/simtel/simtel/msdos/database

Download

cjpos531.zip   (822 K)

That's an Order

OnOrder for Windows ☆☆☆

Invoice-It ☆☆

Wasn't that package supposed to be here today? Or was it tomorrow? Or did I forget to place the order in the first place? Help! If you get confused trying to

OnOrder helps you keep your shipments straight.

remember the who, what, when, and where of your business orders, OnOrder for Windows can help. OnOrder tracks your orders so you'll always know what packages to expect and when to expect them. Plus, OnOrder helps blaze the paper trail by printing envelopes, labels, and reports.

Also at this site, you can download a copy of Invoice-It, which comes in very handy when you need to create **sales invoices**.

How

World Wide Web

Where

www.csusm.edu/cwis/winworld/database.html

Go To

pub/winworld/database

Download

OnOrder:	onord10.zip	(69 K)
Invoice-It:	invit200.zip	(77 K)

People Who Move Food

Food Distribution Association ☆☆

The combined efforts of the National American Wholesale Grocers Association and the International Foodservice Distributors Association—two organizations with members in the U.S., Canada, and twenty other countries—brings you this site for businesses in the food distribution industry. You'll find some statistics here on trends; but the main draws are two monthly newsletters, *NAWGA Review* and *IFDA Report*, plus some links to related Internet sites.

How

World Wide Web

Where

www.nawga-ifda.org

Sic Transit Gloria

International Safe Transit Association ☆☆

People who work for this association must have the advantage of taking out all their hostilities at work. Imagine being able to smash packages for a living. (Kinda like a mailman we once knew.)

The International Safe Transit Association does performance testing of packaging to make sure that the packages you ship will make it to the preferred destination with the contents intact. You'll find information here on how to test your packages to make sure they will arrive safely. For lagniappe, ISTA throws in notices of seminars and conferences, and a small package of links to other packaging sites.

How

World Wide Web

Where

www.ezone.com/ista

For those of you who need to brush up on your Latin, the famous motto above isn't about a woman named Gloria. *Sic transit gloria* means "That's how the glory goes." We were trying to make a pun on "transit." Well, they can't all be gems.

397

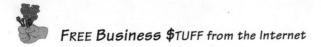

"S" Stands for Shipping

Nedlloyd Transport & Logistics Dictionary ☆☆

The next time at a cocktail party when some wiseguy tries to stump you with, "What's the difference between a quoin, a quay, and a queue," don't just stand there and stammer. Instead, whip out your wireless palmtop, type in the URL of this handy Web dictionary, and rattle off Nedlloyd's definitions. Stops them cold every time.

How

World Wide Web

Where

www.nedlloyd.com/a_z.htm

EDI Stands for Everybody's Doing It

Premenos ☆☆☆☆☆

Actually, EDI stands for *Electronic Data Interchange*. EDI happens when the information for a business transaction goes directly from your computer into another company's computer, with no paperwork changing hands. For example, you could use EDI to send a purchase order directly from your purchasing system into your vendor's sales order system. And EDI can work in the other direction as well—your computer can receive transactions (such as purchase orders) from other companies' computers.

EDI is not for every company. It tends to be most economical if your company has a high volume of transactions, or when you are part of an industry in which every business uses the same off-the-shelf EDI software (such as booksellers, which all use Pubnet as we described in Chapter 8). Many companies use EDI only when a large customer forces them.

If your company decides to use EDI, jump directly to the Premenos website. You'll find far more EDI information and help here than anywhere else on the Net.

From the menu on the Premenos home page, two sections stand out as the most important. The section on standards gives you:

• Understanding EDI - A superquick (only two screens long) overview plus a glossary.

- UN/EDIFACT standards - The *complete* directories of the United Nations EDI standards, the most commonly-used throughout the world. (Hot tip for business software designers: The EDI committees have done half your work for you! Look here before you design a system to find out what fields to include, how long they should be, and what order to put them in.)

- *Henry's Yellow UN/EDIFACT Book* - This entire book is online, in hypertext with links to the directories above. Henry Schlieper describes more than 170 business transactions, one at a time, explaining the components of each. This book is extremely valuable, not just for companies planning EDI, but for businesses looking to buy or build software, and for business planners who need to understand the elements of business transactions. This is the opposite of those *One-Minute Manager* books. If detailed, technically-oriented prose makes you squirm, don't say we didn't warn you.

- ASCX12 standards - These standards are primarily used in the U.S. and Canada and are being merged into the more complete UN/EDIFACT transactions. Click on the list of transaction names to get a description and technical details.

- EDI papers - Several papers on EDI topics, including a FAQ on EDI and the Internet with good questions and accurate, if sometimes shallow, answers.

- Actual EDI implementation plans used by Nissan and Staples.

The section of the Premenos site that gives you lots of free goodies is a group of online directories, which Premenos calls "Electronic Commerce Resources." Go here for links without descriptions of EDI-related Internet resources, a catalog of Value-Added Network providers, an alphabetized but descriptionless directory of a couple of hundred EDI/Electronic Commerce organizations, 12 EDI mailing lists with short descriptions and Web pages where you can subscribe to them, a short list of Web sites for EDI publications, and EDI-related job opportunities.

How

World Wide Web

Where

www.premenos.com

Follow the Money

EDI can automate more than 150 different kinds of business-to-business and business-to-government transactions. In case the concept of Electronic Data Interchange is new to you, here are the names of just a few of the types of business transactions for which EDI standards have been created.

Buying and Selling
Price Change
Price/Sales Catalog
Promotion Announcement
Contract Award
Trading Partner Profile
Request for Quotation
Response to Request for Quotation
Purchase Order
Purchase Order Acknowledgment
Purchase Order Change Request - Buyer Initiated
PO Change Acknowledgment/Request - Seller Init.
Order Status Inquiry
Order Status Report
Cooperative Advertising Agreement
Invoice
Commission Sales Report
Return Merchandise Authorization

Accounting and Money
Electronic Filing of Tax Return Data
Revenue Receipts Statement
Mortgage Loan Default Status
Lockbox
Debit Authorization
Payment Cancellation Request
Credit/Debit Adjustment
Operating Expense Statement
Payment Order/Remittance Advice
Contractor Cost Data Reporting
Uniform Commercial Code filing
Project Cost Reporting

Shipping and Logistics
Warehouse Shipping Order
Inventory Inquiry/Advice
Warehouse Inventory Adjustment Advice
Warehouse Stock Transfer - Receipt Advice

Shipment Delivery Discrepancy Information
Shipment and Billing Notice
Shipping Instructions
Customs Manifest
Customs Release Information
Delivery/Pickup Order
Consolidation of Goods in Container
Rail Carrier Shipment Information
Rail Carrier Freight Details and Invoice
Logistics Reassignment
Air Shipment Information
Air Freight Details and Invoice
Motor Carrier Shipment Status Inquiry
Motor Carrier Loading and Route Guide
Motor Carrier Tariff Information

Insurance
Report of Injury or Illness
Health Care Eligibility/Benefit Inquiry
Health Care Claim Status Request
Property and Casualty Loss Information

Other
Project Schedule Reporting
Product Registration
Product Service Claim
Product Service Claim Response
Planning Schedule with Release Capability
Specifications/Technical Information
Production Sequence

EDI Beginner's Luck

Getting Started with EDI ☆☆☆

If you don't know about EDI and want to know what all the fuss is about, you're in luck. This is the best short introduction that we found. It strips away the high-tech mumbo-jumbo and gives you the basic points with clear explanation. The author, EDI expert Susan Stecklair, also tells you where to go for more information. So uncross your fingers, put down your rabbit's foot and four-leaf clover, and type in this URL.

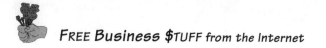
How

World Wide Web

Where

www.catalog.com/napmsv/edi.htm

Pay No Attention to That Man behind the Curtain

bit.listserv.edi-l ☆☆☆

If you want to strip away all the magazine-article politeness and see what's really going on in the EDI trenches, lurk on this newsgroup for a couple of weeks. You'll eavesdrop on some of the top experts in EDI, flinging mud on each other and calling each other names when they disagree over the best ways to do things. You'll also see that these same people will bend over backward to answer anyone's questions on EDI. This lively newsgroup is a mirror of an active email list which is moderated to block spam. We highly recommend it as an excellent way to see the reality behind all the smoke and mirrors that EDI vendors use when trying to dazzle you.

How

Newsgroup

Where

news:bit.listserv.edi-l

If you'd rather read this discussion in the form of email messages instead of a newsgroup, send email to **listserv@uccvma.ucop.edu** with a message saying nothing but **subscribe edi-l Yourfirstname Yourlastname**.

Uncle Sam Wants YOU (to Use EDI)

Electronic Commerce Resource Center ☆☆☆

The star attractions at this government-sponsored Web site are free services for U.S. small-to-medium-sized businesses. The Electronic Commerce Resource Center's mission is to help "U.S. integrated civil-military industries getting started with Electronic Commerce." Now, we're not sure exactly what an "integrated civil-military industry" is—or much less what it is not—but if you think that label might fit your business, c'mon down. You can read the entire *ECRC News* quarterly newsletter, and find out how the ECRC helps businesses with analysis, data conversion, EDI, and systems integration. You might also look at the courses in EDI offered here, and explore the ECRC's extremely short directory of other EDI sites.

How
World Wide Web

Where
www.ecrc.ctc.com

Electronic Commerce Guidebook

BUYER'S GUIDE TO ELECTRONIC COMMERCE ☆☆☆☆

Every time you look up at this site, you can tell yourself, "I just saved $29.00!" That's how much the printed version of the *Buyer's Guide to Electronic Commerce* costs, but the Web version (which gives you everything in the printed version and is more up to date) is free, thanks to sponsorship by the corporations whose logos you'll see on the *Buyer's Guide* home page.

This directory describes hundreds of email, EDI, and electronic reengineering products and services. It also gives you contact information for dozens of special-interest groups worldwide related to these topics. The *Guide* includes a glossary, a calendar of events, and a section called "Electronic Commerce Strategies" which amounts to advertisements for other publications.

How
World Wide Web

Where
ns.wentworth.com/e-com.com/buyersguide

(Hey, you just saved $29.00!)

Where to Find More Logistics & Transport Stuff

We have more logistics and transportation resources for you in this book, but where you'll need to go to find them depends on what kind of resource you need. Someone passionately interested in cargo may not care at all about EDI, and a manufacturing inventory manager may never have to think about customer shipment tracking.

Almost everyone will find something to interest them in our next chapter, *Manufacturing*. We especially recommend a visit to Industry.Net, which can only be described as an industrial-strength resource.

If EDI and Electronic Commerce stir your soul, read the fine print in Chapter 4, *Tools for Internet-Based Businesses*, to expand your horizons.

On the other hand, if cargo and transport make your heart beat faster, thumb through some of the transportation resources in the second half of Chapter 7, *Sales Reps and Road Warriors*.

You can't do yourself any harm by a leisurely test drive of the index to this book. Try looking under the headings **logistics resources, inventory, travel**, and **EDI**.

You'll find a lot more out there on the Net than we have the room to include here. The directories in this chapter will help you discover more, and the find-it resources we share with you in Chapter 2 are always available for those who want to take things just one step further.

FREE $TUFF

If the automobile had followed the same development cycles as the computer, a Rolls-Royce would today cost $100, get a million miles per gallon, and, once a year, explode.

Robert X. Cringely

Manufacturing

With all the grief they get from linking a few devices on the shop room floor, it can be really frustrating for manufacturers to find out how much simpler it is to plug into the Internet and link with the whole planet.

It reminds us of the old complaints that always begin, "If man can go to the moon, how come we can't... (fill in the blank)." In this case, the complaint is, "If I can link my computer with another manufacturer in Hong Kong, how come I can't get my controller to talk to a drill press in the same room?"

We wish we could answer that question, but we can't. Maybe your shop floor equipment would be able to communicate more easily if it were hooked to the Internet. In any case, you'll find that *you* can communicate better once *you* are hooked to the Internet. You can communicate with customers. You can enlarge your supplier base to encompass the planet.

Best of all, you can reach software programs and information that can make your manufacturing operations more efficient and more profitable.

Aside from a few concerns such as quality and project management that are common to all production operations, most manufacturers have needs that are specific to their own type of industry. What we've attempted to do here is supply you with good overall Internet resources that are usable in many types of manufacturing, plus a sampling of resources for specific types of manufacturers (chemicals, electronics, mechanical devices) to give you a hint of the good free stuff that you'll be able to find on the Net for your own specific needs.

Now, roll 'em out!

Industrial-Strength Web Site

Industry.Net ☆☆☆☆☆

Where do we start? Industry.Net's strategy is to offer you enough free stuff for your manufacturing, logistics, and purchasing operations so you will never want to leave. Industry.Net provides so much that it earns honors in anyone's Top Ten List of best business resources on the Net, and probably makes the Top Five.

We could devote an entire chapter to Industry.Net and still not tell you about everything. (No, we are *not* exaggerating!) Instead, we'll focus on where to find Industry.Net's best stuff, including lots of great gems buried in hard-to-find little nooks and crannies.

First steps first. Industry.Net is free, but you must register to use some of its finer resources. Register with a smile, however; because registration gets you extra stuff not on the Web site. Once every six months, Industry.Net sends out via postal mail a buyer's guide directory on disk, with info on 200,000 vendors of products and services for industrial companies, categorized by geographic regions. Every six weeks, you'll also receive the free newsletter *Industry.Net Report*. And, most remarkably, your registration admits you to free seminars on industrial topics held at different U.S. locations. We'll tell you more about those seminars in a moment.

Online Marketplace

If Industry.Net were a town, Online Marketplace would be Main Street. Most of the action on Industry.Net happens here:

- Industry.Net's searchable database of suppliers, products, and services is called the "Regional Business Center Directory and Buying Guide." You can search about 250,000 suppliers by product name, product category, or company name. We applied the same test we used for Thomas Register's Web site way back in Chapter 2. Industry.Net allows you to search by geographic regions of the U.S., but not nationwide. We searched both the Northern California and Pacific States regions for "cassette shells" and for "audio cassettes." Industry.Net found no suppliers, where the Thomas Register found 113. Hmmm. Industry.Net is only second-best.

- Industry.Net News gives you mostly U.S. press releases. Although you can zero in on stories from a particular region, the local ones may hold the most interest for you.

- A directory of free seminars lets you discover exactly what seminars are scheduled for your area of the country. Topics of Industry.Net seminars are tailored to the needs of manufacturers in each area. For instance, Silicon Valley's seminars focus on the electronics industry, while Michigan's cover machine tool and die topics. Some Industry.Net seminars are nothing more than glorified product demos, but many give you good information on important topics.

- Surplus equipment sales.

The Eighteenth Floor

One section of Online Marketplace has product information categorized into "floors," like an industrial Macy's. Take the express elevator to the eighteenth floor for the home pages of dozens of industrial trade organizations. Many of these trade organizations just ask for money. Fortunately, the more forward-looking organizations provide good information for free on the Net. We spent hours digging through every one of these to bring you the cream of the crop:

- **AIM** - The AIM Buying Guide for automatic data collection and ID products and services.

- **IDA** - The Industrial Distribution Association has a "Resources" section, but skip it. It's a bust. Instead, if you want statistics, benchmarks, and trends, head for the "IDA Performance Analysis Summary." You'll find more than 20 tables giving you the lowdown on average company sales, operations, and finances (including prior year comparisons) for IDA's member distributors. IDA also provides benchmark figures for distribution operations.

- **MESA** - Contrary to its name, the Manufacturing Execution Systems Association has nothing to do with guillotines or electric chairs. Instead, MESA members are passionate about accounting-oriented manufacturing systems, software that addresses key business needs disregarded by most manufacturers. Read "White Paper No. 2" for an explanation of the concepts behind manufacturing execution systems. You can find out more by reading "White Paper No. 3: The Control Layer," and by perusing MESA's helpful glossary of terms. Look for this important issue to grow in prominence as a weapon in manufacturers' battle to control profitability.

- **MTI** - The Metal Treating Institute gives the metallically inclined an online version of the *Metal Treating Buyers Guide*, back issues of its *Open Hearth* newsletter, and reports on monthly industry statistics, operational costs, and industry wages and benefits. You'll also find bulletins on regulatory and safety issues.

- **ODVA** - The Open DeviceNet Vendors Association pushes for low-cost communications to connect industrial devices with interchangeable plug-and-play devices from different vendors. You'll find a buyer's guide, files you can download with more information, and free ODVA software.

- **OPC** - Microsoft's organization to compete with ODVA is called OLE for Process Control. You can download OPC specs and read a paper on how great Microsoft is.

- **PMA** - This metalforming group gives you a free online version of *Sources*, a buying guide for metalformed parts, plus the current issue of *Metalforming* (its monthly magazine) and an index to back issues.

- **SMC** - Service-Manufacturing-Commercial calls itself "the voice of smaller business." (We wonder, smaller than what?) Its bimonthly magazine, *Dynamic Business,* is online and features good articles on topics such as "What

Triggers an OSHA Visit?" This organization is local to Pennsylvania, but *Dynamic Business* articles cover subjects of concern to firms across the U.S. You can also search a "products and services" directory of SMC members.

- **VMA** - The Valve Manufacturers Association calls its site "Valves & Actuators Online." It gives you a Valve & Actuator Buying Guide, and a paper called "The Flow Control Industry" that explains valve biz basics.

Industry.Net Linker

This is a very good directory of hotlinks to Internet resources for industrial businesses. You can find sites categorized either by engineering discipline or by manufacturing sector. Industry.Net claims to link to 6,000 resources, and gives pointers to many good ones that we had never heard mentioned elsewhere. Unfortunately, it also misses some obvious ones. For instance, Industry.Net's "Plastics" subdirectory misses GE Plastics' huge Web site.

Industry.Net Professional

Some of Industry.Net's best stuff is in this department, which is divided into several sections:

- Stock Tracking gives you today's stock prices for industrial corporations.
- The Job Opportunities section lists more than 1,000 jobs. Help-Wanted advertisers pay by the month, so not all ads are fresh each week.
- Discussion Groups presents on-Web discussions of different topics. Job hunters go here for more job opportunities.
- Newsgroups gives you the most complete directory we've seen of newsgroups that cover industrial topics, with helpful short descriptions of each.
- The Shareware section looks to hold about 1,700 software programs for DOS and 300 for Windows. This is the best collection of shareware for industry anyplace: 17 bar code programs, 72 process control programs, and 7 programs for purchasing, to give you a brief idea of what you'll find here. You'll find good programs for accounting, engineering, motion control, project management, and oodles of AutoCAD add-ons.

How

World Wide Web

Where

www.industry.net

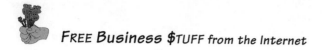

To Succeed, You Must Have a Plan

WebPlan ☆☆☆☆

One very good manufacturing software program is free, and you can get it only from this site. WebPlan is MRP (manufacturing requirements planning) software for Windows NT and Win95. WebPlan allows planning collaboration between multiple planners, multiple plants, and/or between a manufacturer and key suppliers. You can run the software either on your internal Intranet or use it on the Internet to coordinate geographically dispersed sites.

Using WebPlan, different people develop, compare, and modify plans which can then be brought together to create the best synthesis. It produces simulations to answer what-if and what-is questions. Enterprise Planning Systems gives WebPlan away; but to download it, you must register first.

How

World Wide Web

Where

www.enterprise.on.ca/products/mwebpln.htm

Recycled Ideas Can Be Profitable

PartNet ☆☆☆

Why reinvent the wheel? When you need a part, why have it designed from scratch? If you use a standard off-the-shelf part instead of creating a custom component, you save both money and time. PartNet allows designers to specify, find, and select parts from a collection of online parts catalogs. It covers both mechanical and electrical parts. This project is still young, and as it grows it could become a significant design and fabrication resource. There is no fee to use PartNet to find information. Why not use it and save your money and your brain cells to apply to your truly *new* innovations?

How

World Wide Web

Where

part.net

410

A Spot for Bargain-Hunters

Buyers-Sellers Industrial Equipment Database ☆☆☆

Ads aren't free on this sales site (just inexpensive), but it costs you nothing to shop. You'll find some outstanding bargains here, as some companies just want to get rid of excess gear. When we looked, one firm offered excess forestry equipment for free, and several power generators had a price tag of zero! It doesn't get better than that.

Product categories here include A/C and refrigeration equipment; aggregate and mining equipment; asphalt and concrete equipment; construction equipment (cranes, generators, etc.); forestry equipment; fork lifts; and trucks and trailers. Usually you won't find equipment for free here, just bargains. But who knows when you'll get lucky?

How

World Wide Web

Where

www.buyers-sellers.com

Disneyland for Automation Designers

AutomationNet ☆☆☆

Manufacturing engineers who design automation equipment and assembly lines will have a field day at AutomationNet. Click on the humbly named "Product Tree" and you'll find yourself in a giant buyer's guide for automated systems designers. How giant? Well, um, massive. Huge. Really, really, really big. You get the picture.

Another section called "Tech Info" gives you job opportunities for engineers, a fairly complete directory of engineering publications, and a directory of engineering associations. Hit "Cool Web Sites" for a good collection of links to Web sites that cover engineering and robotics, with descriptions of each.

How

World Wide Web

Where

www.automationnet.com/~Azure/default.htm

411

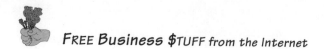
The Wonderful World of Chemistry

Chemistry Sites on the Web ☆☆☆

"Finding something on the Internet is like trying to find the bathroom in a house with 250,000 unmarked doors," says chemical engineer Stephen Heller on this remarkable and entertaining Web page. This is not your garden-variety boring page with just a bunch of links. What you get here is actually a compound site. The foundation is a well-written article by James Krieger from *Chemical & Engineering News.*

Krieger not only does a compelling job of explaining what's on the Net for chemical engineers, he goes beyond that to show how the Internet has *already* transformed the process of chemical research and collaborative engineering projects. This is no stars-in-your-eyes fluff piece. Krieger points out the Net's weak spots along with the good. If you're in the chemicals industry and want to find out how you can use the Net to further your work, this gives you an excellent introduction. Or maybe your boss should see it....

The second blessing delivered at this address is a "Best of the Web" list of the sixty top chem sites with short descriptions of each. Instead of somebody's personal "Dave's Faves" list, this was put together by several top professionals. What it misses in quirkiness, it more than makes up for in breadth and quality.

How

World Wide Web

Where

pubs.acs.org/hotartcl/cenear/951113/pg1.html

Better Netting through Chemistry

Internet Chemistry Resources ☆☆☆

While the site above launches chemical engineers in their career on the Net, a great "Chemistry on the Internet 101" course, advanced-level research begins here. Joseph Warden of Rensselaer Polytechnic Institute built this very good and impressively thorough directory of chemistry resources, providing helpful descriptions to tell you what's special about them. Don't be fooled by the unassuming, simple-looking home page here. You'll find a great deal of information

behind it. Warden's directory is especially good in steering you toward chemical databases, email discussion groups, periodicals, and software.

How

World Wide Web

Where

www.rpi.edu/dept/chem/cheminfo/chemres.html

Use a Paperless Medium to Get More Paper

SCIENTIFIC COMPUTING & AUTOMATION ☆☆

The bad news is that this publication doesn't put all its articles online. The good news is that it does provide a pretty good directory of Internet resources called "Net Links," including such topics as chemical databases (reference databases, graphical periodic tables, spectroscopic data, molecular databases, and others), supercomputing, medical resources, government resources, and visualization. The even better news is that you can sign up here to subscribe without charge to the printed version of the magazine.

How

World Wide Web

Where

gordonpub.loyola.edu

Free Mags for High-Tech Manufacturers

Free Trade Publications ☆☆☆

Here's a spot for computer and electronics manufacturers and engineers—you know, those people who create all this high-tech gear that somebody told us would eliminate paperwork, but actually it just made producing paperwork faster and easier. And when you make something faster and easier to do, you simply generate more of it.

Our revenge is this site, which sends paper back at 'em. At this one spot, you'll find 15 print trade publications in the computer and technology industries that you can subscribe to for free—*if* you are a qualified professional—by simply filling out a form on the Web.

The list includes some excellent publications. One caveat: Most, but not all, of these trade publications will be sent for free only to professionals in the U.S., or in the U.S. and Canada. It's rare to receive them without charge in other countries. You can choose from *VARBusiness, OEM, Electronic Buyers News, Electronic Engineering Times, Solid State Technology, Computer Design, Integrated System Design, Computer Reseller News, Communications Week, Sun Expert, Software Solutions* and others.

How

World Wide Web

Where

www.netline.com/TradePub

Tooling Around

Numerical Control Software for DOS ☆☆☆

Robotics software for operating machine tools and other numerical control devices frequently cost thousands of dollars to design, write, and debug. This source has two files for aiding in NC machine tool operations: cams305.zip is a program that generates control data for machine tools, and cv3d_110.zip is a three-dimensional graphical CNC/CAM control file viewer.

How

World Wide Web

Where

www.coast.net/SimTel/msdos/mfg.html

Download

cams305.zip   (291 K)
cv3d_110.zip   (153 K)

Spend Some Quality Time

American Society of Quality Control ☆☆☆☆

Okay, all you quality hounds, hop to it. This site is one big directory, and will keep you pointing and clicking for hours. You'll find quality plans for dozens of industries and business activities. You can research project-management techniques and systems. You can read up on quality-related job opportunities and pop your resume into a resume bank. You can find out about W. Edwards Deming, the American quality guru whom Japanese manufacturers credit with giving them the strategies to capture world markets.

You can also find out about software for quality management. (If your business produces software, you can read about SQE, Software Quality Engineering, and the techniques of Clean Room Software Engineering.) You can learn from online tutorials, and download slide presentations and lesson plans if you teach quality classes yourself. You can read even more in the newsletter, articles, and journals archive.

As you can see, there is a tremendous amount of stuff here. And surprisingly, for the subject matter, the quality is very uneven. To improve the quality of its overwhelming site, we wish the ASQC would put in place some kind of guidance system, or at least add short descriptions to the dozens of links here.

How

World Wide Web

Where

www.quality.org/qc

Where Quality Is Job Number One

TQM in Manufacturing and Service Industries ☆☆☆

This "TQM in Manufacturing and Service Industries" mailing list is moderated, meaning there is no spam. It generates a high volume of messages dealing with every aspect of Total Quality Management, both technical and strategic issues. This is, without a doubt, the most philosophical business mailing list. Sometimes it gets quite deep.

Sample topics: Business Strategic Game; Certifying Distributors; Deming's Point #11 vs. MBO; Hal Popplewell's Variance Issue; HELP: ISO 9000 in software development; Organizational Disorders; p and pn attribute charts; Profit and CEOs; Profit Maximization; Profit Sharing; Strategic Planning Software; Cheating.

How

Email

Where

listserv@pucc.princeton.edu

Message

SUBSCRIBE QUALITY Yourfirstname Yourlastname

This mailing list is mirrored to the newsgroup **bit.listserv.quality**.

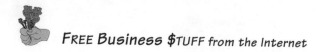

FREE Business $TUFF from the Internet

Quality Conquers the World

Quality Function Deployment Discussion Group ☆☆☆

QFD evolved in Japan as a way to include customer needs in every stage of design, manufacturing, delivery, and support of both products and services. Mostly used in the U.S. and Japanese auto industries, QFD is gaining adopters in the electronics, aerospace, and software industries worldwide. This email discussion group claims participants from around the world. It is the best place to keep up with what's new in the promising quality management technique.

How

Email

Where

majordomo@quality.org

Message

subscribe QFD-L

Belly Up to the Bar

Wbar Bar Code Generator ☆☆☆☆

Wbar, a bar code generating program, makes it a snap to create many different types of bar codes to insert into any Windows program that accepts bitmaps or metafiles.

Follow the comprehensive documentation to quickly get up to speed, then simply position the cursor in the window where you want to place the barcode and click. You'll be prompted for the type of bar code you want, and you're finished.

How

World Wide Web

Where

www.coast.net/SimTel/win3/barcode.html

Download

wbar19.zip   (47 K)

See Here, You CAD

CAD for Windows ☆☆☆

Computer-aided design has been around for over a decade, but as personal computers have become more versatile, these programs once relegated to only

the most demanding drafters and architects have come into their own as powerful, fun, and easy-to-use design tools.

You can take out a second mortgage to buy the latest version of AutoCAD on the market and spend the rest of your life trying to learn all of its bells and whistles, and you'll still only scratch the surface. But if your needs are a little less demanding, you can find some excellent shareware CAD programs at this site.

To be certain, the programs available here won't give you the same versatility or options available in the best-selling CAD programs available off the shelf, but then you will be much happier with the prices of the shareware versions.

A couple of the programs you'll find here are GammaCAD, a full-featured CAD program for Windows, and CAD/Draw, which promises to be as easy to use as it is powerful (also for Windows).

How

World Wide Web

Where

www.acs.oakland.edu/oak/SimTel/win3/cad.html

Download

GammaCAD:	gcad110.zip	(1,022 K)
Tommy Software CAD/Draw (English)	tscd320e.zip	(2,691 K)
Tommy Software CAD/Draw (German)	tscd320d.zip	(2,744 K)

Keep Your Eye on the Other Guy

MANUFACTURING IT INFORMER III

This Web site serves you daily news articles—mostly covering the U.S., Canada, the U.K., and Australia—about hardware and software for manufacturers. You'll find out what products are new from vendors, which manufacturer bought what product (or built it in-house), how much the product costs, and what the manufacturer plans to do with it. A story like this is especially interesting when the manufacturer in question is your top competitor.

Normally a subscription to the *Manufacturing IT Informer* costs $300 a year, but you can get a free trial subscription that lasts until the end of the month. Our tip: Subscribe right on or after the first of the month so your free trial lasts as many days as possible.

How

World Wide Web

Where

For fastest performance, use the site closest to you:

U.S.: www.keyway.net/mmp/manufac

U.K.: www.pavilion.co.uk/mmp/manufac

Follow the Money, Stupid

Invested Costing Database ☆☆☆

If Ross Perot ever achieves immortality by being included in *Bartlett's Familiar Quotations*, it will probably be for one line he said that has been quoted by everyone in every place from Marvel Comics to the *New York Times*: "Follow the money, stupid." We're not sure if Perot added that tagline of "stupid" or somebody else did, but still, we bet Perot wishes he had earned royalties just for uttering that one phrase. Not that he particularly needs more royalties.

If you want to be rich like Perot someday, you'd better follow your business' money. This Windows software program helps by tracking how much money you are investing in any ongoing project. At any point, you can pull reports on your job's cost to date. And you don't need big ears to do it.

How

World Wide Web

Where

www.csusm.edu/winworld/database.html

Download

invested.zip   (101 K)

For Faster Design-to-Production, Get Primed!

Agile & Advanced Manufacturing ☆☆☆☆

Would you like a process that gives you a much faster design-to-production cycle? A collaboration of manufacturers in the U.S. and Europe is creating such a process, and then demonstrating that it works by rapidly designing and producing precision electromechanical devices.

This site explains the strategies they use to get these results, and gives you the tools to replicate their approach in your own plant. This project's name is A-PRIMED. If you want an explanation of A-PRIMED, visit this site, find the A-PRIMED name (near the top of the page), and click on it. That unobtrusive link is apparently the only way for you to reach the background information.

The rest of the home page gives you links to directories, tools, news, and publications about and for A-PRIMED manufacturers.

How

World Wide Web

Where

www.sandia.gov/agil/home_page.html

Where to Find More Manufacturing Mouseclicks

If you ever make it out of Industry.Net alive and can even *think* of wanting more manufacturing resources from the Internet than we gave you in this chapter—don't worry, we've got 'em for you.

Good first stops might be the preceding two chapters, Chapter 14 on purchasing and Chapter 15, which covers logistics. The purchasing chapter includes a resource where you can license new manufacturing technologies. In Chapter 15, pay close attention to the EDI resources. If you have a high volume of transactions with your customers and/or your suppliers, EDI might be a strategy for you to consider. If you are a very small business, probably not.

Chapter 2, *How to Find Business Stuff on the Internet*, includes one resource that almost every U.S. manufacturer can use, the Thomas Register of American Manufacturers. It's a great supply source. If you are interested in Internet strategies for manufacturers, you may want to take a look at CommerceNet's Manufacturing Working Group, also in Chapter 2.

Two resources in Chapter 3, which covers *Business News*, are especially useful for manufacturers. The ClariNet newsgroups include several newsgroups that bring you daily news stories about manufacturing in different industries. EPRI's newsletter has good information on plant maintenance and power.

Whether your business is large or small, if you want software you could do worse than the SBA Shareware Archive, featured in Chapter 5, *Entrepreneurs,*

Startups, and Home Businesses. Even though Industry.Net's software archive is larger, the SBA Archive includes several programs that are not carried by Industry.Net's archive.

Chapter 13 on *Business Law, Trademarks, Copyrights, and Patents* has several places you might want to search. We mention that the Gama legal forms archive provides a Product Licensing Contract that you can download and use, but you might find handy several other legal forms from Gama as well. (Hey, a download is cheaper than a lawyer any day.) Check out the Internet Patent News Service for news of new technologies you can license, and the KuesterLaw Technology Law site if you are in a technology-based industry.

When all else fails, turn to the **manufacturing** heading in the index. Yeah, you knew we were going to say that. So why did you ask?

FREE $TUFF

Whenever there are great strains or changes in the economic system, it tends to generate crackpot theories, which then find their way into the legislative channels.

David Stockman

A Free Lunch for Economists

Economists often say, "There is no such thing as a free lunch." Meaning that somehow, you always pay for what you get.

This chapter proves them wrong. You can't get lunch here, but you can get free software, free newsletters, thousands of free data sets, free charts, free help in finding a job (maybe your interviewer will buy you lunch), and excellent sources of free advice from experts. Okay, so you had to pay for your Internet connection. But weren't you going to do that anyway to play games and download *Star Trek* screen savers? If this chapter's wealth of economics resources isn't perfectly free, at least it's a disproportionately high return on a comparatively minuscule investment.

Actually, you might be inclined to think that this chapter won't be of much use to your business. Not all businesses need economic resources. But many businesses do. Marketers use economic statistics to find new kinds of customers and to monitor current markets. International trade pros apply this data to compare trends country-by-country. Investors sniff out solid investments. Because your company doesn't keep an economist on staff, don't jump to the conclusion that this chapter holds nothing you can use.

Before we get to the good stuff, a few words about the very last resource in this chapter. It's an archive of jokes about economics and economists. In the first chapters of this book, we promised that every resource listed would be strictly for business and will help put money in your pocket. You may think a humor archive would be stretching things a bit. But let's face it, economics can be a dry subject. What if you get asked to make a speech on an economic topic? Or to deliver a paper on "Econometricians and Post-Modern Statistical Dingus Norms?" Wouldn't you want to liven things up a bit? Add a joke from this archive, and your audience will laugh. An impressed headhunter will make you a job offer. Then your boss will have to give you a raise just to keep you on staff. So don't go knocking this joke archive until you've had an opportunity to put it to use.

But maybe you're looking forward to the economics jokes. Before you race to the end of this chapter looking for them, check out the more serious resources first. You'll find extremely valuable sources of data, information, and software, more than you can fit on your plate. Save the jokes for dessert.

The Most Helpful Guide to Econ on the Net

Resources for Economists on the Internet ☆☆☆☆☆

This monumental guide to economics and economics-related resources was created by economist Bill Goffe. Three things make Goffe's guide different from others on the Net:

1. Goffe doesn't list junk, only "items that either offer a substantial amount of information, or are specialized to a specific area."
2. Few Internet directories on any topic match this site's awe-inspiring size.
3. Goffe gives excellent descriptions of almost all resources.

Goffe's descriptions really set his guide apart. They save you time and point out new possibilities. A two- or three-sentence rundown describes most resources. Major resources receive a lengthy, section-by-section explanation, often revealing alternative access methods, search engine tricks, or hidden treasures not described by the resource itself. For a free sample of one of Goffe's descriptions, check out his review of Netlib in the next sidebar.

Goffe's site is well organized. He has grouped resources under more than 30 headings:

- U.S. Macro & Regional Data
- Finance and Financial Markets
- Economic Consulting and Forecasting Services
- Data Archives, Newsletters
- Economic Societies and Associations
- Program Libraries, Information about the Economics Profession
- And so forth

The main drawback to this site, though, is an organizational problem. Resources for Economists on the Internet was probably designed as a Gopher site first and then ported into the World Wide Web. Each of Goffe's category headings presents you with a list of resource names with no descriptions. To get to his descriptions, you must click on a link to receive several single pages, each carrying only one description. This may not sound too annoying, but prepare yourself for a lot of back-and-forth click-and-wait when you visit this site.

For the most part, Goffe does not review email discussion groups. He just presents them, under the heading "Mailing Lists," with instructions on where and how to subscribe. Check this section out. Goffe gives you more than 100 email groups, several of which I found nowhere else on the Net. You'll find these economics email lists and more:

- Workshop on Information Systems Economics
- *The Electronic Journal of Finance*
- Political Economics
- Labor Economics, Ecological Economics
- LABOR-L [Labor and the Global Economy]
- ISLMECON [Islamic Economy]
- Forensic Economics
- Economics of Pensions and Retirement
- MEMSNET [Mineral Economics and Management Society]

Goffe excels at finding lists that discuss international economics and world trade. Some examples of lists include:

- *Discussao sobre economia brasileira*
- Eastern Business Network
- International Trade, *Ekonomika* [Czech Republic]
- General Economics Issues in Eastern Europe/CIS
- POLEC-ITA [Italian economic policy]
- Australian-Economics-L, Latin-America Economy

Browsing this site is an education in itself. Anyone interested in economics, finance, or international trade should tune in.

How

World Wide Web

Where

Original site:	netec.wustl.edu/EconFAQ/EconFAQ.html
Texas mirror:	coba.shsu.edu/EconFAQ/EconFAQ.html
U.K. mirror:	netec.mcc.ac.uk/~adnetec/EconFAQ/EconFAQ.html
Singapore:	www.ntu.ac.sg/nbs/ae/EconFAQ/EconFAQ.shtml
Australia:	www.uwa.edu.au/EconFAQ/EconFAQ.html

In addition to the four mirror sites listed above, Resources for Economists on the Internet are mirrored at several other sites around the world. The sites are all listed on the information page. If one site is slow, try the next one closest to you.

Bill Goffe Reviews Netlib

Netlib is a numerical software library with approximately 50 megabytes of code. The routines, mostly in FORTRAN, are generally of high quality (many were developed at U.S. national labs or by professional numerical analysts). The popularity of Netlib is attested by the number of times it has been contacted—at last count, nearly eight million times.

Packages include Linpack, Eispack, and its successor, Lapack (including a pre-release version in C), fftpack, the Harwell sparse matrix routines, Hompack, Lanczos, and Minpack. There are many other more specialized libraries. Code is used from various texts (but not *Numerical Recipes*) and from the *ACM Transactions on Mathematical Software* (more than 500 different routines here alone). Also, many directories are organized not by package, but by subject (each entry is code by different authors). Finally, various tools are supplied for FORTRAN and C users.

In all, nearly 150 directories cover almost every imaginable area in numerical computation. Any user of numerical methods would be well advised to become familiar with these directories.

Netlib is available via email, FTP, Gopher, and the Web. Introductory material on Netlib can be found in the first entries of the Web, FTP, and Gopher interfaces. For an email introduction, write **send index** in the body of a message addressed to one of the sites listed below, and in return you will receive general directions.

You can search the contents of Netlib through email (the method is explained in the email directions) and the Web interface. The latter is more flexible, but you must carefully read the directions.

The Netlib2 FTP site, Web, and Gopher sites contain uncompressed files. You can find these files at:

www.netlib.org

ftp://netlib2.cs.utk.edu

ftp://netlib.att.com/netlib

ftp://unix.hensa.ac.uk/pub/netlib

ftp://draci.cs.uow.edu.au/netlib

(or)

FREE Business $TUFF from the Internet

Email:
netlib@ornl.gov
netlib@research.att.com
netlib@unix.hensa.ac.uk
netlib@nac.no
netlib@draci.cs.uow.edu.au

Easier and Faster Econ Stuff

FinWeb ☆☆☆☆☆

If you're interested in financial economics, investment, and banking resources, visit FinWeb. Professor James Garven of the University of Texas at Austin gives excellent short descriptions of all resources he lists in this directory. Like Bill Goffe, Garven hand-picks only useful resources and omits time-wasting garbage. Garven lists fewer resources than Goffe's Resources for Economists on the Internet (described earlier), and he provides less description per resource than Goffe. These drawbacks are compensated for: FinWeb is easier and faster to navigate because it all springs off one page. It also covers more banking resources. FinWeb is a part of RiskWeb, a risk management and insurance site.

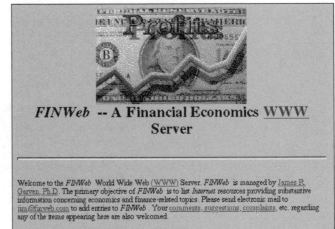

FINWeb -- A Financial Economics WWW Server

Welcome to the *FINWeb* World Wide Web (WWW) Server. *FINWeb* is managed by James R. Garven, Ph.D. The primary objective of *FINWeb* is to list *Internet* resources providing substantive information concerning economics and finance-related topics. Please send electronic mail to jim@finweb.com to add entries to *FINWeb* . Your comments, suggestions, complaints, etc. regarding any of the items appearing here are also welcomed.

Hand-picked profit-building resources for financial economics, investment, and banking.

How

World Wide Web

Where

www.finweb.com

426

NetEc: The Most Econ Stuff on the Net

NetEc ☆☆☆☆☆

NetEc is a joint project of academics, government economists, and bankers from 18 organizations in 7 countries. This ambitious resource centralizes world-wide economic information in four sub-resources:

- **CodEc** - A repository of free software for econometrics and economics
- **WebEc** - A Web site linking all Internet economic resources
- **WoPEc** - An archive of all economics working papers on the Net
- **BibEc** - A database of summaries of all printed economics working papers

Each of these component sub-resources are reviewed in detail below. NetEc also includes a single search engine that can search all these resources except for WebEc. The search engine will search only one of the three sub-resources at a time, not two or three together. (If you want to go directly to the NetEc search engine, go to **netec.mcc.ac.uk/~adnetec/local/search.html**.) For more details on the NetEc search engine, see the WoPEc description below.

How

World Wide Web

Where

U.K.: netec.mcc.ac.uk/netec.html

U.S.: netec.wustl.edu/netec.html

By email, you can get the FAQ for NetEc. The FAQ is available in English, French, and German by emailing to **netec@netec.mcc.ac.uk** or in Spanish by emailing to **netec@mozart.econom.uv.es**. The body of your email message should contain nothing but the word **NetEc**.

NetEc 2: A Little Free Code

CodEc ☆☆☆

When I checked, NetEc's economics software repository only held 20 free computer programs (only 4 for DOS and Windows, none for Macs). The bad news about this site is that it offers few programs. The good news is that there is quality control here. These programs have been used and *really* do work. Some of them are quite elaborate. You'll find routines for Mathematica, Matlab, Estima, and GAUSS, as well as stand-alone programs. You'll also find links to other software archives with statistical and mathematical software.

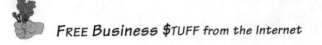

How

World Wide Web

Where

netec.mcc.ac.uk/~adnetec/CodEc/codec.html

NetEc 3: The Host with the Most

WebEc ☆☆☆☆☆

WebEc is one of the three biggest directories of economics resources on the Internet. This directory contains the largest number of resources. (The other two are Bill Goffe's site and FinWeb.) The difference is that the other two are picky, but this one wants to include *everything*. That means WebEc is the most comprehensive guide to economics on the Internet, but some of WebEc's resources are—how shall I say it—of limited usefulness. Even so, you'll still find hundreds of good, solid resources at WebEc. Most directories have short (but helpful) descriptions. For some economics email discussion groups and announcement lists, you'll find more information here than anyplace else. In all, WebEc is an extremely useful site for any business that needs economics resources.

How

World Wide Web

Where

netec.wustl.edu/webec.html

NetEc 4: Paper, Mister?

WoPEc ☆☆☆☆

This database gives you access to more than 1,500 working papers in economics, and makes the complete text available on the Internet. Papers are mostly in English, but also in German, Spanish, Italian, Dutch, and French. There are two ways you can find a WoPEc paper. If you know what organization makes the paper available on the Net, you can find the institution on a WoPEc list and then browse a catalog of papers for that specific institution, broken down by series. Otherwise (which is most of the time), you can use the NetEc search engine.

This makes the search function the most important part of WoPEc (and of BibEc below). If you can't find a paper, it may just as well not exist. This search engine has almost no instructions, so read the description here carefully. It is the only documentation you will get on how to use WoPEc. The screen for the search engine tells you to type in a keyword. WoPEc searches only the *titles* of the papers, not the actual *contents* of the papers. The search screen doesn't tell you this helpful information, but it will also let you search by author name(s), or by author name(s) and keyword(s). Just type the author name on the regular entry line (with your keyword or keywords, if you have one or more). It's safest to stick to author last names only. If you type in "Charles Dickens," for example, WoPEc will not only give you all papers written by Dickens, but all papers written by anyone named Charles.

Result of search in the NetEc-database

This is a searchable index of information.
Note: *This service can only be used from a forms-capable browser.*

Enter keyword(s): [startup]   [Search] [Reset]

Select an index to search: [WoPEc Database ▼]

Here is the result of your search using the keyword(s) **"startup"**:

1: 📄 Firms Started as Franchises have Lower Survival Rates than Independent Small Business Startups
     Score: **1000**, Lines: **28**, Size: **1 kbytes**, Type: **HTML file**

This search was performed by wwwwais 2.5.

A simple search engine gives you access to more than 1,500 economics papers on the Net. Here is the result of a search for the word "startup."

Your search results will bring you only a paper's title, size in bytes, and type. See the illustration for an example. From this skimpy results page, a link for each paper takes you to a second page with author name, author's organization, and other data. The second page doesn't tell you the year the paper was issued or other standard bibliographic data. This search function is a step in the right direction, but still needs a little fine tuning. The information in the papers themselves makes WoPEc a rich and rewarding site.

How

World Wide Web

Where

netec.wustl.edu/~adnetec/WoPec.wopec.html

If you'd like to be informed of new economics papers as they appear online, you can subscribe to WoPEc's email announcement list. Email to **wopec-announce@glider.econ3.uni-bonn.de** for information.

NetEc 5: Abstract Art

BibEc ☆☆☆☆

Bill Goffe calls BibEc "one of the most valuable resources for economists on the Internet." What you have here are abstracts (or, as we businesspeople call them, summaries) of thousands of working papers in economics from around the world: U.S. Federal Reserve, NBER, Centre for Economic Policy, and dozens of other organizations. Note that you do not get the *text* of the papers, just their *summaries*. These summaries are all indexed and searchable, either via Gopher or by using the same NetEc search engine described above as part of WoPEc. (Read instructions above before using.)

Surprisingly, papers in WoPEc are not always included in BibEc. If you want to make a thorough search for a topic, you'll need to search twice, once in BibEc and once in WoPEc. You'll find the search engine at:

netec.mcc.ac.uk/~adnetec/local/search.html

How

Gopher

Where

gopher://netec.mcc.ac.uk:70/11/NetEc/BibEc

Free Math Software, Anyone?

Netlib ☆☆☆☆

Many businesses have no use for mathematical software, but many businesses do. Whether for economic analyses, marketing statistics, or factory machine control, if your business needs math software, Netlib's immense library of free software, papers, and  databases may be your preferred place to shop. It includes software from several different organizations. The National High-Performance Software Exchange (NHSE) is part of this site. For an in-depth look at Netlib, read Bill Goffe's detailed report earlier in this chapter.

How

World Wide Web

Where

www.netlib.org

Economics for Mathheads

sci.econ.research Newsgroup ☆☆☆

Visit this moderately active newsgroup for questions, answers, technical papers, and news covering the mathematical side of economics. If you're not comfortable with terms like "stochastic regressor theory," go elsewhere. This group is moderated and 99 percent spam-free. Most postings are by professionals and graduate students.

Sample topics include: Markowitz optimization with transaction costs; Assessed values and transaction prices; Cost Benefit Analysis Request for Proposals; business cycle survey paper; Cox-Huang martingale representation technique under incomplete market?; Differentiable preference "close to" arbitrary preferences; Government spending multipliers.

How

Newsgroup

Where

news:sci.econ.research

The Business of Statistics

sci.stat.consult Newsgroup ☆☆☆☆

This active newsgroup, moderated and spam-free, is for statistics consultants and anyone else in the statistics field. You'll find more discussion of software here than **sci.stat.math**, the other statistics newsgroup. Also, you'll find more job opportunities and consulting contract offers here. Some messages in this group are duplicated in **sci.stat.math**.

Sample topics include: Analysis of large data sets; Bonferroni reference; Clustering—cutting the dendogram; Compute ASE in SPSS LOGLIN; EpiInfo—>STATA file conversion; Market Research Job Opportunity; Help—Bivariate Piosson; Multivariate vs. Univariate tests help desperately needed; Philadelphia Area SAS Opportunities; EDP Contract Services; ROC curves analysis software wanted; Shareware DOS Stat Software?

How
Newsgroup

Where
news:sci.stat.consult

The Science of Statistics

sci.stat.math Newsgroup ☆☆☆

This group discusses the mathematical side of statistics, along with some inappropriate rant messages. (The message below titled "Ignorance and drug screening" is an example of rant in the wrong place.) Some messages here are duplicates of those in the **sci.stat.consult** newsgroup.

Sample topics include:

- Ridge Regression Question
- Experiments with GA and neural nets
- Ignorance and drug screening
- Markov Chains
- Math Books (Sale)
- More fiddling with GA-NN
- Multivariate versus univariate tests help desperately needed
- S function for Gelman-Rubin
- Statistical evaluation of psychological testing
- Testing for (tied-down) Wiener Process
- UCD Statistics Web Server

How
Newsgroup

Where
news:sci.stat.math

Hey, JOE, Whaddya Know?

Job Openings for Economists (JOE) ☆☆☆☆

The printed newsletter *JOE* contains the same material as this electronic version, but the electronic *JOE* is searchable. Job openings are divided into three categories:

1. U.S. academic.

2. Non-U.S. academic.

3. Non-academic (worldwide).

The last time I looked, category 3 alone listed more than 100 positions. *JOE* is so rich in job opportunities because of the great pressure within the economics field to use it as the first hiring source. Before you use this Gopher site, read its directions on how to make a search. Especially pay close attention to the unusual classification codes used to describe job openings.

How

Gopher

Where

gopher://vuinfo.vanderbilt.edu:70/11/employment/joe

Euro JOE

Job Openings for Economists in Europe ☆☆☆

This site contains two sections. One links to *JOE*, and the second contains job openings of its own. The last time I looked, I found only 12 openings. Only one position was in the private industry, and the rest were academic. But the advantage of this site is that job openings are emailed here and posted immediately, so they show up sooner than the once-a-month *JOE* listings. Euro JOE is worth checking out. This site will soon move to a Web address.

How

Gopher

Where

gopher://otto.ww.tu-berlin.de:70/11/Economics/jobs

 If you have a job opening to post on this site, email it to: **job-offer@otto.ww.tu-berlin.de**.

Papers with a European Flavour

Centre for Economic Performance ☆☆☆

This site provides more theoretical economics information than practical, but it's quite good. Based at the London School of Economics and Political Science, it presents research on labour markets, unemployment, wages, human

resources, entrepreneurship, international trade, and transition economies. You'll find downloadable discussion papers on topics such as:

- "R&D in Oligopolistic Industries"
- "Why Is Consumption So Seasonal?"
- "Accounting for Strikes"
- "Economic Policies, Employment and Labour Markets in Transition in Central and Eastern Europe"
- "Regional Migration in Britain, 1975-1992"
- "Japanese Capitalism, Anglo-Saxon Capitalism"
- "The British Disease Overcome? Living Standards, Productivity and Educational Attainment, 1979-1994"

You can download some papers directly from the Web. For others, you can read abstracts on the Web and order papers for free via email.

How
World Wide Web

Where
cep.lse.ac.uk

God Save the Queen—with Interest

Her Majesty's Treasury ☆☆☆

H.M. Treasury's Web site presents daily press releases, economic forecasts, speeches, and minutes of the Chancellor's monthly interest rate meetings with the Governor of the Bank of England. You can subscribe here to *Economic Briefing*, a free printed newsletter. (You remember, the kind you receive by post.) This Web site also includes articles from past issues.

A unique section of this site is titled "The Treasury's Contacts with Industry Scheme." Whether your company is small or large, one to three Treasury officials will visit your British business. They investigate how Treasury economic policies affect industries. Good idea, bringing bureaucrats into the real world. This site shows how your company can receive a visit, too.

How
World Wide Web

Where
www.hm-treasury.gov.uk

You can also subscribe to two email announcement lists from H.M. Treasury. One sends you all Treasury press releases. The other sends you notices of any new Treasury Internet services. For both, email to **maillist@hm-treasury.gov.uk**. For press releases, make your message: **SUBSCRIBE PRESS**, or for Internet services: **SUBSCRIBE WHATSNEW**.

Chart of Darkness

Dr. Ed Yardeni's Economic Network ☆☆☆☆

You'll find good-quality, original material at this site, which Bill Goffe rates as "excellent." Yardeni is chief economist of Deutsche Morgan Grenfell. Here he presents, in Adobe Acrobat format, dozens of charts on U.S. macroeconomics, financial, and industrial data such as:

- Imports
- Exports
- Trade deficit
- Bank loans
- Debit and borrowing
- Consumer surveys
- Auto production and sales
- Retail sales
- Employment
- National Association of Purchasing Management surveys
- Federal Reserve Bank surveys
- Inventories
- GDP

In addition to charts, you'll also find country surveys on Japan, the U.K., and Canada. In addition to the above goodies, customers of Deutsche Morgan Grenfell can access several restricted-access files with additional material.

How
World Wide Web

Where
www.webcom.com/~yardeni

It's Penn & Teller—Not!

Penn World Tables ☆☆☆☆

We have data for you here. Lots of data. In fact, you can download data from 152 countries on 29 subjects, including:

- Population
- Real GDP per capita
- Consumption percentage of GDP
- Investment percentage of GDP
- Exchange rate
- Producer durables
- Construction, Real Gross National Product (which sounds like something from *The Simpsons*)
- Standards of living

Check out "Value-added PWT Services." It presents cool pre-made lists of countries sorted by GDP per capita, by population size, by total GDP, and by total capital stock.

How

World Wide Web

Where

www.cansim.epas.utoronto.ca:5680/pwt/html

This'll Keep Your Spreadsheets Busy

EconData ☆☆☆☆

One problem with the economic data series produced by the World Bank, IMF, and government agencies is that they come in 93 skedillion different formats, which you must convert to use. Here you can get different types of macro data, but all in one format:

- Balance of payments
- Flow of funds
- Employment
- Consumer Price Index
- Producer Price Index

- Industrial production
- And other national, state, local, and world data

You access the data with PC programs and can easily convert it to spreadsheet format. Included at this site is PDG, a public domain DOS software program you can use to read the series, perform regression, and produce graphs. You'll find hundreds of thousands of time series here.

How

World Wide Web

Where

www.inform.umd.edu:8080/Educational_Resources/
AcademicResourcesByTopic/EconomicsResources/EconData/Data/

Royal Canadian Counted Police

Statistics Canada ☆☆☆

Statistics Canada contains everything that is Canadian and counted. You can get Canadian census tables, plus a lot more. This site adds new services and information often (although it's not all free). From this Web site, Statistics Canada provides a useful email help desk. It's called Information Request Service. Email your questions about statistics and receive answers from a Statistics Canada staffer. You can take part in an email discussion group on Canadian statistics. Just email to **listproc@statcan.ca** with the message **subscribe statcan Yourfirstname Yourlastname**. Be sure to leave the "Subject" line of your message blank.

You can also get a free subscription to *The Daily*, Statistics Canada's official release bulletin, emailed to you each work day. Send email to **listproc@statcan.ca** with the message **subscribe daily Yourfirstname Yourlastname**. Again, leave your "Subject" line blank. This Web site has an archive of back issues of *The Daily* that you can search through with Architext software. Francophones will be pleased to hear that Statistique Canada is available in both English and in French. Wait a minute—How come they don't have Wayne Gretzky's hockey stats?

How

World Wide Web

Where

www.statcan.ca

437

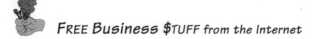
The Face of Net Statistics

Statistical Agencies on the Internet ☆☆☆

This site uses face symbols to review and rate more than two dozen statistical resources on the Net, both free resources and those that charge a fee. The site's main drawback is the lack of descriptions to its links. Other than that, this is a cute time-saver.

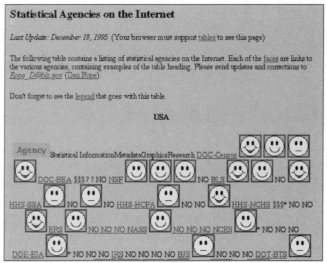

On the face of it, this is a quick guide to statistics stuff on the Net.

How

World Wide Web

Where

www.science.gmu.edu/csi779/drope/govstats.html

One Lump or 75,000?

Central Statistical Office ☆☆☆☆

"Contains more statistics than a John Motson football commentary," said the *Yorkshire Evening Post*, and it's true. The CSO produces U.K. government economic forecasts and indexes, including the Retail Price Index, the Producer Price Index, and many labor and business indexes. You'll find those on this site, plus the valuable CSO Databank. It contains more than 75,000 time series, some seasonally adjusted, from CSO, other government organizations, and the Bank of England. You can access data you need from directories or from a search engine. To run these datasets, you need a Windows software program called Navidata, available for free here. Navidata also prepares charts and graphs.

This site also lists job opportunities, and has a useless tiny page of links. A time-saving tip: If the CSO homepage is slow loading because of the excessive use of graphics files, you can kill all the graphics files on the homepage and still use the text links. Now, can somebody link economic performance to football stats?

How

World Wide Web

Where

www.emap.com\cso

My Business Cycle Is a Harley

Media Logic's Business Cycle Indicators ☆☆☆☆

Free samples of spreadsheet-ready U.S. aggregated data are the attraction at this site. U.S. Business Cycle Indicators are 256 data series from 1948 to the present, mostly derived from data issued monthly by the Bureau of Economic Analysis. You can also download attractive color charts generated by Media Logic's software. Data is available in **.wks** format for spreadsheets. Data series include:

- Composite indexes
- Labor and employment
- Factory output and capacity use
- Sales and orders
- Capital investment
- Inventories, prices
- Money
- Credit
- Interest rates
- Stock prices
- Imports
- Exports

- International comparisons
- Currency exchange rates
- Plus many more

How

World Wide Web

Where

www.mlinet.com/bci/bci.html

The World's Bank's SID Is a Good Guy

The World Bank ☆☆☆

Some people know Sid as the mean kid who tortured toys in *Toy Story*, but to the World Bank, SID stands for Social Indicators of Development. SID is a database of more than 90 demographic and economic indicators for 170 countries. This site has a time series from 1965-1994, and a search engine so you can find them. This page also gets you to TIDES, Trends in Developing Economies, which reports on countries that borrow from the World Bank. At another site (**www.worldbank.org/html/iec/cp/pink.html**) you can read the World Bank's monthly *Pink Sheet* of commodity prices from around the world. This latter site also links to the bank's Latin America and Caribbean Region Technical Department, which features reports on those regions in English and in Spanish. Nothing about toys, though. Sorry, Sid.

How

World Wide Web

Where

www.ciesin.org/IC/wbank/sid-home.html

Income, Revenu, Ingresos, Einkommen

Panel Study of Income Dynamics ☆☆☆

A detailed annual survey of U.S. individuals and their families has accumulated a heap of data since 1968. You'll find information here on salaries, health care, marriage, childbirth, adoption, and personal and family expenditures. The site is free, but you must register to use the data. It's useful for discovering and analyzing consumer trends. Instructions are available in English, French, Spanish, and German.

A Free Lunch for Economists

How
World Wide Web

Where
www.umich.edu/~psid

Drop into My LAB; See What's on the Slab

Bureau of Labor Statistics (LABSTAT) ☆☆☆☆

The many resources offered by LABSTAT remind me of two books of the Bible: the Book of Numbers and the Book of Jobs. Numbers first, hundreds of thousands of time sets:

- Average Price Data
- Collective Bargaining
- Consumer Price Index
- Employee Benefit Survey
- International Price Index
- Special Export Comparison Index
- Occupational Injury and Illness Rates
- International Labor Statistics
- Department Store Inventory Price Index
- Producer Price Index; Major Sector Productivity and Costs Index
- State and Area Employment
- Hours, and Earnings
- Work Stoppage Data
- And on and on

Whew! You can retrieve data using either BLS series IDs or by filling in Web forms.

Other numbers here include news releases, "Economy at a Glance" (a quick overview of key numbers in the U.S. economy) which is a searchable bibliography of research papers on labor and human resources that you can download from the Net, U.S. regional economic statistics, and the *Current Population Survey*.

441

The Book of Jobs is well-represented by a free online version of the 600-page book *Occupational Outlook Handbook*, useful for both job hunters and human resources managers. It profiles more than 250 occupations that account for 7 out of 8 U.S. jobs. It covers each job in detail, and projects workplace demand for that job until 2005.

As a bonus for your salespeople, "About BLS" includes upcoming purchase contracts that are open for bidding by your sales force.

How

World Wide Web

Where

stats.bls.gov

Research Heaven, Complete with Angels

U.S. Census Bureau ☆☆☆☆☆

Not only is the Census Bureau research heaven for economists, it also provides useful information for marketers and for anyone in the import/export game. Best of all, this massive but confusingly organized library of data provides live, human librarians who help you find what you need. (If this is heaven, maybe they're guardian angels.)

First, the easy part. From the Census home page, you can go several ways. Here's what you'll find:

- **Data Access Tools** - Several tools to help you find and extract data from different Census Bureau sources, including map-creation software, a U.S. Gazetteer to search for place names, the WWW Thematic Mapping System (An ISDN or faster connection will help with its 100 K or larger files. It works best with Netscape, and lets you choose data sets and see maps by areas you define.), 1990 Census Lookup, Data Extraction System (also known as SIPP-On-Call, it lets you extract custom data for reports).

- **Economy** - Scads of numbers on agriculture, manufacturing, construction, County Business Patterns, Current Industrial Reports, international trade, payroll, employment, and organizational data on more than 6 million U.S. businesses, and the North American Industrial Classification System (which will replace the old SIC codes).

- **Geography** - Tiger digital map database, Census Tract Street Index, GeoWeb, and other map resources that generate detailed maps on the fly.

- **Job Opportunities** - The Census Bureau regional offices: Atlanta, Boston, Charlotte, Chicago, Detroit, Kansas City, New York, Philadelphia, and Seattle.

- **Subjects** - An alphabetical index to some of the topics scattered across this site.

- **Search** - If you need facts and figures, this is where you want to go. You can search by place names, by point-and-click maps, and by several different "Word" searches. Most of the time you'll want one of the "Word" searches, especially the Textfile Index, which gets you to thousands of reports you can't otherwise reach from the Web. Look up your product type, your industry, or what activity you want to do. Chances are you'll get dozens of hits from this WAIS search engine.

Census Bureau WAIS Search

Search of : Primary HTML / Web Page File Index (HTML)

This is a searchable index. Enter search keywords:

Note: You can enter a new query, of the same index(es), in the keywords box above.

The following 39 item(s) match your query 'Export':

- HTTP or FTP - 'International Trade Overview' - Size: < 1 Kbyte , Type: HTML file
- HTTP or FTP - 'U.S. Commodity Exports and Imports as Related to Output (OEI)' - Size: < 1 Kbyte , Type: HTML file
- HTTP or FTP - 'U.S. International Trade Statistics' - Size: < 1 Kbyte , Type: HTML file
- HTTP or FTP - 'abt900.html: (No title)' - Size: 1 Kbytes , Type: HTML file
- HTTP or FTP - 'Foreign Trade Division Classification Schedules' - Size: 1 Kbytes , Type: HTML file
- HTTP or FTP - 'Foreign Trade Division Classification Schedules' - Size: 1 Kbytes , Type: HTML file
- HTTP or FTP - 'AES SATELLITE BROADCAST' - Size: 2 Kbytes , Type: HTML file
- HTTP or FTP - 'Correct way to fill out the Shipper's Export Declaration' - Size: 2 Kbytes

At the Census Bureau, you can use several different text search engines like this one, or search with point-and-click maps of the U.S., its states, and their counties.

- **Bulletin Board Systems** - Click here to feel like you've entered *The Twilight Zone*. This yanks you off the Web via Telnet to the BEA Electronic Forum, a valuable (ugly-looking) goldmine of resources. When you get in, you'll see a nearly blank screen. Don't panic. Press your "Enter" key to see instructions. This is a free site, but you must register to use it. After registering, you will be asked to "JOIN a Special Interest Group (SIG)." You *must* join one group to get in. Each group can access everything here, but your choice determines which Census Bureau experts will answer your questions. Most readers of this book will want to choose the INDUSTRY Special Interest Group. Once in, you can review TUTORIALS on how to use this system,

SPECIAL FUNCTIONS (detailed instructions on the system), files of information (download FILELIST.EXE for a compressed DOS catalog of everything here), and your Special Interest Group. Your group is like a newsgroup or an email discussion group. You can read other people's questions and answers, and you can ask your own questions, which will be answered by Census Bureau experts (see IMPORT/EXPORT example below). Sometimes your fellow visitors to this site will add helpful comments.

How

World Wide Web

Where

www.census.gov

Besides the Special Interest Groups described above, the Census Bureau also runs more traditional email discussion groups. All have Census Bureau experts on tap, except the last two, which are read-only announcement groups where you read news and can't argue back. To subscribe to any of these groups, email to **majordomo@census.gov** with the message **subscribe listname**, substituting a name in boldface for the word "listname."

- **agfs** - Questions and answers about agricultural statistics
- **ces** - Discussion of the Center for Economic Studies
- **compendia** - Questions and answers about *U.S. Statistical Abstracts*
- **econweb** - Discussion of the Census Bureau's World Wide Web site and its resources
- **ftd** - Questions and answers about foreign trade facts and figures
- **internet-users-group** - Discussion about all Census Internet offerings
- **metadata** - Discussion of the Bureau's Metadata product
- **press-release** - Census Bureau news releases
- **product-announce** - New Bureau products and their prices

Want even more from the Census Bureau? If you are comfortable with FTP, try **ftp://ftp.census.gov** for more data files, including many that are preformatted for spreadsheets.

Census Angels Help Find Your Data

Subject: IMPORT/EXPORT DATA

Looking for import/export data on the product my company manufactures. We manufacture rotary actuators (power hinge). I can't seem to find any Census data on U.S. production or import/export. Can you help?

Subject: REPLY TO MSG# 15485 (IMPORT/EXPORT DATA)

Our Foreign Trade Information office (301-763-5140) should be able to help you with quantity and value information for a product after they figure out the harmonized system code for the product, which is probably the hardest part of the search. They have data on 15,000 imported products and 8,000 exported ones. Data is available monthly, with Feb 94 being the most recent.

Economy Sized Humor

Jokes About Economists and Economics ☆☆☆

Why did God create economists? In order to make weather forecasters look good. If you liked that one, A) you're not an economist, B) you're not a weather forecaster, and C) you'll love Jokes about Economists and Economics.

For reasons known only to the lunatics who manage this site, hundreds of jokes, riddles, and stories that poke fun at economists are stored here.

How

World Wide Web

Where

www.etla.fi/pkm/joke.html

Three Econometricians Went Hunting...

Three econometricians went hunting, and came across a large deer. The first econometrician fired, but missed, by a meter to the left. The second econometrician fired, but also missed, by a meter to the right. The third econometrician didn't fire, but shouted in triumph, "We got it! We got it!"

Where to Find More Free Economics Stuff

You'll find Internet resources useful to economists scattered throughout this book. Look especially in the chapters on *More Profitable Investing* and *Doing Business Internationally*.

For instance, the *More Profitable Investing* chapter includes a newsletter called "Briefing" that includes economic and market forecasts. The *Doing Business Internationally* chapter includes information on the Japanese economy from the Economic Planning Agency of Japan.

If you're looking for more software, check out Free C and C++ for Numerical Computing in the *Manufacturing* chapter; many of its math routines are useful for economics calculations.

For interesting discussions of gender economics, you'll find an email discussion group of the same name in the *For Businesswomen* chapter.

And, as a last resort, you can always look up **economics resources** in the index.

FREE $TUFF

Men always try to keep women out of business so they won't find out how much fun it really is.

Vivien Kellems

For Businesswomen

According to Dun & Bradstreet, U.S. women-owned businesses employ 35 percent more workers than all the Fortune 500 corporations put together employ worldwide. That figure will only go up, because more women open more businesses every day.

Within less than one century—a mere eyeblink in human history—we have moved from the Victorian misconception of stupid, helpless women with no sexual desire and less management aptitude, to a time that enables women rise to become heads of state and presidents of corporations. And do very well at it, thank you.

It's sometimes hard to remember how different life was for working women a century ago, or even fifty years ago. When Vince's mother graduated from college in 1950 with a degree in chemistry, many people still questioned the need for a woman to earn a college degree, let alone one in a scientific field. Wouldn't she just get married and have children and waste that degree anyhow? Well, Vince's mom did get married and did have eight babies (or you wouldn't be reading this book), but she still worked as a chemist and published research papers. It took decades of success stories by millions of women like Vince's mother to turn people's attitudes around. A big ship takes a long time to make a U-turn.

After years of hard work by businesswomen to build a firm foundation, more women today reach higher levels of success in more industries than at any other time in the history of the human race. More than half of all new businesses started in the U.S. are started by women. Some professional fields—such as publicity and human resources management—are now dominated by women.

This is the best time ever to be a female in business, but women still face problems. Some are geographical and cultural. Women have made great success in business in some countries, such as the United States, Canada, and the Scandinavian countries. But much of the world does not yet take women seriously in business. Even in more "enlightened" countries, some people are still uncomfortable working with women. This vestigal attitude will die out, but it will take generations of work to remove it completely.

But who has the patience to wait? With that in mind, we have some Internet resources to help you with today's challenges.

There are many, many Web sites and email discussion groups on the Internet for women. Most deal with non-business aspects of life. Of the dozens of resources dealing with women, work, and money, most offer nothing for free. Not a free sample. Not a free newsletter. No even free information. Most just want your money. Even excellent women's professional groups such as Women In Communications (which we highly recommend to women in media and PR, even though you have to *pay* for it) present a Web page that tells you how to join without giving so much as a free taste of what the association has to offer.

We believe that you'll see this change quickly over the next year, as existing women's business Web sites grow in richness, and as greater competition forces organizations to add information to differentiate themselves. We hope that one of these sites develops a truly comprehensive directory of women's business resources on the Net. The Small Business Administration's (SBA) directory is currently the most complete, but it is a long way from all-encompassing. (We'll be glad to consult with someone to build a better one.)

Yes, although there is plenty of room for growth, you'll still find some very good resources on the Net for women in business. You'll find resources that provide background information. You'll find others that provide how-to information. Some Web sites help women get business loans, and others generate sales leads. Several places help prevent workplace discrimination and harassment, and work to smash that promotion-blocker, the glass ceiling. Others concentrate on personal finances, or on helping balance your work and your personal life.

We can't help but wonder how a struggling businesswoman from the beginning of this century would feel if she were given this same information and assistance, all just by pressing a keyboard with her fingertips. Perhaps she would regard it as magic. Perhaps it still is.

Ownership Is Power

SBA Office of Women's Business Ownership ☆☆☆☆

This is a valuable site for all businesswomen worldwide. For U.S. women entrepreneurs, it will often prove to be the most rewarding site on the Net.

Every woman, however, can profit from a visit to the SBA's "Outside Resources Hotlist." The Hotlist is by far the most complete directory we found of women's business resources on the Net—and not just U.S. Web sites, but resources worldwide. Resources are not described, so you can't tell the winners from the turkeys, but the selection offered is wide.

Other sections of this site focus on the needs of U.S. businesswomen, and in particular of women who own or want to own their own businesses. The SBA offers you a helping hand, and it's a big hand. President Clinton greatly expanded the SBA's offerings for women. Under Clinton, more than 27,000 woman-owned businesses have received more than $3.8 billion in SBA-guaranteed loans. He also expanded government purchases from women. In 1994, women-owned businesses received $4.9 billion in federal government purchasing contracts. We're not talking about small change here, but what could be a big boost for your business.

Sections at this information-packed SBA Web site include:

- **Most Commonly Asked Questions** - This good FAQ, tailored for women, addresses the basic questions that you need to know before you start a business.

- **Demonstration Training Program** - More than 47,000 women have used this program. It teaches you the skills you need to open your own business. It targets socially and economically disadvantaged women, providing financial, management, marketing, and technical assistance.

- **Women's Network for Entrepreneurial Training** - This excellent program provides mentoring and support groups for women business owners. We highly recommend it.

- **Women's Prequalification Pilot Loan Program** - This special program helps women get business loans more easily.

- **Other Financial Resources** - This page lists and describes additional SBA programs to help you get business loans and bonds. These programs are all available to women, but are not targeted specifically to women.

- **Intragency Committee on Women's Business Enterprise** - There's not much on this page. Look on the SBA's home page for something better: *Intragency Committee for Women-Owned Businesses Newsletter*, which is actually the annual report of this committee. You'll find economic statistics, outlines of all federal government programs available for women's businesses (with contact phone numbers for all of them), sources for more statistical data on women's businesses, and several short case histories of women-owned businesses.

- **Federal Procurement Program for Women-Owned Businesses** - We already discussed the billions of dollars that Uncle Sam spends every year

with women-owned businesses. Go here to find the first steps on how your business can get its share.

- **SBA's Women's Business Ownership Representatives** - The SBA has people all around the country who help businesswomen locally. This page tells you how to reach the ones closest to you.

- **Statistics on Women-Owned Businesses**

How

World Wide Web

Where

www.sbaonline.sba.gov/womeninbusiness

For Women Who Manage

National Association of Female Executives ☆☆☆☆

With more than a quarter of a million members, the National Association of Female Executives (NAFE) is the world's largest organization of women in business.

EXECUTIVE FEMALE MAGAZINE **and more.**

NAFE's Web site is still evolving, and it's growing fast. Some parts are not all they could be, but we're sure that will change. One of the best parts of the site is the collection of articles from the bi-monthly *Executive Female Magazine.* Don't miss Wendy Crisp's well-written columns. When we checked, *Executive Female Magazine* offered no archive of stories from past issues, but it did provide unexpected sources of more information: many articles attach several additional stories following the text of the original article. Continue scrolling

down after you finish the article to see if you're a lucky winner. Look under "Entrepreneurial Problem Solver" for good short case histories. A separate department reports on government news and regulations.

Besides *Executive Female Magazine*, other sections of this Web site are "Cafe NAFE," providing chat, "daily" woman-related news (a week old when we checked), and a directory of Net resources. This directory had categories for Astronomy, Art and Art Museums, and Government—but *no business!* A subdirectory of Women's Resources also neglected listing business resources. In spite of these oversights, NAFE still provides a good resource for executive women.

How

World Wide Web

Where

www.nafe.com

Newsstand for Working Women

Women's Web ☆☆☆☆

What's the largest circulation business magazine? Could it be *Forbes*? Maybe *Fortune*? Or perhaps the more international magazine *The Economist*? If you chose any of the above, you're incorrect. The correct answer is *Working Woman*, which was the first business magazine ever to have more than 1,000,000 subscribers.

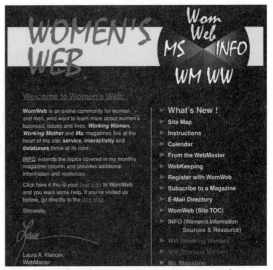

The online sites for Ms., WORKING WOMAN, and WORKING MOTHER are all at the Women's Web site.

Working Woman has a Web site in common with two other publications, *Working Mother* and *Ms*. The Web site provides some (not all) articles and departments from each magazine, plus searchable databases and bonus features not found in the printed versions. For instance,

Working Woman gives you its Top Woman-Owned Companies database and the Hottest Careers for Women. You can search *Working Mother*'s Best Companies For Working Mothers in database format, or browse it as a catalog of companies.

The site plans to add chat features for all magazines and other articles and information, as well. If you sometimes carry one of these magazines in your purse, you'll also want to add its Web address to your bookmark file.

How

World Wide Web

Where

www.womweb.com

Where San Francisco Businesses Click

Bay Area Businesswomen's Calendar ☆☆☆

More than just a calendar of events, this site is a combination directory and online businesswomen's magazine. It includes *Businesswomen's Directory*, a directory of San Francisco Bay Area women-owned businesses categorized by field; a calendar of monthly events; another calendar of ongoing events (it would go easier on readers if the two were combined); classified ads; and monthly columns, including Charlotte Brown's no-nonsense Tech Talk, book reviews (not of business books when we looked), food, astrology, and business topics.

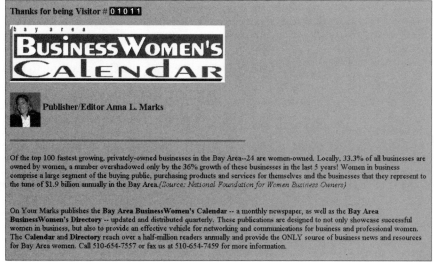

Thanks for being Visitor # 0 1 0 1 1

bay area
BusinessWomen's Calendar

Publisher/Editor Anna L. Marks

Of the top 100 fastest growing, privately-owned businesses in the Bay Area--24 are women-owned. Locally, 33.3% of all businesses are owned by women, a number overshadowed only by the 36% growth of these businesses in the last 5 years! Women in business comprise a large segment of the buying public, purchasing products and services for themselves and the businesses that they represent to the tune of $1.9 billion annually in the Bay Area. *(Source: National Foundation for Women Business Owners)*

On Your Marks publishes the **Bay Area BusinessWomen's Calendar** -- a monthly newspaper, as well as the **Bay Area BusinessWomen's Directory** -- updated and distributed quarterly. These publications are designed to not only showcase successful women in business, but also to provide an effective vehicle for networking and communications for business and professional women. The **Calendar** and **Directory** reach over a half-million readers annually and provide the ONLY source of business news and resources for Bay Area women. Call 510-654-7557 or fax us at 510-654-7459 for more information.

A good mousestop for business in the San Francisco Bay Area.

453

A section called "Monthly Highlights" provides news stories. Another directory lists women-owned restaurants in the Bay Area. Other sections include profiles of local women business owners (written like ads and not useful as case histories), and a short directory of mostly non-business resources.

How

World Wide Web

Where

www.slip.net/~bizwomen

Breaking the Barriers I

Glass Ceiling Commission ☆☆☆

You'll mostly find background information at this site, but there is some how-to instruction as well. This is the report of the 21-member board appointed by President Clinton to study the invisible barrier that prevents women from reaching senior management positions in corporations. You can read the summary of the report on the Web and then download the complete report, which includes twelve actions your company can take to eliminate the glass ceiling where you work. You can download the report in either Postscript format (both PC and Mac) or Adobe Acrobat format.

In addition, this site presents 17 additional reports on the glass ceiling. Most just *describe* the problem (Like telling a drowning woman, "You're drowning!" It's accurate, but not a big help.), but the better reports propose steps to remedy the situation. (Yes! Throw me a lifesaver!) You might want to keep this important distinction in mind if you read these:

- Successful Initiatives for Breaking the Glass Ceiling to Upward Mobility for Minorities and Women
- Impact of Corporate Restructuring and Downsizing on the Managerial Careers of Minorities and Women
- Barriers to Workplace Advancement Experienced by Women in Low-Paying Occupations
- Use of Enforcement Techniques in Eliminating Glass Ceiling Barriers
- Impact of Family-Friendly Policies on the Glass Ceiling
- Preparedness, Career Advancement, and the Glass Ceiling
- Barriers to Workplace Advancement Experienced by White Women Workers

How

World Wide Web

Where

www.ilr.cornell.edu/library/e_archive/glassceiling

Breaking the Barriers II

DATALINE GLASS CEILING NEWSLETTER ☆☆

This newsletter was published from 1991 to 1994, so it contains no current information. It reported on lawsuits against corporations for glass ceiling discrimination, cases in which women were denied rightfully earned promotions, while men with lesser qualifications were promoted in their place. You'll find true horror stories here, both in terms of what happened to women at work, and the sometimes worse things that happened after they fought back. This newsletter has no how-to information. Use it for background purposes, or if you want late-night reading that in its own way is as scary as a Steven King story. His stories are fiction; these are true.

How

World Wide Web

Where

www.cyberwerks.com/dataline

When Reasonableness Doesn't Make It

The Rise—and Fall—of the Reasonable Woman ☆☆

If you are thinking of filing a sexual harassment lawsuit, read this article first. Written by attorney Barbara Kate Repa, it discusses the Reasonable Woman Standard used in sexual harassment cases. Ms. Repa explains why the Reasonable Woman Standard used to be employed frequently, and why it is less-often applied successfully in newer lawsuits.

How

World Wide Web

Where

www.e1c.gnn.com/gnn/bus/nolo/nn214.html

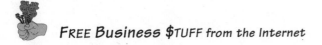

Make Your Work a Little Better Place

Gender Issues ☆☆☆

If you're looking for information and ideas on women's needs and the workplace, you'll find no better reference spot on the Net. The contents of this directory are organized into several subdirectories. Four of them cover women and work:

- **Glass Ceiling** - A collection of documents and links to sites with information on glass ceiling barriers to women.
- **Sex Discrimination** - A collection of antidiscrimination documents.
- **Sexual Harassment** - A very good collection of documents, reports, and links to other sites, reporting on this problem and telling what to do about it.
- **Women in the Workforce** - The largest and best section of the Gender Issues directory presents more than twenty publications on this topic, mostly from the Women's Bureau. You may be especially interested in "Working Woman's Guide to Her Job Rights," and "Work and Family Needs," a large report that lists many different types of benefits and work policies that companies can put into place to make work better for women.

How

World Wide Web

Where

www.inform.umd.edu:8080/Educational_Resources/

AcademicResourcesByTopic/WomensStudies/GenderIssues

If You Just Can't Get Enough Biz Info

Women's Wire Archives ☆☆☆

Women's Wire is a very good Internet service for women, but it seems to dollop out its business information one spoonful at a time. You certainly won't be overwhelmed by data at Women's Wire. The site features regularly changing business sections that include a personal finance article called "Cash Flo," a profile interview with a successful businesswoman (easy to read; about the depth of a *People* article), and a good business Q&A column called "Biz Shrink." In "Biz Shrink," Laura Gates answers questions on topics such as finding qualified women job candidates, marketing your company, dealing with difficult men, and feeling underpaid and what to do about it.

If you're hungry for more business insight than you can find on the current Women's Wire pages, you might want to browse the Women's Wire Archives, where you can read several articles instead of only a spoonful.

How

World Wide Web

Where

Cash Flo: www.women.com/wwire/archives/html/qacashhome.html

Biz Shrink: www.women.com/wwire/archives/html/qabizhome

Profiles: www.women.com/wwire/archives/html/profilehome.html

This Site Makes You Work

BizWomen ☆☆

There is good information at this site, but you will have to dig for it. Whether or not you decide it is worth the effort is up to you, but we'll do our best to point out the good as well as the—um—less worthwhile, to be polite about it.

First, we'll point out four resources here we did not check. BizWomen includes four email discussion groups for businesswomen, which may be very good. You can subscribe to all four at this Web site:

- **business-bw** is for discussing women and business
- **technology-bw** is for discussing technology
- **finance-bw** if for finances and investments; it may be about personal finances rather than business finances, if the rest of this site is any clue
- **career-bw** is for discussing your career

We assumed BizWomen's "R&R" section would cover "Rest & Relaxation," which is normally what "R&R" stands for. But it actually provides "References & Resources" specifically for women in businesses. You'll find a directory here of off-Net contact information for 19 organizations. The directory omits Web links for organizations that have them. A suggested reading directory lists eight books, without details on most.

A section called "WIN" presents an email service called "My Online Mentor." It was not yet working when we visited, but this service sounds like a good idea. Another section, "WWWomen," tries to sell you Web ad space. Not worth it. "BizNews" forces you to slog through way too many layers of menus to get to a little information. In spite of its name, "BizNews" provides no news, but mediocre articles. Its "Entrepreneurs" subsection is mere self-promotion, and "BizNews Digest" has news stories that, when we looked, were four months old.

BizWomen's "Q&A" is the worst we've seen, out of date and with almost no information. "Emporium" links to a handful of direct merchants.

Much better is the "Link to Link" directory of directories. Quality is inconsistent, though. The best sections are "Online References" and "Business Opportunities." We are still trying to figure out why the U.S. Copyright Office was categorized as "News."

How

World Wide Web

Where

www.bizwomen.com

What Is the Lifetime Value of Your Customer?

WomenBiz ☆☆

Don't mistake this site for the one we just discussed! The names of WomenBiz and BizWomen are confusingly similar, but they are quite different. This one, WomenBiz, *says* it is for women business owners, but the information here is useful for any businessperson. You'll find a not-very-active discussion area, "Technology U Can Use" (a skippable ad), "Money Matters" (tax tips and junk ads), and the best section, "BizTips." This last section apparently lets anyone write and post any kind of article at all. The quality ranges from extremely useful to spam ads that waste perfectly good electrons. We recommend "How to Determine the Lifetime Value of a Customer" and the introduction to "Business Plans." Customer value is an extremely important figure for any business to know, and surprisingly few do. Skip any articles with "FREE" in all caps in their titles—they are just Webspam. Any story here you read that mentions Murray Broach is useless. Other articles vary in quality, and new ones will appear. You'll want to make your own evaluations of those.

How

World Wide Web

Where

www.fsa.com/womenbiz

Spinning a Business on the Web?

Spiderwoman ☆☆☆

There are unique hassles for women starting a business on the Web, an area where men are definitely in the majority. (For right now, anyhow!) Chances are when you meet other women in this male-dominated field, after sharing a few stories you will instantly feel a bond of camraderie. Here's a way to get to know a whole group of kindred souls. Spiderwoman is an email discussion group for women who manage or design Web sites. If you want to ask questions about Web development, consulting, HTML, integrating your business with your social life, or if you just want to share war stories, this active group of Web women could be just the place for you.

How
Email

Where
majordomo@lists.primenet.com

Message
subscribe spiderwoman

You Want Stats, We Got Stats

Women- and Minority-Owned Business Surveys ☆☆

In 1992, 5,888,883 women-owned businesses in the United States racked up sales of $642,484,352,000. That ain't chicken feed.

If you need more statistics on women-owned businesses in the U.S., here is a place to turn. The U.S. Census Bureau gives you overall information, plus comparisons of women-owned businesses with companies overall, and data by state and by industry.

How
World Wide Web

Where
www.census.gov/ftp/pub/econ/www/mu0200.html

Women-Owned Banks

Minority Bank Monitor ☆☆

We think more women should own banks. If you share this ambition, this is a
site to visit. The consulting company of Creative Investment Research Monitor did in-depth studies of women- and minority-owned banks. You can download the report (it's a 505 K file) and also read CRIM's library of articles on
minority banks and brokers.

How

World Wide Web

Where

www2.ari.net/cirm

Women and Technology: Breaking the Myth

Business Women's Network ☆☆

This research organization prefers to charge for information, but you will find
two free goodies at its site. One is a lengthy summary of its *Women and Technology Report*, which reports statistics and trends on women's use of computers and software, effectively dismissing the myth that women are inherently
computer-impaired. Number two is a directory of the twenty largest business
and professional women's organizations. It lists the membership size of each,
and provides contact information, and for organizations with Web sites, you'll
find links to their home pages.

How

World Wide Web

Where

www.tpag.com/BWN.html

I Am Woman, Hear Me Code

Women Undergrads in Computing ☆☆

Women who work in computer science already know what many women currently studying the field may not realize: There ain't many of you out there.
Long dominated by the male species, the computer science field is now providing skyrocketing job opportunities—especially for women.

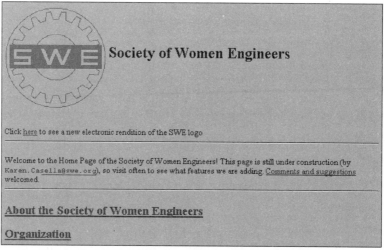

The Society for Women Engineers is just one of the many links at the Women Undergrads in Computer Science Web page.

Here's a Web site devoted to giving women the resources they need to learn more about undergrad and graduate degrees in computer science, internships and scholarships available, organizations and mailing lists devoted to women in computer science, and lots more.

How

World Wide Web

Where

infomac1.science.unimelb.edu.au/cielle/women/wucs.html

Talking about a Steady Cashflow

Woman's Guide to Pension Rights ☆☆☆

Pensions are more important to women than men due to the simple fact that most women live longer than men. This means you'll depend on retirement funds and pensions for more years than most men do. The American Association of Retired Persons (AARP) produced this good, detailed guide. It explains your own pension plans and your husband's pension plans. It tells how to find what you will be paid. If you don't yet know about this important topic, visit this site. Don't throw away what may be twenty years of income by not taking a few simple steps now.

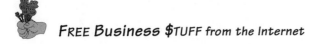
How

World Wide Web

Where

www.magicnet.net/benefits/articles/guide.html

Sales Leads for California Businesswomen

ABAG Contracts Exchange: Women-Owned Businesses

The Association of Bay Area Governments (ABAG)—a group of local governments and public agencies from the San Francisco area—provides this site to help women-owned businesses sell to ABAG members. This service is free for your business, and could be a valuable way for you to make sales. We say "could be" because we don't know. This service was not yet complete as we went to press, but it looks promising, so we wanted to tell you about it.

How

World Wide Web

Where

www.abag.ca.gov/bayarea/commerce/ace/ace_mwbe.html

Where to Find More Resources for Women

Most of the resources in this book are gender-neutral. There may be vestigal prejudices against women in fields such as manufacturing, but on the Internet, no one knows that you aren't an ex-football player. That levels the playing field.

Turn to *More Profitable Investing* for resources covering investing and personal finance for women. This is an important area to understand. Women have very different financial needs than men. If you want to know about these differences, we suggest you visit the MoneyWorld site described in Chapter 11 and read its guide to personal finance for women. MoneyWorld is a British site, but its guide can be an eye-opener for anyone from any country.

In this same chapter, you might want to register for free use of PAWWS so you can read Nancy Dunnan's column, "The Buck Starts Here." You'll find Ms. Dunnan in the *MoneyTalk Magazine* section of PAWWS.

If you have children, you may want to visit the Personal Finance Center, also described in *More Profitable Investing*. It has a section called "Parent Soup," which covers money matters for parents.

FREE $TUFF

Five Star Sites

FREE *Business* $TUFF *from the Internet*

Chapter	Site Name	Address
Accounting and Finance	International Accounting Network	anet.scu.edu.au/net
	Kaplan's AuditNet Resource List	www.unf.edu/students/jmayer/arl.html
	Credit Management Information and Support	www.teleport.com/ ~ richh
Business Law, Trademarks, Copyrights, and Patents	*The Legal List Internet Desk Reference*	www.lcp.com
	Legal Information Institute	www.law.cornell.edu/
Business News	ClariNet	See sidebar on page 69.
	Compilation of News Sites	www-leland.stanford.edu/ ~ jmaier/inetnews.htm
Doing Business Internationally	Accent Software	www.accentsoft.com
	Travlang	www.travlang.com
Entrepreneurs, Startups, and Home Businesses	Small Business Administration	www.sbaonline.sba.gov
	Business Network International	www.bninet.com
A Free Lunch for Economists	FinWeb	www.finweb.com
	Resources for Economists on the Internet	netec.wustl.edu/EconFAQ/EconFAQ.html
	NetEc	U.S.: netec.wustl.edu/netec.html
		(or) U.K.: netec.mcc.ac.uk/netec.html
	U.S. Census Bureau	www.census.gov
	WebEc	netec.wustl.edu/webec.html
For Retailers	RETEX Retail Technology Consortium	www.retex.com
How to Find Business Stuff on the Internet	Yahoo	www.yahoo.com
	Alta Vista	altavista.digital.com
	Lycos	www.lycos.com
	InfoSeek	www.infoseek.com
	The Business Guide to the Internet	www.helsinki.fi/ ~ lsaarine/ssbusg.html
	Thomas Register of American Manufacturers	www.thomasregister.com/home.html
	Hoover's Company Profiles	www.hoovers.com
	Internet Fax Server	U.S.: www.tpc.int/faxsend.html
		(or) U.K.: www.balliol.ox.ac.uk/fax/faxsend.html
	bit.listserv.buslib-l business librarians newsgroup	bit.listserv.buslib-l
Logistics and Transportation	Premenos	www.premenos.com
Manufacturing	Industry.Net	www.industry.net
Marketing, Advertising, and Publicity	*DM News* Online Edition	www.dmnews.com

Chapter	Site Name	Address
More Profitable Investing	EDGAR	edgar.stern.nyu.edu/edgar.html
	Investor In Touch	smokey.money.com/ssnhome.html
Tools for Internet-Based Business		
	Budget Web Index	digiserve.com/mercer/lowcost
	The List of Internet Access Providers	thelist.com
	Thomas Ho's Favorite Electronic Commerce Resources	www.engr.iupui.edu/ ~ ho/interests/commenu.html
	A1 Index	www.a1co.com/home.html
	Winzip	www.winzip.com/winzip
	Selena's Public Domain CGI Scripts	www.eff.org/ ~ erict/Scripts

Index

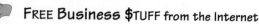